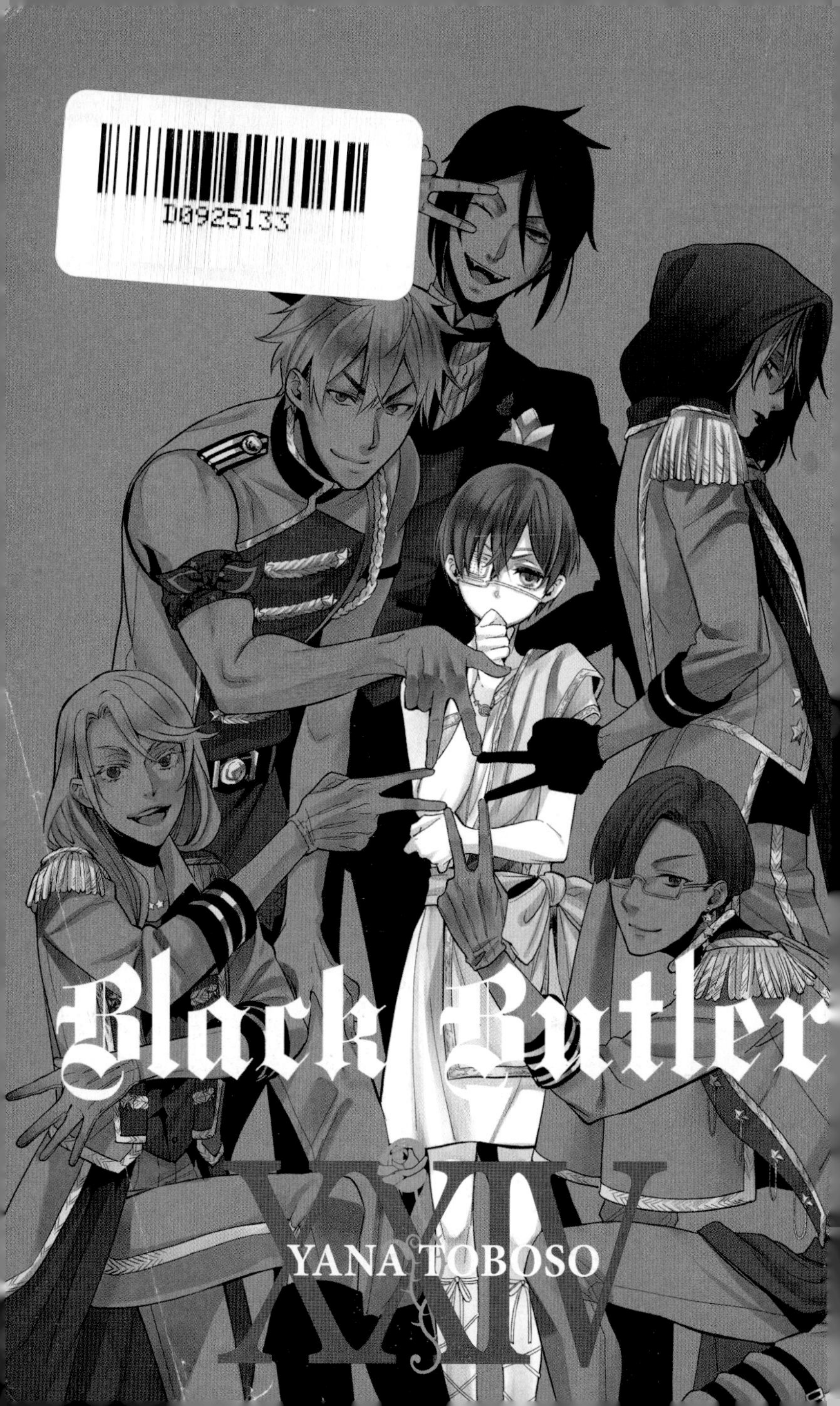
Black Butler
XXIV
YANA TOBOSO

Contents

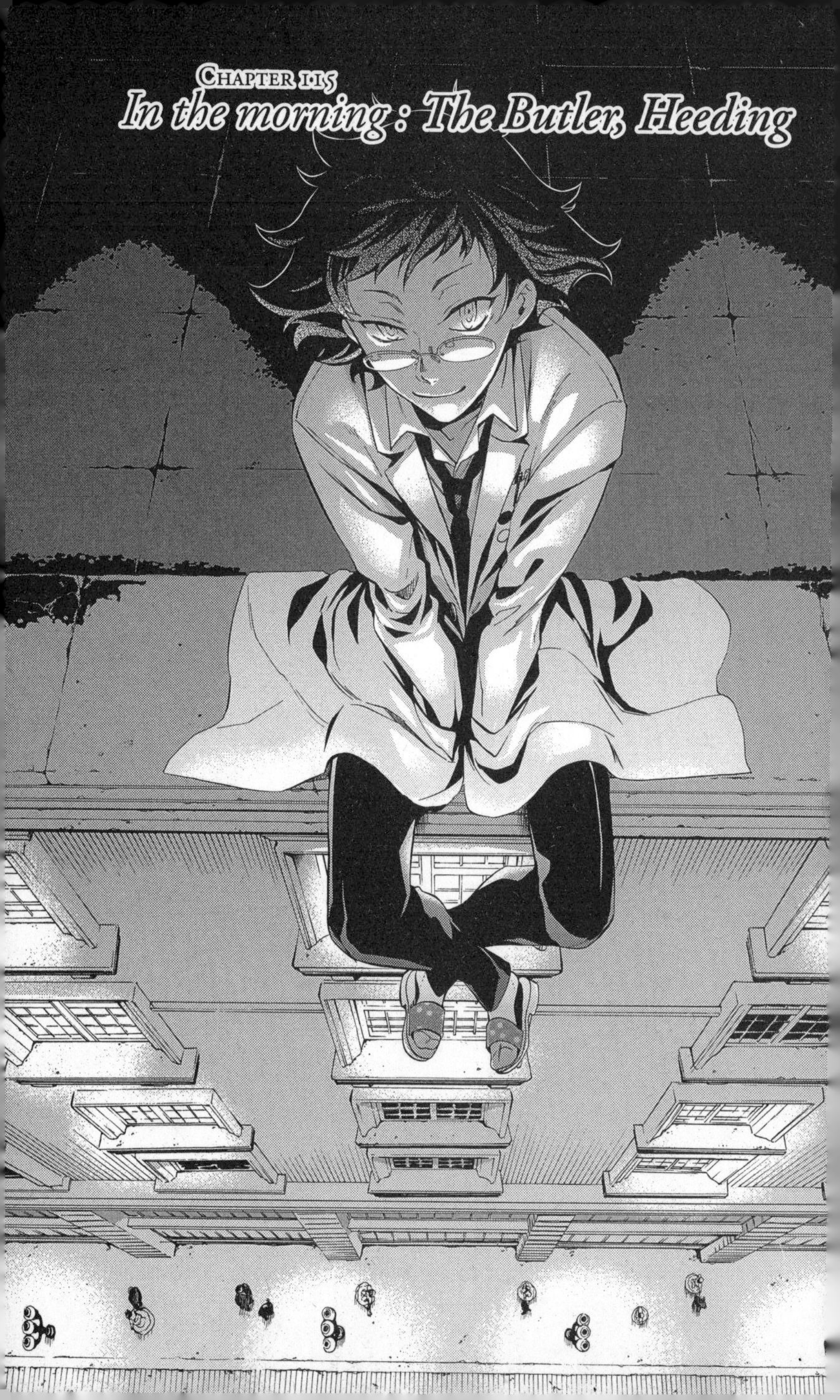
Chapter 115
In the morning : The Butler, Heeding

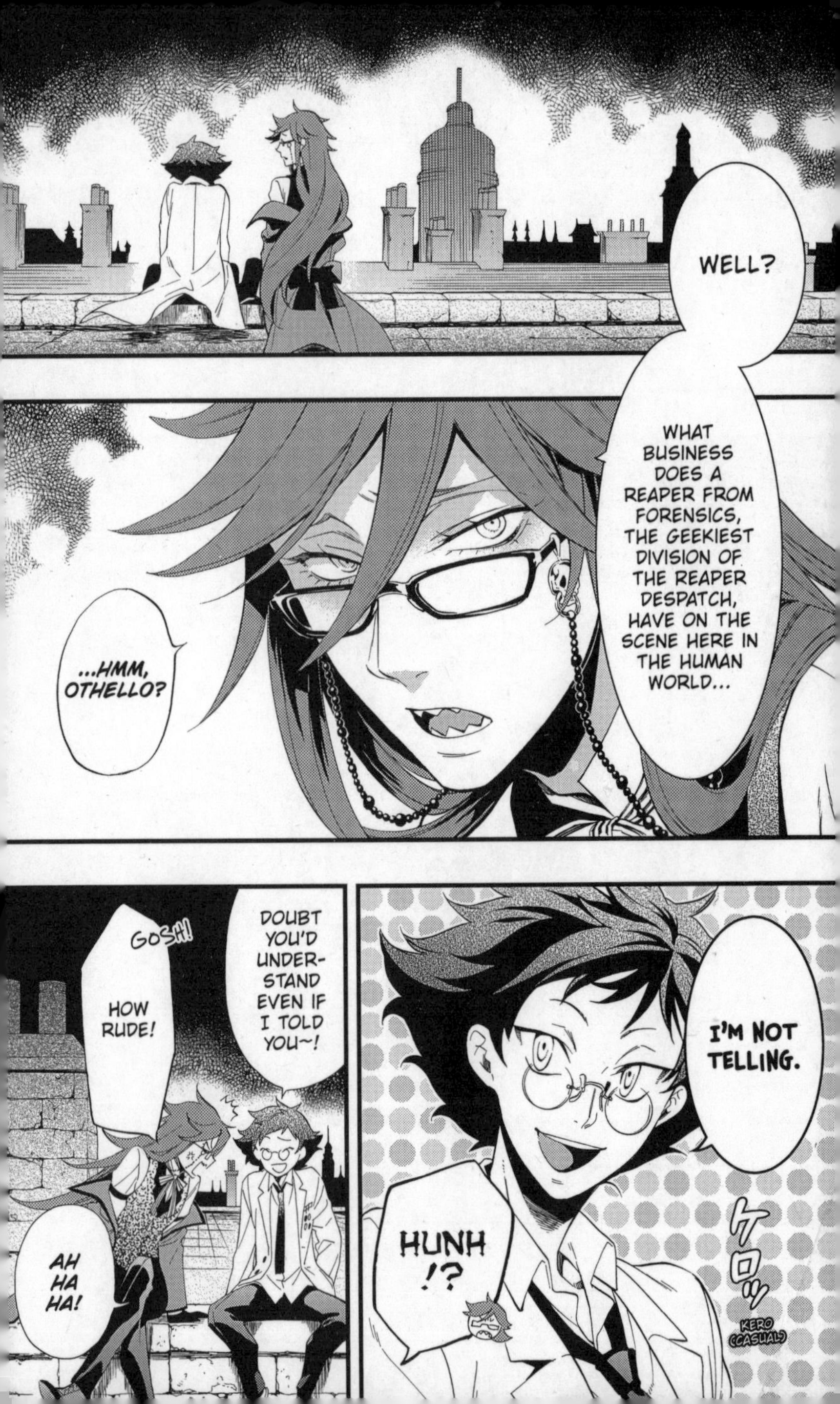
WELL?
WHAT BUSINESS DOES A REAPER FROM FORENSICS, THE GEEKIEST DIVISION OF THE REAPER DESPATCH, HAVE ON THE SCENE HERE IN THE HUMAN WORLD...
...HMM, OTHELLO?
I'M NOT TELLING.
HUNH !?
ケロッ
KERO (CASUAL)
DOUBT YOU'D UNDER-STAND EVEN IF I TOLD YOU~!
GOSH!
HOW RUDE!
AH HA HA!

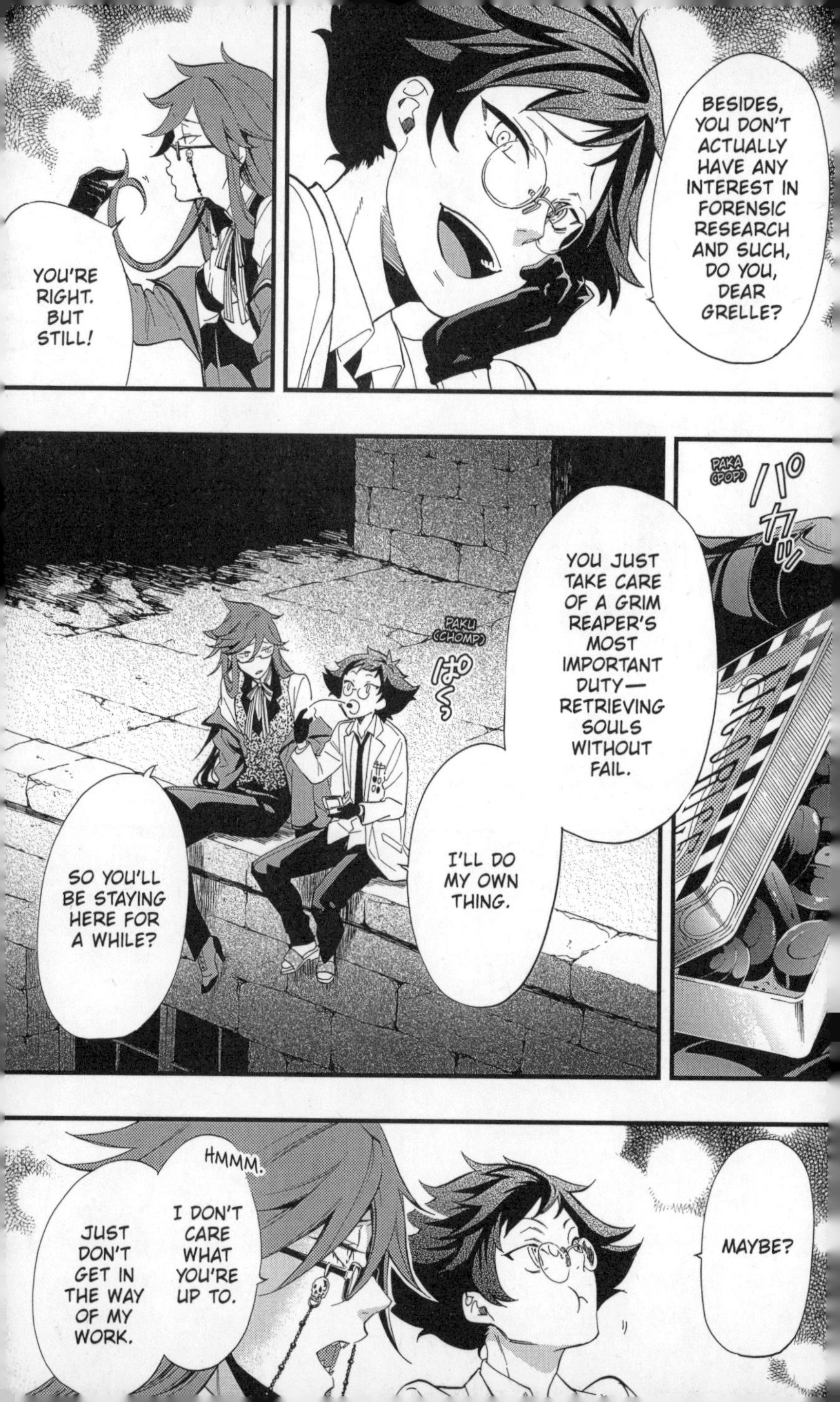
BESIDES, YOU DON'T ACTUALLY HAVE ANY INTEREST IN FORENSIC RESEARCH AND SUCH, DO YOU, DEAR GRELLE?
YOU'RE RIGHT. BUT STILL!
PAKA (POP)
YOU JUST TAKE CARE OF A GRIM REAPER'S MOST IMPORTANT DUTY— RETRIEVING SOULS WITHOUT FAIL.
I'LL DO MY OWN THING.
PAKU (CHOMP)
SO YOU'LL BE STAYING HERE FOR A WHILE?
MAYBE?
HMMM.
I DON'T CARE WHAT YOU'RE UP TO.
JUST DON'T GET IN THE WAY OF MY WORK.

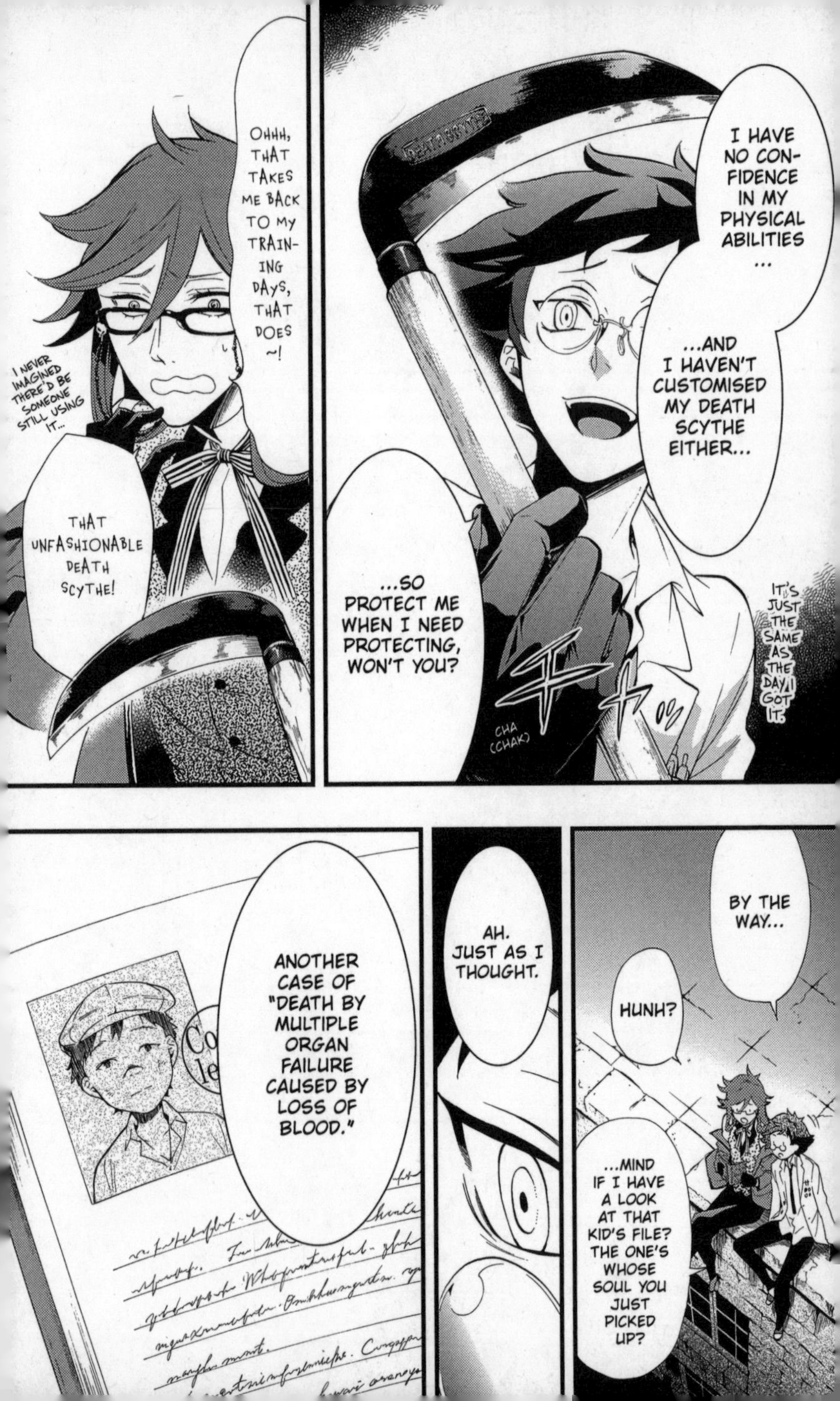
I HAVE NO CONFIDENCE IN MY PHYSICAL ABILITIES ...
...AND I HAVEN'T CUSTOMISED MY DEATH SCYTHE EITHER...
IT'S JUST THE SAME AS THE DAY I GOT IT.
...SO PROTECT ME WHEN I NEED PROTECTING, WON'T YOU?
CHA (CHAK)
OHHH, THAT TAKES ME BACK TO MY TRAINING DAYS, THAT DOES ~!
I NEVER IMAGINED THERE'D BE SOMEONE STILL USING IT...
THAT UNFASHIONABLE DEATH SCYTHE!
BY THE WAY...
HUNH?
...MIND IF I HAVE A LOOK AT THAT KID'S FILE? THE ONE'S WHOSE SOUL YOU JUST PICKED UP?
AH. JUST AS I THOUGHT.
ANOTHER CASE OF "DEATH BY MULTIPLE ORGAN FAILURE CAUSED BY LOSS OF BLOOD."

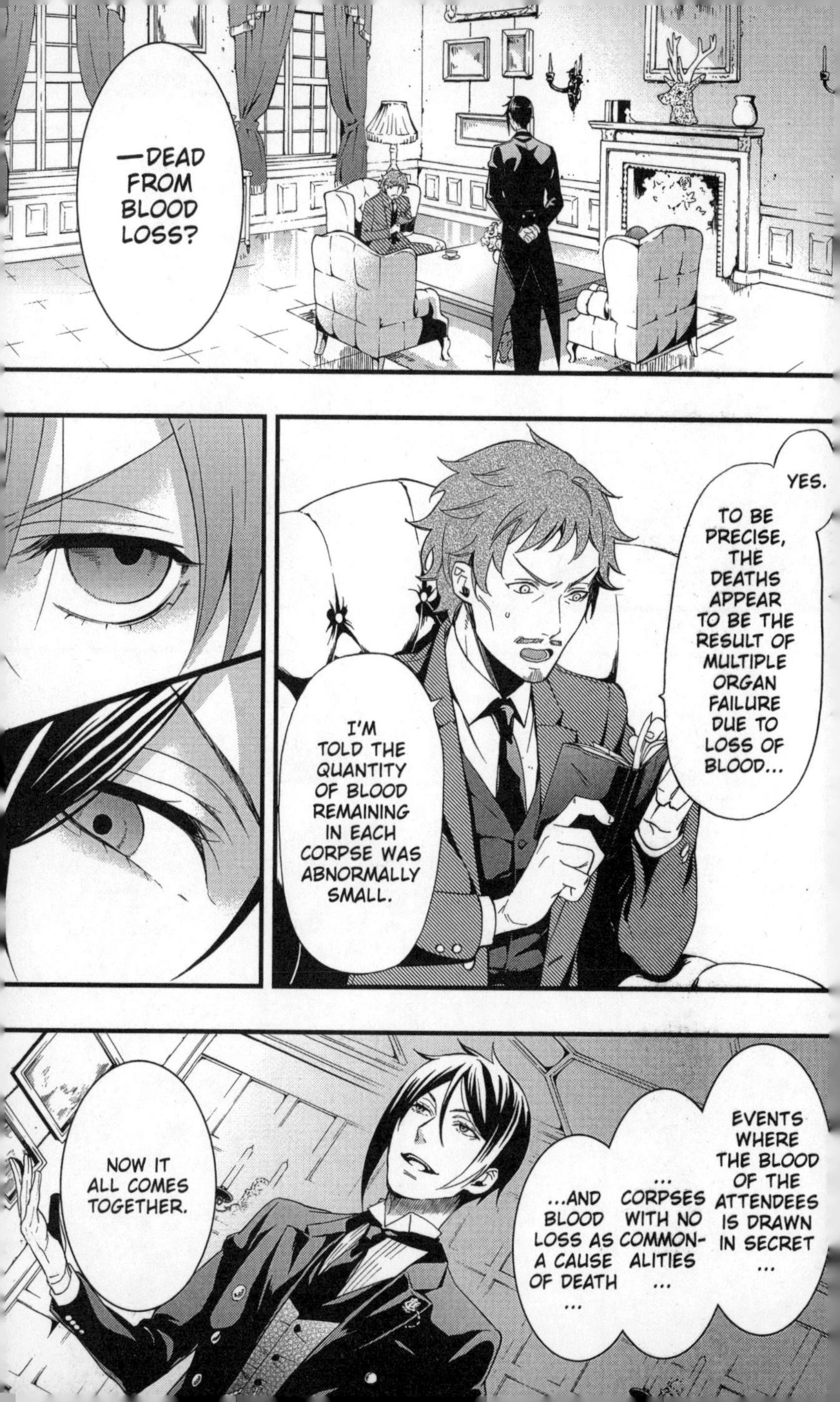
—DEAD FROM BLOOD LOSS?
YES.
TO BE PRECISE, THE DEATHS APPEAR TO BE THE RESULT OF MULTIPLE ORGAN FAILURE DUE TO LOSS OF BLOOD...
I'M TOLD THE QUANTITY OF BLOOD REMAINING IN EACH CORPSE WAS ABNORMALLY SMALL.
EVENTS WHERE THE BLOOD OF THE ATTENDEES IS DRAWN IN SECRET...
...CORPSES WITH NO COMMON-ALITIES...
...AND BLOOD LOSS AS A CAUSE OF DEATH...
NOW IT ALL COMES TOGETHER.

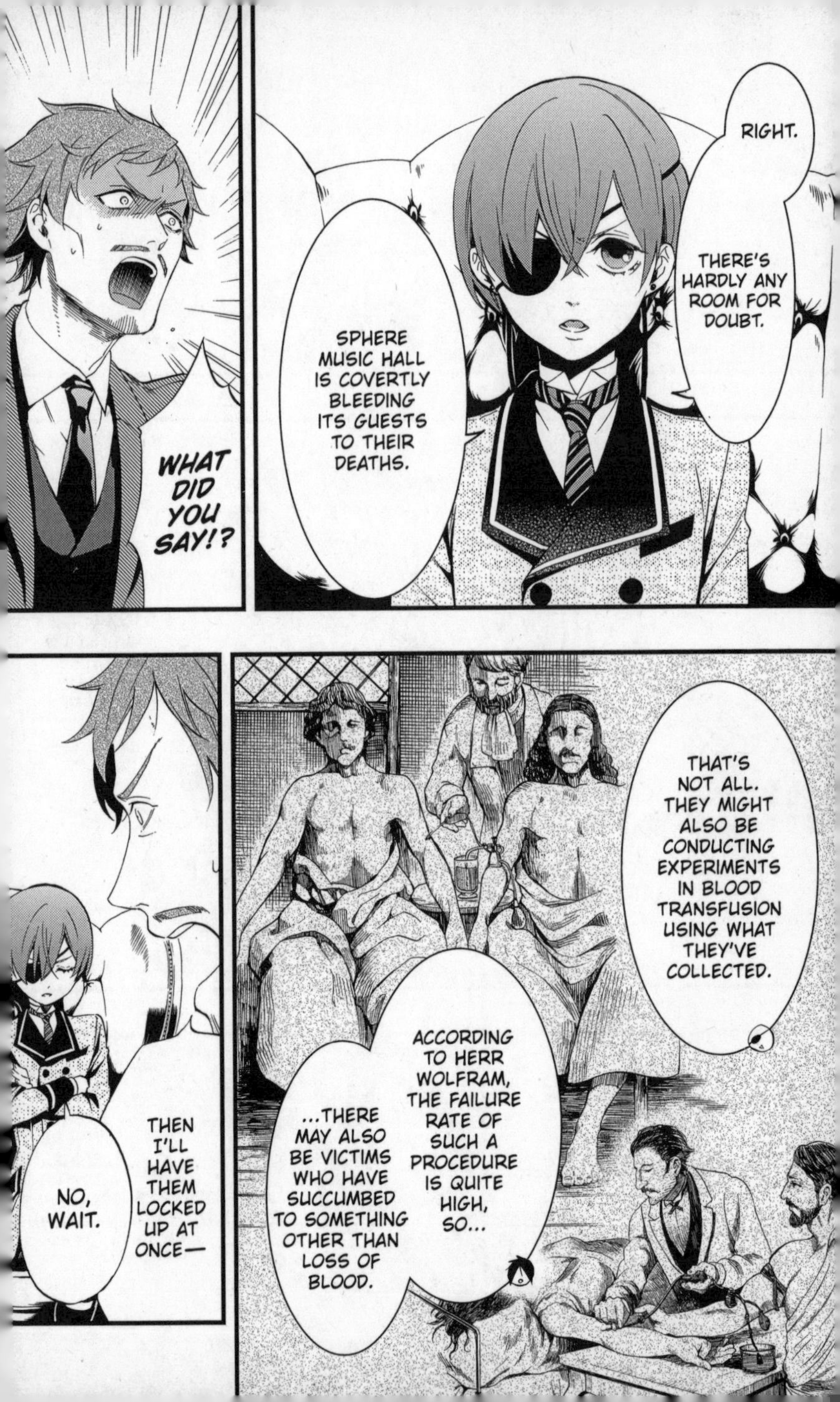
RIGHT.
THERE'S HARDLY ANY ROOM FOR DOUBT.
SPHERE MUSIC HALL IS COVERTLY BLEEDING ITS GUESTS TO THEIR DEATHS.
WHAT DID YOU SAY!?
THAT'S NOT ALL. THEY MIGHT ALSO BE CONDUCTING EXPERIMENTS IN BLOOD TRANSFUSION USING WHAT THEY'VE COLLECTED.
ACCORDING TO HERR WOLFRAM, THE FAILURE RATE OF SUCH A PROCEDURE IS QUITE HIGH, SO...
...THERE MAY ALSO BE VICTIMS WHO HAVE SUCCUMBED TO SOMETHING OTHER THAN LOSS OF BLOOD.
THEN I'LL HAVE THEM LOCKED UP AT ONCE—
NO, WAIT.

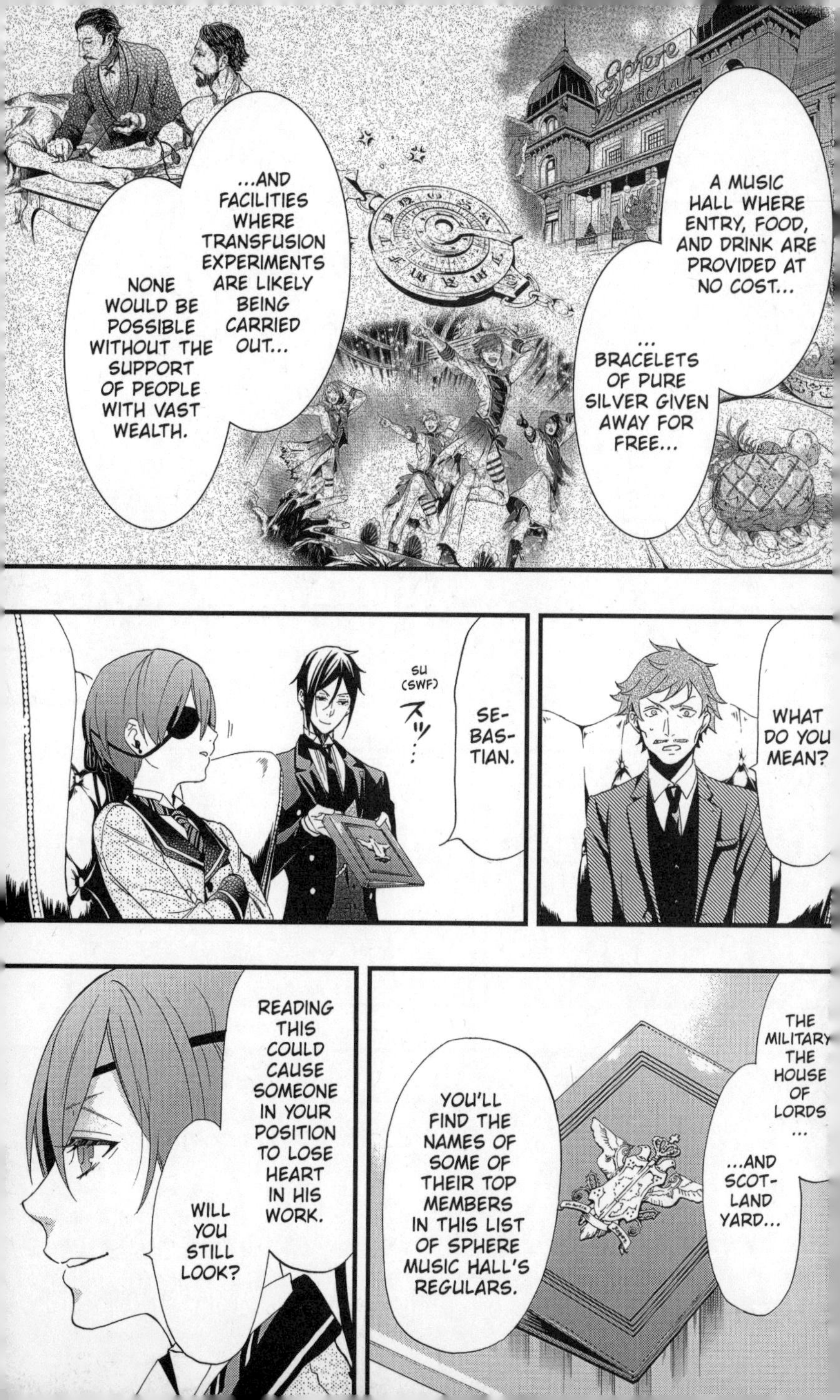
Sphere Music Hall
A MUSIC HALL WHERE ENTRY, FOOD, AND DRINK ARE PROVIDED AT NO COST...
... BRACELETS OF PURE SILVER GIVEN AWAY FOR FREE...
...AND FACILITIES WHERE TRANSFUSION EXPERIMENTS ARE LIKELY BEING CARRIED OUT...
NONE WOULD BE POSSIBLE WITHOUT THE SUPPORT OF PEOPLE WITH VAST WEALTH.
WHAT DO YOU MEAN?
SU (SWF)
スッ…
SE-BAS-TIAN.
THE MILITARY THE HOUSE OF LORDS ...
...AND SCOT-LAND YARD...
YOU'LL FIND THE NAMES OF SOME OF THEIR TOP MEMBERS IN THIS LIST OF SPHERE MUSIC HALL'S REGULARS.
READING THIS COULD CAUSE SOMEONE IN YOUR POSITION TO LOSE HEART IN HIS WORK.
WILL YOU STILL LOOK?

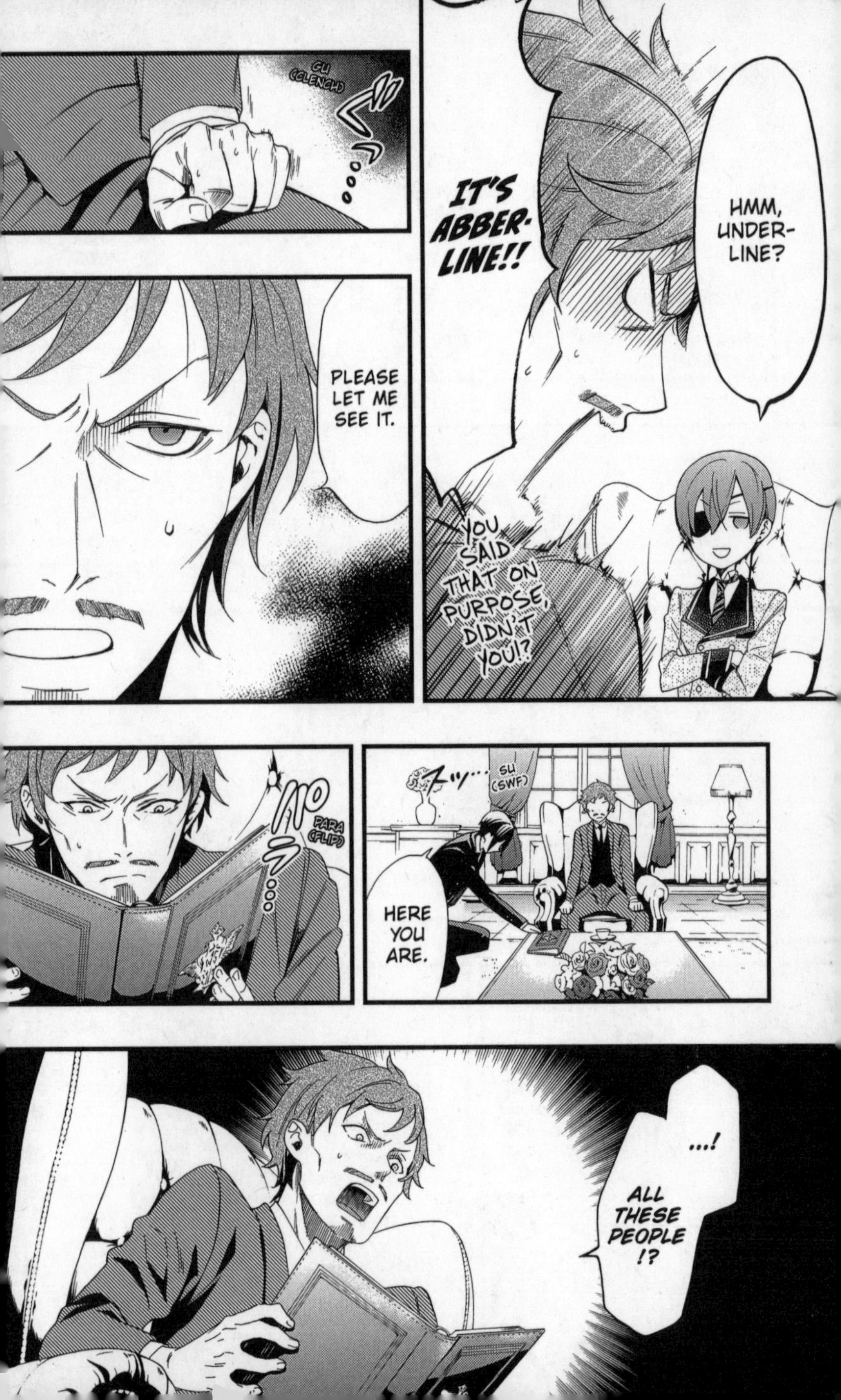

HMM, UNDER-LINE?
IT'S ABBER-LINE!!
YOU SAID THAT ON PURPOSE, DIDN'T YOU!?
GU (CLENCH)
PLEASE LET ME SEE IT.
SU (SWF)
HERE YOU ARE.
PARA (FLIP)
...!
ALL THESE PEOPLE!?

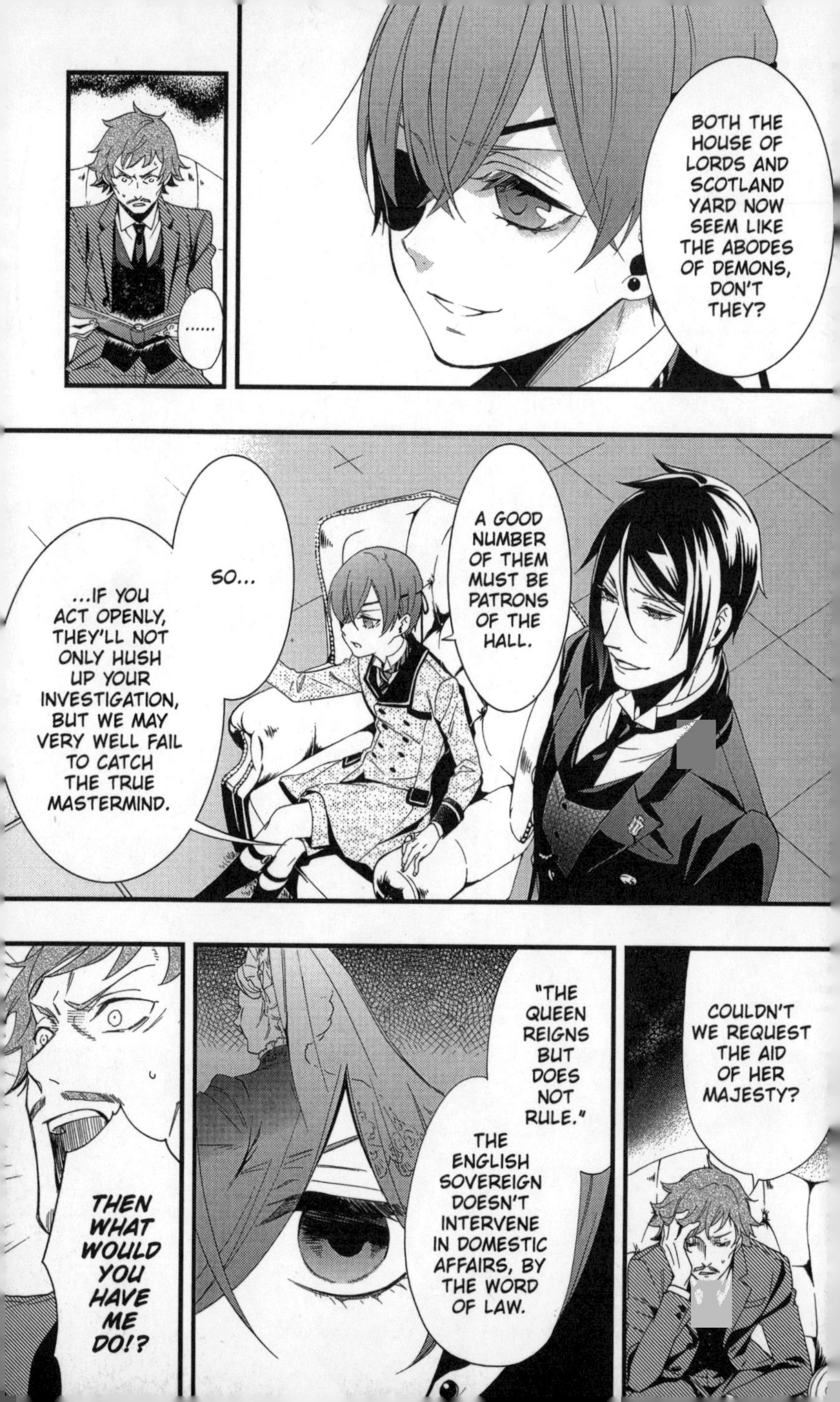
BOTH THE HOUSE OF LORDS AND SCOTLAND YARD NOW SEEM LIKE THE ABODES OF DEMONS, DON'T THEY?
......
A GOOD NUMBER OF THEM MUST BE PATRONS OF THE HALL.
SO...
...IF YOU ACT OPENLY, THEY'LL NOT ONLY HUSH UP YOUR INVESTIGATION, BUT WE MAY VERY WELL FAIL TO CATCH THE TRUE MASTERMIND.
COULDN'T WE REQUEST THE AID OF HER MAJESTY?
"THE QUEEN REIGNS BUT DOES NOT RULE."
THE ENGLISH SOVEREIGN DOESN'T INTERVENE IN DOMESTIC AFFAIRS, BY THE WORD OF LAW.
THEN WHAT WOULD YOU HAVE ME DO!?

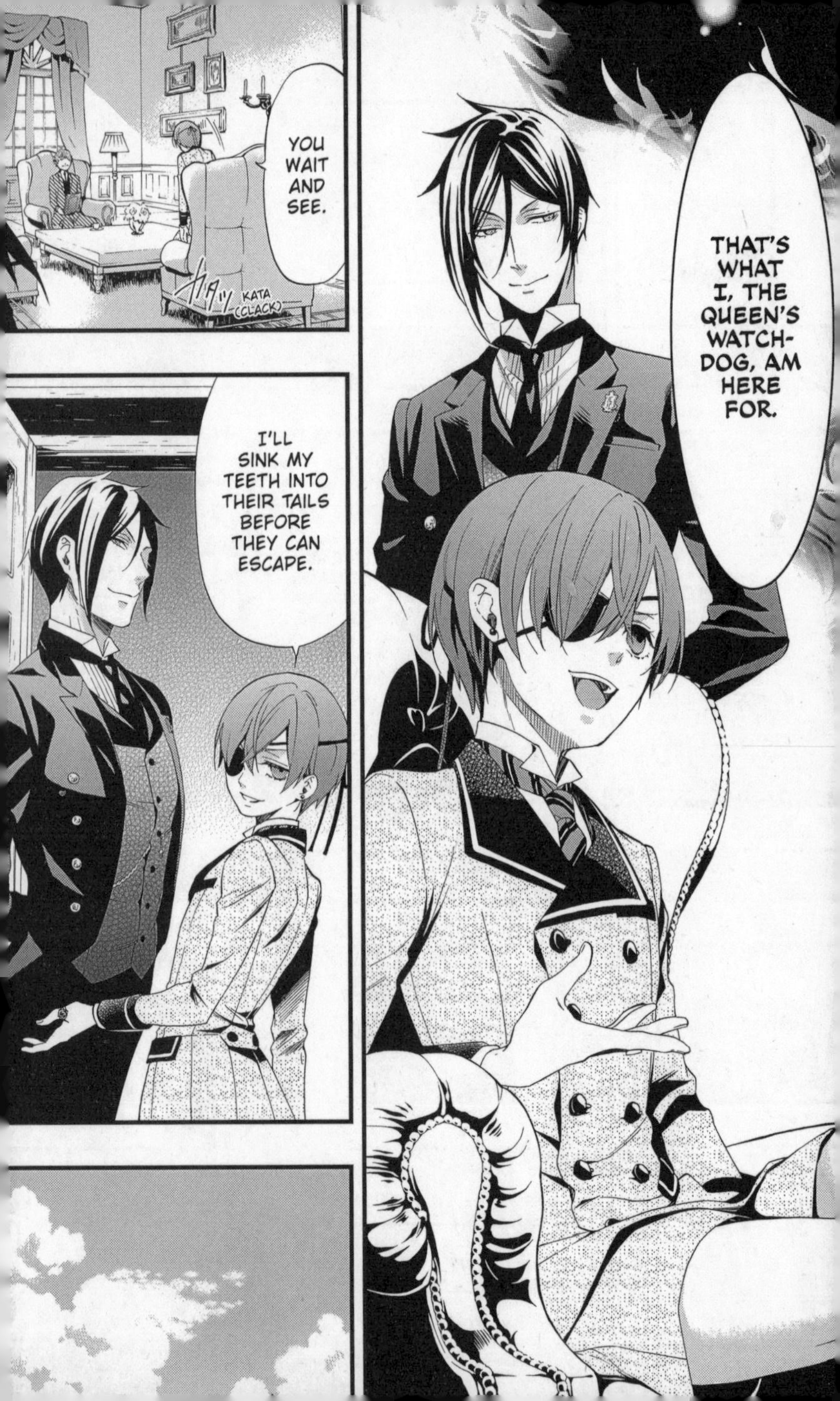
THAT'S WHAT I, THE QUEEN'S WATCH-DOG, AM HERE FOR.
YOU WAIT AND SEE.
KATA (CLACK)
I'LL SINK MY TEETH INTO THEIR TAILS BEFORE THEY CAN ESCAPE.

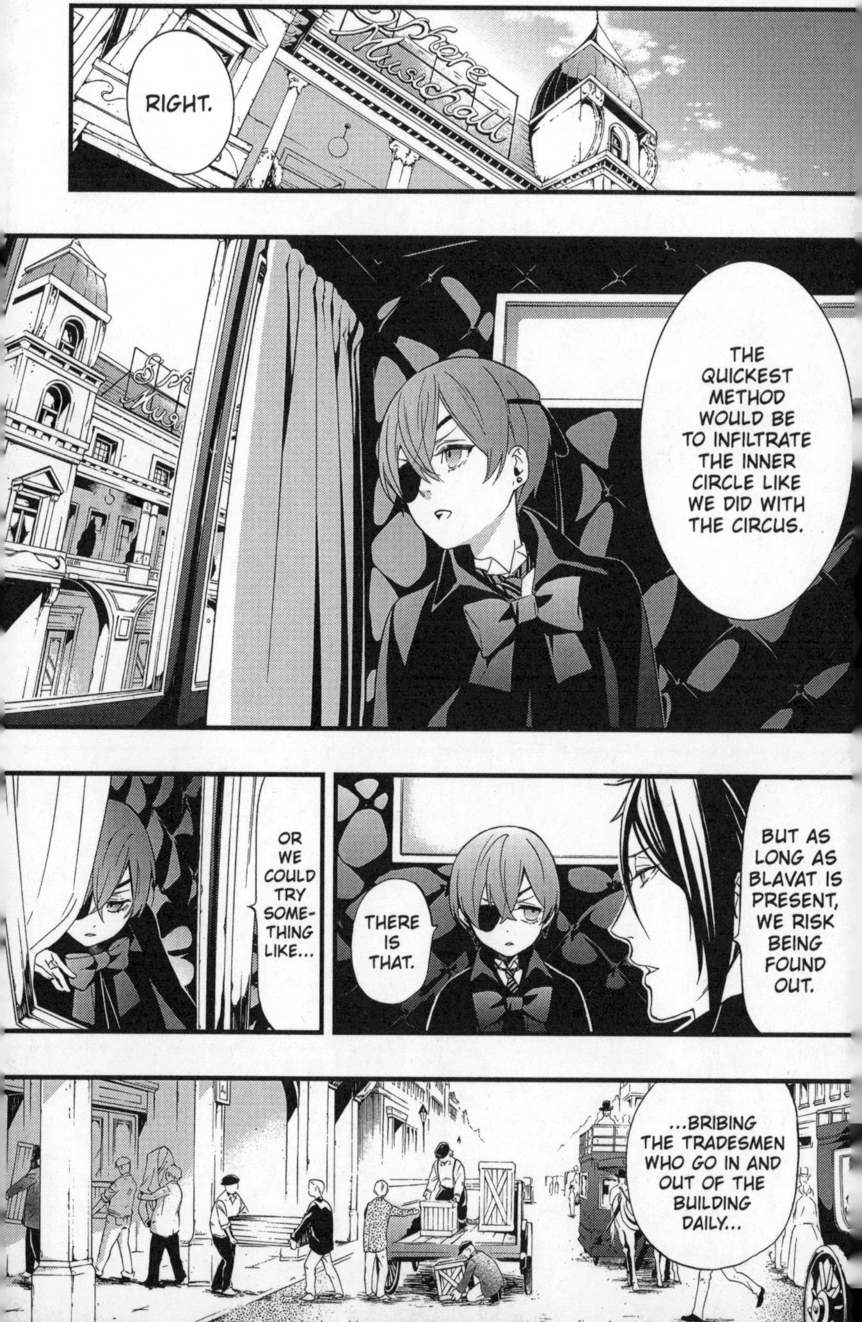
Sphere Musichall
RIGHT.
THE QUICKEST METHOD WOULD BE TO INFILTRATE THE INNER CIRCLE LIKE WE DID WITH THE CIRCUS.
BUT AS LONG AS BLAVAT IS PRESENT, WE RISK BEING FOUND OUT.
THERE IS THAT.
OR WE COULD TRY SOME-THING LIKE...
...BRIBING THE TRADESMEN WHO GO IN AND OUT OF THE BUILDING DAILY...

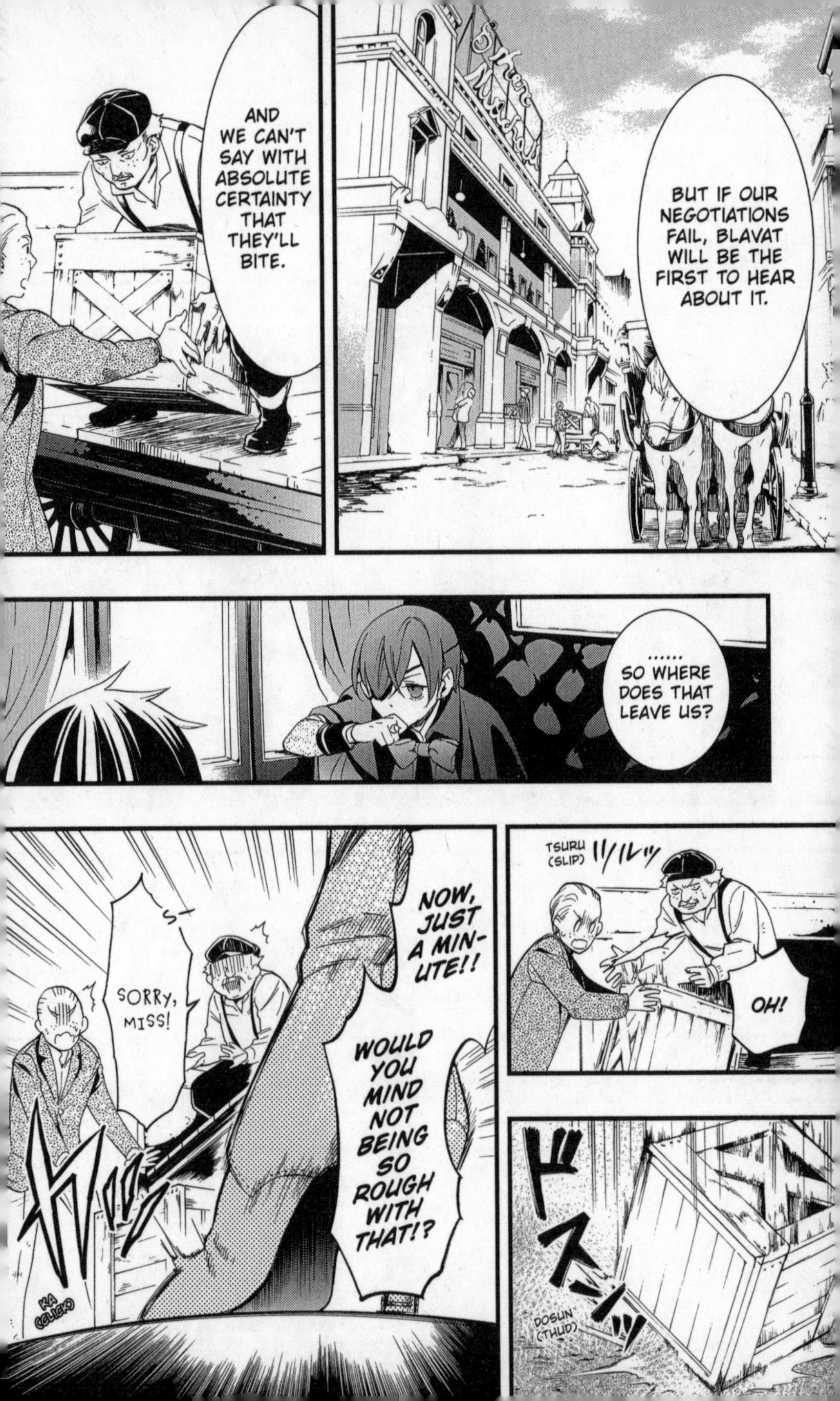
BUT IF OUR NEGOTIATIONS FAIL, BLAVAT WILL BE THE FIRST TO HEAR ABOUT IT.
AND WE CAN'T SAY WITH ABSOLUTE CERTAINTY THAT THEY'LL BITE.
...... SO WHERE DOES THAT LEAVE US?
TSURU (SLIP)
OH!
DOSUN (THUD)
NOW, JUST A MIN-UTE!!
WOULD YOU MIND NOT BEING SO ROUGH WITH THAT!?
S-
SORRY, MISS!
KA (CLICK)

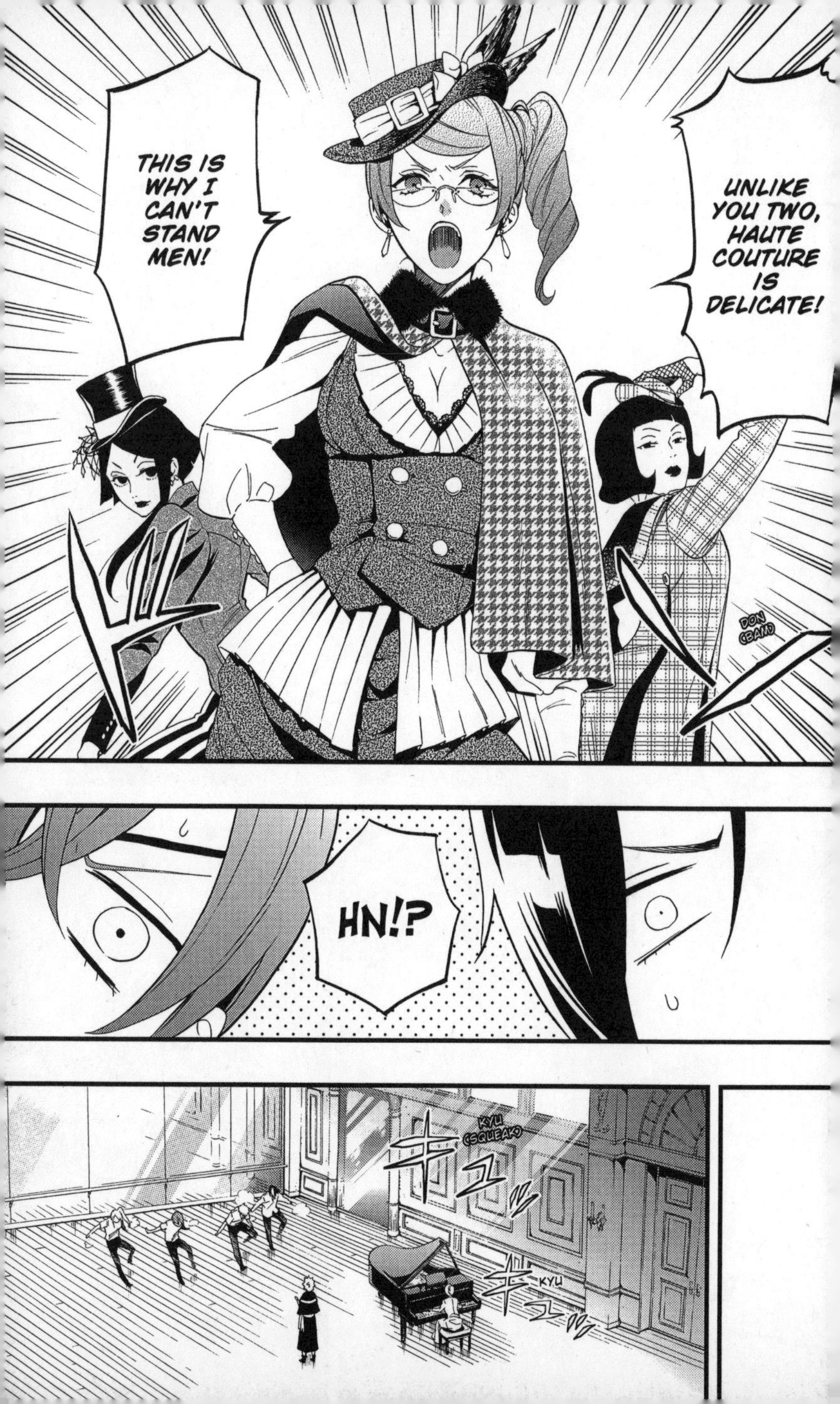
UNLIKE YOU TWO, HAUTE COUTURE IS DELICATE!
THIS IS WHY I CAN'T STAND MEN!
DON (BAM)
HN!?
KYU (SQUEAK)
KYU

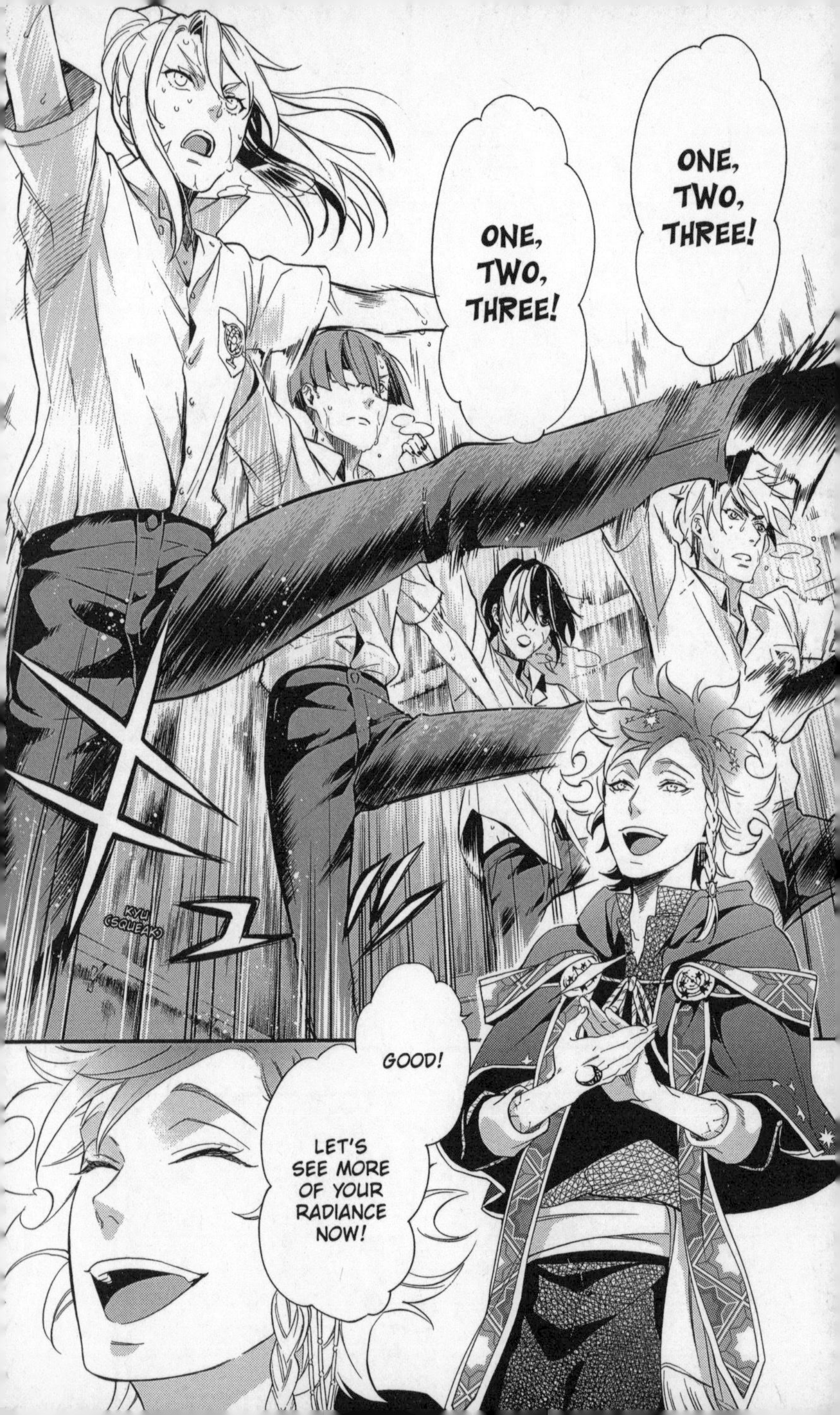
ONE, TWO, THREE!
ONE, TWO, THREE!
KYU (SQUEAK)
GOOD!
LET'S SEE MORE OF YOUR RADIANCE NOW!

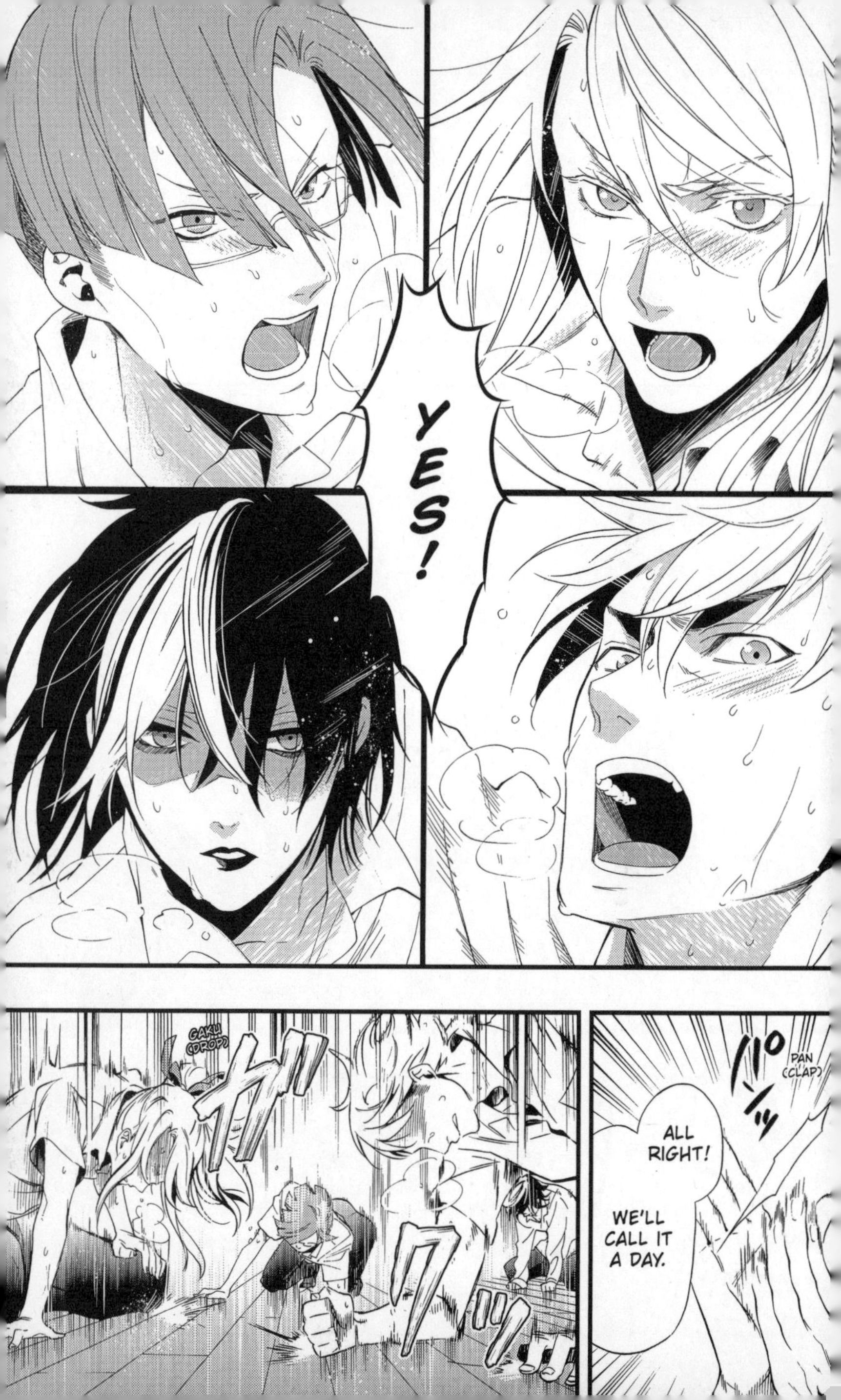
YES!
PAN (CLAP)
ALL RIGHT!
WE'LL CALL IT A DAY.
GAKU (DROP)

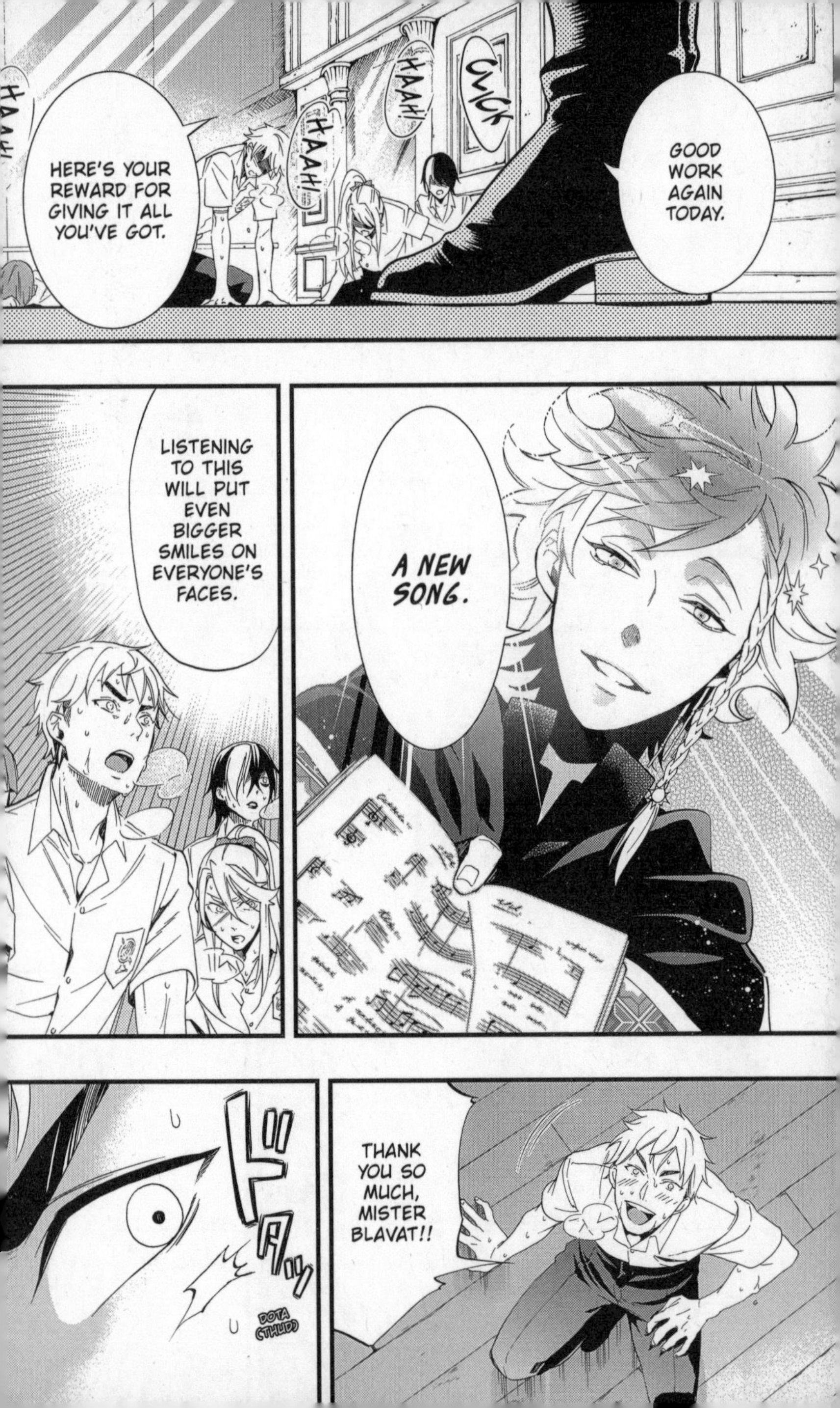
GOOD WORK AGAIN TODAY.
CLICK
HAAAH!
HAAAH!
HERE'S YOUR REWARD FOR GIVING IT ALL YOU'VE GOT.
A NEW SONG.
LISTENING TO THIS WILL PUT EVEN BIGGER SMILES ON EVERYONE'S FACES.
THANK YOU SO MUCH, MISTER BLAVAT!!
DOTA (THUD)

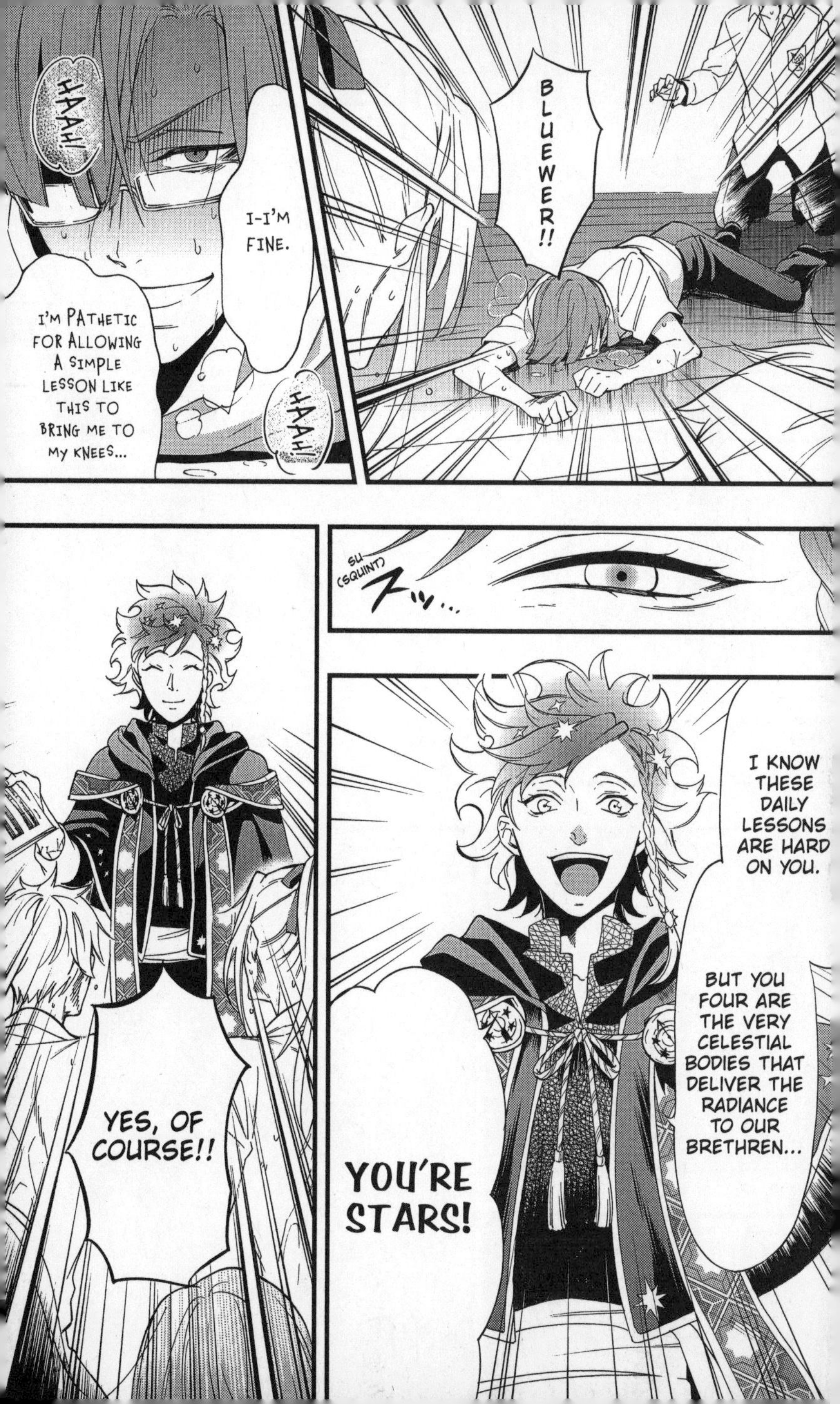
BLUEWER!!
HAAH!
I-I'M FINE.
I'M PATHETIC FOR ALLOWING A SIMPLE LESSON LIKE THIS TO BRING ME TO MY KNEES...
HAAH!
SU (SQUINT)
スッ...
I KNOW THESE DAILY LESSONS ARE HARD ON YOU.
BUT YOU FOUR ARE THE VERY CELESTIAL BODIES THAT DELIVER THE RADIANCE TO OUR BRETHREN...
YOU'RE STARS!
YES, OF COURSE!!

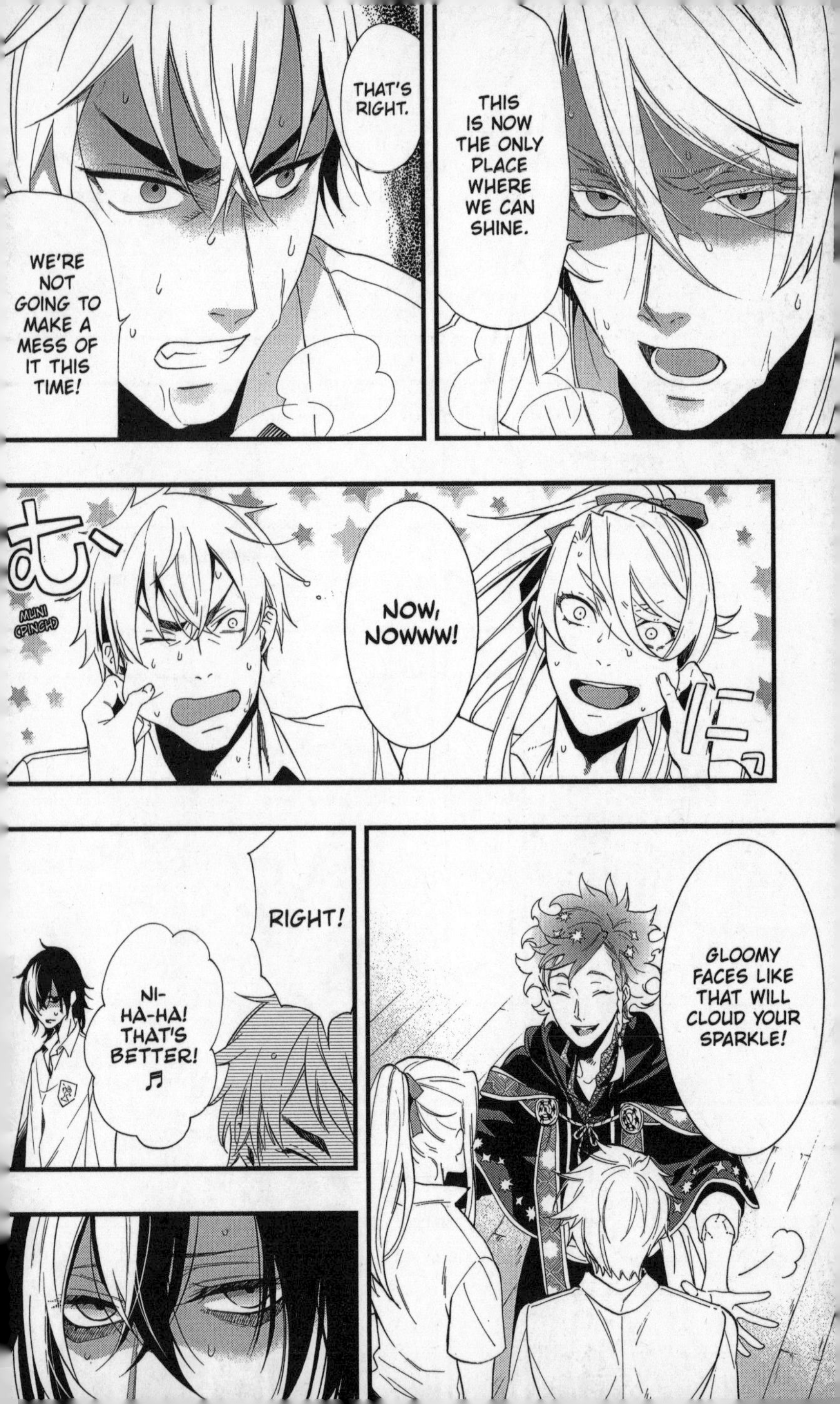

THIS IS NOW THE ONLY PLACE WHERE WE CAN SHINE.
THAT'S RIGHT.
WE'RE NOT GOING TO MAKE A MESS OF IT THIS TIME!
NOW, NOWWW!
む
MUNI (PINCH)
GLOOMY FACES LIKE THAT WILL CLOUD YOUR SPARKLE!
RIGHT!
NI-HA-HA! THAT'S BETTER! ♬

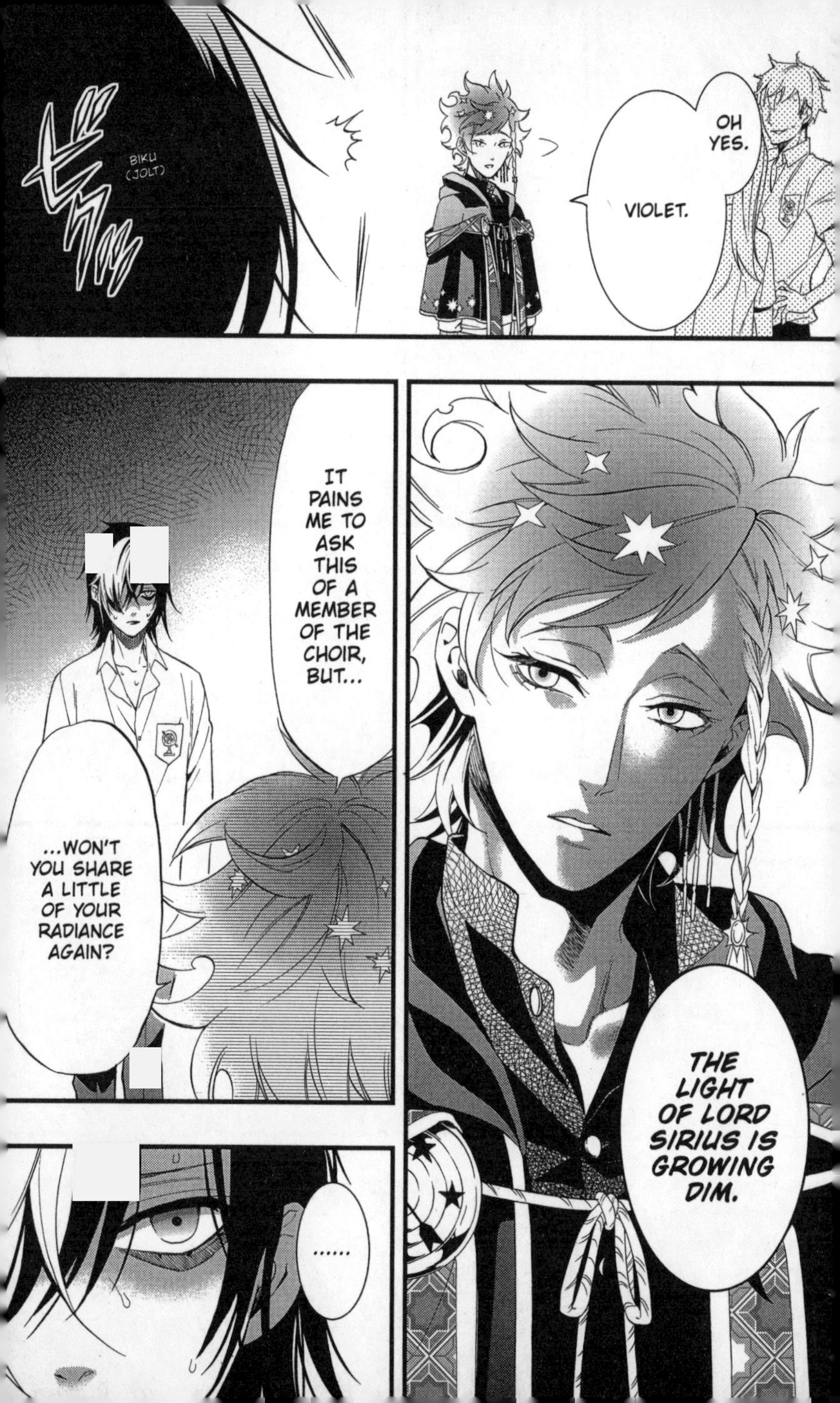
OH YES.
VIOLET.
BIKU (JOLT)
THE LIGHT OF LORD SIRIUS IS GROWING DIM.
IT PAINS ME TO ASK THIS OF A MEMBER OF THE CHOIR, BUT...
...WON'T YOU SHARE A LITTLE OF YOUR RADIANCE AGAIN?
......

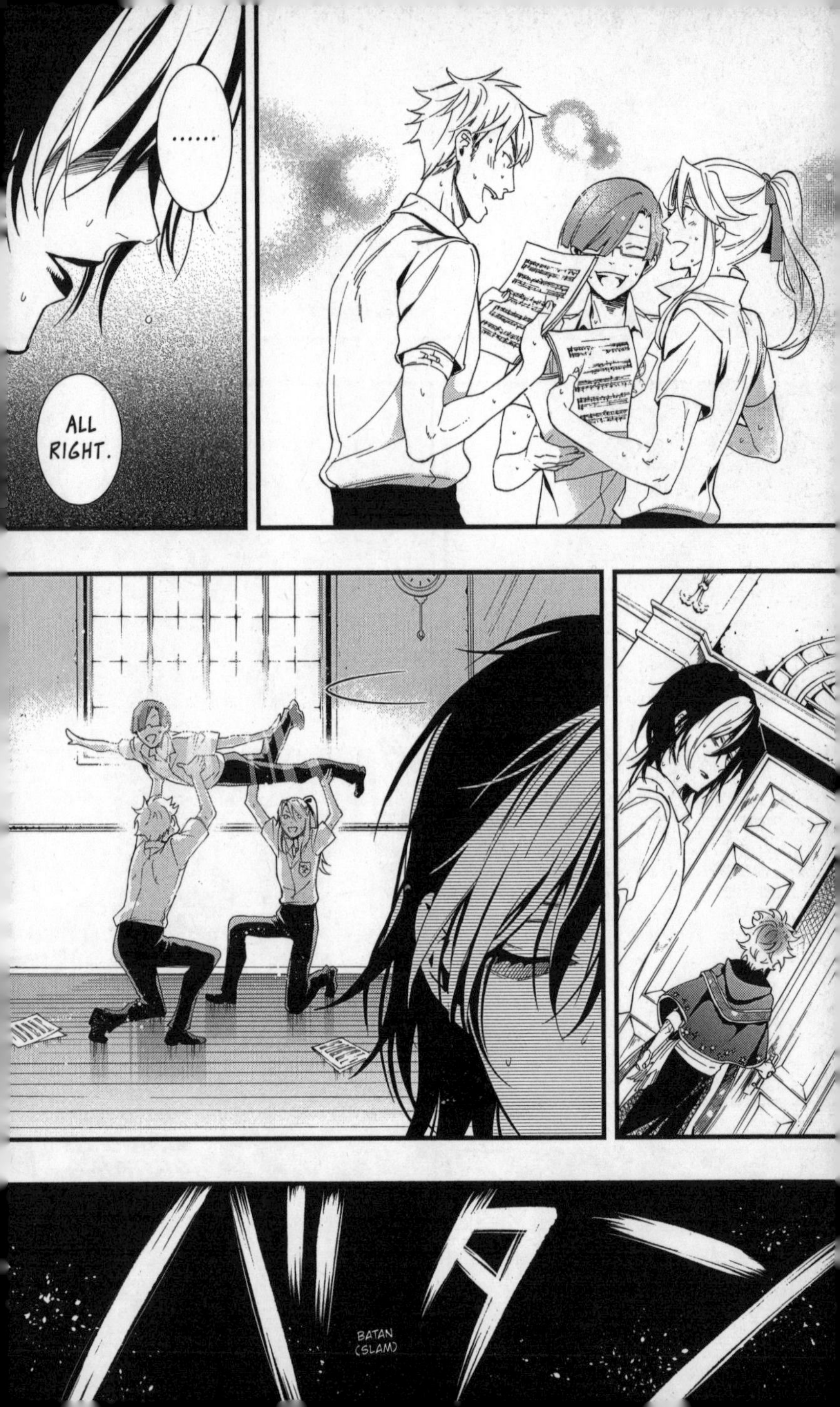

......
ALL RIGHT.
BATAN
(SLAM)

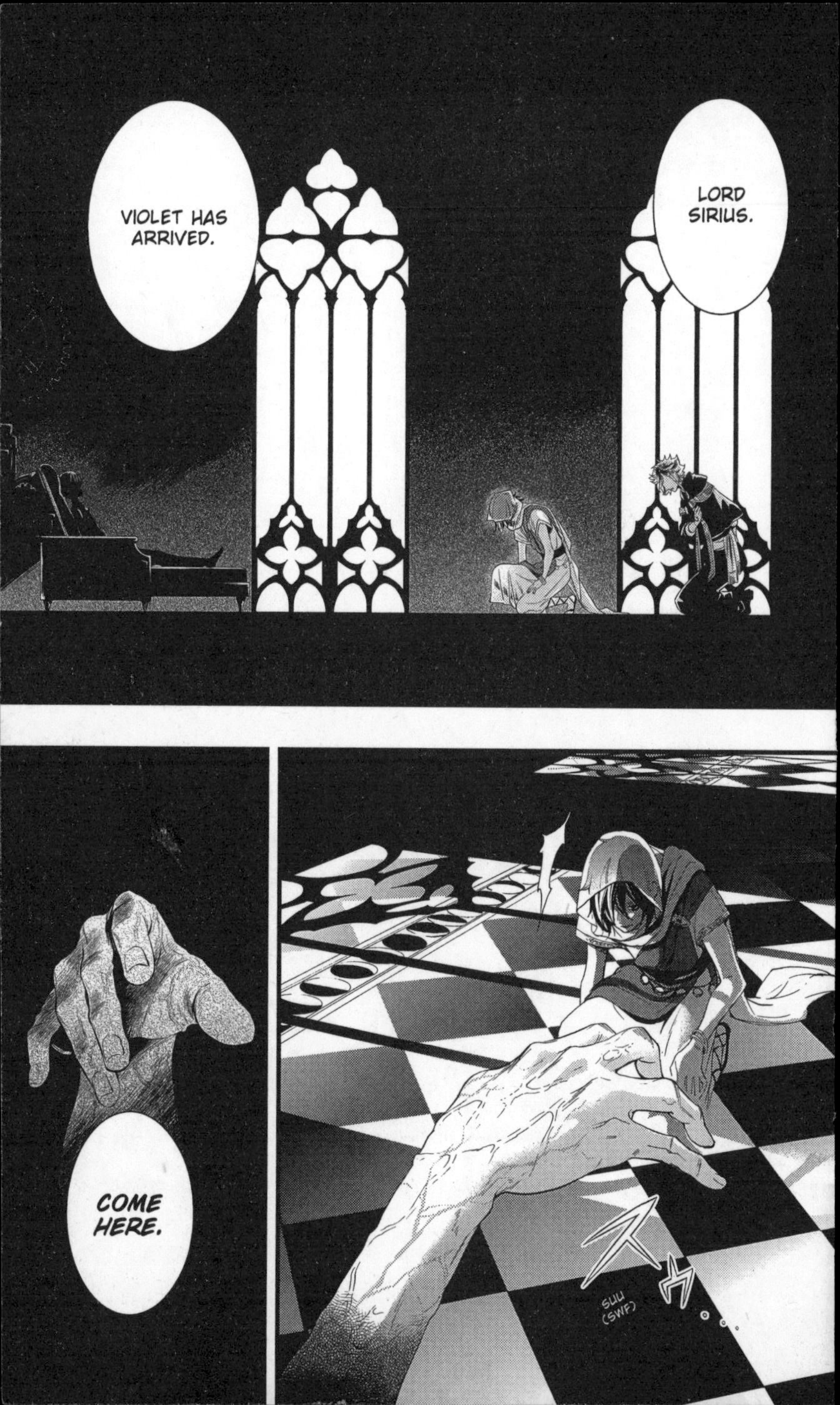
LORD SIRIUS.
VIOLET HAS ARRIVED.
SUU (SWF)
COME HERE.

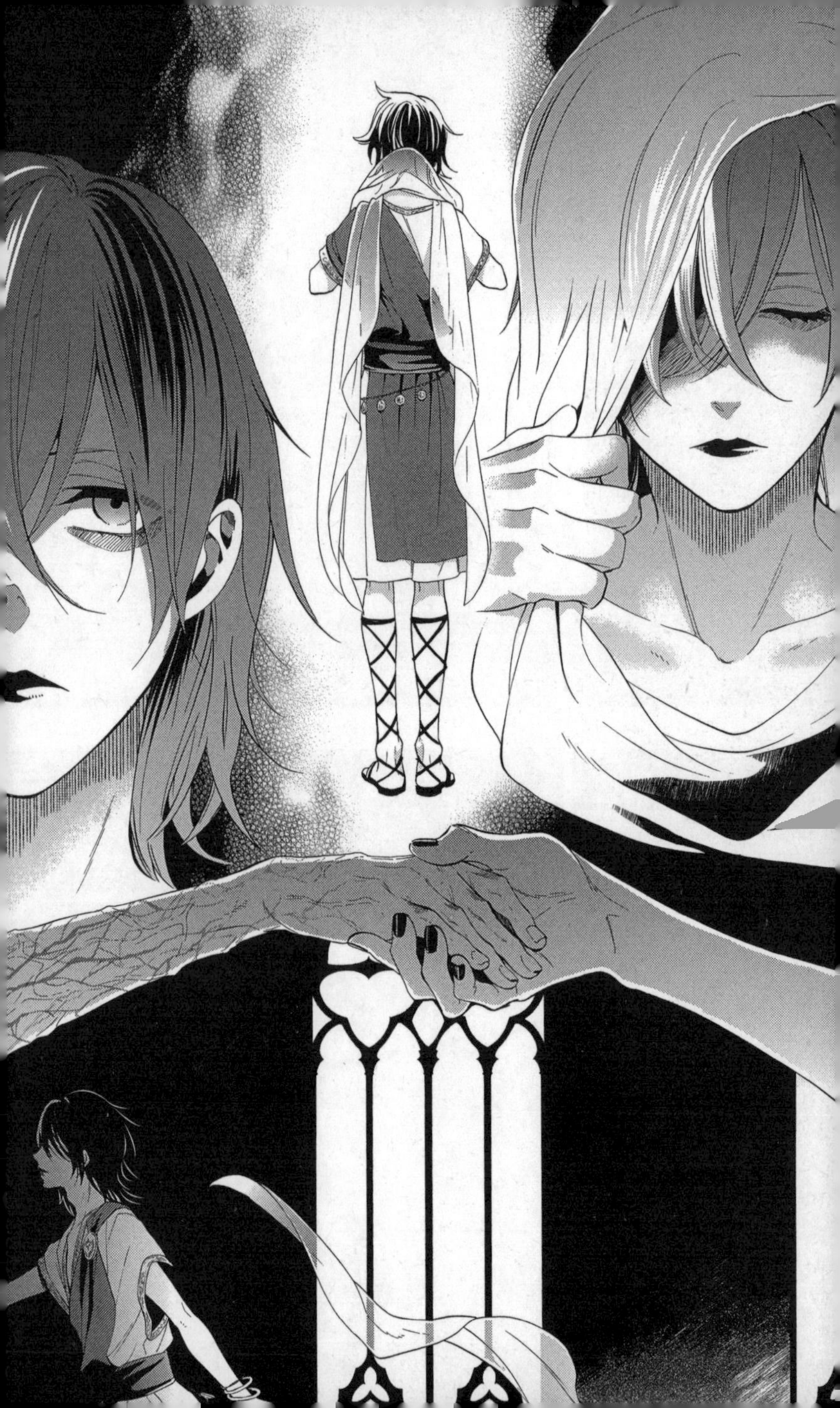

Black Butler

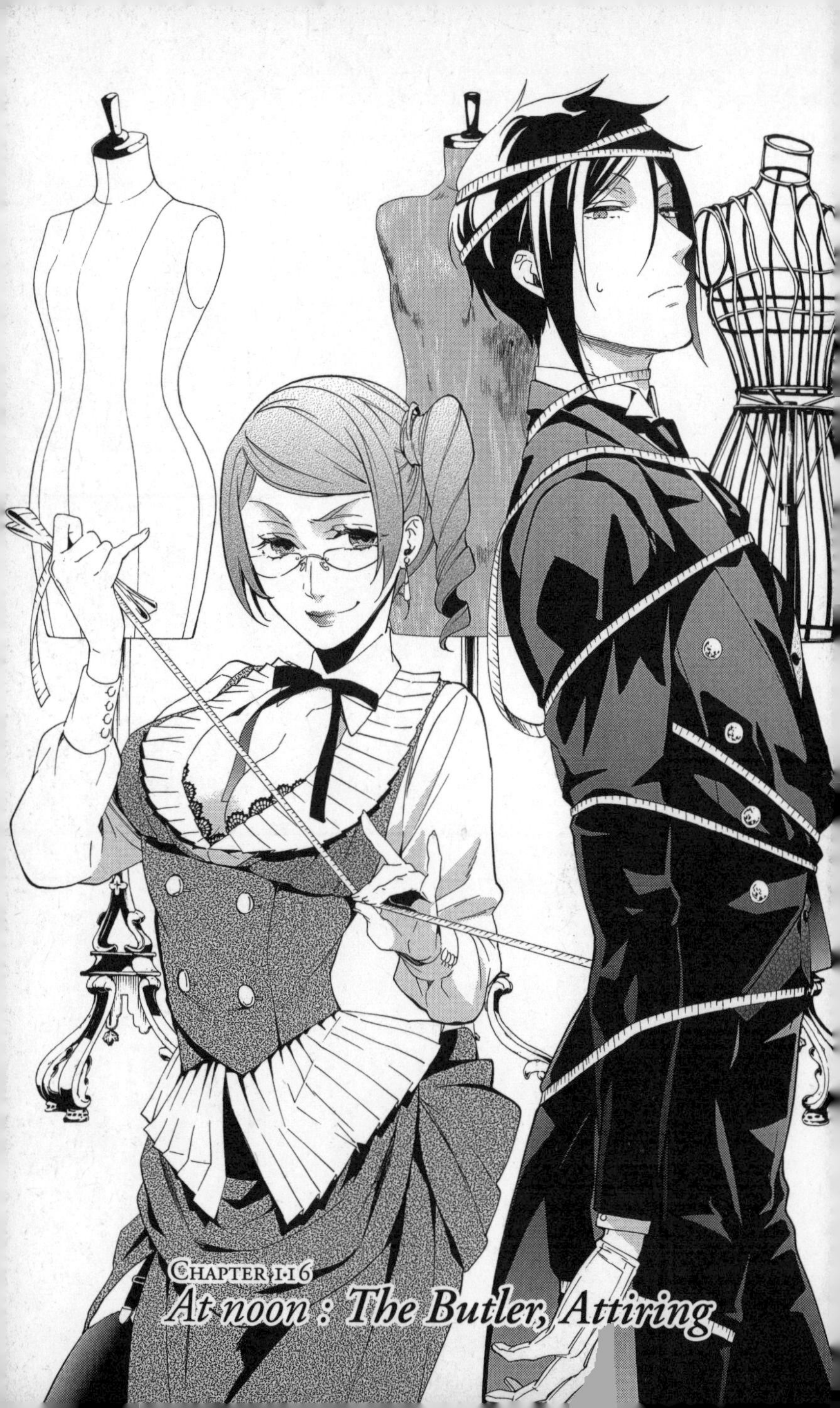
CHAPTER 116
At noon : The Butler, Attiring

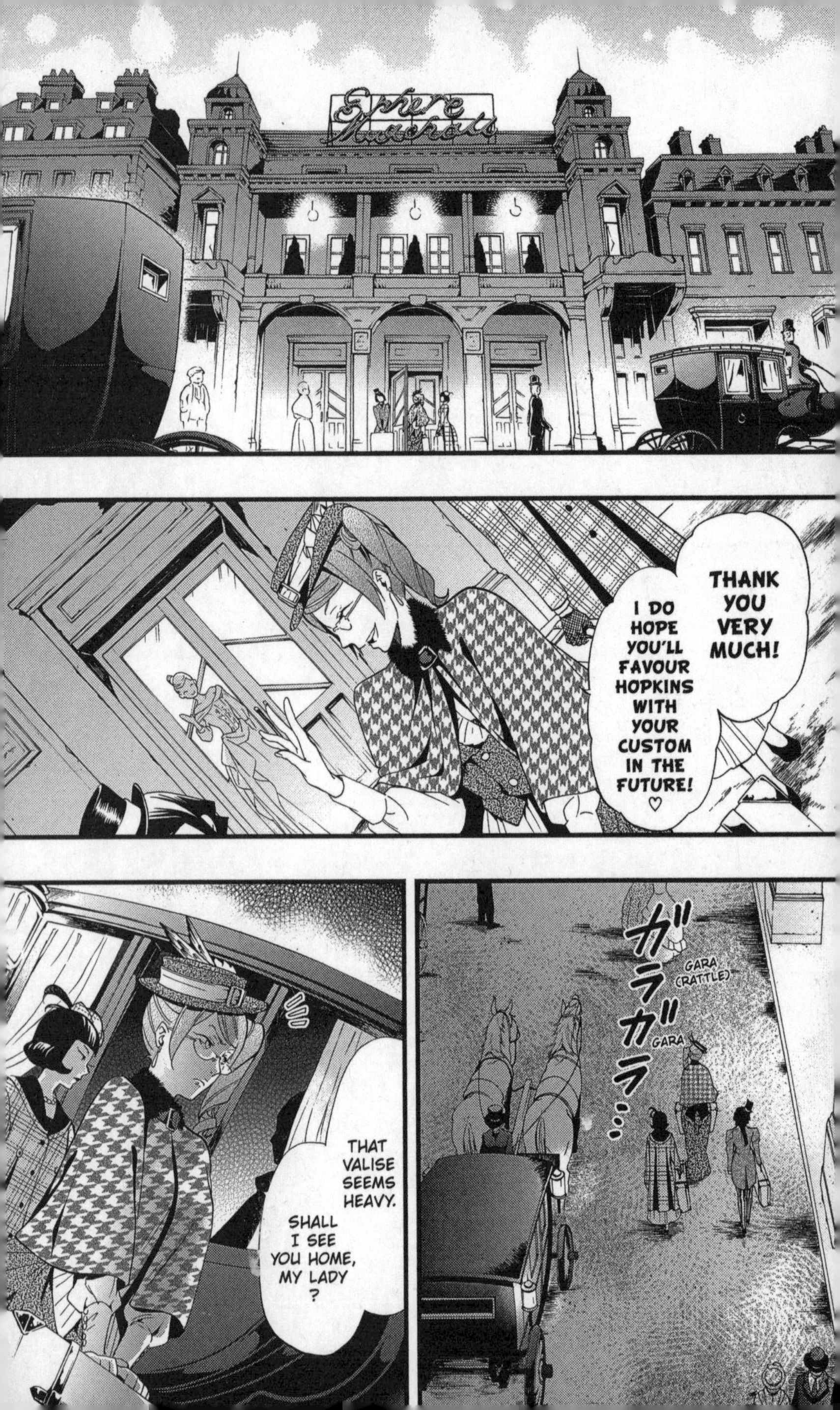
THANK YOU VERY MUCH!
I DO HOPE YOU'LL FAVOUR HOPKINS WITH YOUR CUSTOM IN THE FUTURE! ♡
ガラガラ…
GARA (RATTLE)
GARA
THAT VALISE SEEMS HEAVY.
SHALL I SEE YOU HOME, MY LADY?

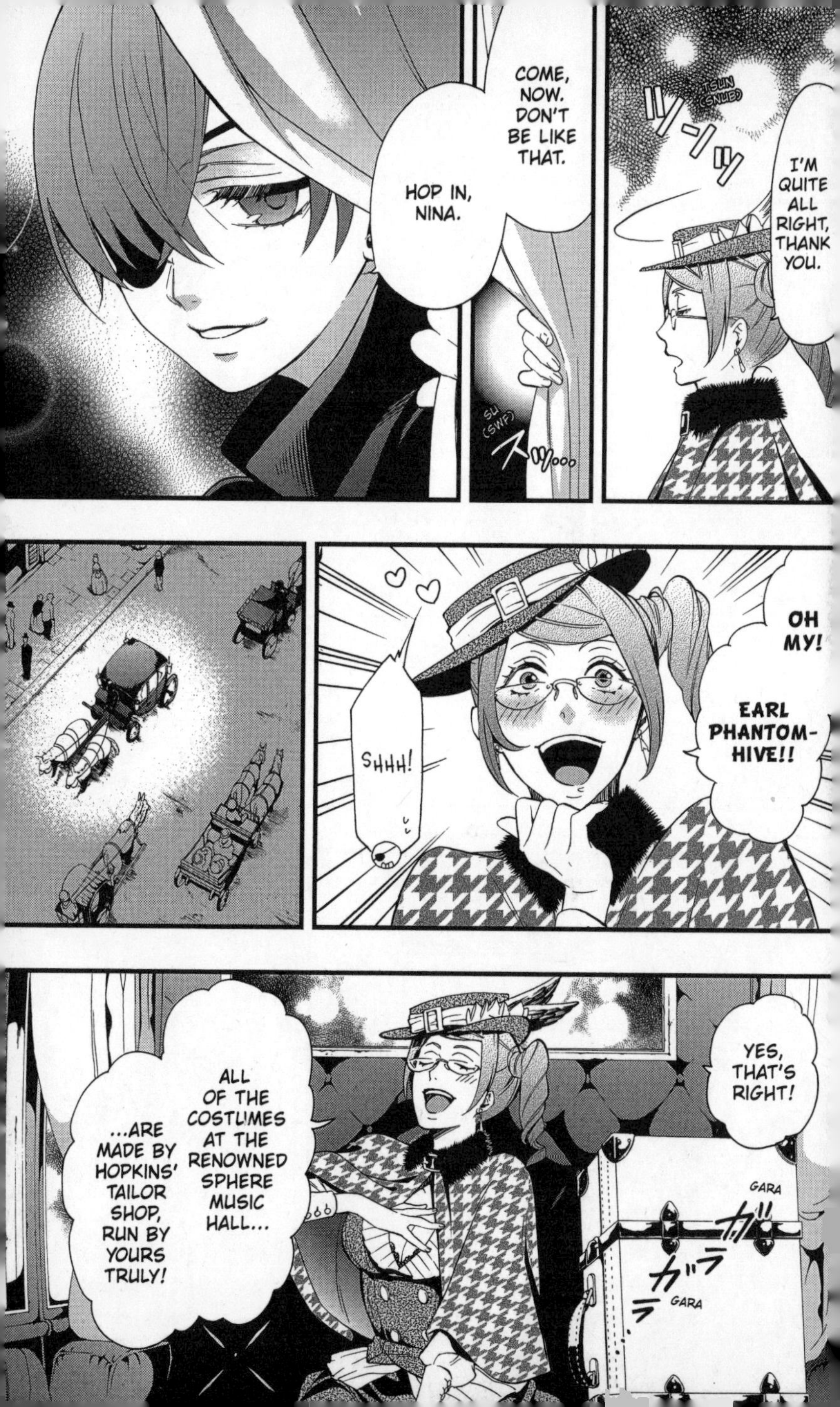
TSUN (SNUB)
I'M QUITE ALL RIGHT, THANK YOU.
COME, NOW. DON'T BE LIKE THAT.
HOP IN, NINA.
SU (SWP)
OH MY!
EARL PHANTOM-HIVE!!
SHHH!
YES, THAT'S RIGHT!
GARA
GARA
ALL OF THE COSTUMES AT THE RENOWNED SPHERE MUSIC HALL...
...ARE MADE BY HOPKINS' TAILOR SHOP, RUN BY YOURS TRULY!

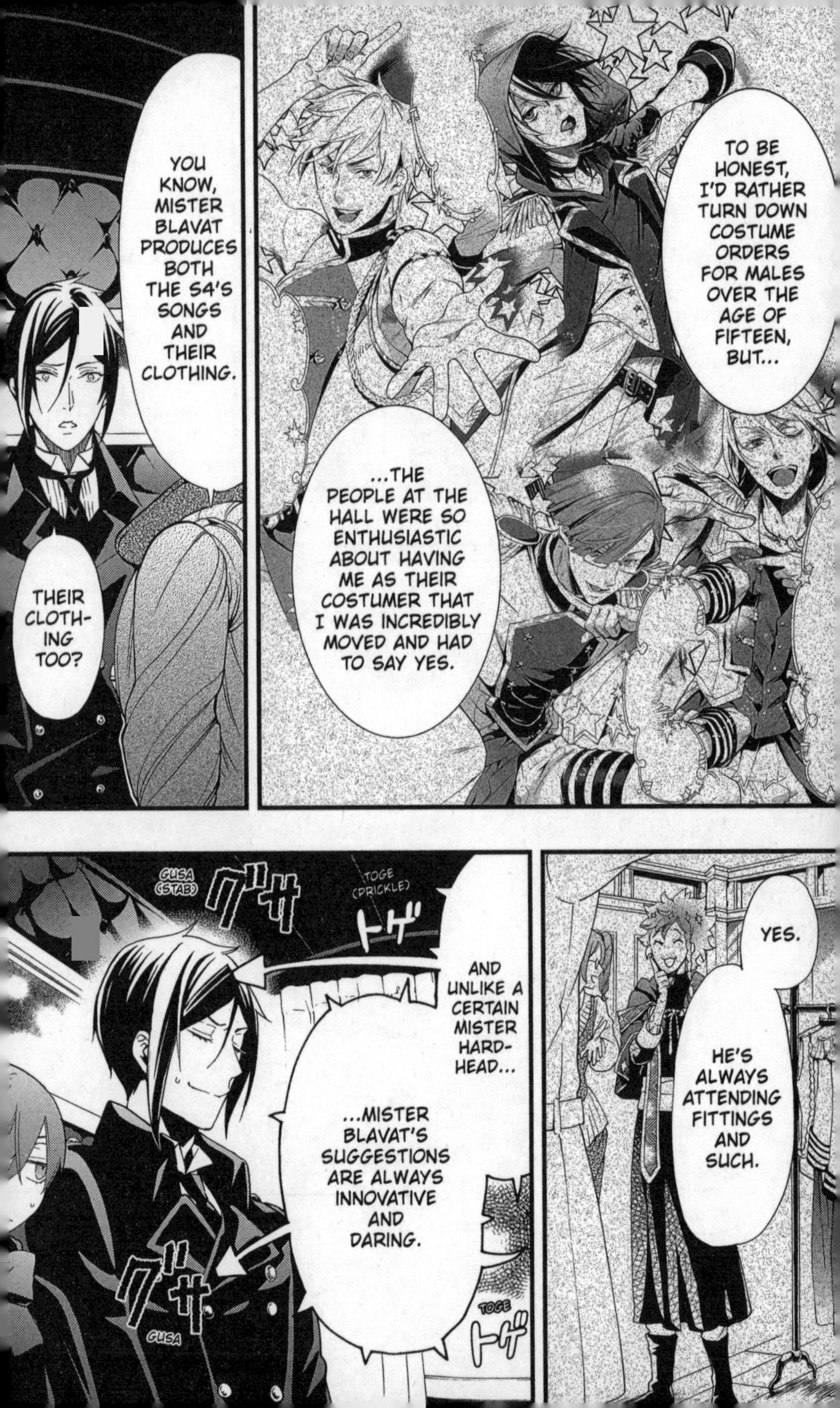
TO BE HONEST, I'D RATHER TURN DOWN COSTUME ORDERS FOR MALES OVER THE AGE OF FIFTEEN, BUT...
...THE PEOPLE AT THE HALL WERE SO ENTHUSIASTIC ABOUT HAVING ME AS THEIR COSTUMER THAT I WAS INCREDIBLY MOVED AND HAD TO SAY YES.
YOU KNOW, MISTER BLAVAT PRODUCES BOTH THE S4'S SONGS AND THEIR CLOTHING.
THEIR CLOTH-ING TOO?
YES.
HE'S ALWAYS ATTENDING FITTINGS AND SUCH.
TOGE (PRICKLE)
トゲ
GUSA (STAB)
グサ
AND UNLIKE A CERTAIN MISTER HARD-HEAD...
...MISTER BLAVAT'S SUGGESTIONS ARE ALWAYS INNOVATIVE AND DARING.
TOGE
トゲ
グサ
GUSA

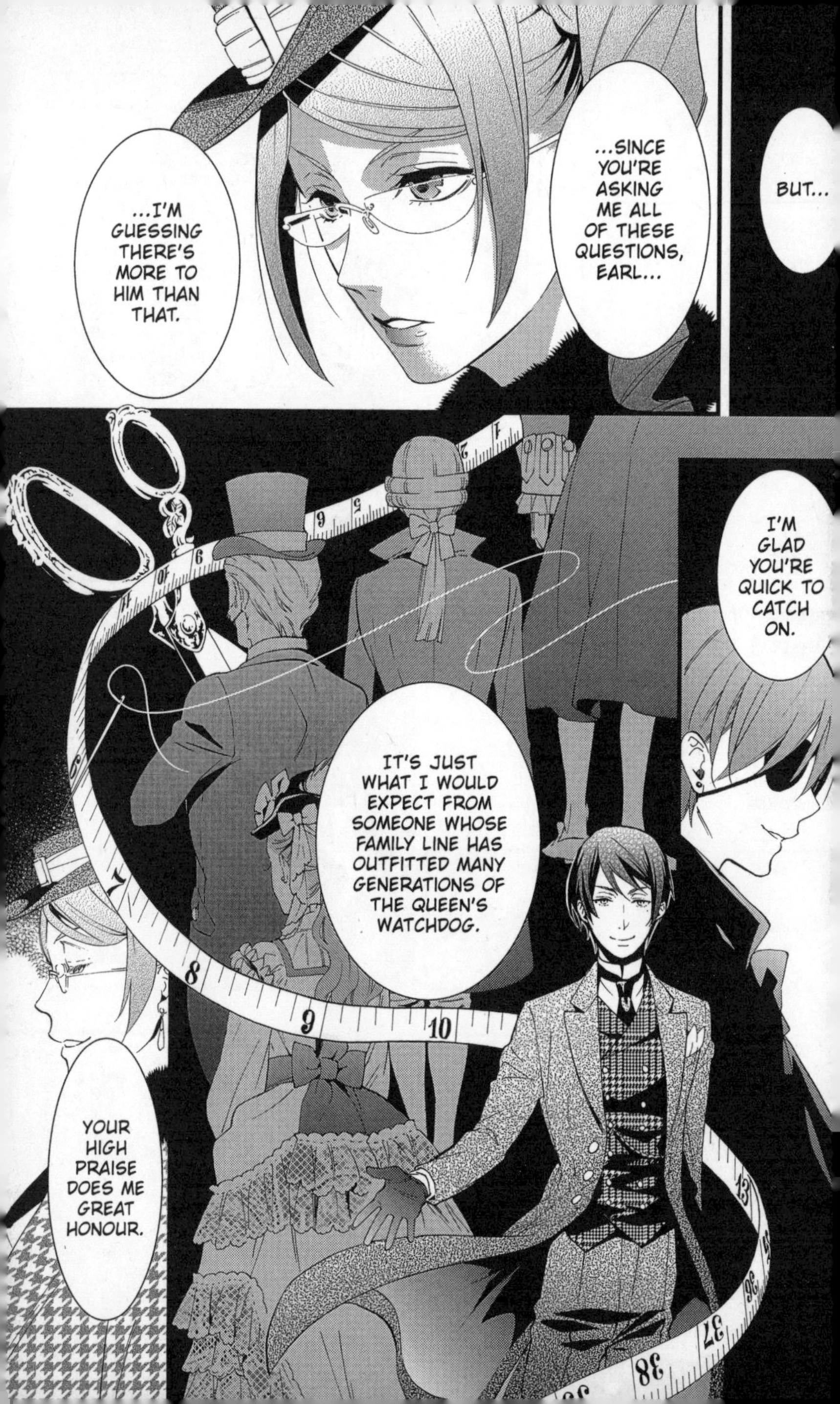
BUT...
...SINCE YOU'RE ASKING ME ALL OF THESE QUESTIONS, EARL...
...I'M GUESSING THERE'S MORE TO HIM THAN THAT.
I'M GLAD YOU'RE QUICK TO CATCH ON.
IT'S JUST WHAT I WOULD EXPECT FROM SOMEONE WHOSE FAMILY LINE HAS OUTFITTED MANY GENERATIONS OF THE QUEEN'S WATCHDOG.
YOUR HIGH PRAISE DOES ME GREAT HONOUR.

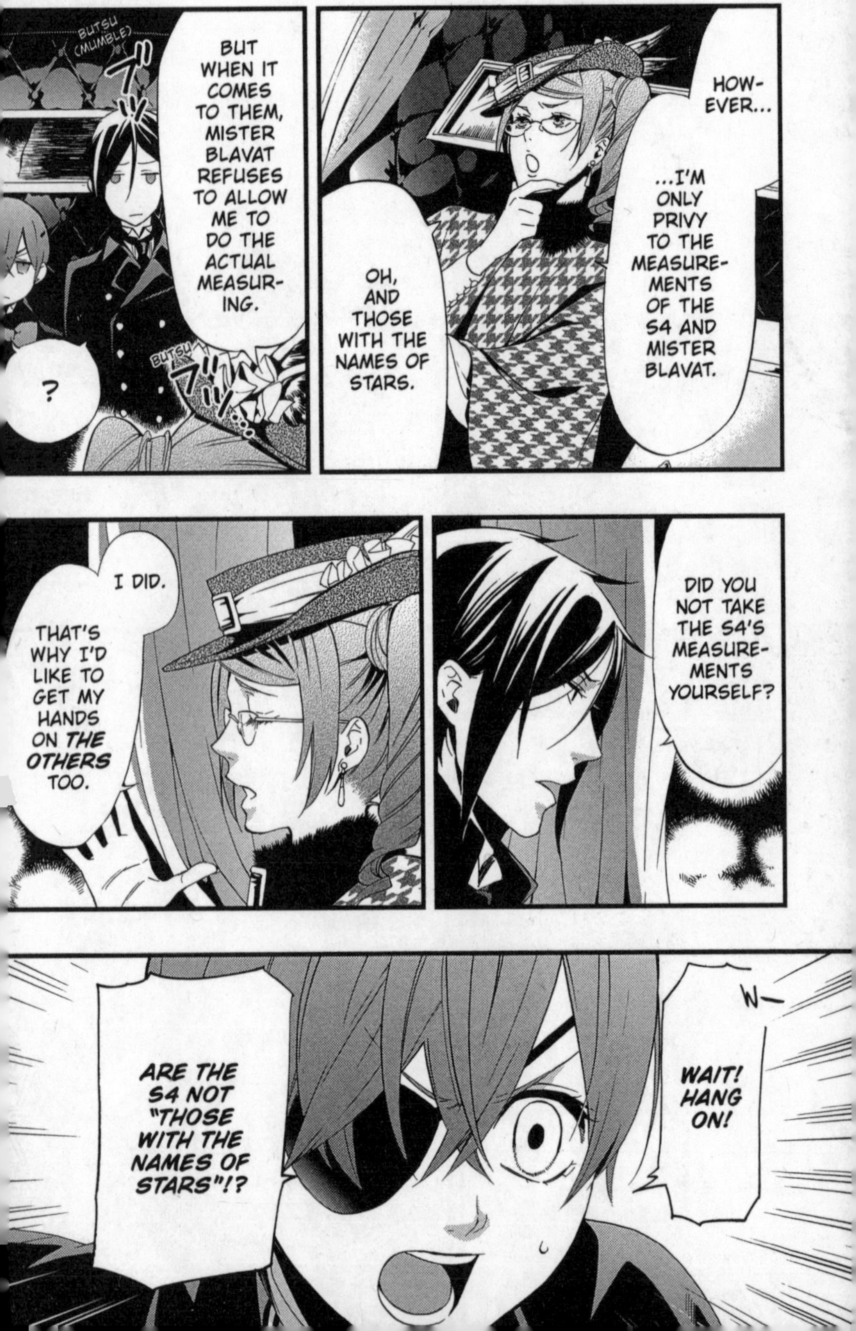
HOW-EVER...
...I'M ONLY PRIVY TO THE MEASUREMENTS OF THE S4 AND MISTER BLAVAT.
OH, AND THOSE WITH THE NAMES OF STARS.
BUTSU (MUMBLE)
BUT WHEN IT COMES TO THEM, MISTER BLAVAT REFUSES TO ALLOW ME TO DO THE ACTUAL MEASURING.
BUTSU
?
DID YOU NOT TAKE THE S4'S MEASUREMENTS YOURSELF?
I DID.
THAT'S WHY I'D LIKE TO GET MY HANDS ON *THE OTHERS* TOO.
W—
WAIT! HANG ON!
ARE THE S4 NOT "THOSE WITH THE NAMES OF STARS"!?

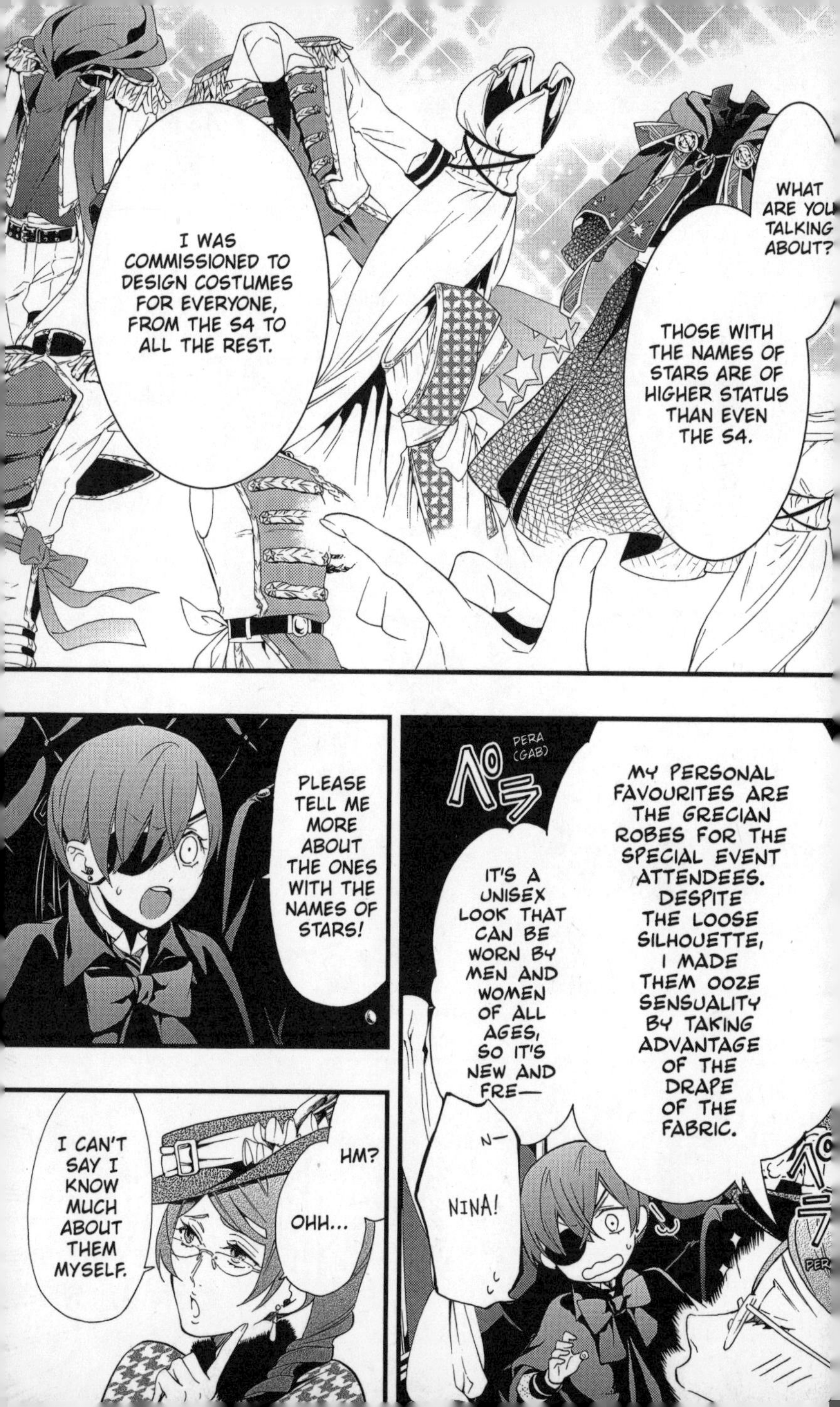

WHAT ARE YOU TALKING ABOUT?
THOSE WITH THE NAMES OF STARS ARE OF HIGHER STATUS THAN EVEN THE S4.
I WAS COMMISSIONED TO DESIGN COSTUMES FOR EVERYONE, FROM THE S4 TO ALL THE REST.
PERA (GAB)
MY PERSONAL FAVOURITES ARE THE GRECIAN ROBES FOR THE SPECIAL EVENT ATTENDEES. DESPITE THE LOOSE SILHOUETTE, I MADE THEM OOZE SENSUALITY BY TAKING ADVANTAGE OF THE DRAPE OF THE FABRIC.
IT'S A UNISEX LOOK THAT CAN BE WORN BY MEN AND WOMEN OF ALL AGES, SO IT'S NEW AND FRE—
N—
NINA!
PER
PLEASE TELL ME MORE ABOUT THE ONES WITH THE NAMES OF STARS!
HM?
OHH...
I CAN'T SAY I KNOW MUCH ABOUT THEM MYSELF.

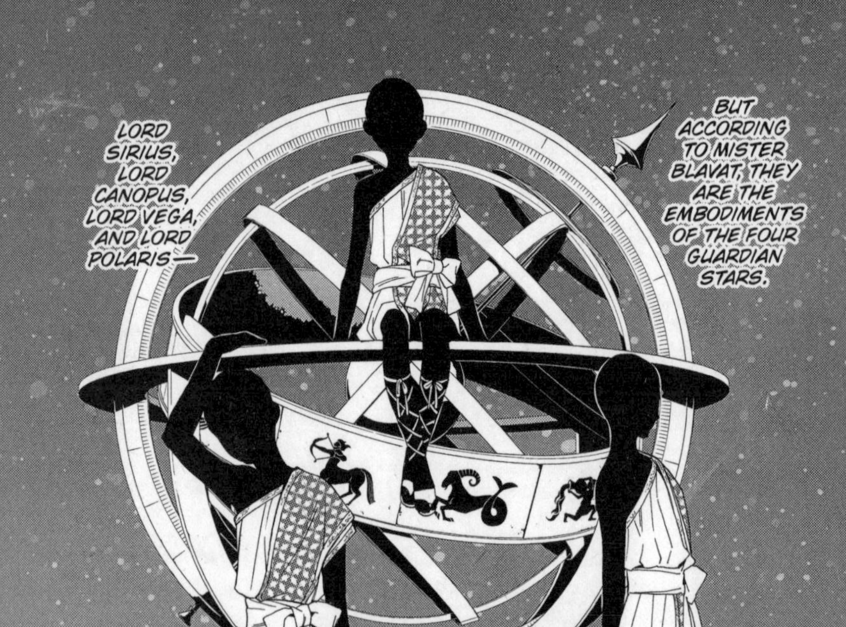
LORD SIRIUS, LORD CANOPUS, LORD VEGA, AND LORD POLARIS—
THAT IS HOW THE FOUR INDIVIDUALS ARE ADDRESSED.
BUT ACCORDING TO MISTER BLAVAT, THEY ARE THE EMBODIMENTS OF THE FOUR GUARDIAN STARS.

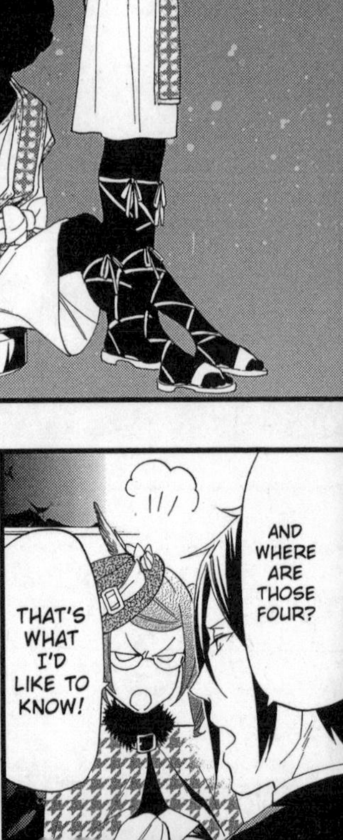
AND WHERE ARE THOSE FOUR?
THAT'S WHAT I'D LIKE TO KNOW!

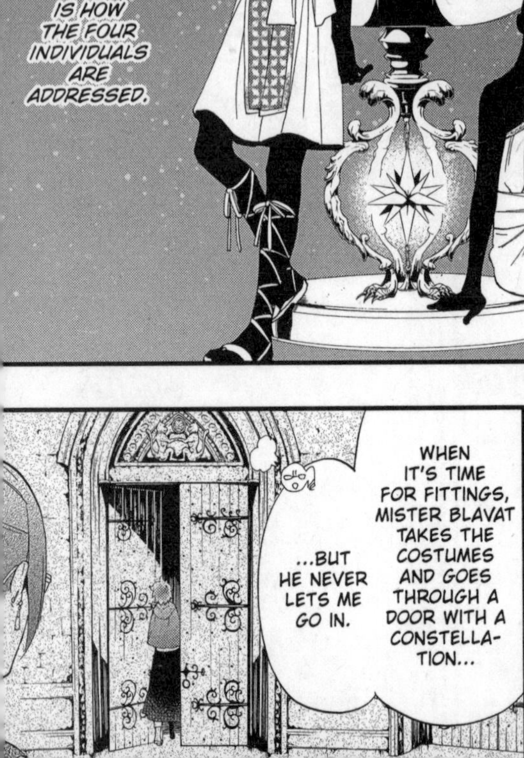
WHEN IT'S TIME FOR FITTINGS, MISTER BLAVAT TAKES THE COSTUMES AND GOES THROUGH A DOOR WITH A CONSTELLATION...
...BUT HE NEVER LETS ME GO IN.

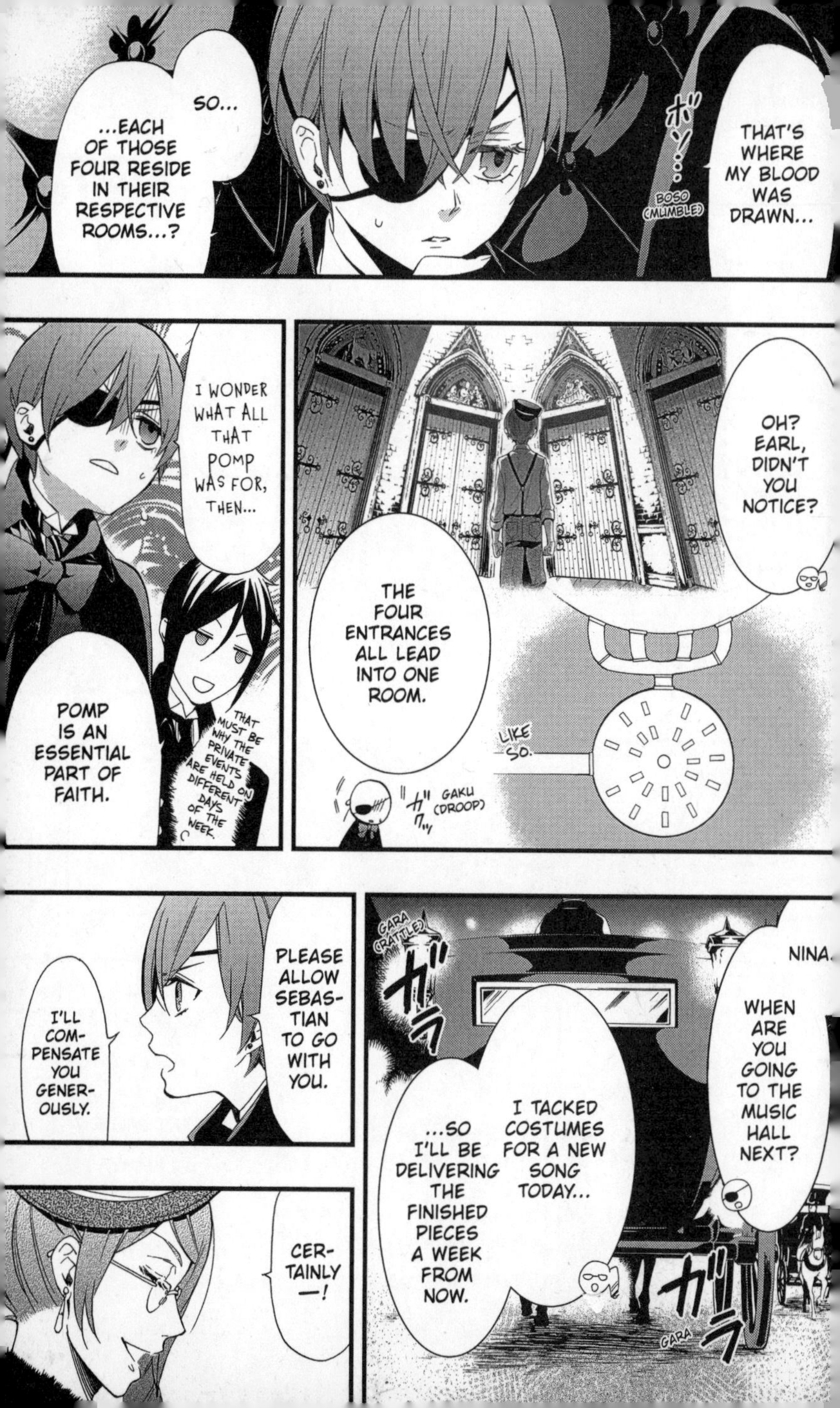
THAT'S WHERE MY BLOOD WAS DRAWN...
BOSO (MUMBLE)
SO...
...EACH OF THOSE FOUR RESIDE IN THEIR RESPECTIVE ROOMS...?
OH? EARL, DIDN'T YOU NOTICE?
THE FOUR ENTRANCES ALL LEAD INTO ONE ROOM.
LIKE SO.
GAKU (DROOP)
I WONDER WHAT ALL THAT POMP WAS FOR, THEN...
THAT MUST BE WHY THE PRIVATE EVENTS ARE HELD ON DIFFERENT DAYS OF THE WEEK.
POMP IS AN ESSENTIAL PART OF FAITH.
GARA (RATTLE)
NINA.
WHEN ARE YOU GOING TO THE MUSIC HALL NEXT?
I TACKED COSTUMES FOR A NEW SONG TODAY...
...SO I'LL BE DELIVERING THE FINISHED PIECES A WEEK FROM NOW.
GARA
PLEASE ALLOW SEBASTIAN TO GO WITH YOU.
I'LL COMPENSATE YOU GENEROUSLY.
CERTAINLY—!

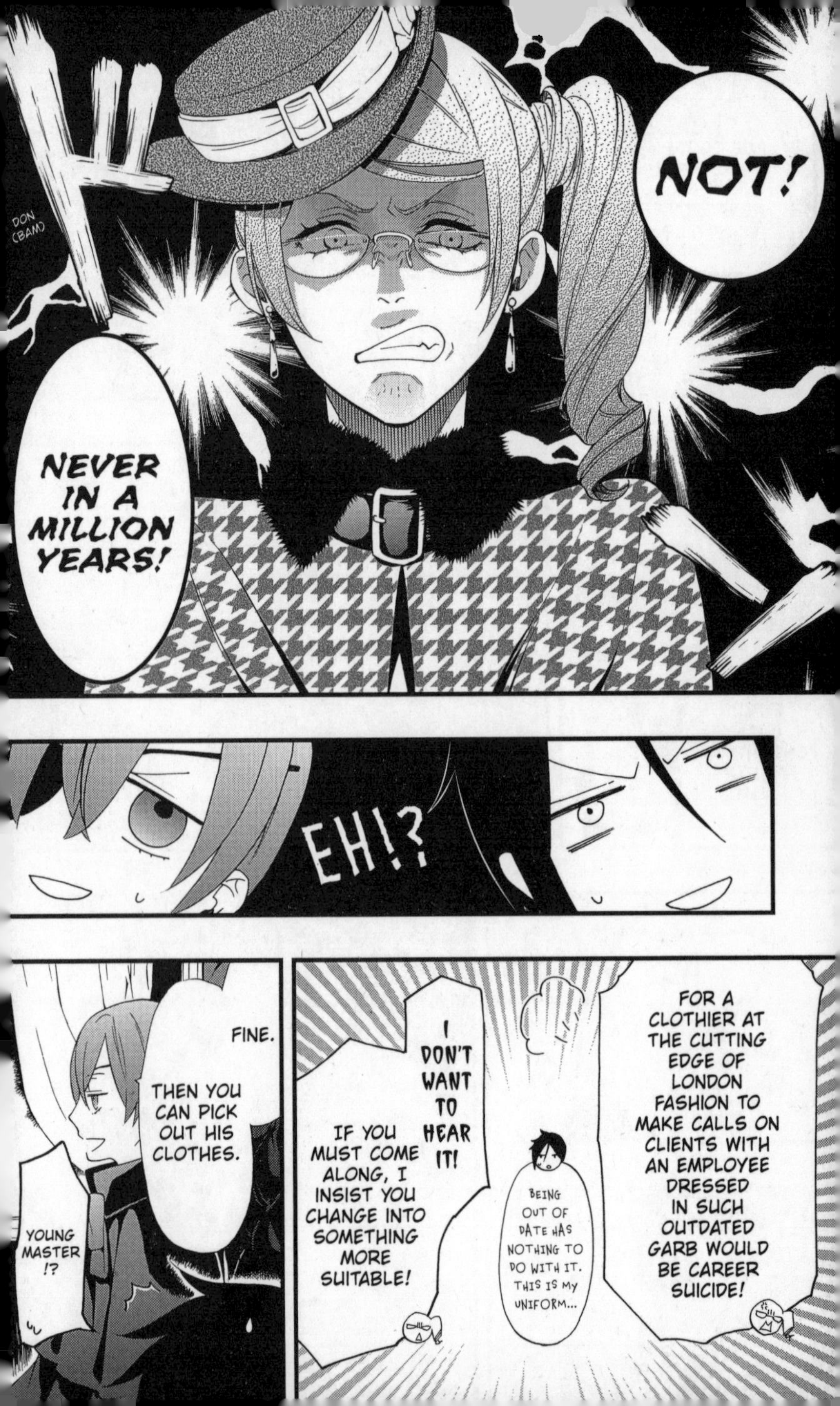
NOT!
NEVER IN A MILLION YEARS!
DON (BAM)
EH!?
FOR A CLOTHIER AT THE CUTTING EDGE OF LONDON FASHION TO MAKE CALLS ON CLIENTS WITH AN EMPLOYEE DRESSED IN SUCH OUTDATED GARB WOULD BE CAREER SUICIDE!
BEING OUT OF DATE HAS NOTHING TO DO WITH IT. THIS IS MY UNIFORM...
I DON'T WANT TO HEAR IT!
IF YOU MUST COME ALONG, I INSIST YOU CHANGE INTO SOMETHING MORE SUITABLE!
FINE.
THEN YOU CAN PICK OUT HIS CLOTHES.
YOUNG MASTER !?

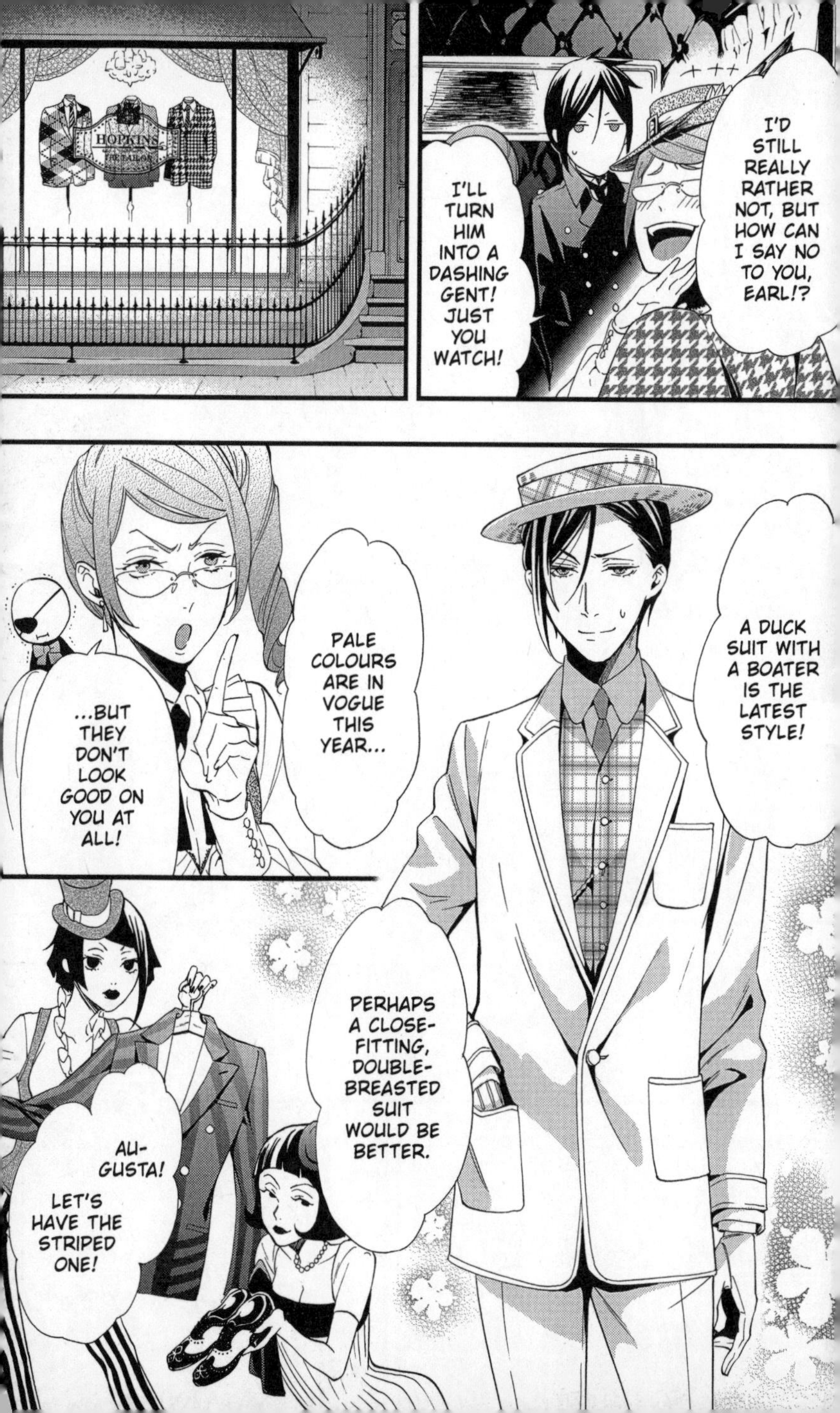
I'D STILL REALLY RATHER NOT, BUT HOW CAN I SAY NO TO YOU, EARL!?
I'LL TURN HIM INTO A DASHING GENT! JUST YOU WATCH!
HOPKINS
THE TAILOR
A DUCK SUIT WITH A BOATER IS THE LATEST STYLE!
PALE COLOURS ARE IN VOGUE THIS YEAR...
...BUT THEY DON'T LOOK GOOD ON YOU AT ALL!
PERHAPS A CLOSE-FITTING, DOUBLE-BREASTED SUIT WOULD BE BETTER.
AU-GUSTA!
LET'S HAVE THE STRIPED ONE!

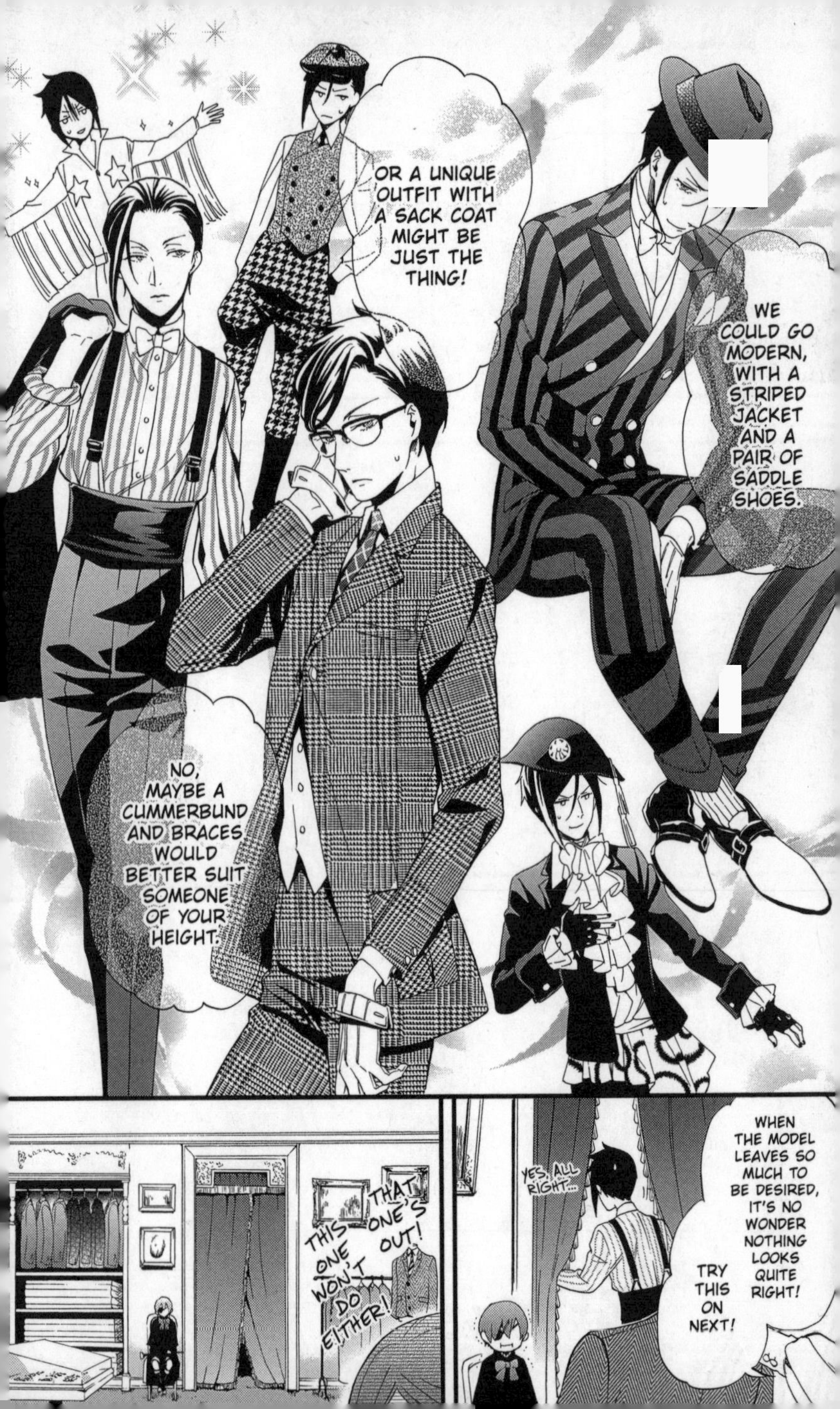
WE COULD GO MODERN, WITH A STRIPED JACKET AND A PAIR OF SADDLE SHOES.
OR A UNIQUE OUTFIT WITH A SACK COAT MIGHT BE JUST THE THING!
NO, MAYBE A CUMMERBUND AND BRACES WOULD BETTER SUIT SOMEONE OF YOUR HEIGHT.
WHEN THE MODEL LEAVES SO MUCH TO BE DESIRED, IT'S NO WONDER NOTHING LOOKS QUITE RIGHT!
TRY THIS ON NEXT!
YES, ALL RIGHT...
THAT ONE'S OUT!
THIS ONE WON'T DO EITHER!

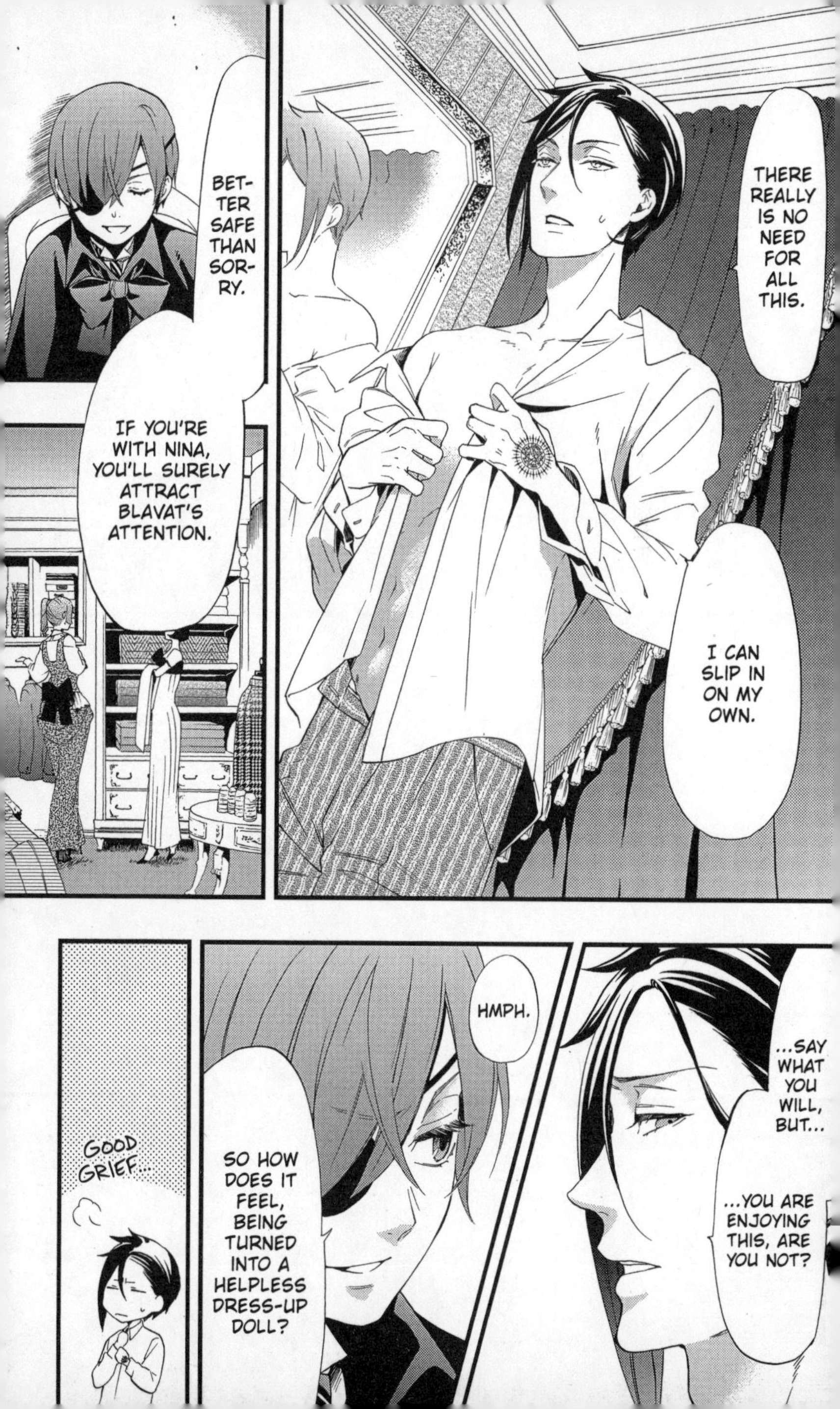
THERE REALLY IS NO NEED FOR ALL THIS.
I CAN SLIP IN ON MY OWN.
BET-TER SAFE THAN SOR-RY.
IF YOU'RE WITH NINA, YOU'LL SURELY ATTRACT BLAVAT'S ATTENTION.
...SAY WHAT YOU WILL, BUT...
...YOU ARE ENJOYING THIS, ARE YOU NOT?
HMPH.
SO HOW DOES IT FEEL, BEING TURNED INTO A HELPLESS DRESS-UP DOLL?
GOOD GRIEF...

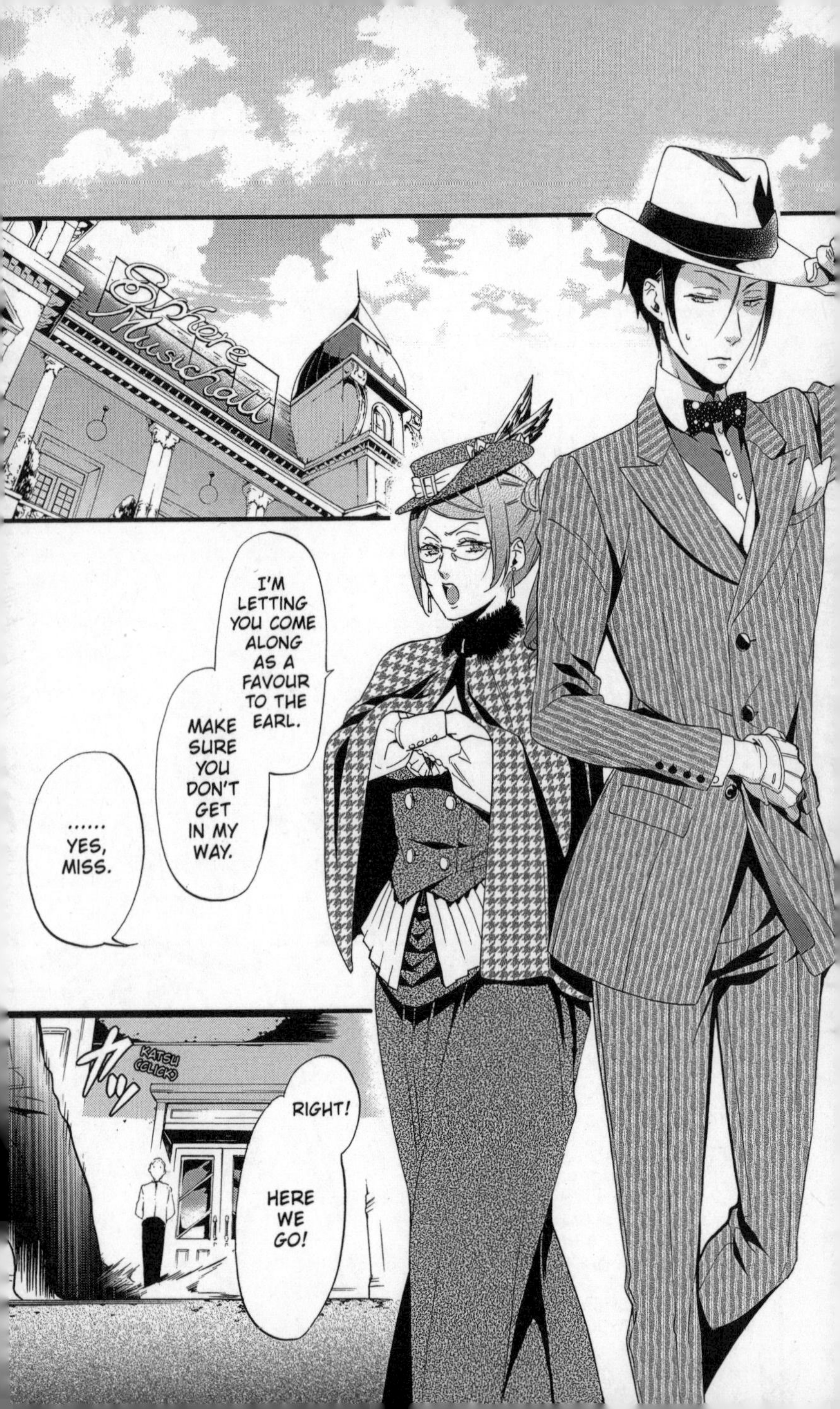
Sphere Musichall
I'M LETTING YOU COME ALONG AS A FAVOUR TO THE EARL.
MAKE SURE YOU DON'T GET IN MY WAY.
...... YES, MISS.
RIGHT!
HERE WE GO!
KATSU (CLICK)

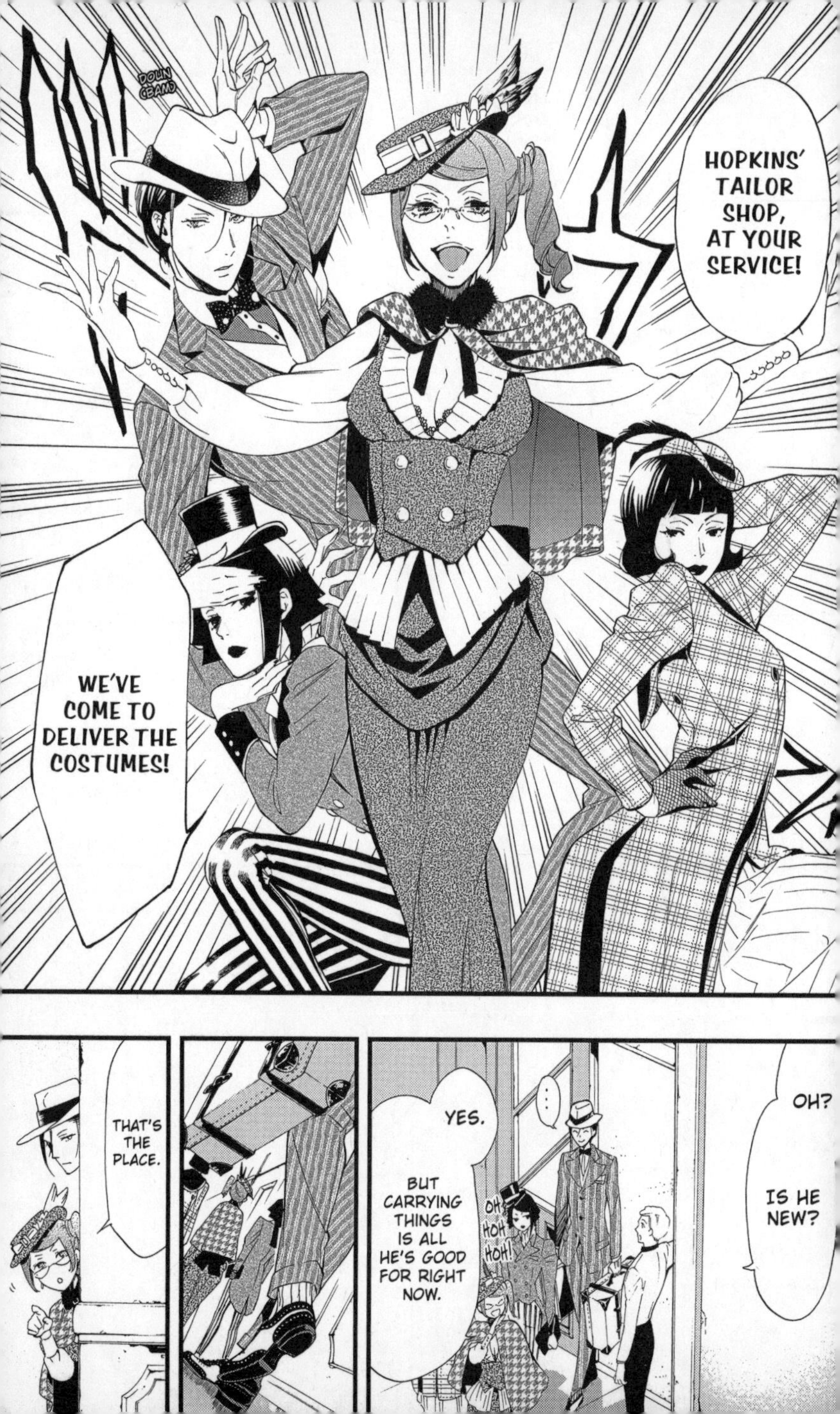
HOPKINS' TAILOR SHOP, AT YOUR SERVICE!
DOUN (BAM)
WE'VE COME TO DELIVER THE COSTUMES!
OH?
IS HE NEW?
...
YES.
BUT CARRYING THINGS IS ALL HE'S GOOD FOR RIGHT NOW.
OH HOH HOH!
THAT'S THE PLACE.

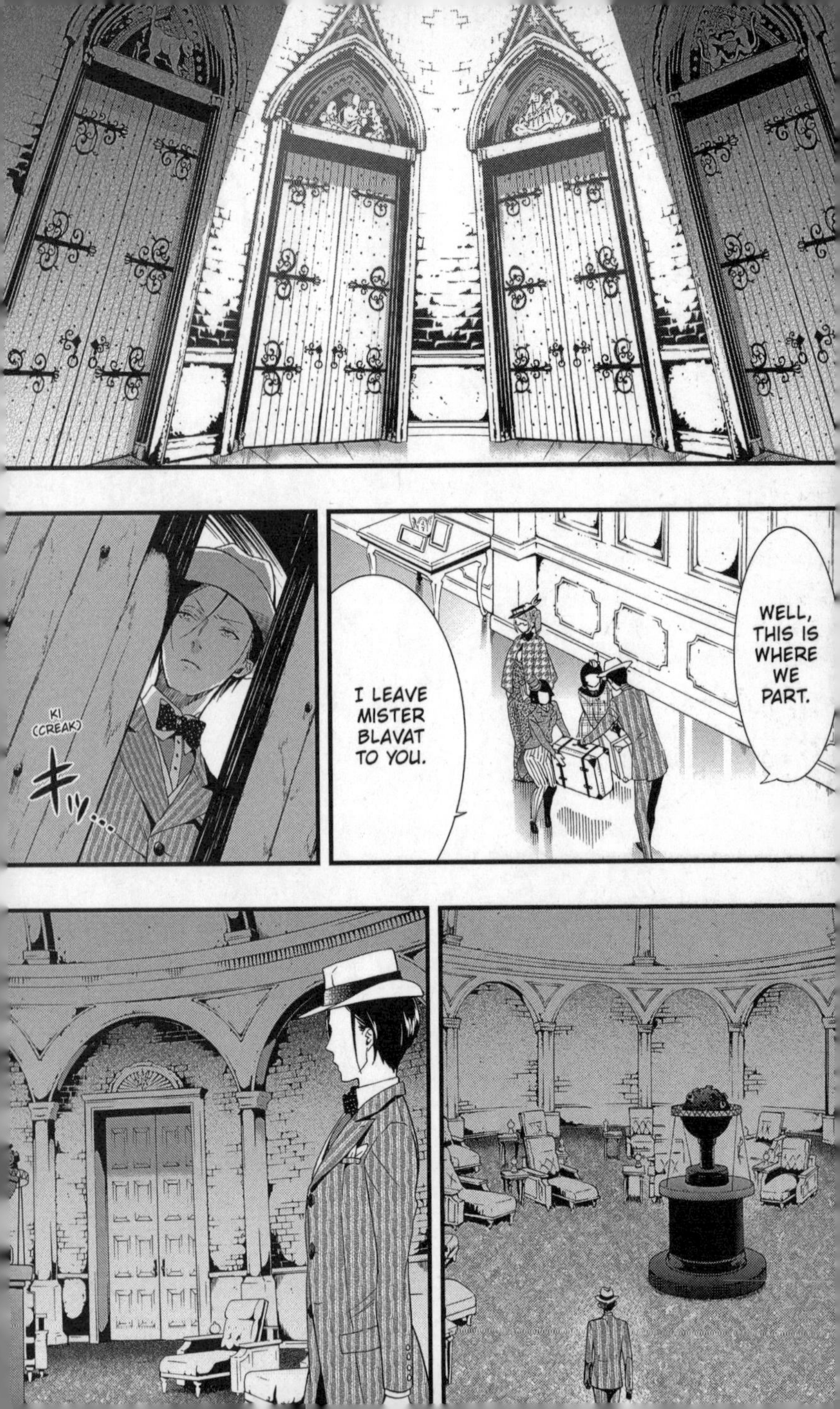
WELL, THIS IS WHERE WE PART.
I LEAVE MISTER BLAVAT TO YOU.
KI (CREAK)
キッ...

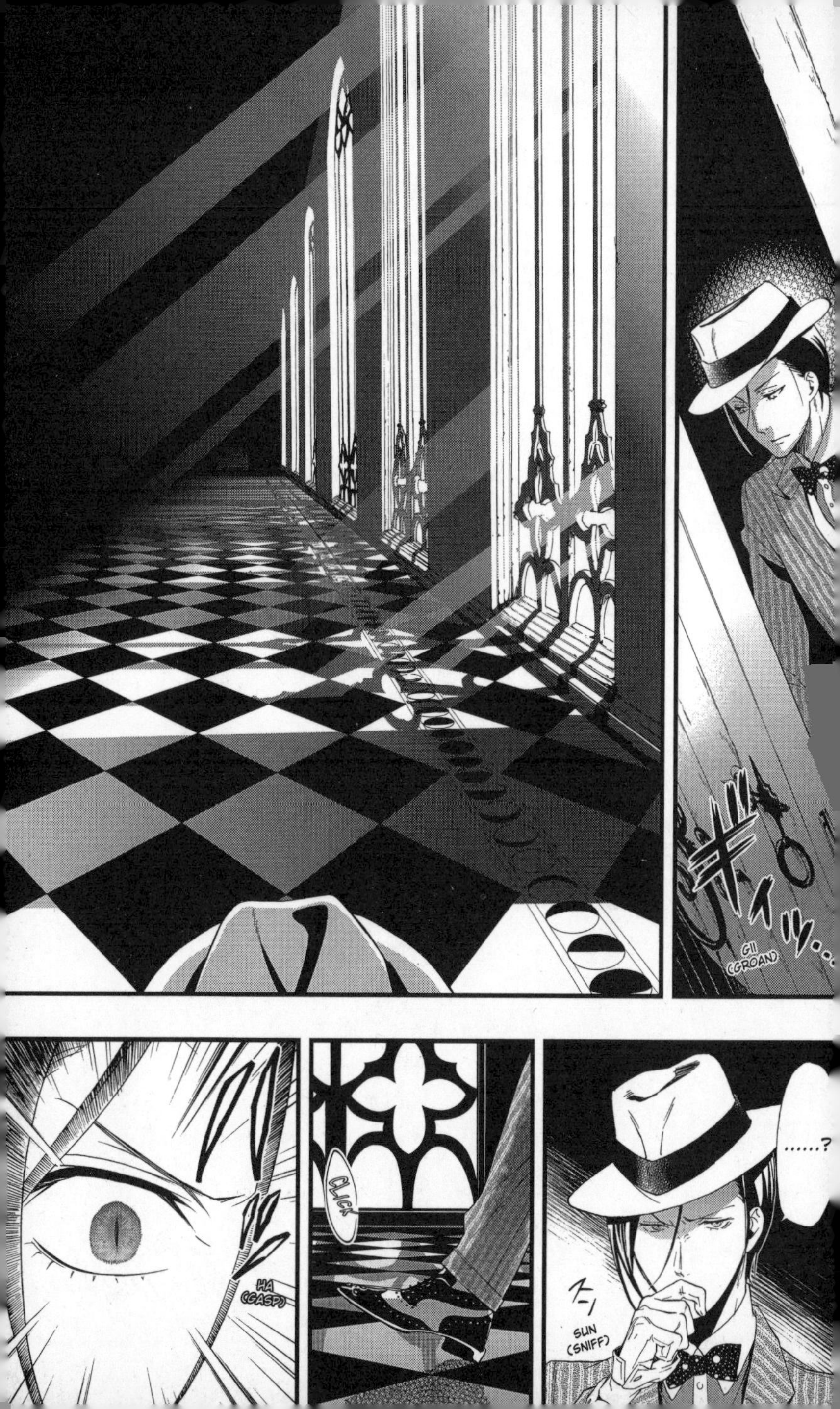

GII (GROAN)
......?
SUN (SNIFF)
CLICK
HA (GASP)

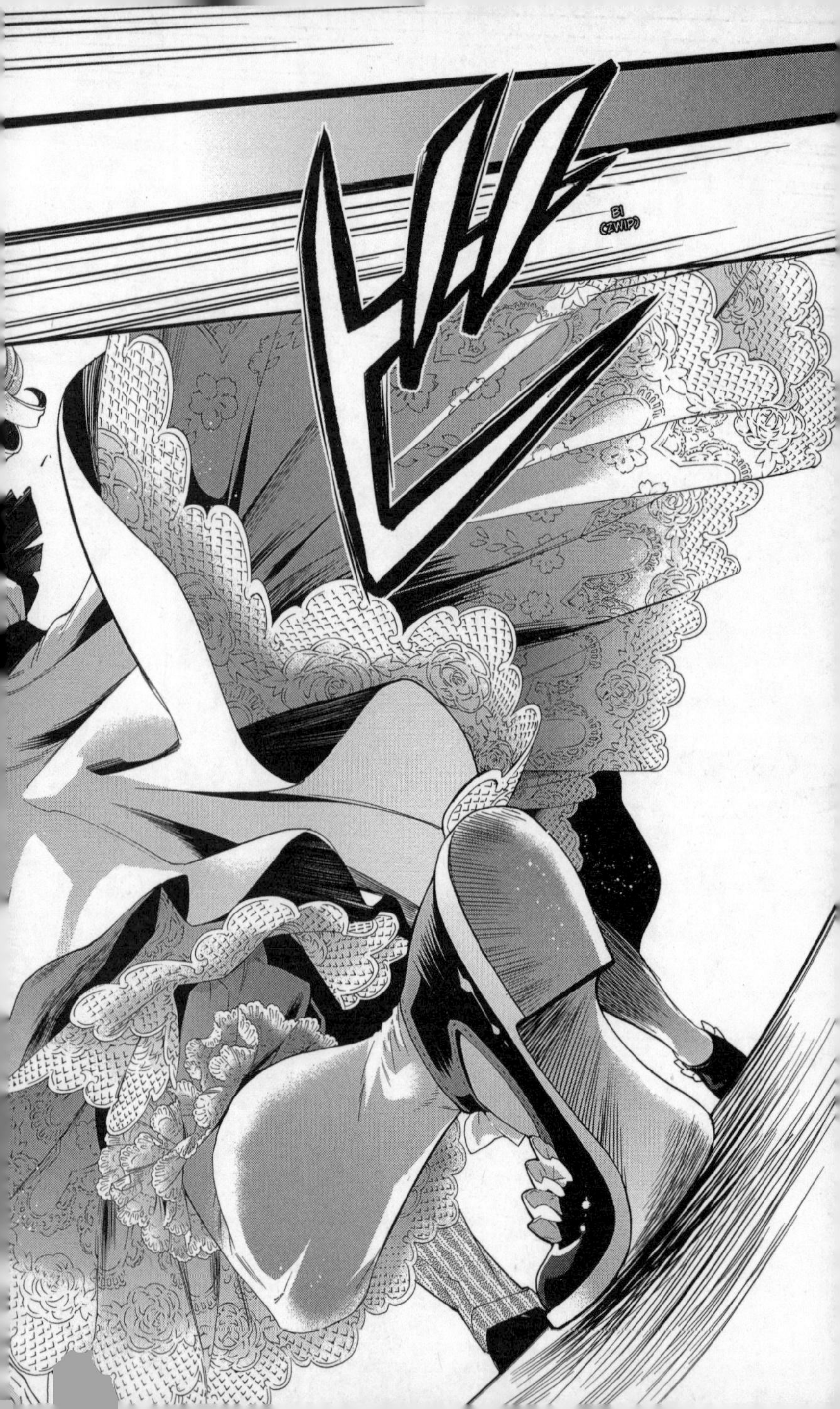
BI
(ZWIP)

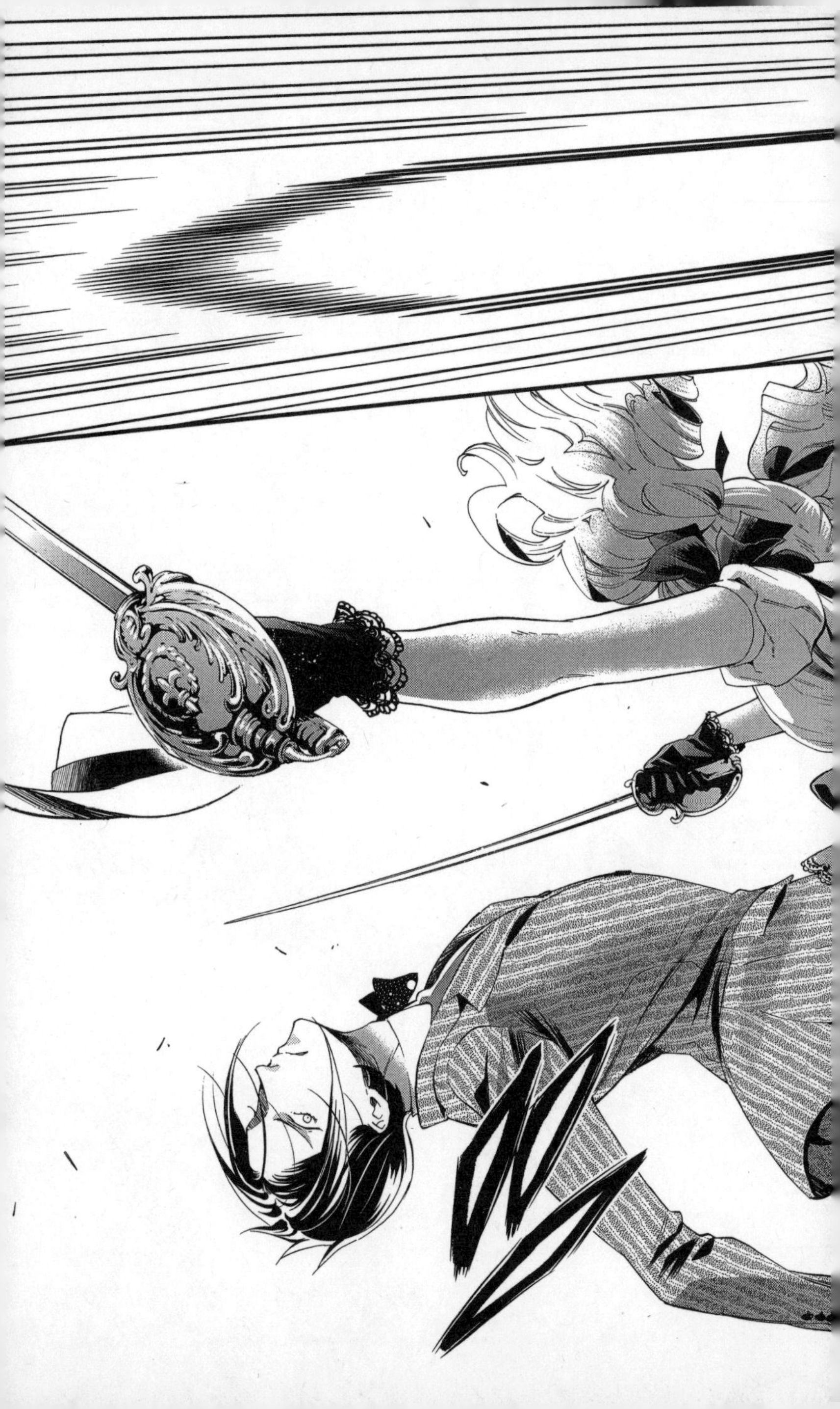

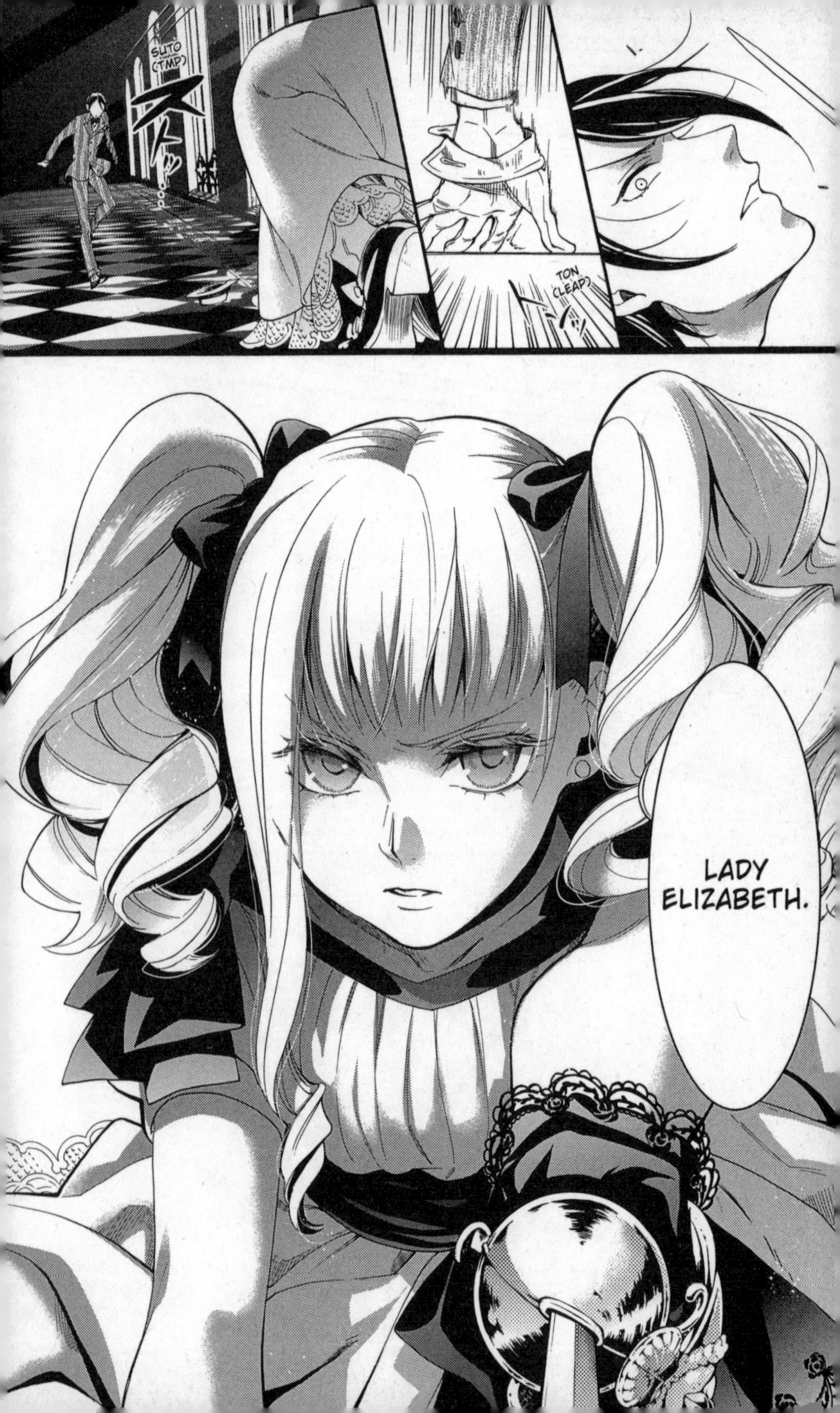
TON (LEAP)
SUTO (TMP)
LADY ELIZABETH.

Black Butler

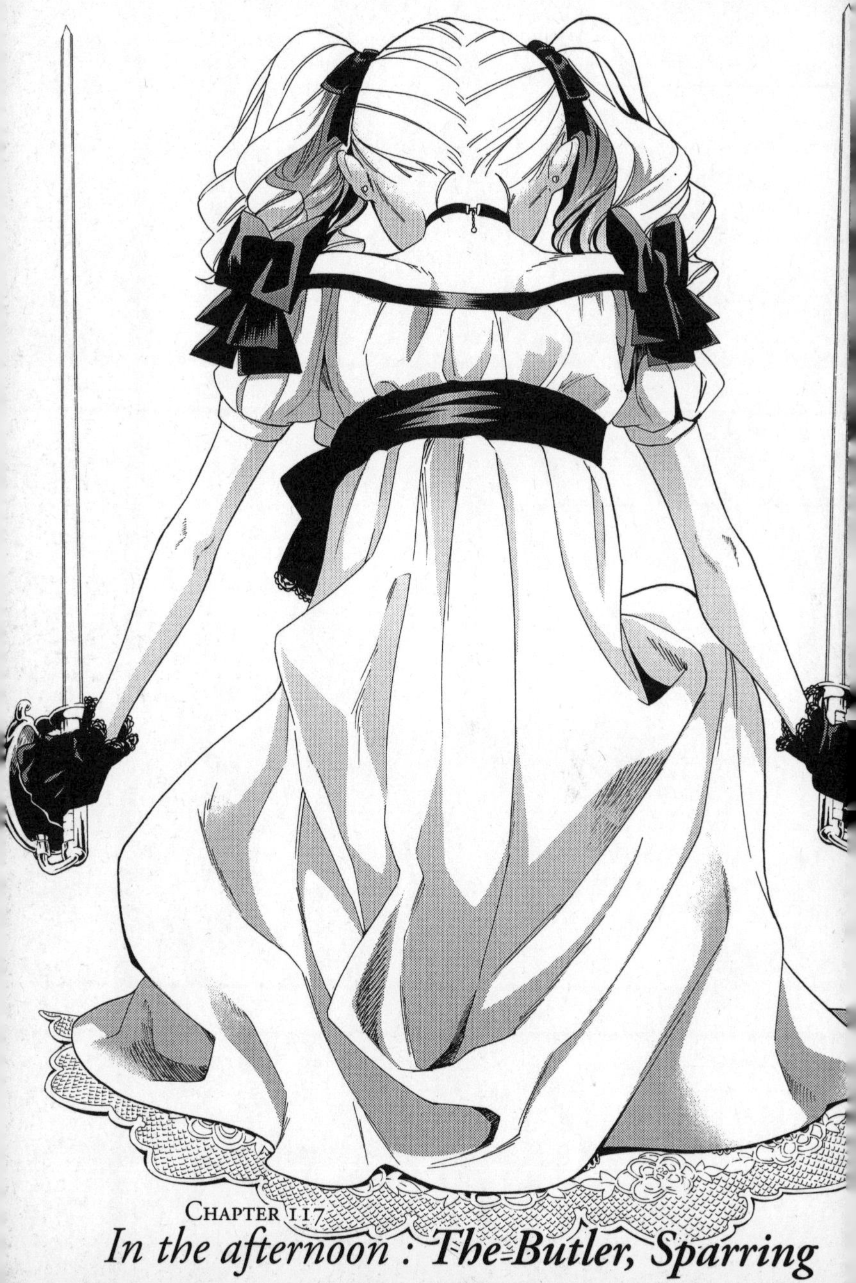

Chapter 117
In the afternoon : The Butler, Sparring

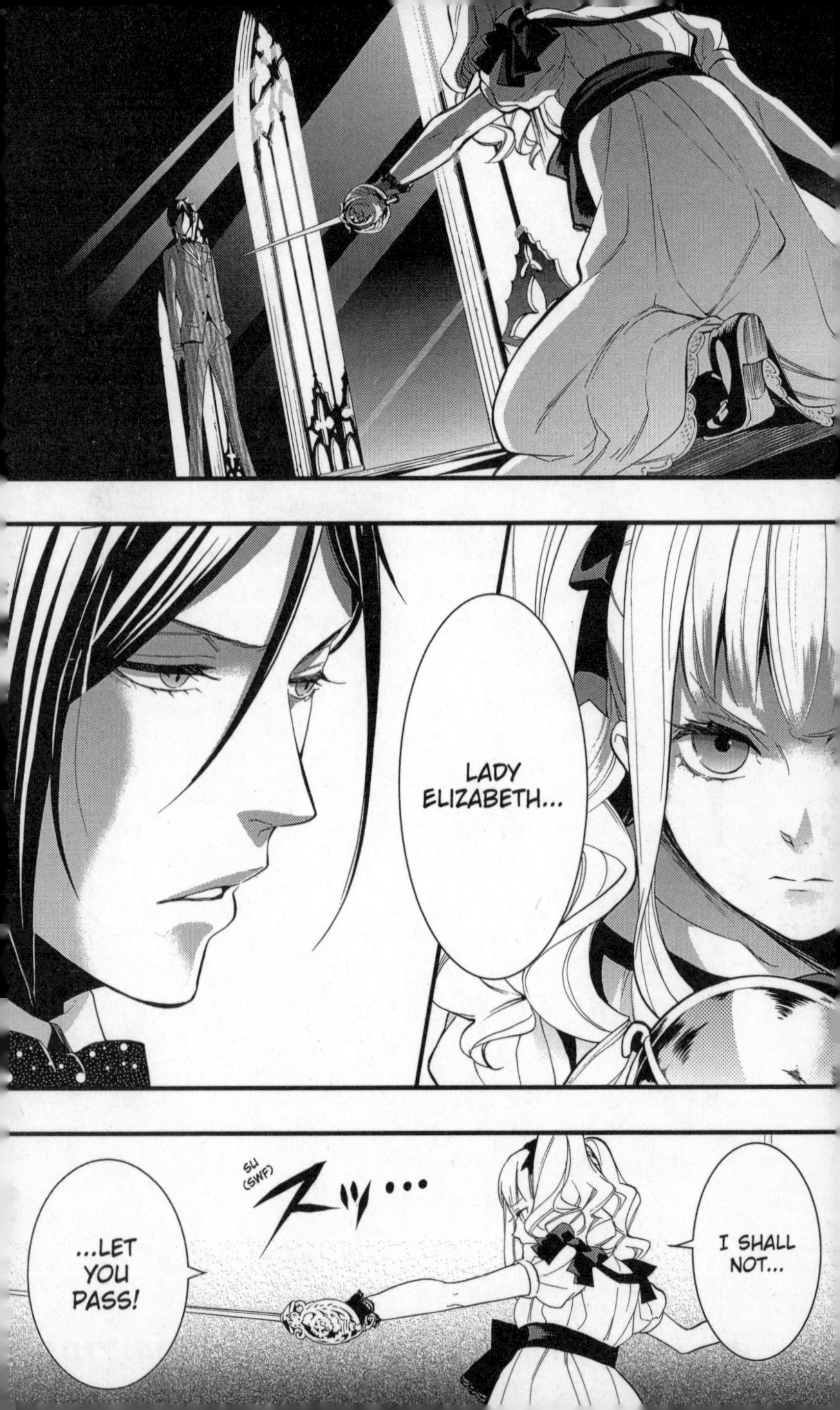
LADY ELIZABETH...
I SHALL NOT...
SU (SWF)
スッ…
...LET YOU PASS!

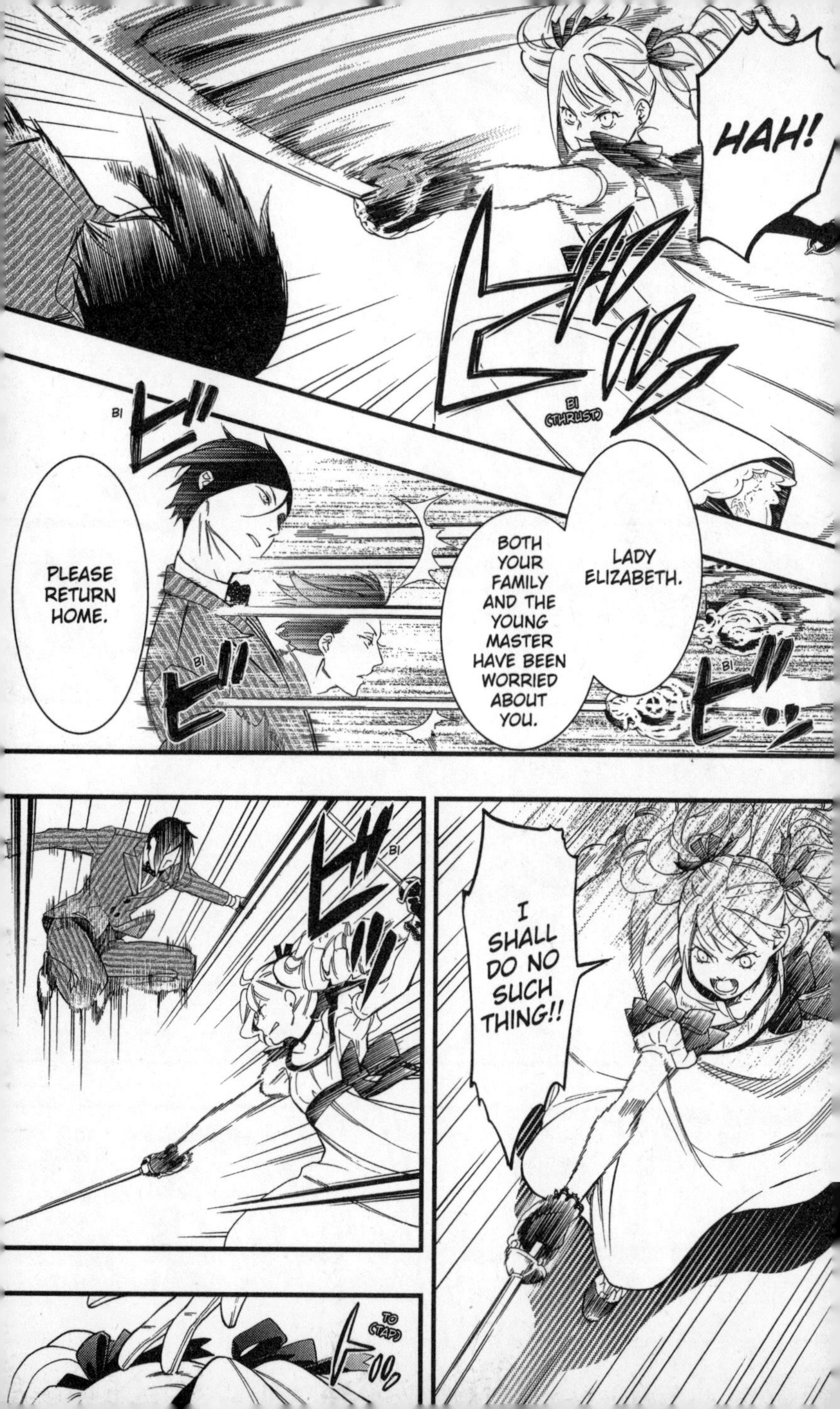
HAH!
BI (THRUST)
LADY ELIZABETH.
BI
BOTH YOUR FAMILY AND THE YOUNG MASTER HAVE BEEN WORRIED ABOUT YOU.
BI
PLEASE RETURN HOME.
BI
I SHALL DO NO SUCH THING!!
BI
TO (TAP)

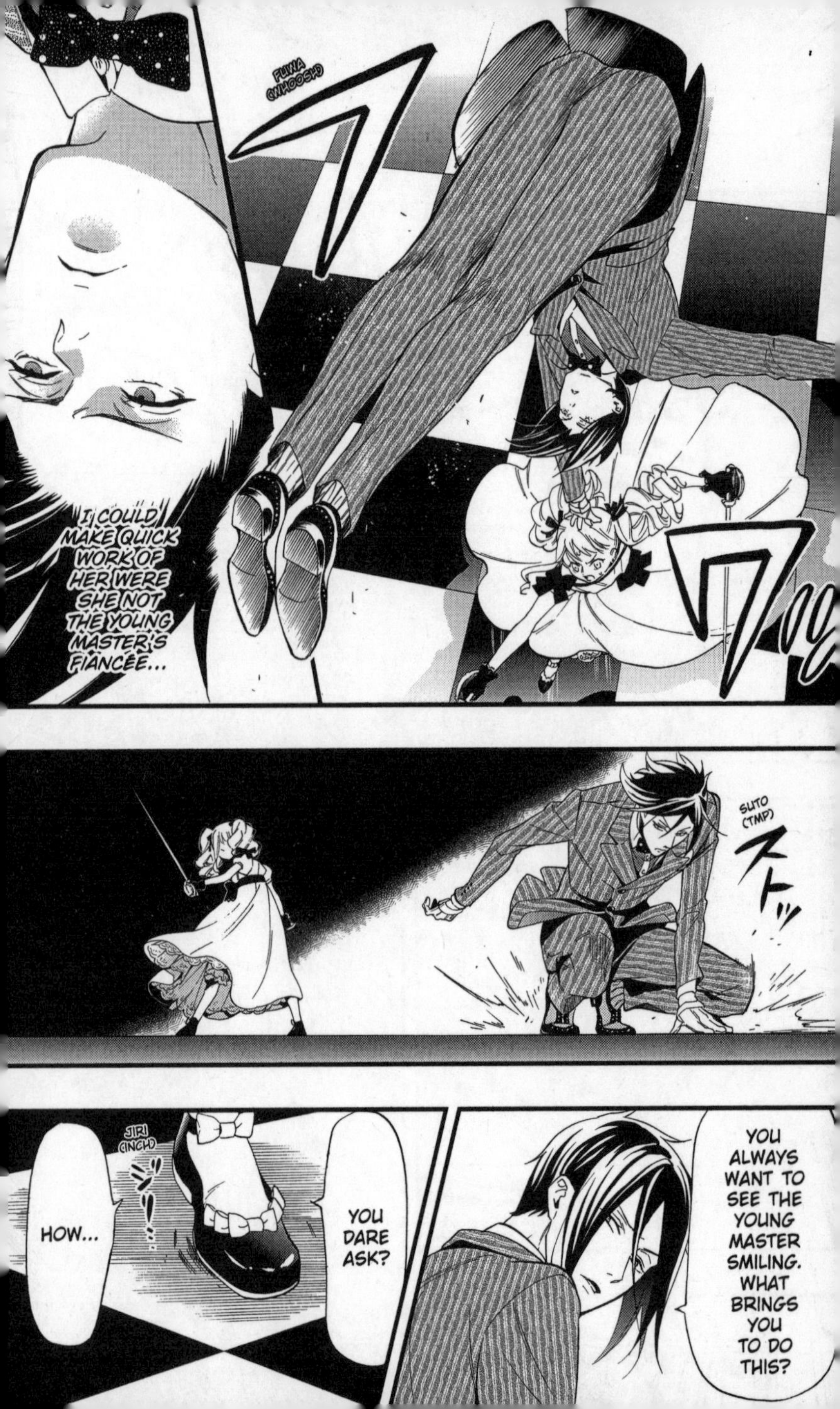

PUWA (WHOOSH)
I COULD MAKE QUICK WORK OF HER WERE SHE NOT THE YOUNG MASTER'S FIANCÉE...
SUTO (TMP)
YOU ALWAYS WANT TO SEE THE YOUNG MASTER SMILING. WHAT BRINGS YOU TO DO THIS?
JIRI (INCH)
YOU DARE ASK?
HOW...

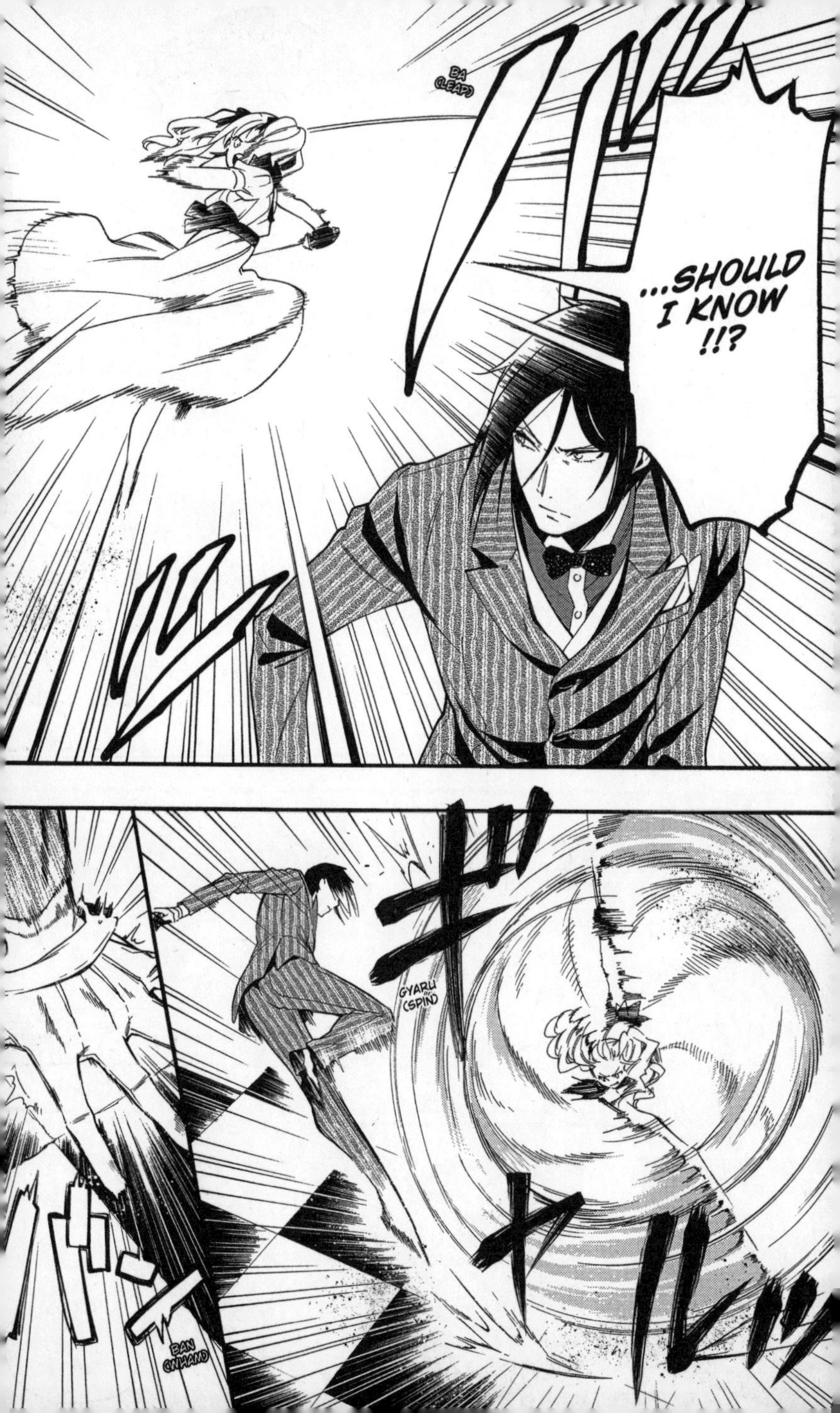
BA (LEAP)
...SHOULD I KNOW !!?
GYARU (SPIN)
BAN (WHAM)

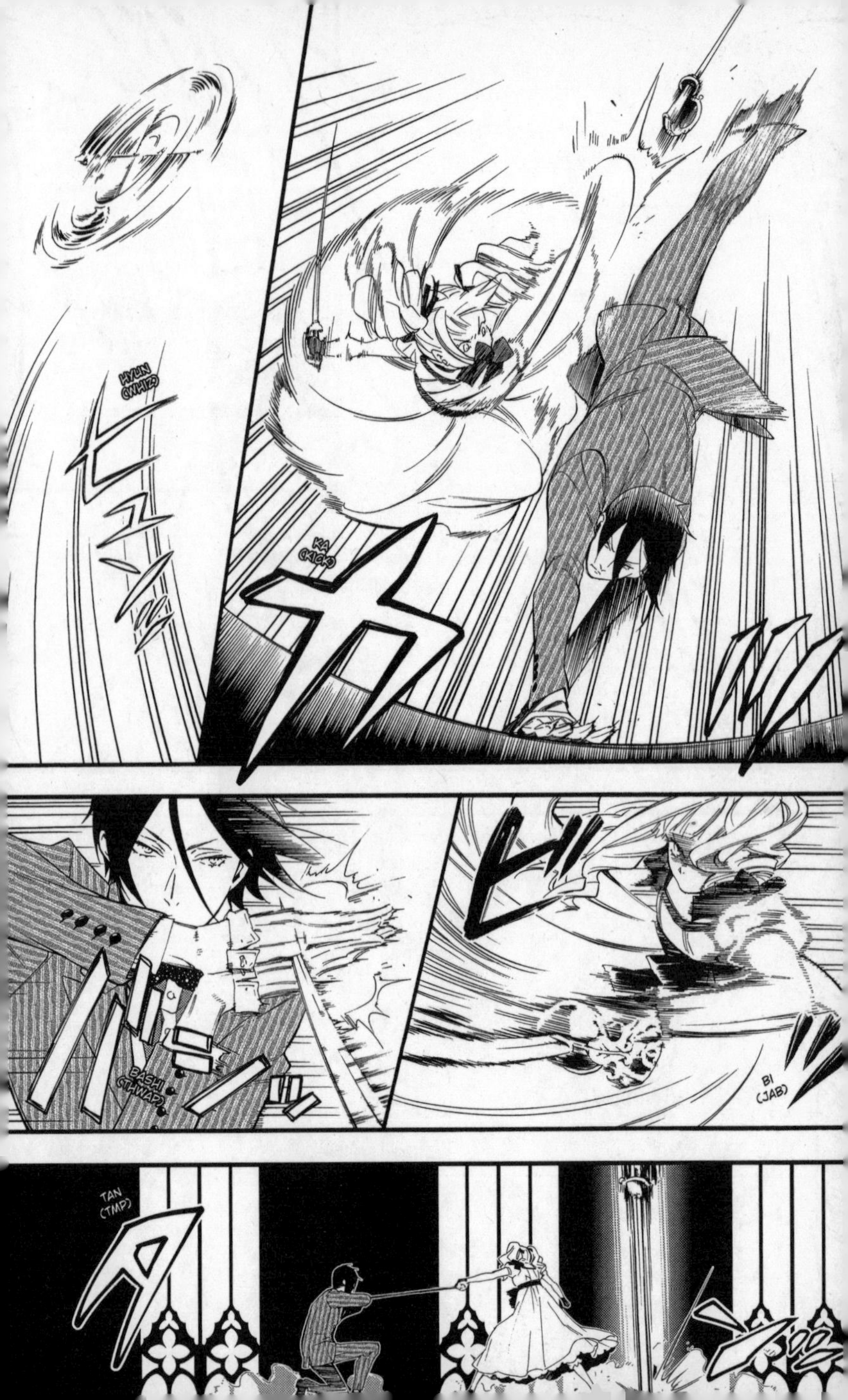
KA (KICK)
HYUN (WHIZ)
BI (JAB)
BASHI (THWAP)
TAN (TMP)

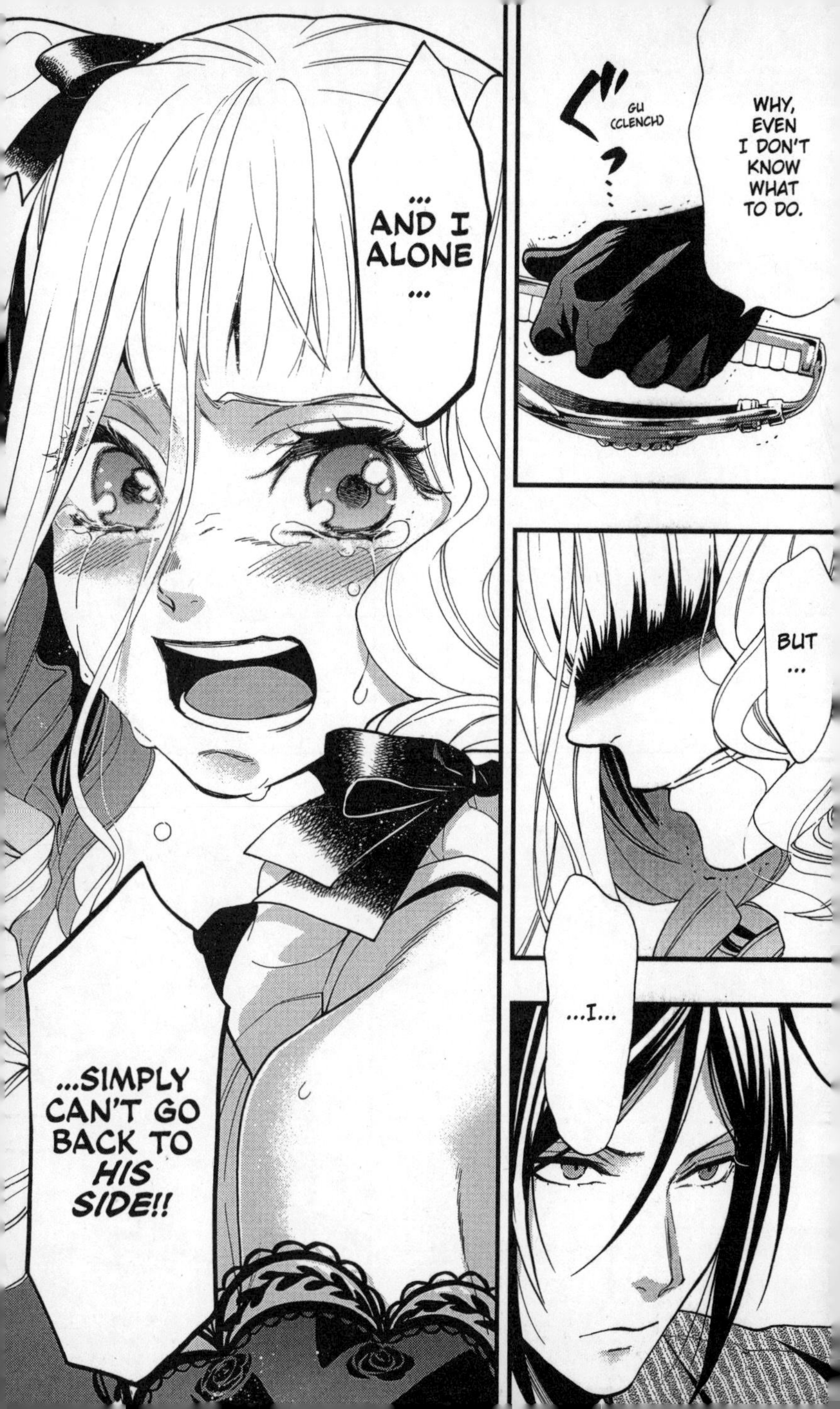
WHY, EVEN I DON'T KNOW WHAT TO DO.
GU (CLENCH)
BUT ...
...I...
... AND I ALONE ...
...SIMPLY CAN'T GO BACK TO *HIS SIDE!!*

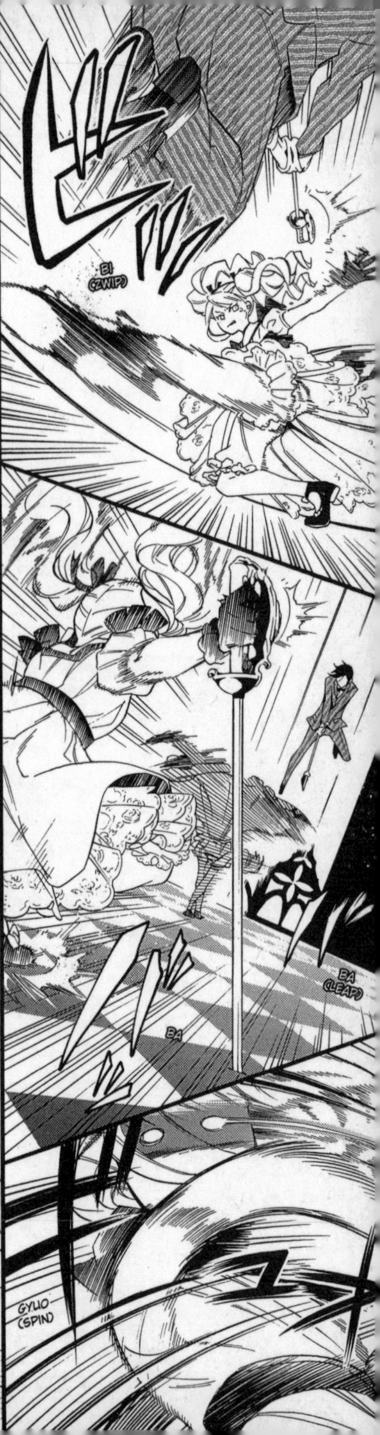
BI
(ZWIP)
BA
(LEAP)
BA
GYUO
(SPIN)
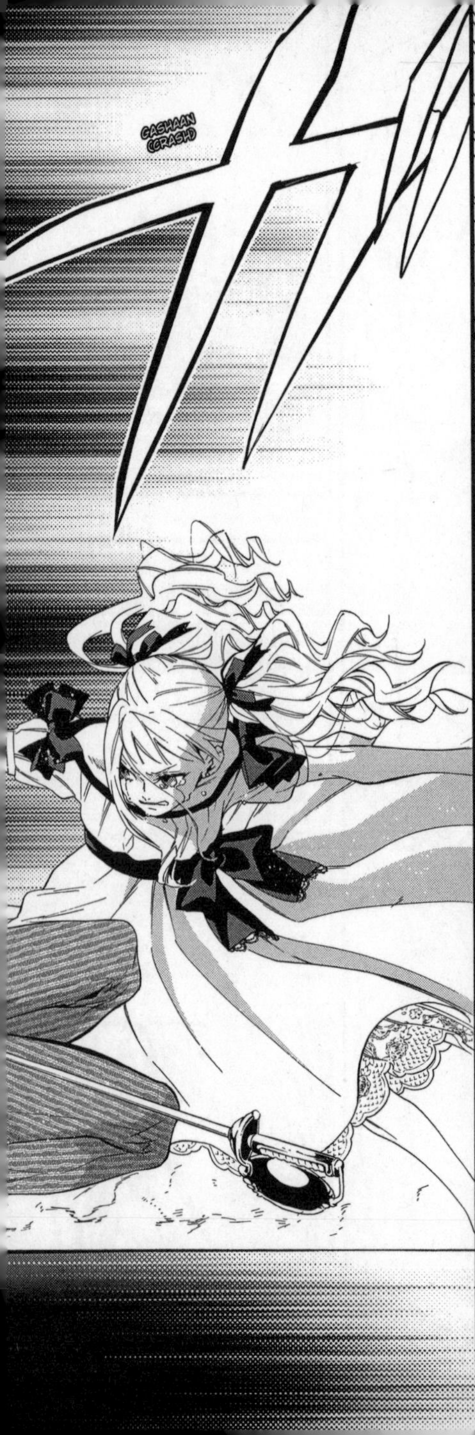
GASHAAN
(CRASH)

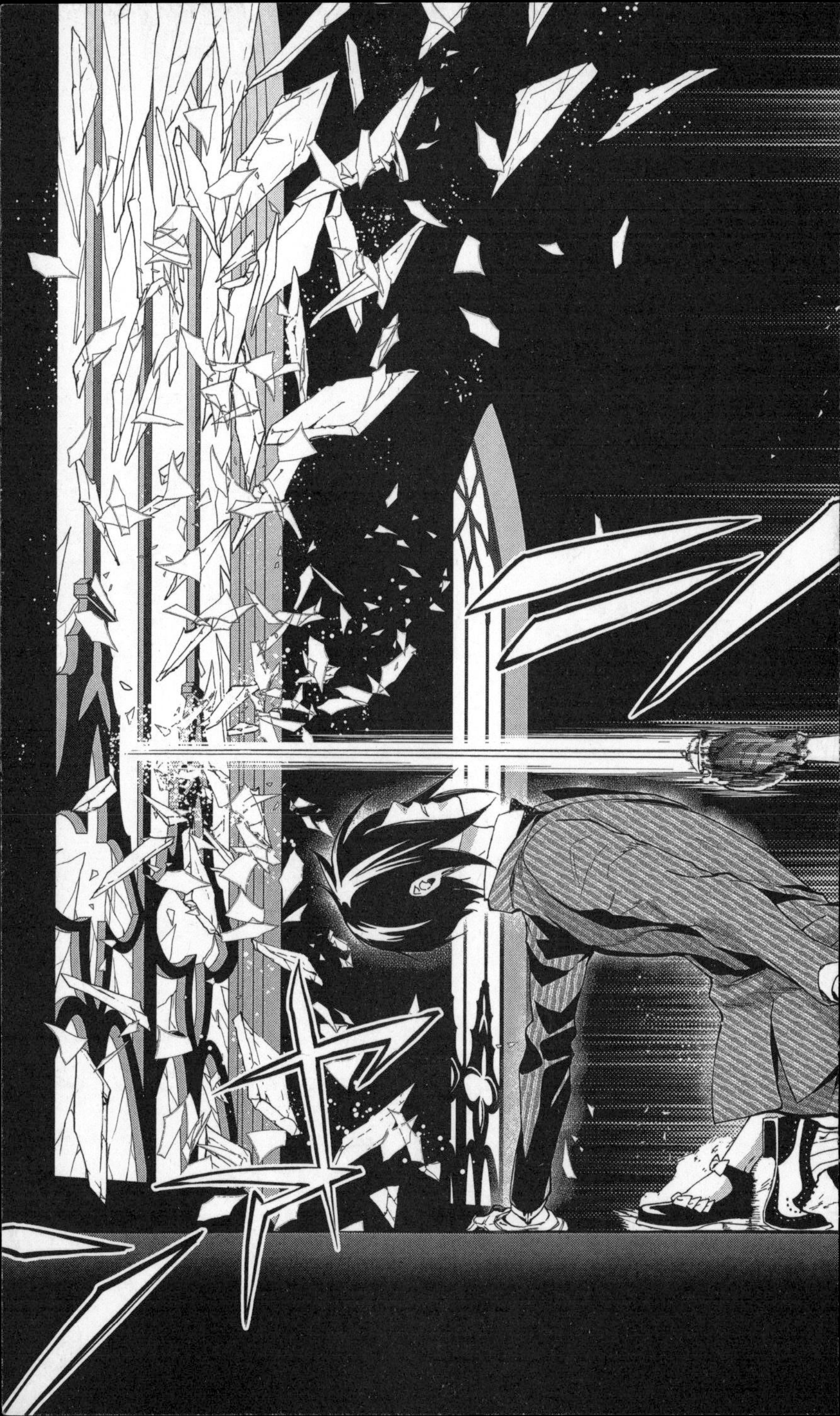

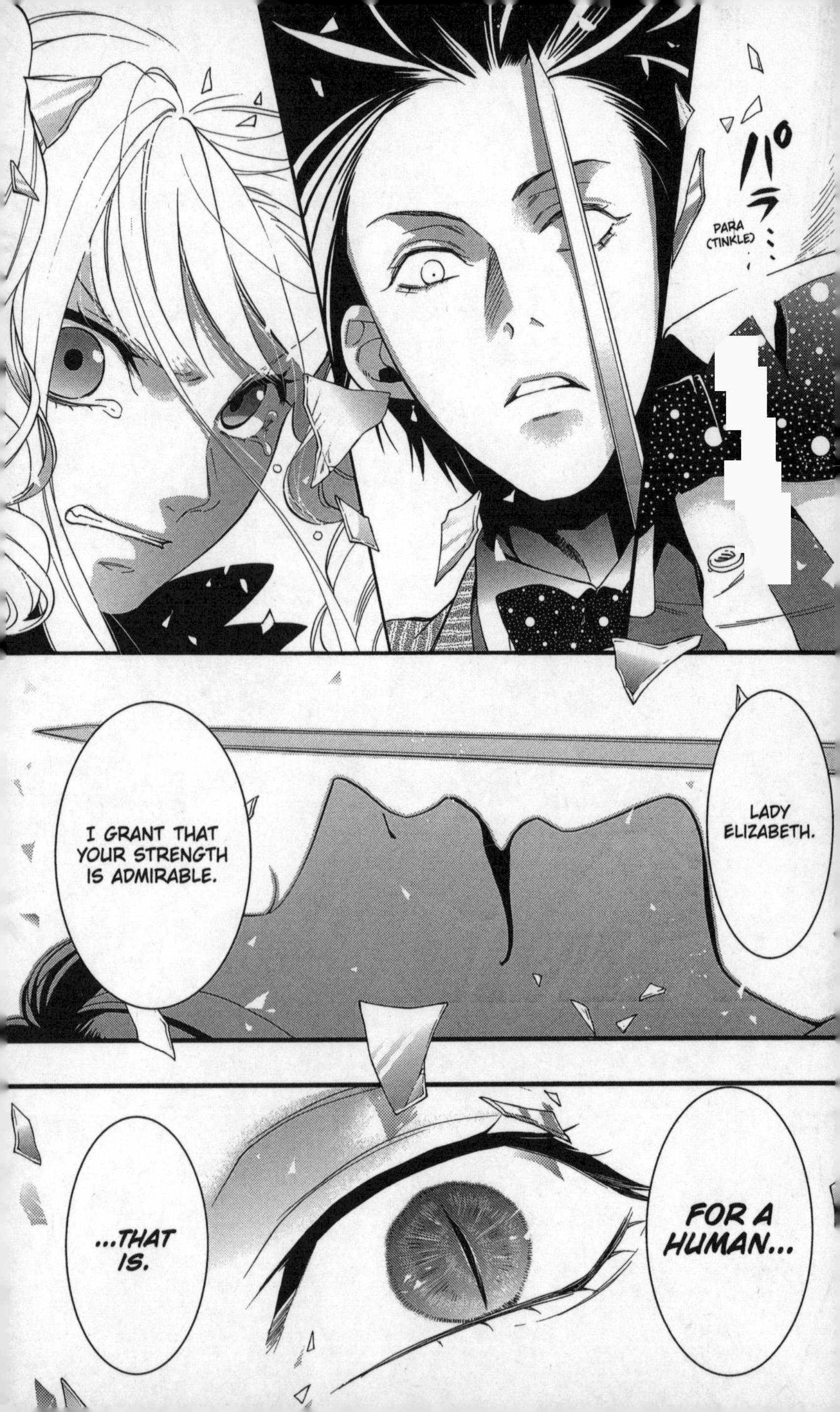
パラ
PARA (TINKLE)
LADY ELIZABETH.
I GRANT THAT YOUR STRENGTH IS ADMIRABLE.
FOR A HUMAN...
...THAT IS.

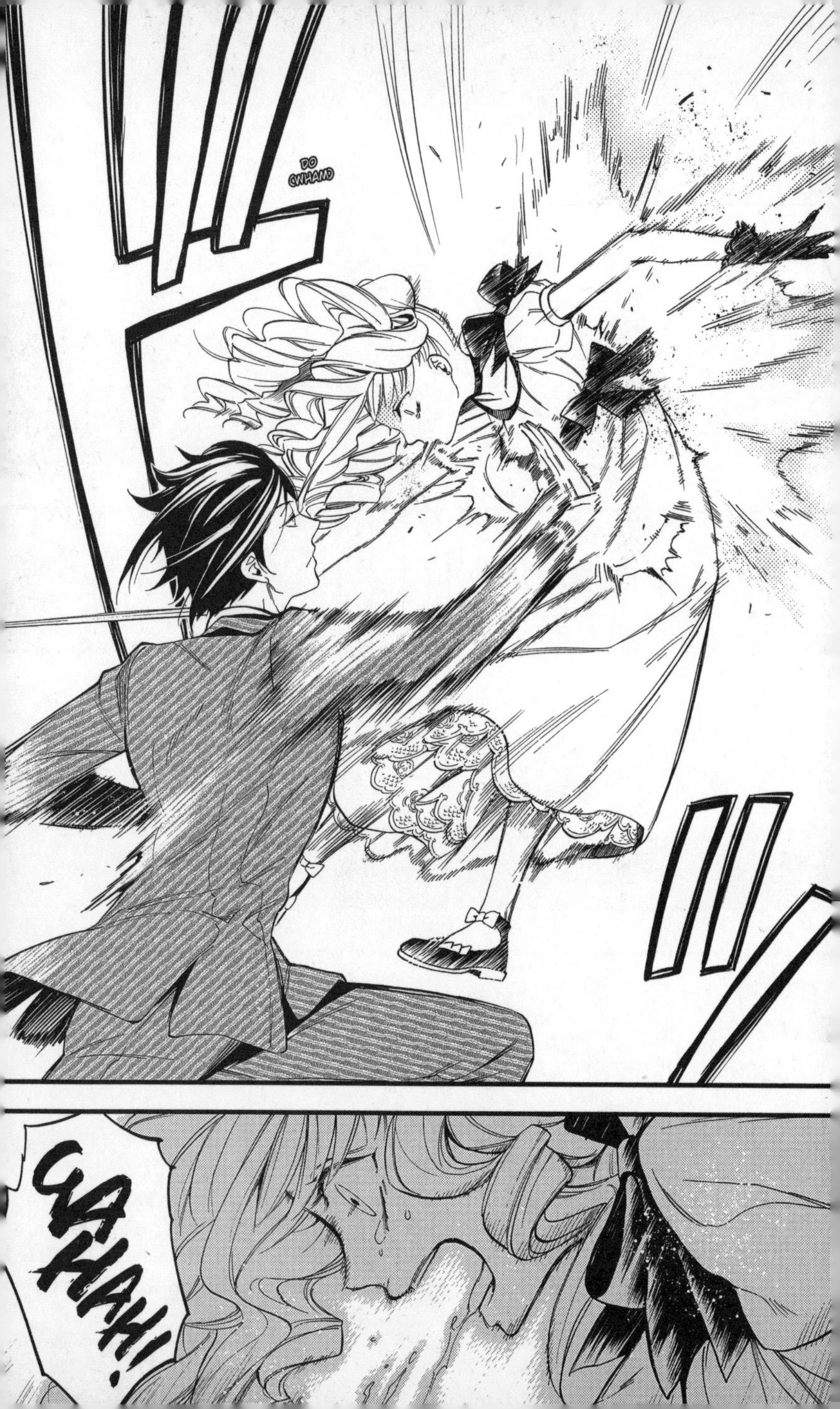
DO
(WHAM)
GAHH!

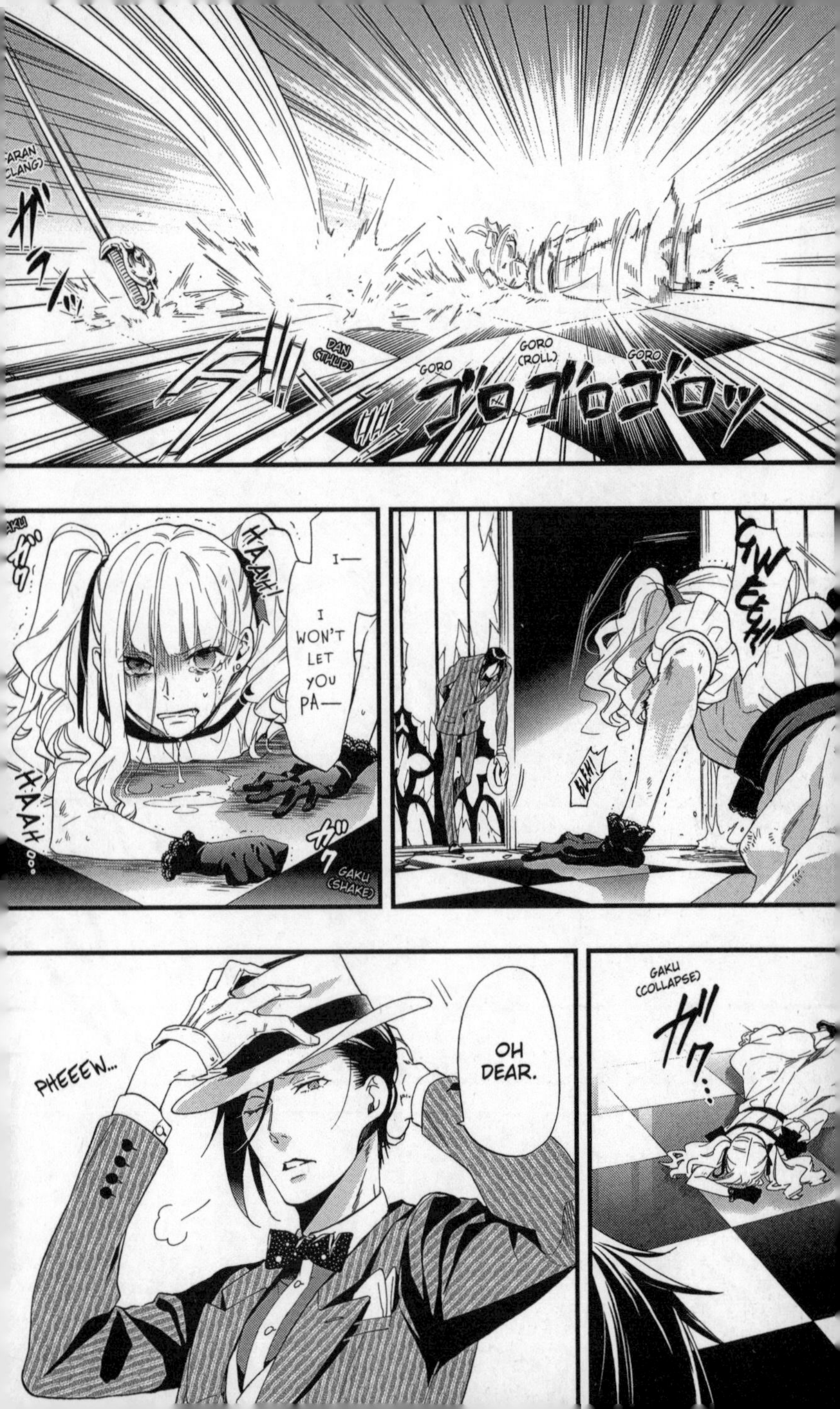
GORO
GORO (ROLL)
GORO
DAN (THUD)
ARAN
CLANG)
GWEEUH!
BLEH!
HAAAH!
I—
I WON'T LET YOU PA—
GAKU (SHAKE)
HAAAH...
GAKU (COLLAPSE)
OH DEAR.
PHEEEW...

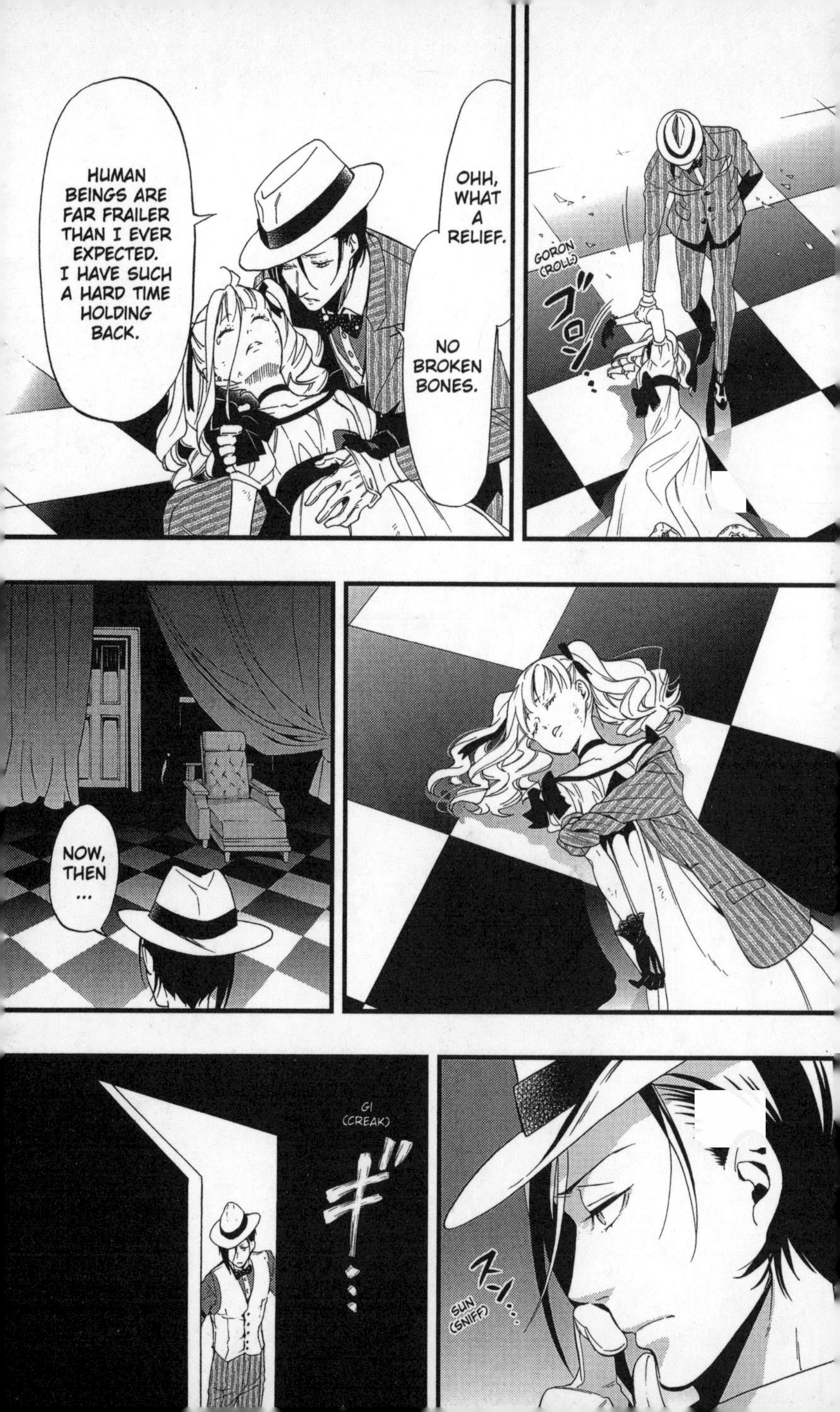
GORON (ROLL)
OHH, WHAT A RELIEF.
NO BROKEN BONES.
HUMAN BEINGS ARE FAR FRAILER THAN I EVER EXPECTED. I HAVE SUCH A HARD TIME HOLDING BACK.
NOW, THEN ...
SUN (SNIFF)
GI (CREAK)

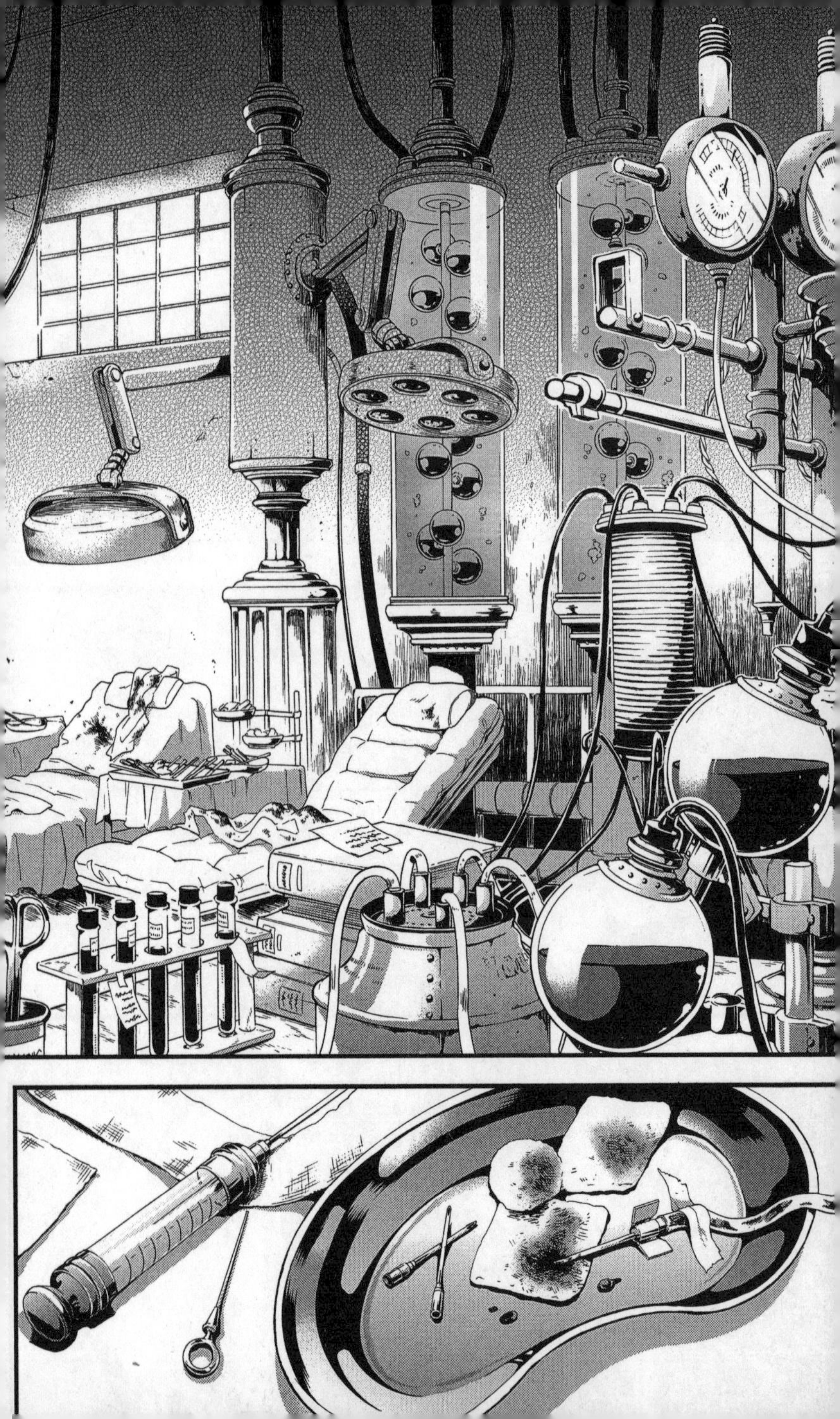

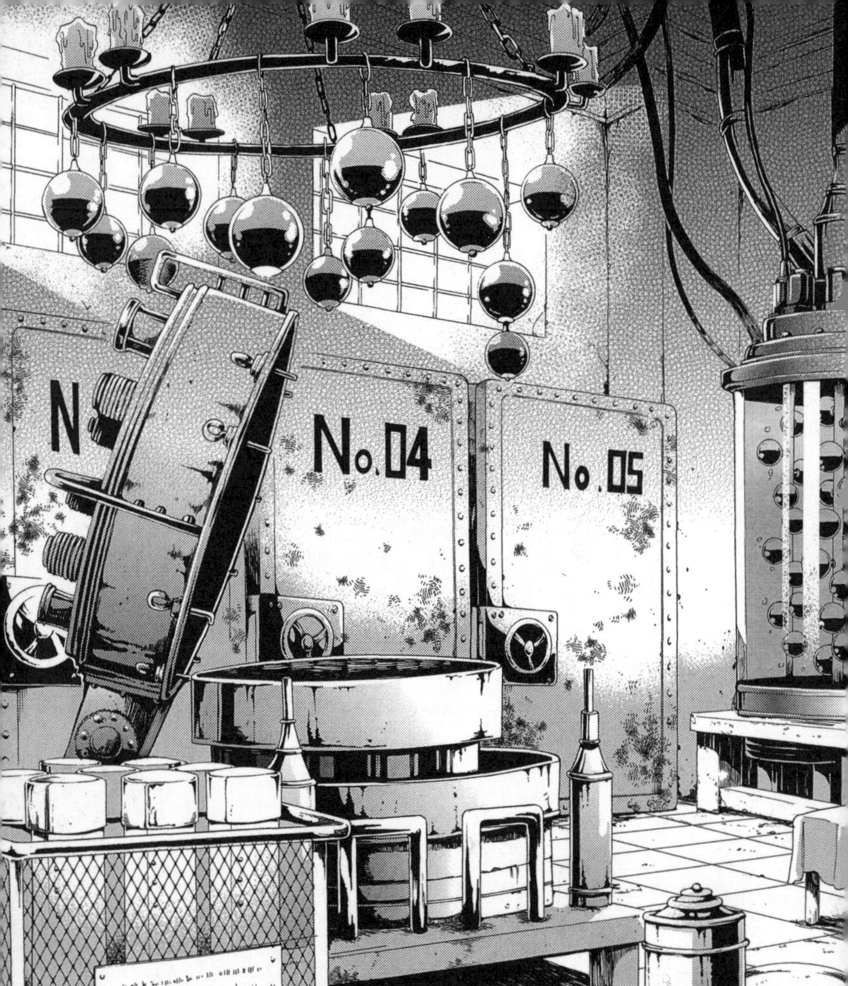
No.04
No.05
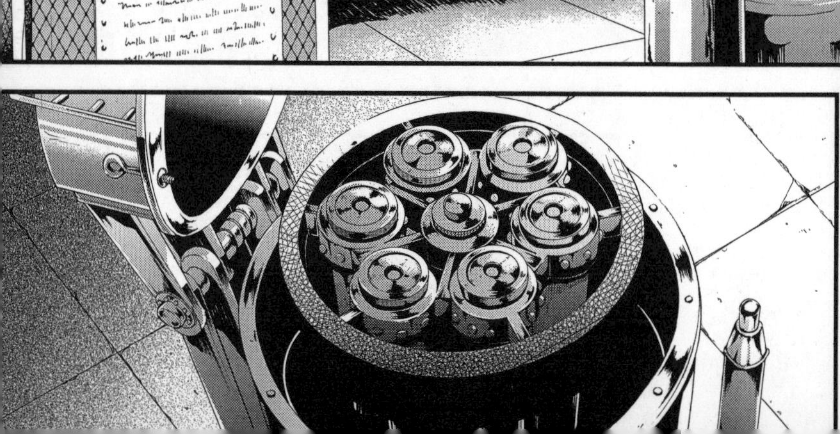

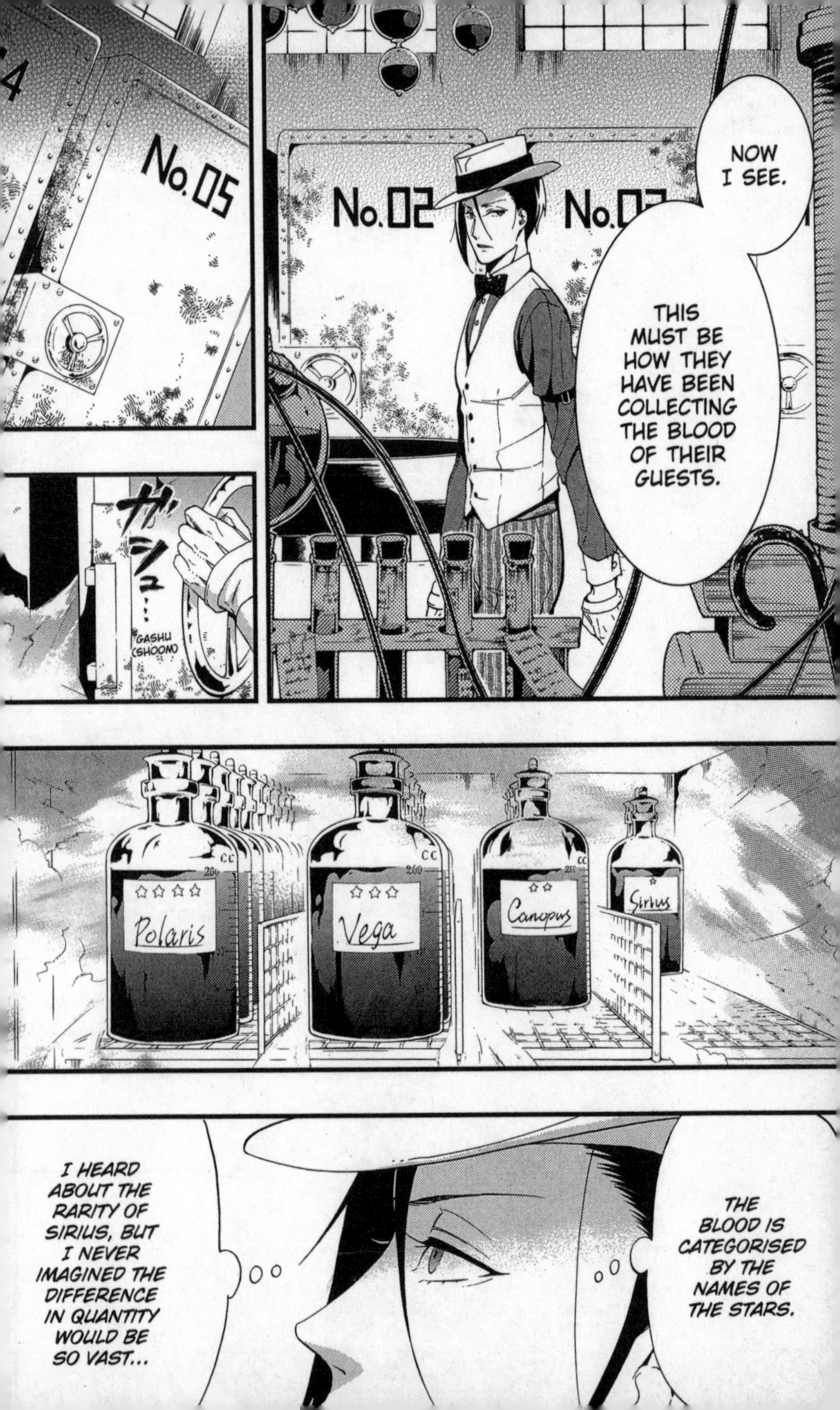

No.02
No.03
NOW I SEE.
THIS MUST BE HOW THEY HAVE BEEN COLLECTING THE BLOOD OF THEIR GUESTS.
No.05
ガシュ…
GASHU (SHOOM)
Polaris
Vega
Canopus
Sirius
THE BLOOD IS CATEGORISED BY THE NAMES OF THE STARS.
I HEARD ABOUT THE RARITY OF SIRIUS, BUT I NEVER IMAGINED THE DIFFERENCE IN QUANTITY WOULD BE SO VAST…

GACHA
(KACHAK)

KASHA
(RATTLE)

NOW TO FIND THE SPECIAL FOUR NAMED AFTER THE STARS...

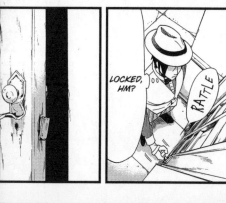

LOCKED, HM?

RATTLE

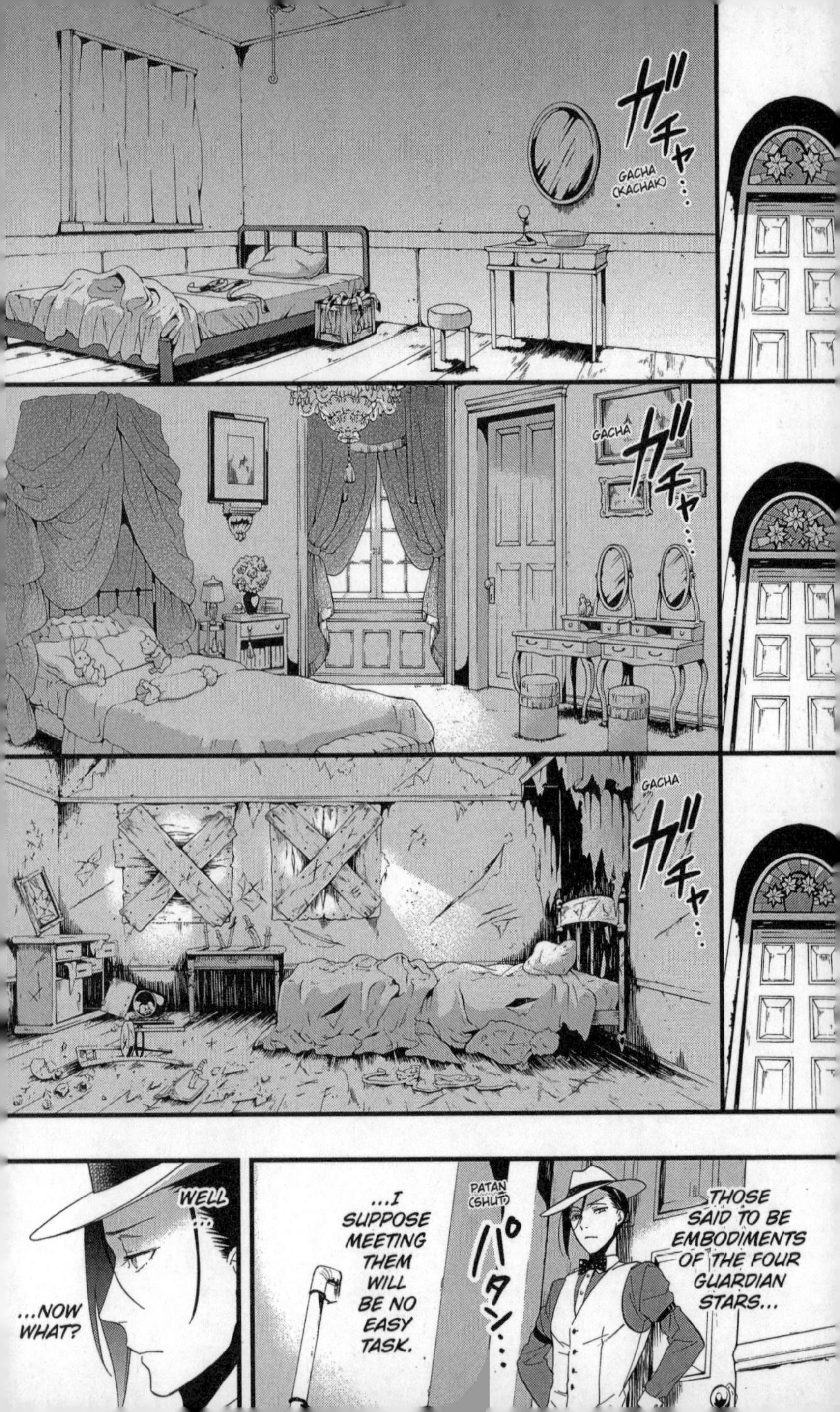
ガチャ…
GACHA (KACHAK)
GACHA
ガチャ…
GACHA
ガチャ…
THOSE SAID TO BE EMBODIMENTS OF THE FOUR GUARDIAN STARS...
PATAN (SHUT)
パタン…
...I SUPPOSE MEETING THEM WILL BE NO EASY TASK.
WELL...
...NOW WHAT?

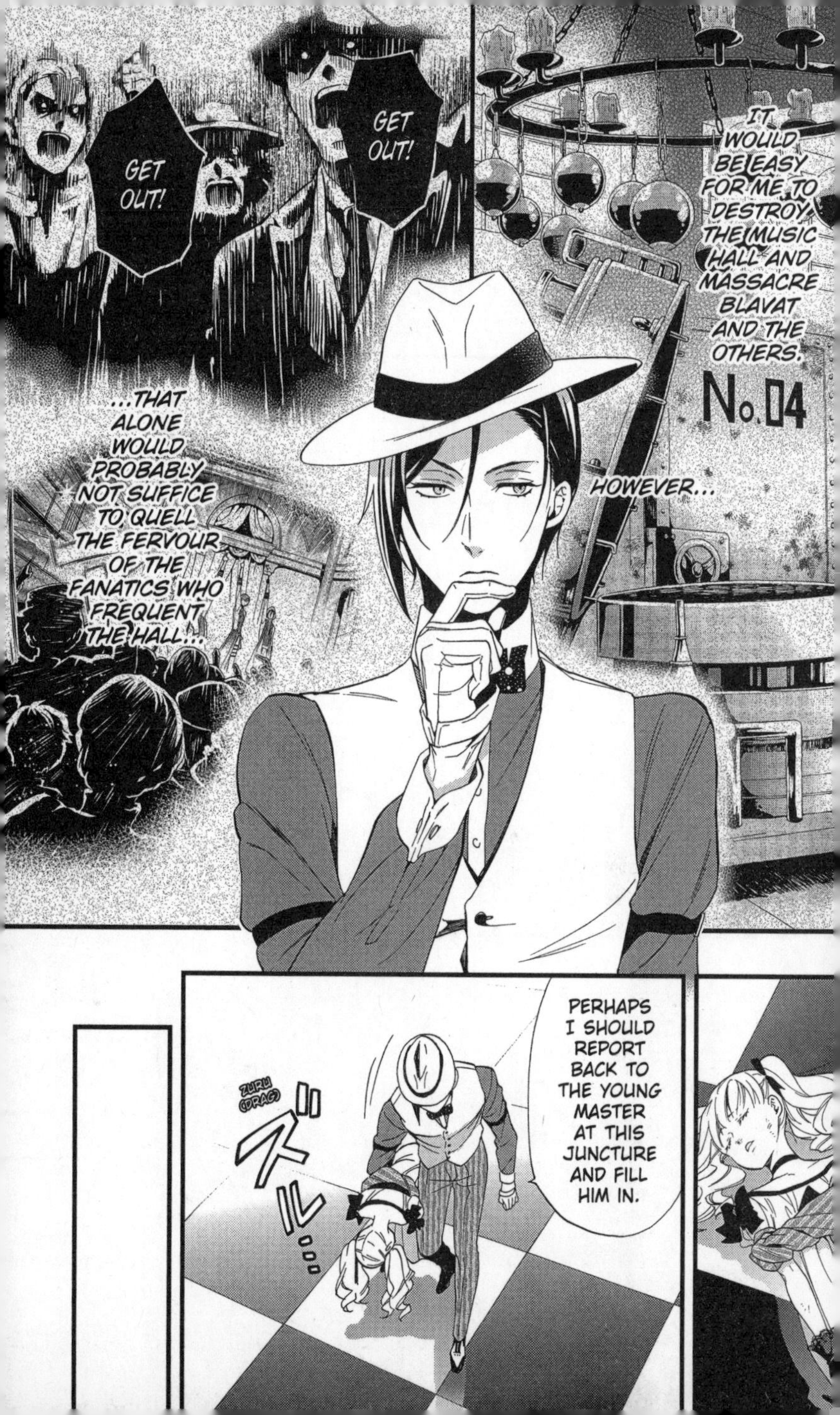
IT WOULD BE EASY FOR ME TO DESTROY THE MUSIC HALL AND MASSACRE BLAVAT AND THE OTHERS.
No. 04
GET OUT!
GET OUT!
HOWEVER...
...THAT ALONE WOULD PROBABLY NOT SUFFICE TO QUELL THE FERVOUR OF THE FANATICS WHO FREQUENT THE HALL...
PERHAPS I SHOULD REPORT BACK TO THE YOUNG MASTER AT THIS JUNCTURE AND FILL HIM IN.
ZURU (DRAG)

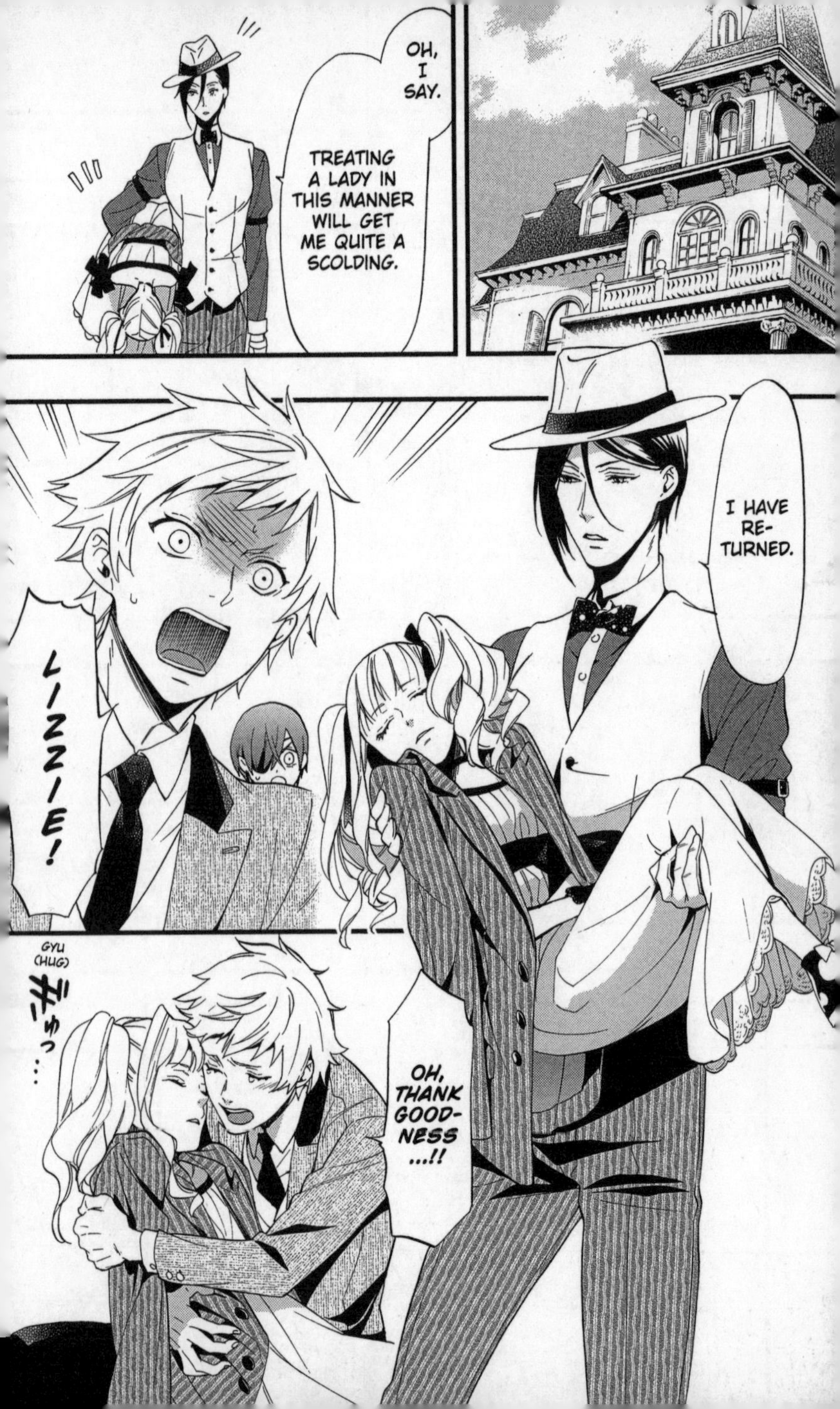
OH, I SAY.
TREATING A LADY IN THIS MANNER WILL GET ME QUITE A SCOLDING.
I HAVE RE-TURNED.
LIZZIE!
GYU (HUG)
ぎゅっ…
OH, THANK GOOD-NESS ...!!

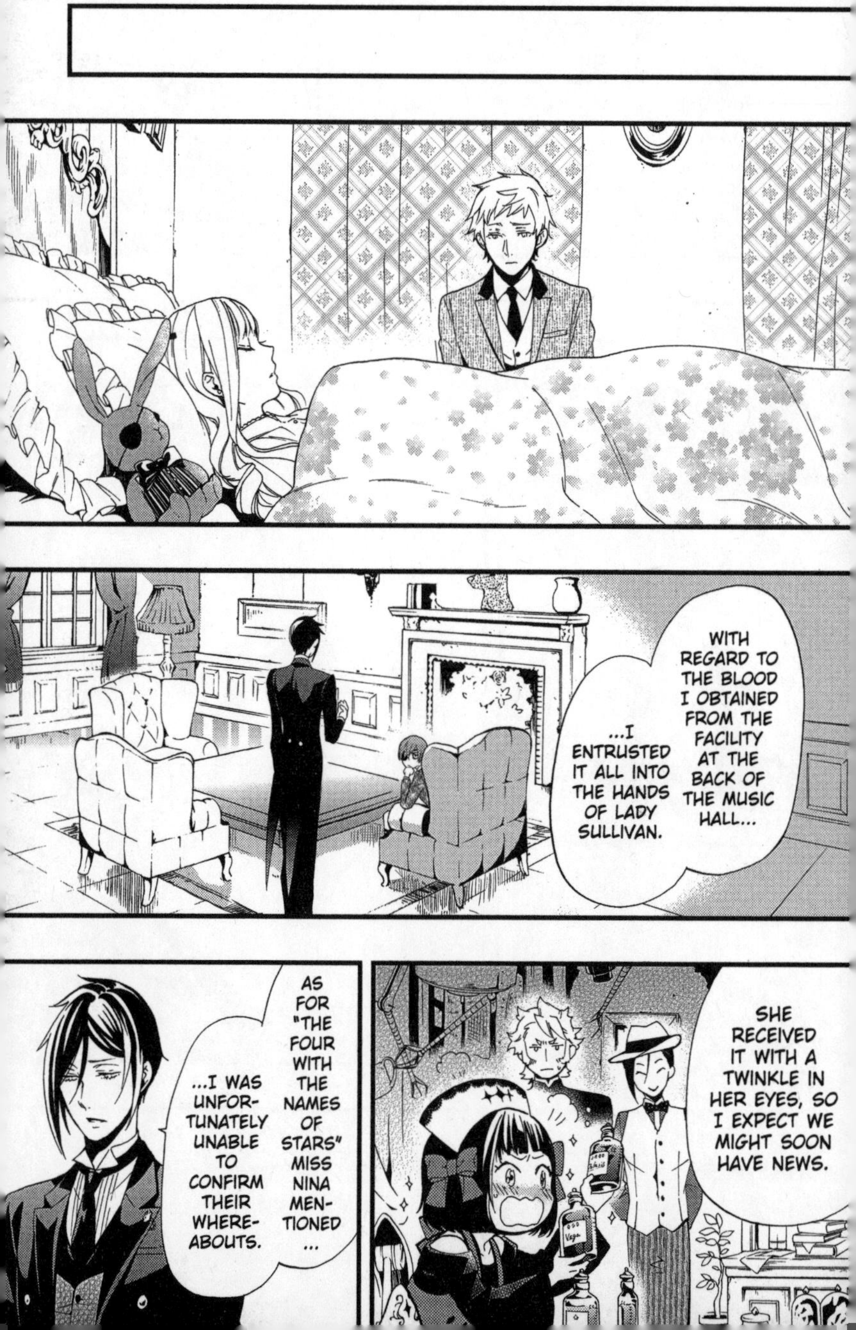
WITH REGARD TO THE BLOOD I OBTAINED FROM THE FACILITY AT THE BACK OF THE MUSIC HALL...
...I ENTRUSTED IT ALL INTO THE HANDS OF LADY SULLIVAN.
SHE RECEIVED IT WITH A TWINKLE IN HER EYES, SO I EXPECT WE MIGHT SOON HAVE NEWS.
AS FOR "THE FOUR WITH THE NAMES OF STARS" MISS NINA MENTIONED...
...I WAS UNFORTUNATELY UNABLE TO CONFIRM THEIR WHEREABOUTS.

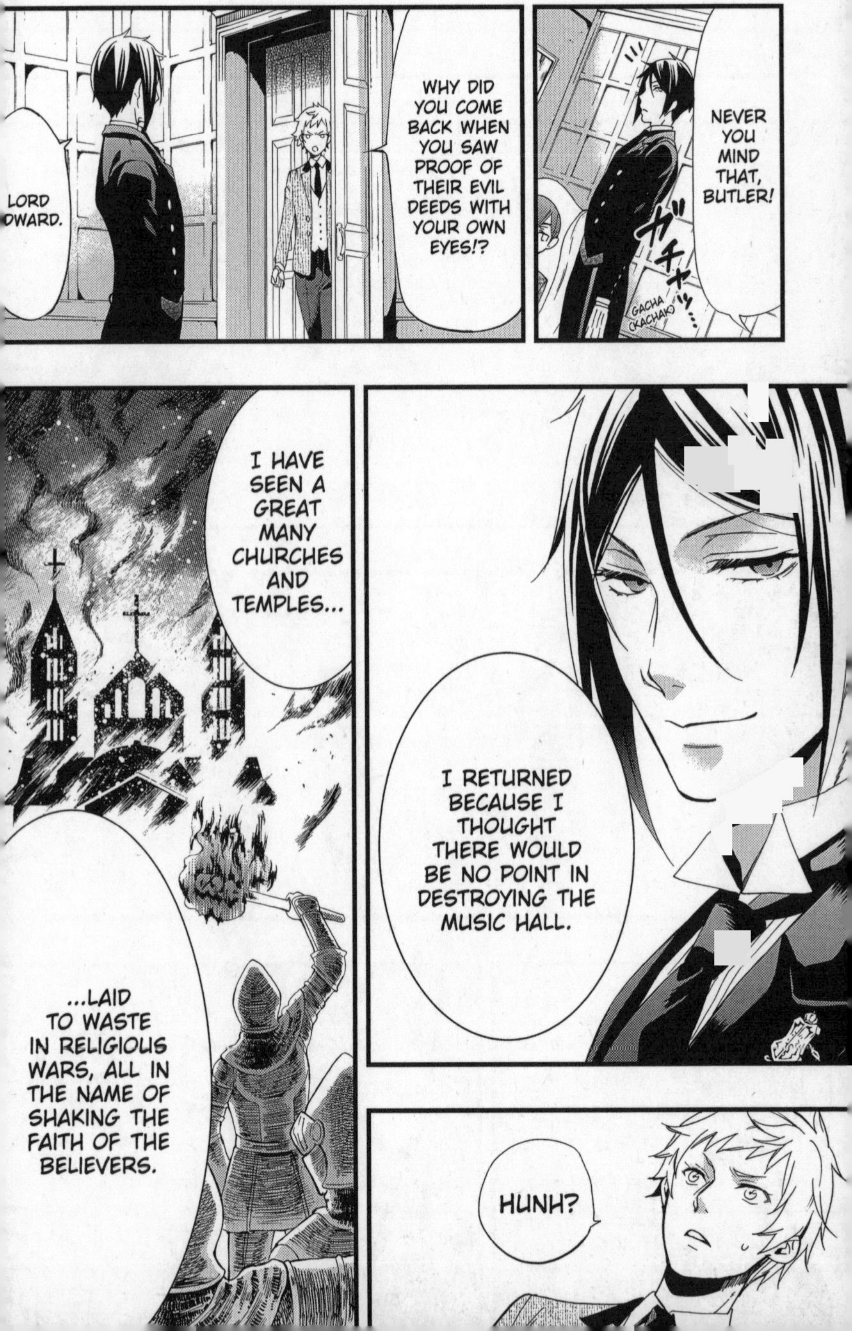
NEVER YOU MIND THAT, BUTLER!
ガチャッ…
GACHA (KACHAK)
WHY DID YOU COME BACK WHEN YOU SAW PROOF OF THEIR EVIL DEEDS WITH YOUR OWN EYES!?
LORD DWARD.
I RETURNED BECAUSE I THOUGHT THERE WOULD BE NO POINT IN DESTROYING THE MUSIC HALL.
HUNH?
I HAVE SEEN A GREAT MANY CHURCHES AND TEMPLES...
...LAID TO WASTE IN RELIGIOUS WARS, ALL IN THE NAME OF SHAKING THE FAITH OF THE BELIEVERS.

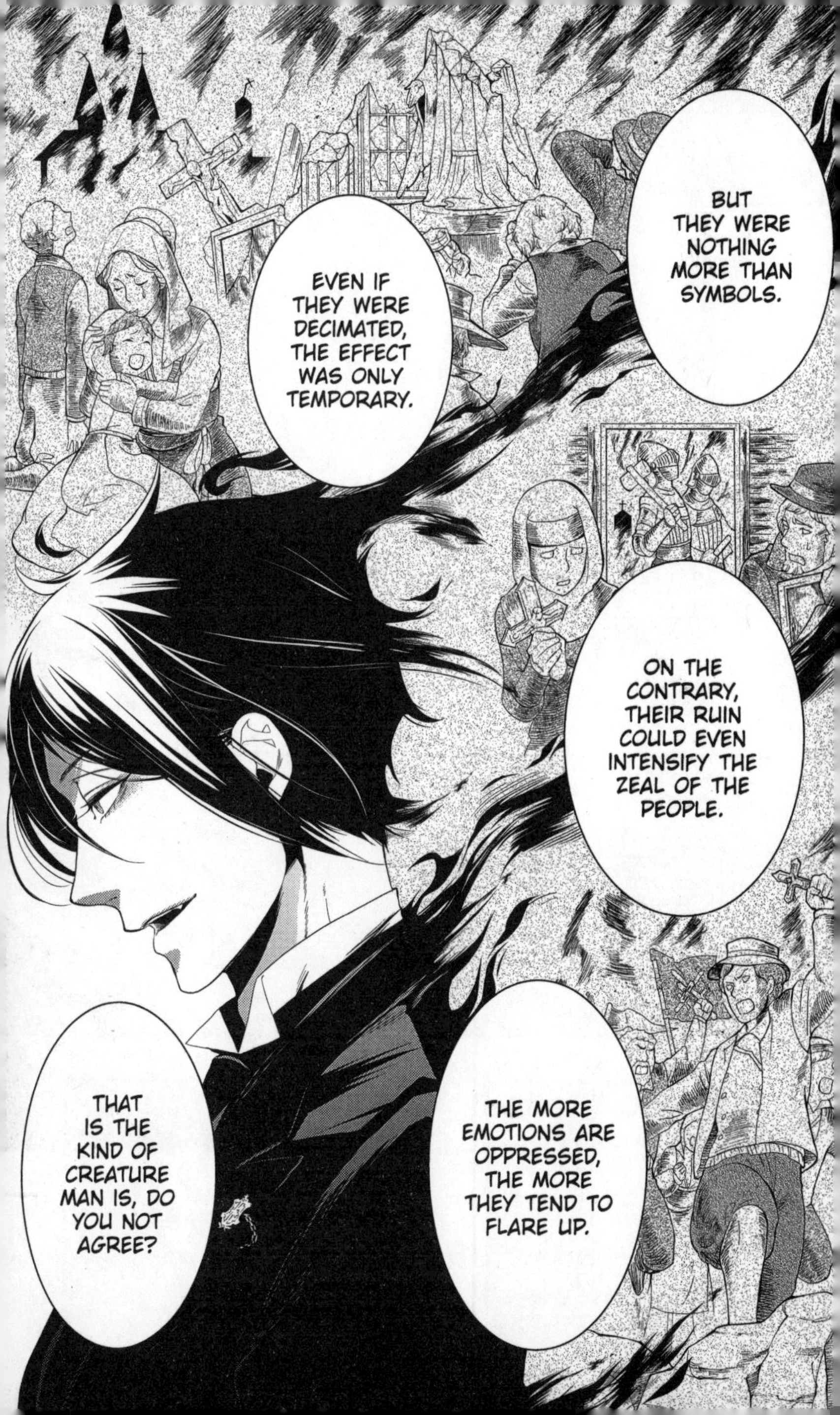
BUT THEY WERE NOTHING MORE THAN SYMBOLS.
EVEN IF THEY WERE DECIMATED, THE EFFECT WAS ONLY TEMPORARY.
ON THE CONTRARY, THEIR RUIN COULD EVEN INTENSIFY THE ZEAL OF THE PEOPLE.
THE MORE EMOTIONS ARE OPPRESSED, THE MORE THEY TEND TO FLARE UP.
THAT IS THE KIND OF CREATURE MAN IS, DO YOU NOT AGREE?

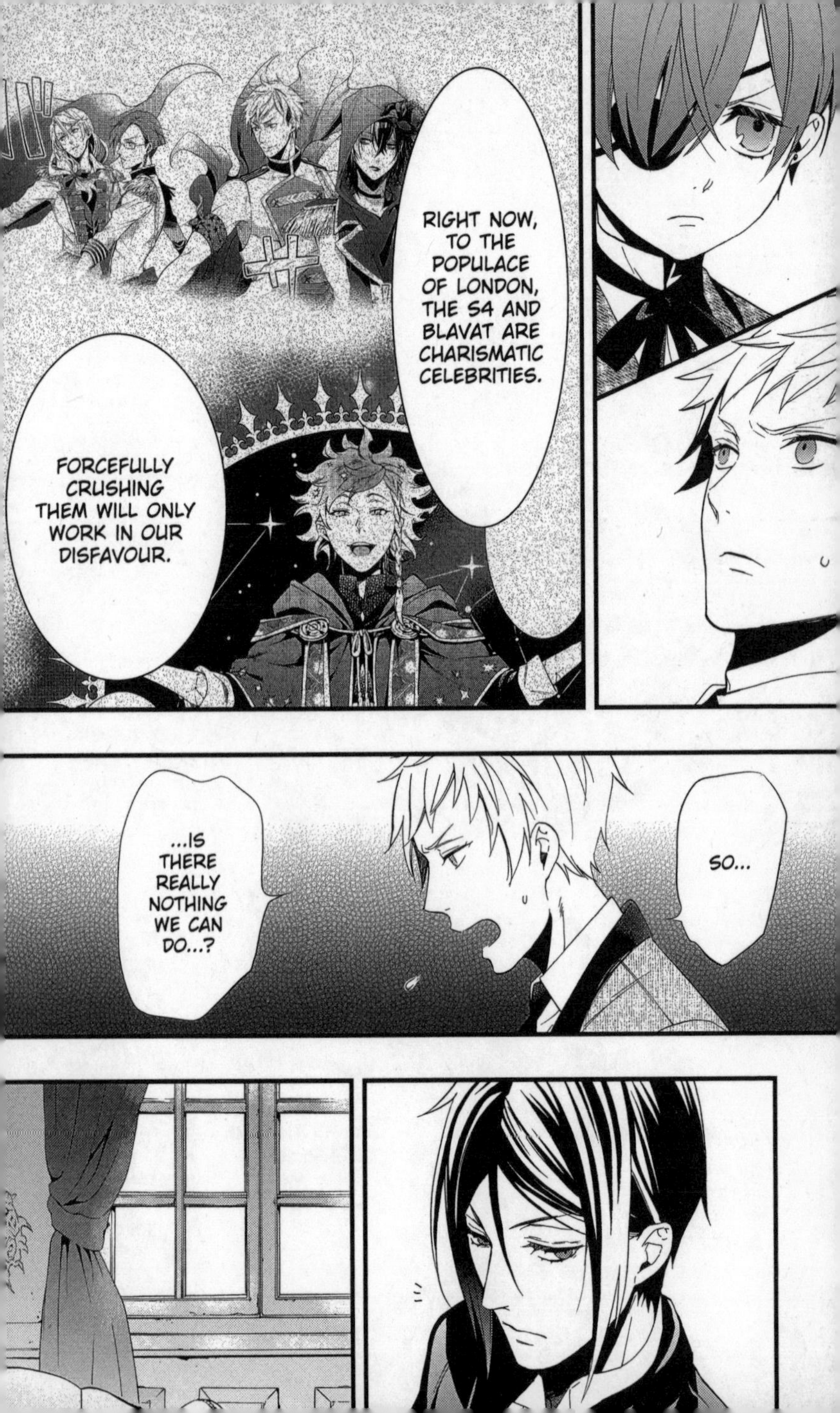
RIGHT NOW, TO THE POPULACE OF LONDON, THE S4 AND BLAVAT ARE CHARISMATIC CELEBRITIES.
FORCEFULLY CRUSHING THEM WILL ONLY WORK IN OUR DISFAVOUR.
SO...
...IS THERE REALLY NOTHING WE CAN DO...?

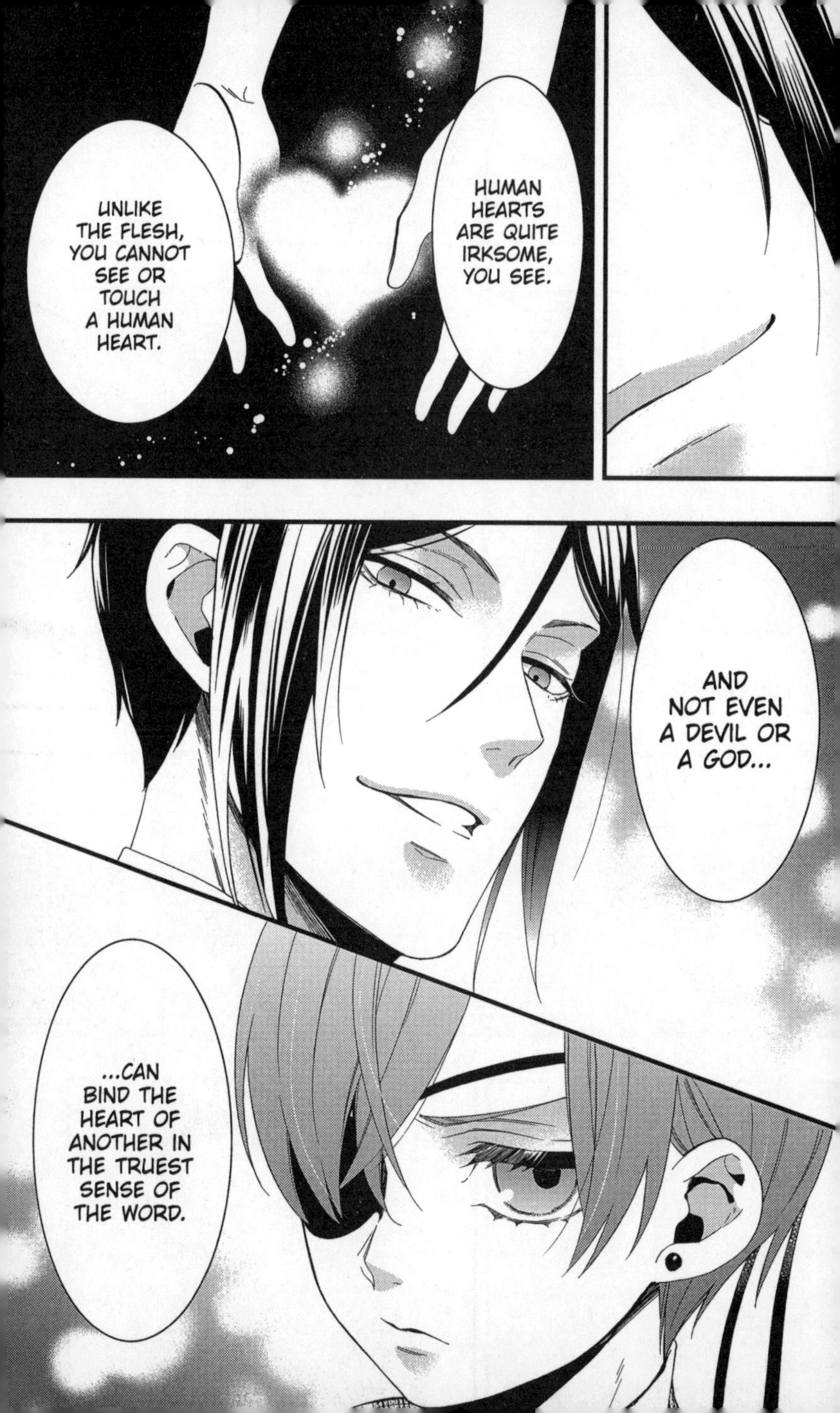
HUMAN HEARTS ARE QUITE IRKSOME, YOU SEE.
UNLIKE THE FLESH, YOU CANNOT SEE OR TOUCH A HUMAN HEART.
AND NOT EVEN A DEVIL OR A GOD...
...CAN BIND THE HEART OF ANOTHER IN THE TRUEST SENSE OF THE WORD.

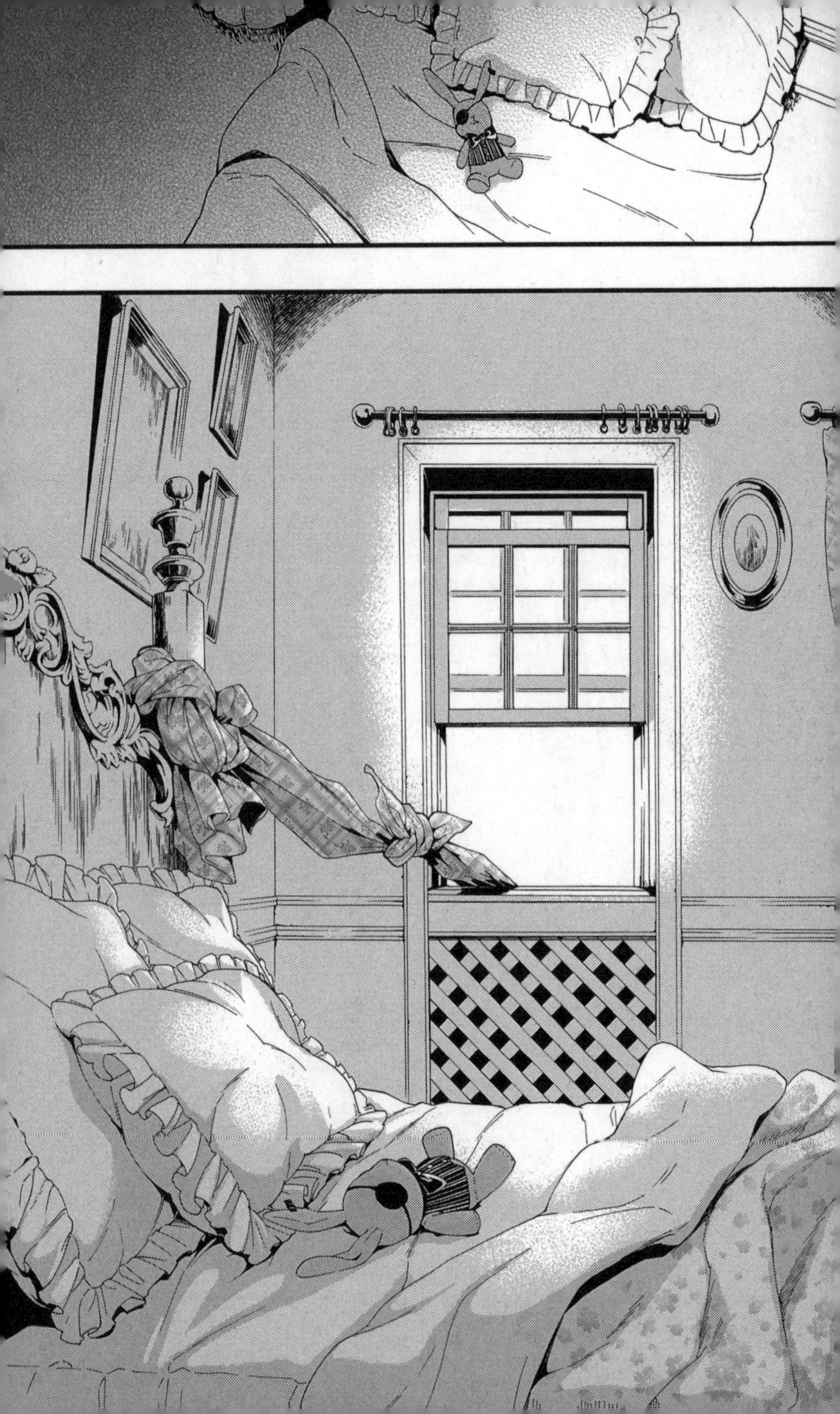

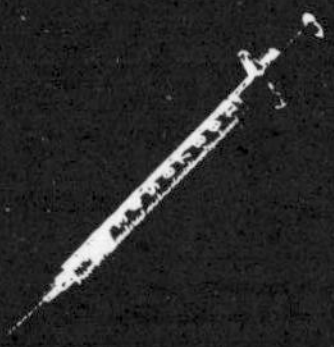

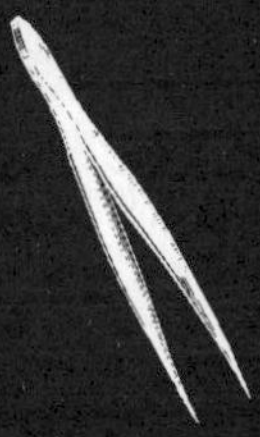

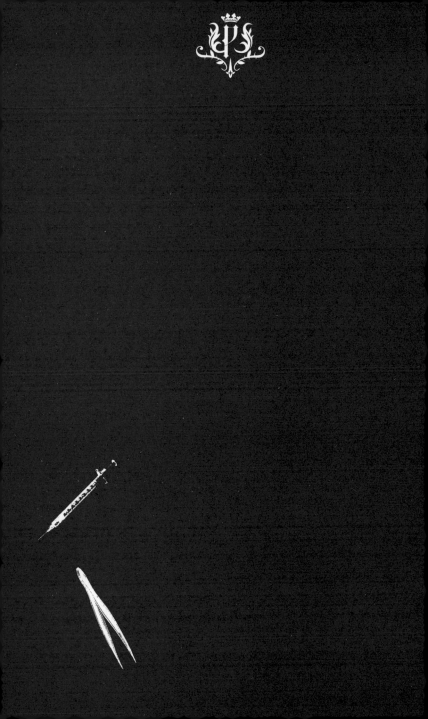

Black Butler

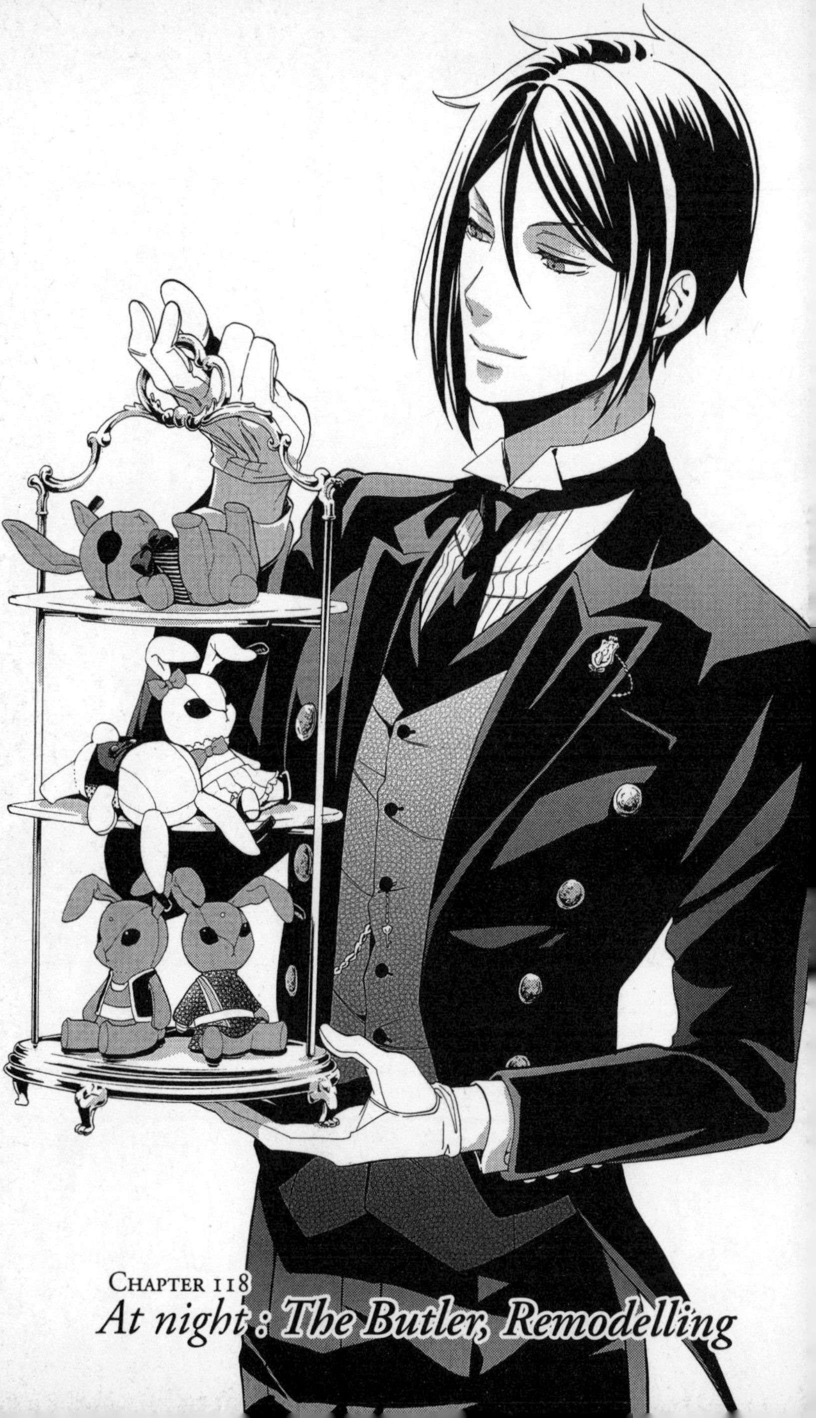

CHAPTER 118

At night : The Butler, Remodelling

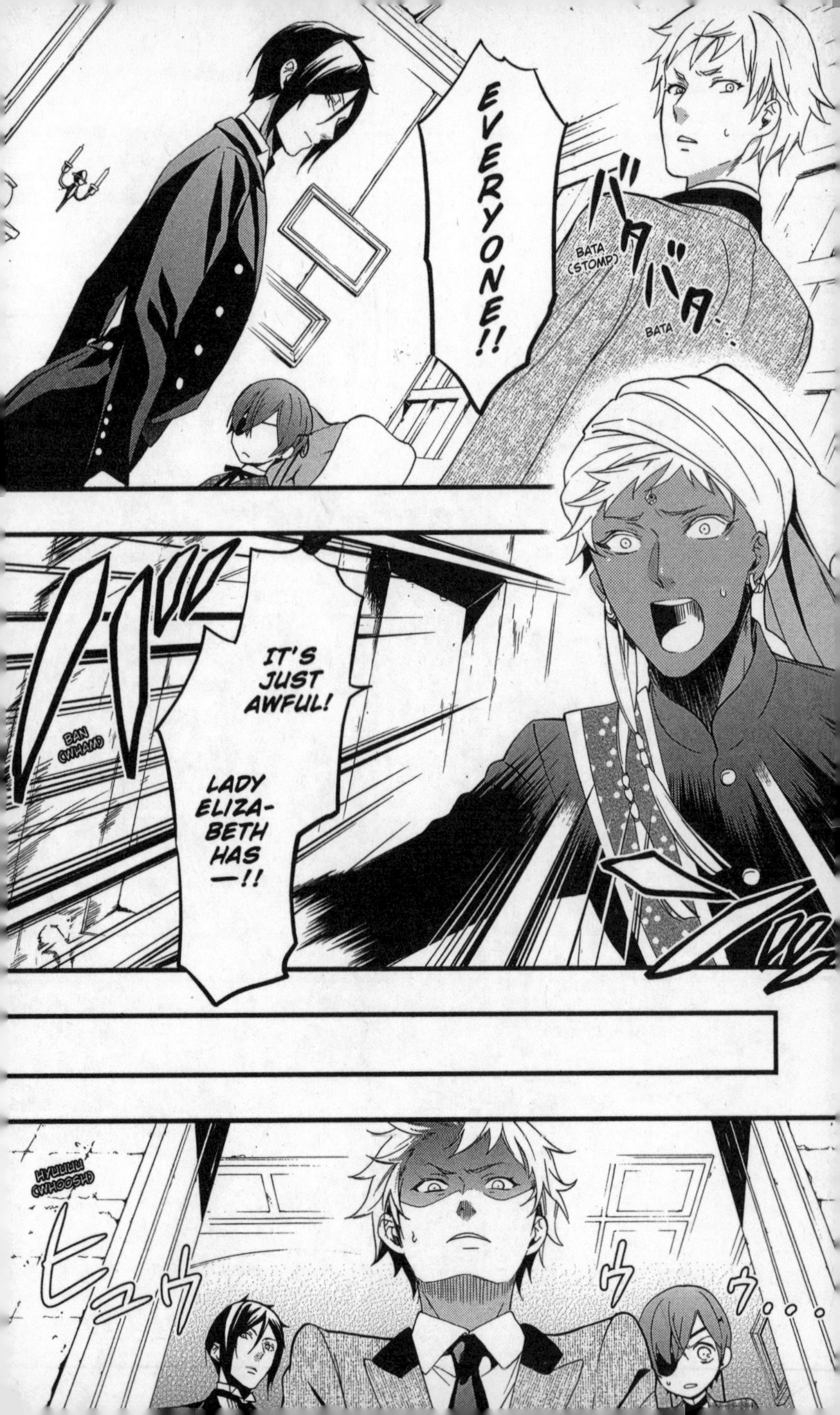
BATA (STOMP)
BATA
EVERYONE!!
IT'S JUST AWFUL!
LADY ELIZA-BETH HAS—!!
BAN (WHAM)
HYUUUU (WHOOSH)

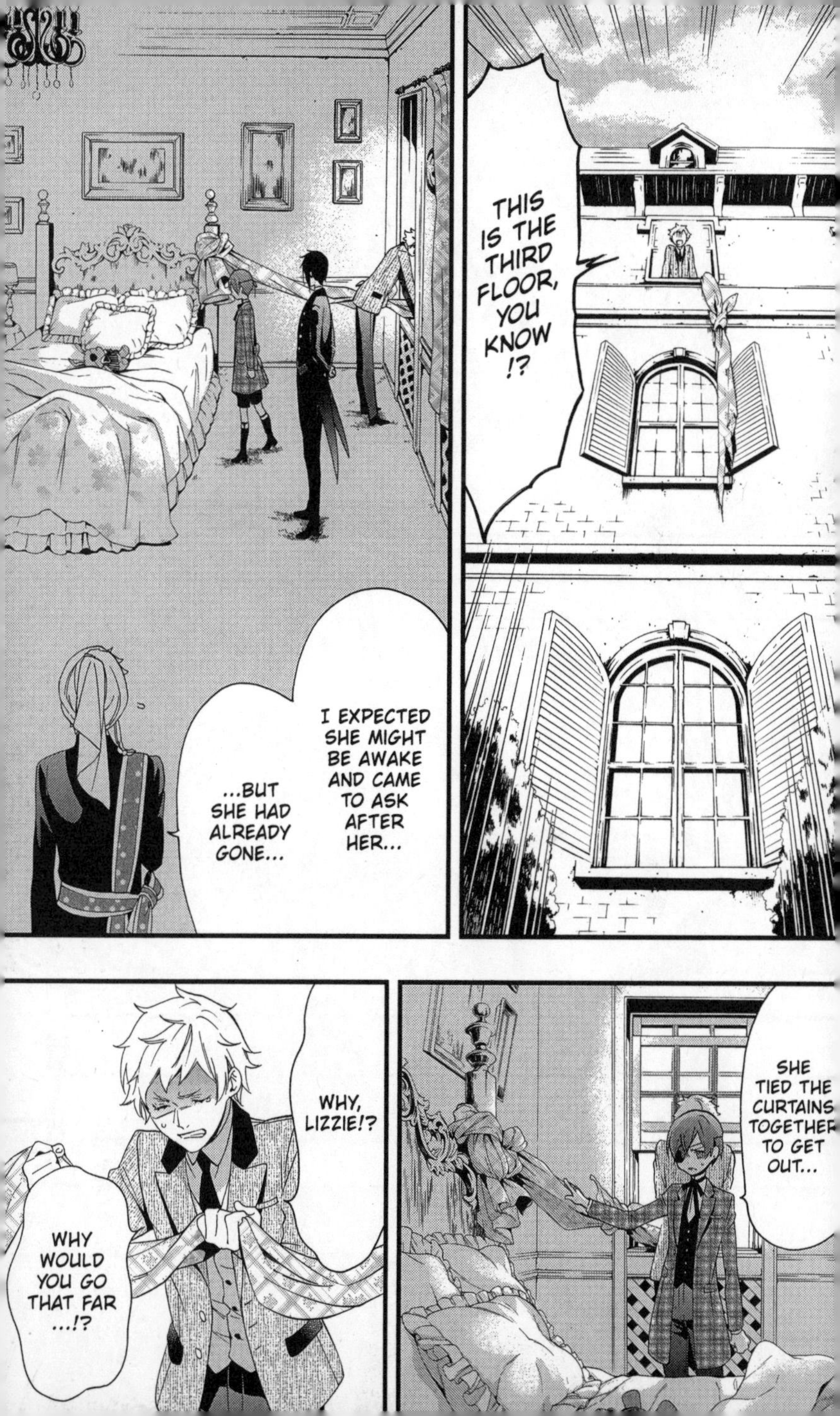
THIS IS THE THIRD FLOOR, YOU KNOW !?
I EXPECTED SHE MIGHT BE AWAKE AND CAME TO ASK AFTER HER...
...BUT SHE HAD ALREADY GONE...
SHE TIED THE CURTAINS TOGETHER TO GET OUT...
WHY, LIZZIE!?
WHY WOULD YOU GO THAT FAR ...!?

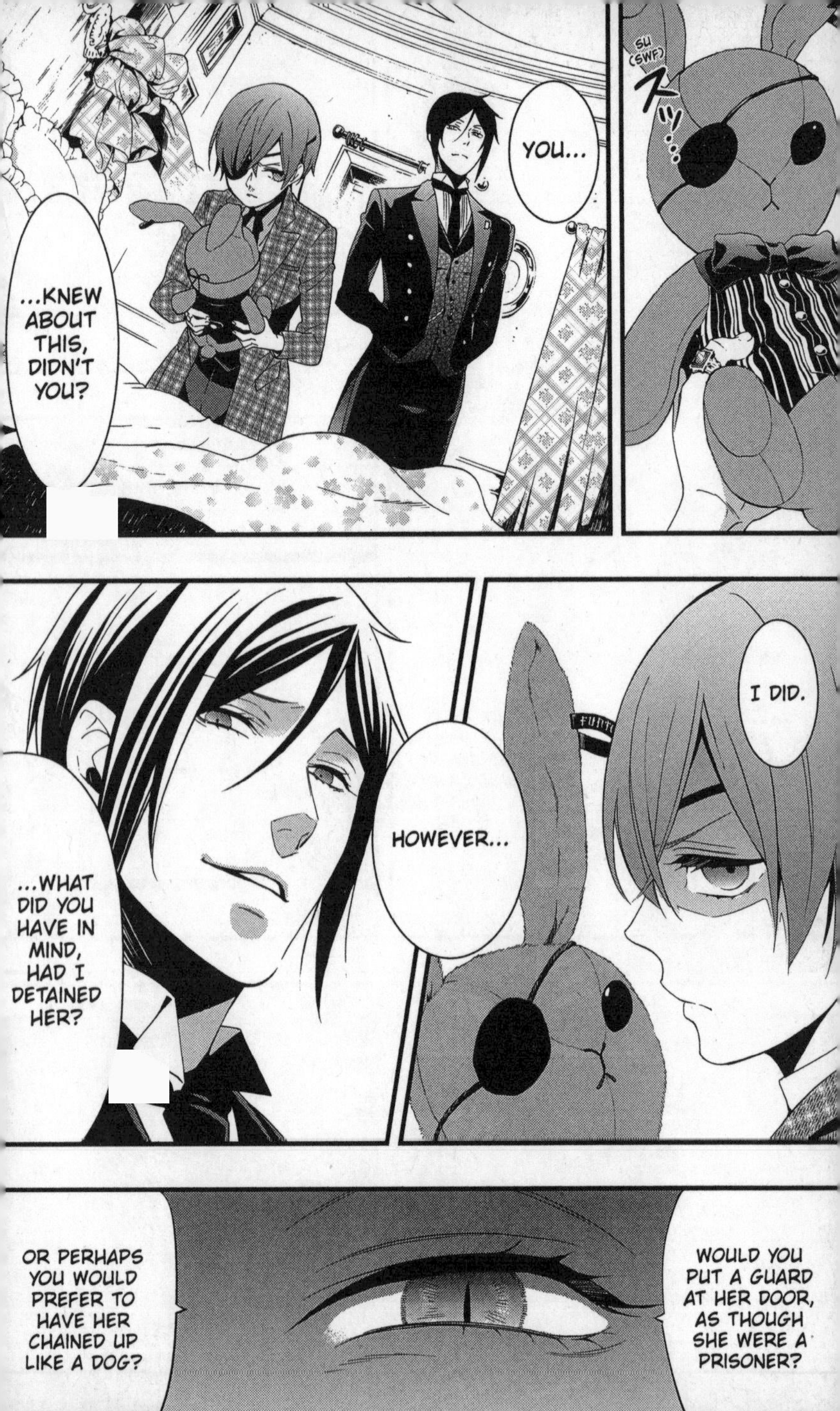
SU (SWF)
YOU...
...KNEW ABOUT THIS, DIDN'T YOU?
I DID.
HOWEVER...
...WHAT DID YOU HAVE IN MIND, HAD I DETAINED HER?
WOULD YOU PUT A GUARD AT HER DOOR, AS THOUGH SHE WERE A PRISONER?
OR PERHAPS YOU WOULD PREFER TO HAVE HER CHAINED UP LIKE A DOG?

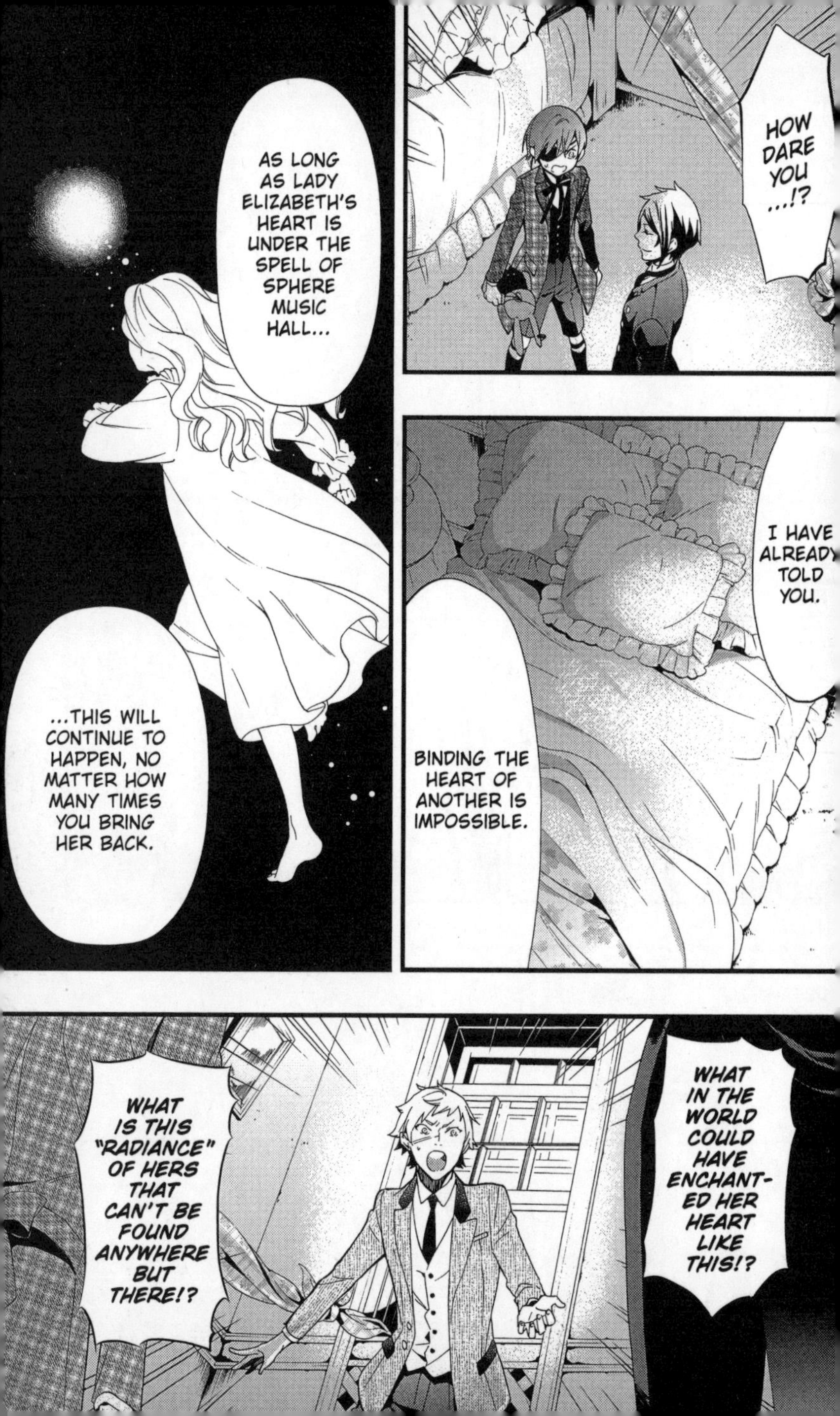
HOW DARE YOU ...!?
I HAVE ALREADY TOLD YOU.
BINDING THE HEART OF ANOTHER IS IMPOSSIBLE.
AS LONG AS LADY ELIZABETH'S HEART IS UNDER THE SPELL OF SPHERE MUSIC HALL...
...THIS WILL CONTINUE TO HAPPEN, NO MATTER HOW MANY TIMES YOU BRING HER BACK.
WHAT IN THE WORLD COULD HAVE ENCHANTED HER HEART LIKE THIS!?
WHAT IS THIS "RADIANCE" OF HERS THAT CAN'T BE FOUND ANYWHERE BUT THERE!?

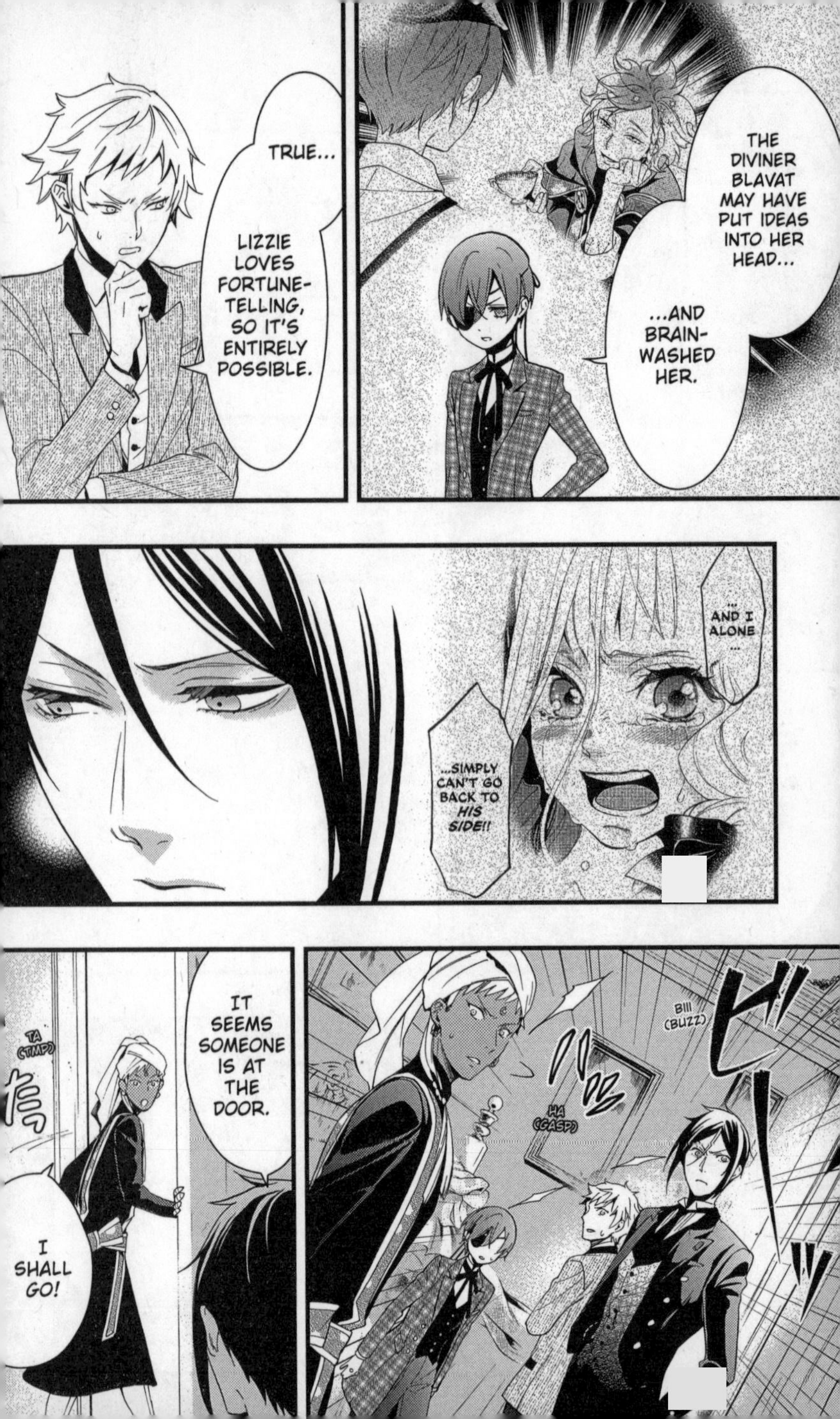
THE DIVINER BLAVAT MAY HAVE PUT IDEAS INTO HER HEAD...
...AND BRAIN-WASHED HER.
TRUE...
LIZZIE LOVES FORTUNE-TELLING, SO IT'S ENTIRELY POSSIBLE.
...AND I ALONE...
...SIMPLY CAN'T GO BACK TO *HIS* SIDE!!
BIII (BUZZ)
HA (GASP)
IT SEEMS SOMEONE IS AT THE DOOR.
TA (TMP)
I SHALL GO!

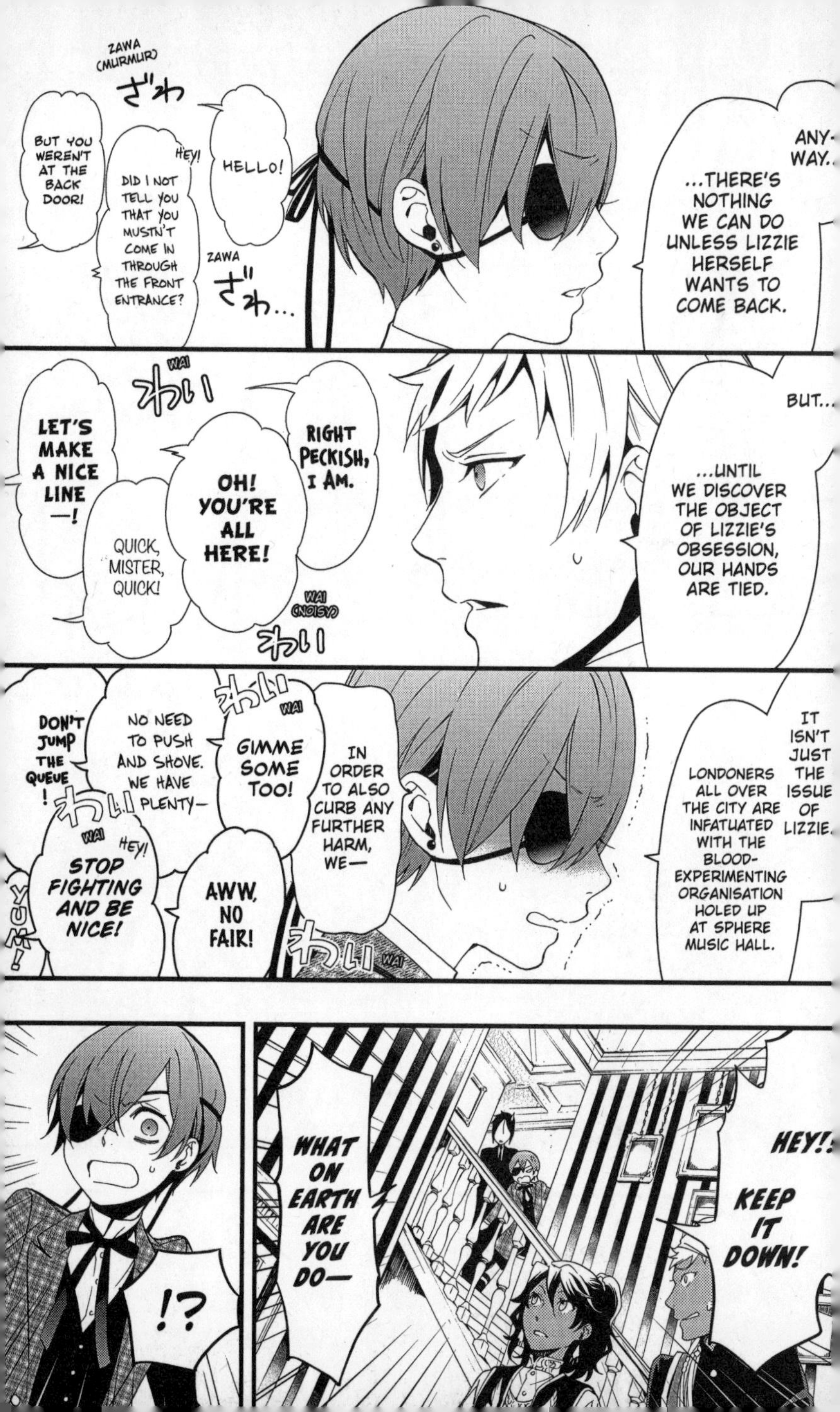
ANY-WAY.
...THERE'S NOTHING WE CAN DO UNLESS LIZZIE HERSELF WANTS TO COME BACK.
ZAWA (MURMUR)
ざわ
HELLO!
HEY!
DID I NOT TELL YOU THAT YOU MUSTN'T COME IN THROUGH THE FRONT ENTRANCE?
BUT YOU WEREN'T AT THE BACK DOOR!
ZAWA
ざわ...
BUT...
...UNTIL WE DISCOVER THE OBJECT OF LIZZIE'S OBSESSION, OUR HANDS ARE TIED.
RIGHT PECKISH, I AM.
WAI
わい
OH! YOU'RE ALL HERE!
QUICK, MISTER, QUICK!
LET'S MAKE A NICE LINE—!
WAI (NOISY)
わい
IT ISN'T JUST THE ISSUE OF LIZZIE.
LONDONERS ALL OVER THE CITY ARE INFATUATED WITH THE BLOOD-EXPERIMENTING ORGANISATION HOLED UP AT SPHERE MUSIC HALL.
IN ORDER TO ALSO CURB ANY FURTHER HARM, WE—
WAI
わい
GIMME SOME TOO!
NO NEED TO PUSH AND SHOVE. WE HAVE PLENTY—
DON'T JUMP THE QUEUE!
WAI
わい
AWW, NO FAIR!
HEY!
STOP FIGHTING AND BE NICE!
YUM!
WAI
わい
HEY!!
KEEP IT DOWN!
WHAT ON EARTH ARE YOU DO—
!?

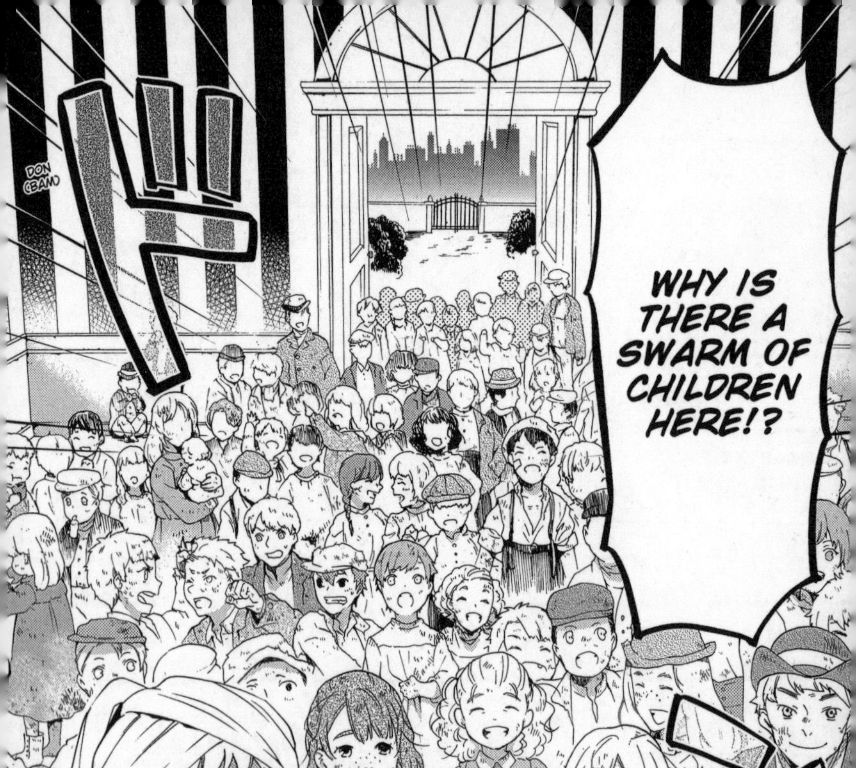
WHY IS THERE A SWARM OF CHILDREN HERE!?
DON (BAM)

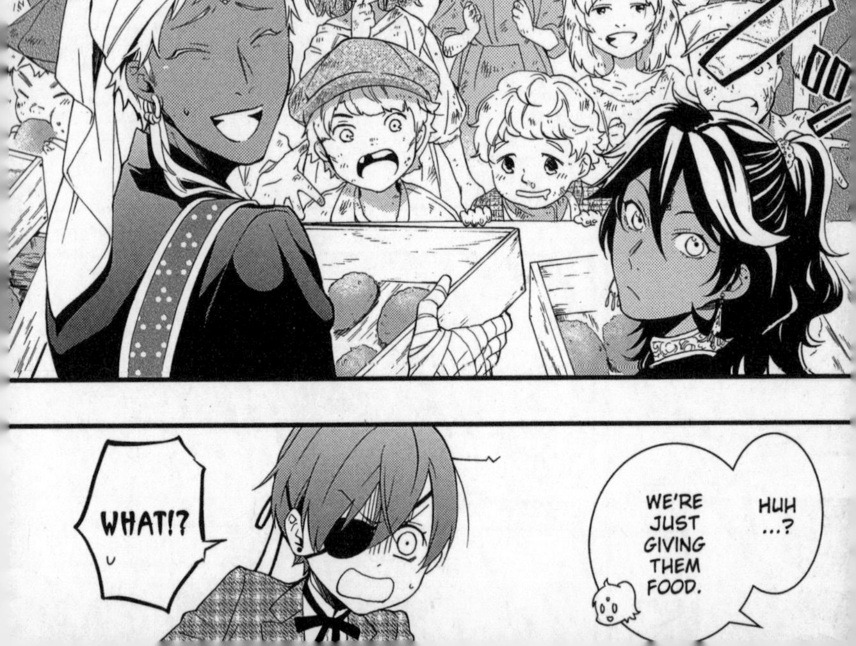
HUH ...?
WE'RE JUST GIVING THEM FOOD.
WHAT!?

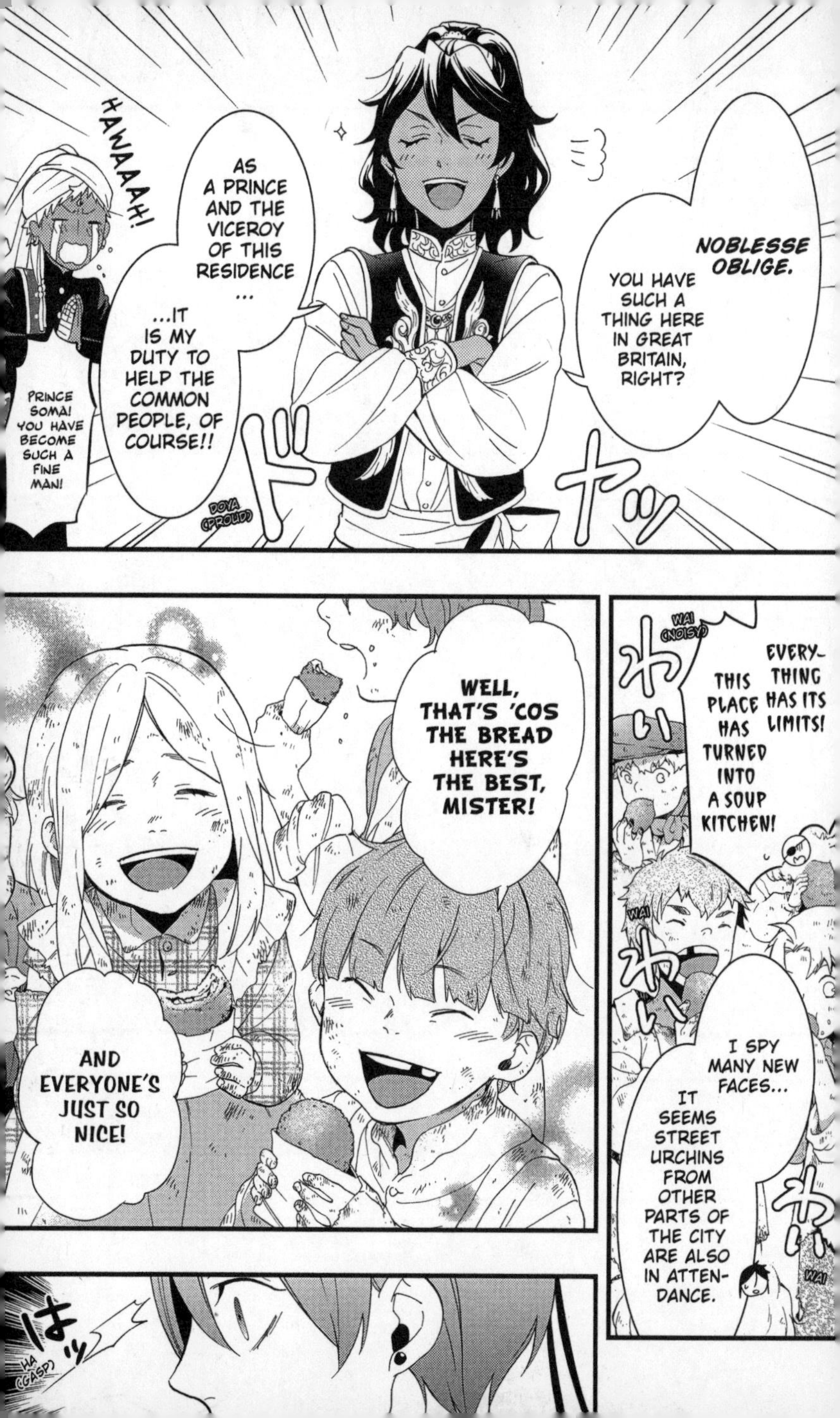
NOBLESSE OBLIGE.
YOU HAVE SUCH A THING HERE IN GREAT BRITAIN, RIGHT?
AS A PRINCE AND THE VICEROY OF THIS RESIDENCE...
...IT IS MY DUTY TO HELP THE COMMON PEOPLE, OF COURSE!!
DOYA (PROUD)
HAWAAAAH!
PRINCE SOMA! YOU HAVE BECOME SUCH A FINE MAN!
WAI (NOISY)
EVERY-THING HAS ITS LIMITS!
THIS PLACE HAS TURNED INTO A SOUP KITCHEN!
WAI
I SPY MANY NEW FACES...
IT SEEMS STREET URCHINS FROM OTHER PARTS OF THE CITY ARE ALSO IN ATTEN-DANCE.
WAI
WELL, THAT'S 'COS THE BREAD HERE'S THE BEST, MISTER!
AND EVERYONE'S JUST SO NICE!
HA (GASP)

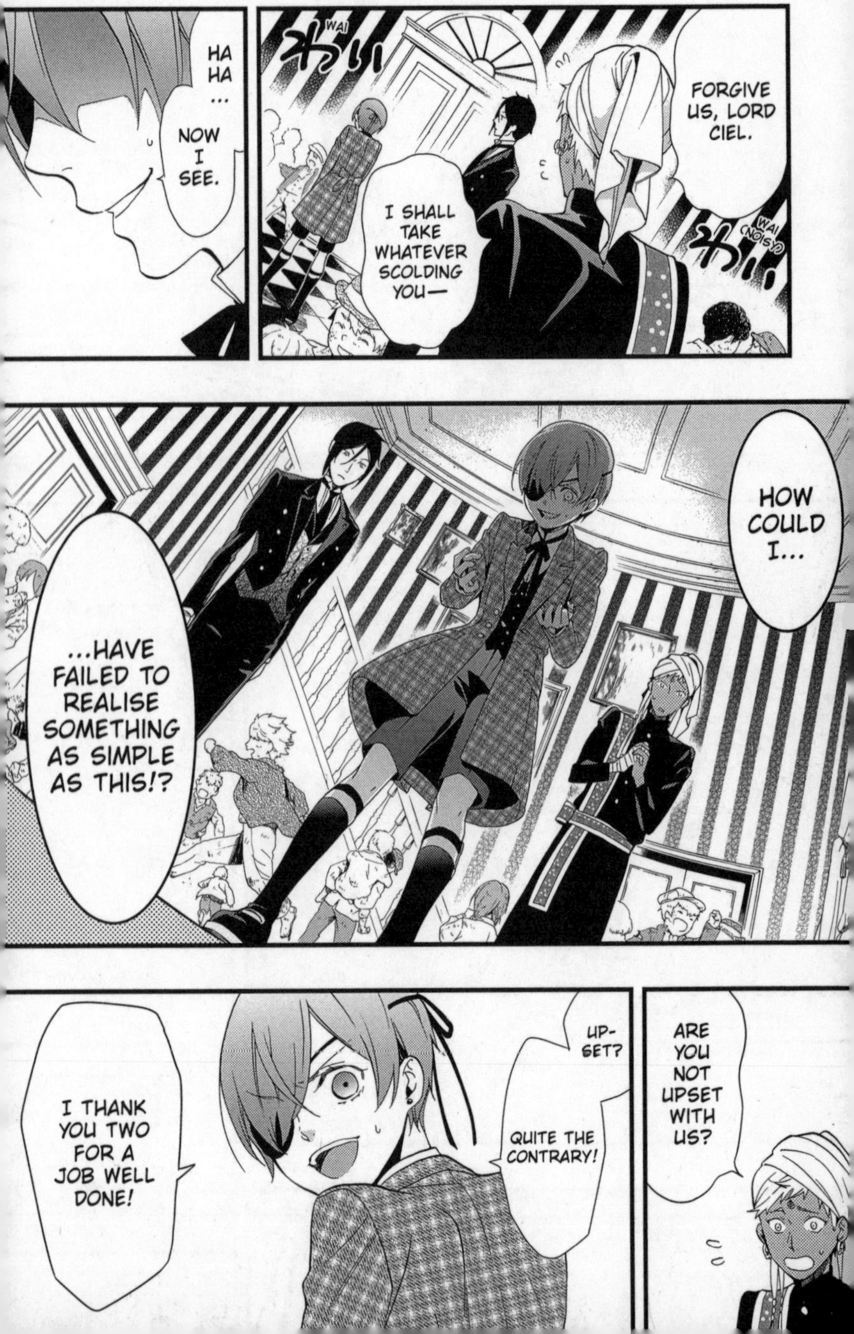
WAI
FORGIVE US, LORD CIEL.
I SHALL TAKE WHATEVER SCOLDING YOU—
WAI (NOISY)
HA HA ...
NOW I SEE.
HOW COULD I...
...HAVE FAILED TO REALISE SOMETHING AS SIMPLE AS THIS!?
ARE YOU NOT UPSET WITH US?
UP-SET?
QUITE THE CONTRARY!
I THANK YOU TWO FOR A JOB WELL DONE!

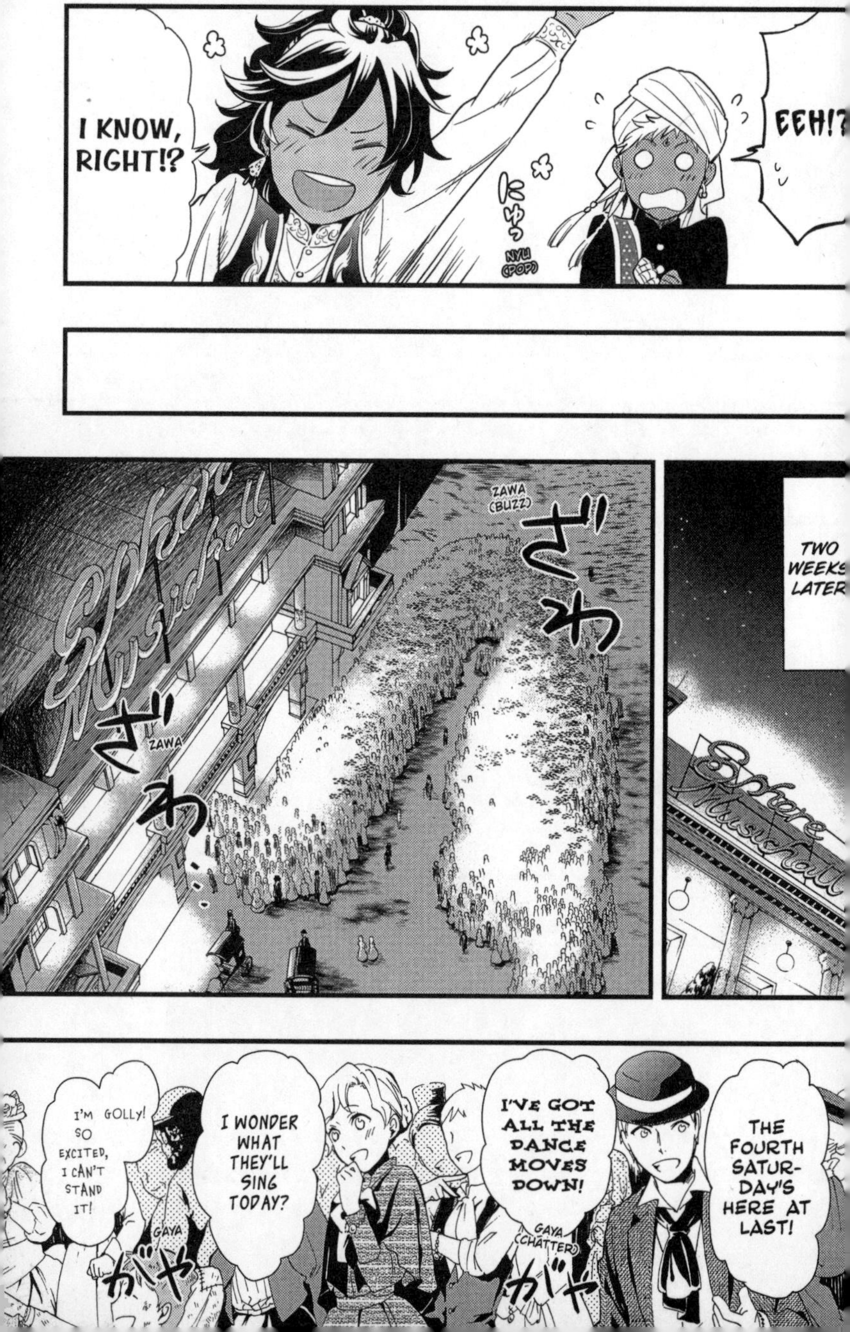
EEH!?
にゅっ
NYU (POP)
I KNOW, RIGHT!?
TWO WEEKS LATER
ざわ
ZAWA (BUZZ)
ざわ
ZAWA
THE FOURTH SATURDAY'S HERE AT LAST!
I'VE GOT ALL THE DANCE MOVES DOWN!
がや
GAYA (CHATTER)
I WONDER WHAT THEY'LL SING TODAY?
GOLLY!
I'M SO EXCITED, I CAN'T STAND IT!
がや
GAYA

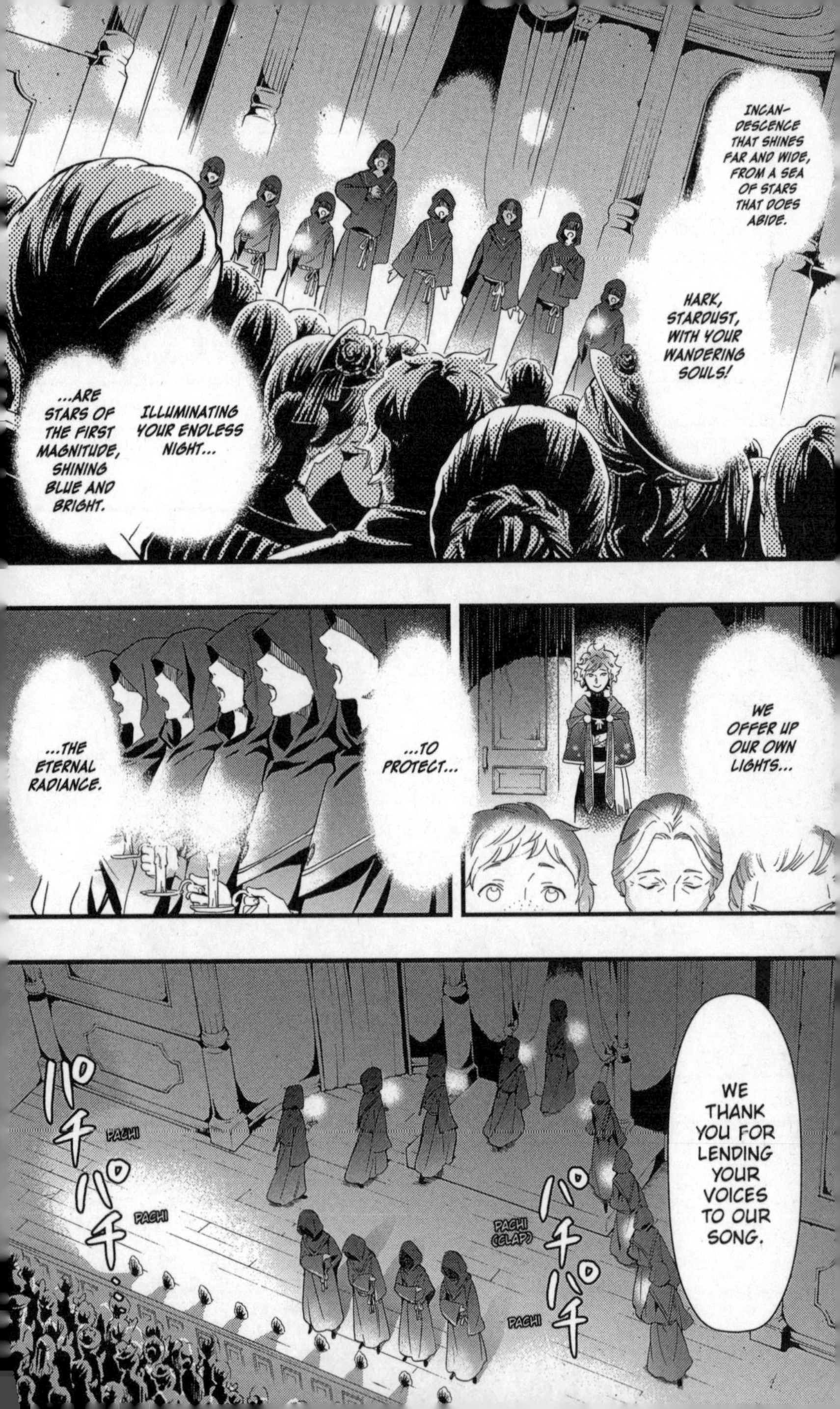
INCANDESCENCE THAT SHINES FAR AND WIDE, FROM A SEA OF STARS THAT DOES ABIDE.
HARK, STARDUST, WITH YOUR WANDERING SOULS!
ILLUMINATING YOUR ENDLESS NIGHT...
...ARE STARS OF THE FIRST MAGNITUDE, SHINING BLUE AND BRIGHT.
WE OFFER UP OUR OWN LIGHTS...
...TO PROTECT...
...THE ETERNAL RADIANCE.
WE THANK YOU FOR LENDING YOUR VOICES TO OUR SONG.
パチパチ
PACHI (CLAP)
PACHI
パチパチ…
PACHI
PACHI

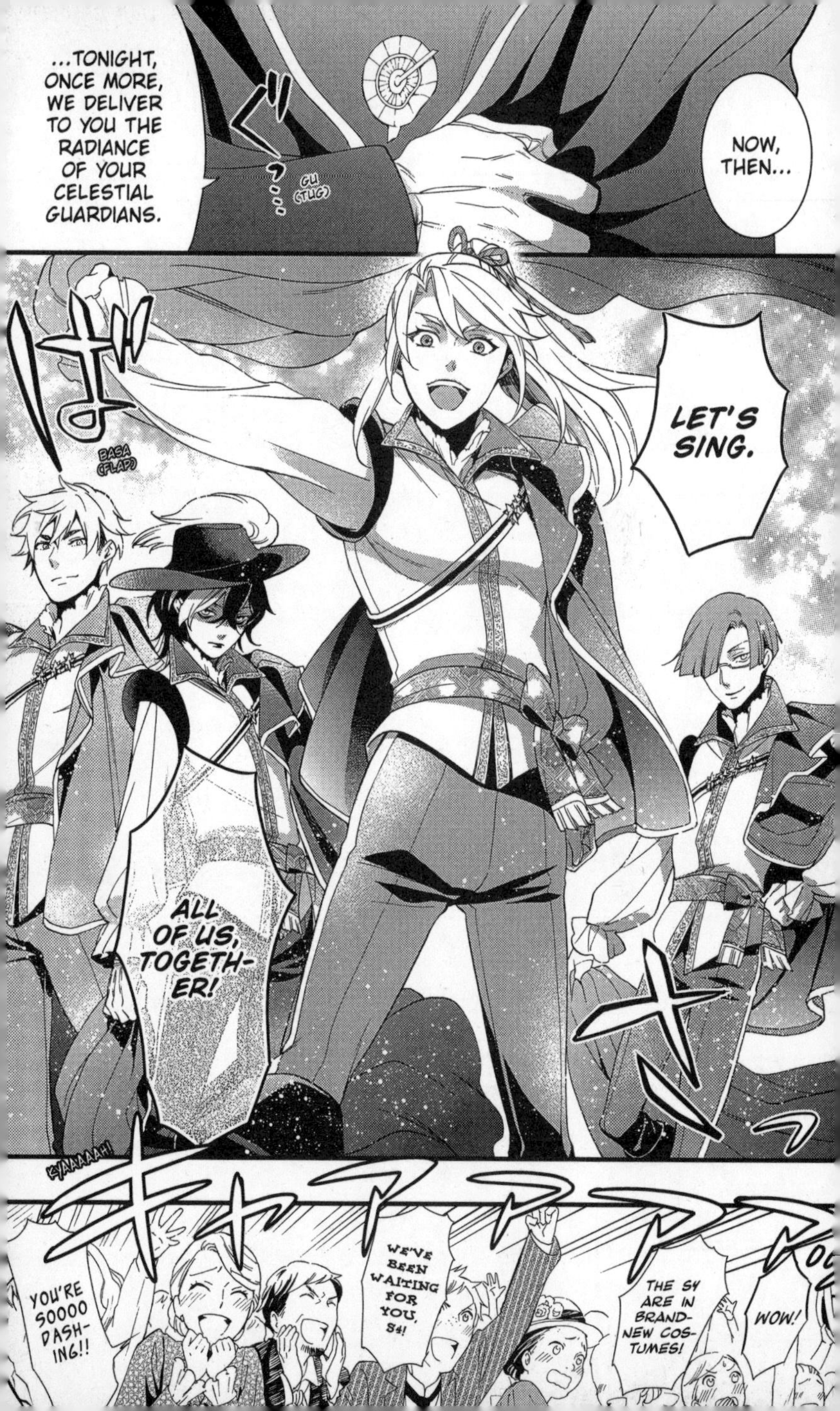
NOW, THEN...
GU (TUG)
...TONIGHT, ONCE MORE, WE DELIVER TO YOU THE RADIANCE OF YOUR CELESTIAL GUARDIANS.
LET'S SING.
BASA (FLAP)
ALL OF US, TOGETH-ER!
KYAAAAAH
WOW!
THE S4 ARE IN BRAND-NEW COS-TUMES!
WE'VE BEEN WAITING FOR YOU, S4!
YOU'RE SOOOO DASH-ING!!

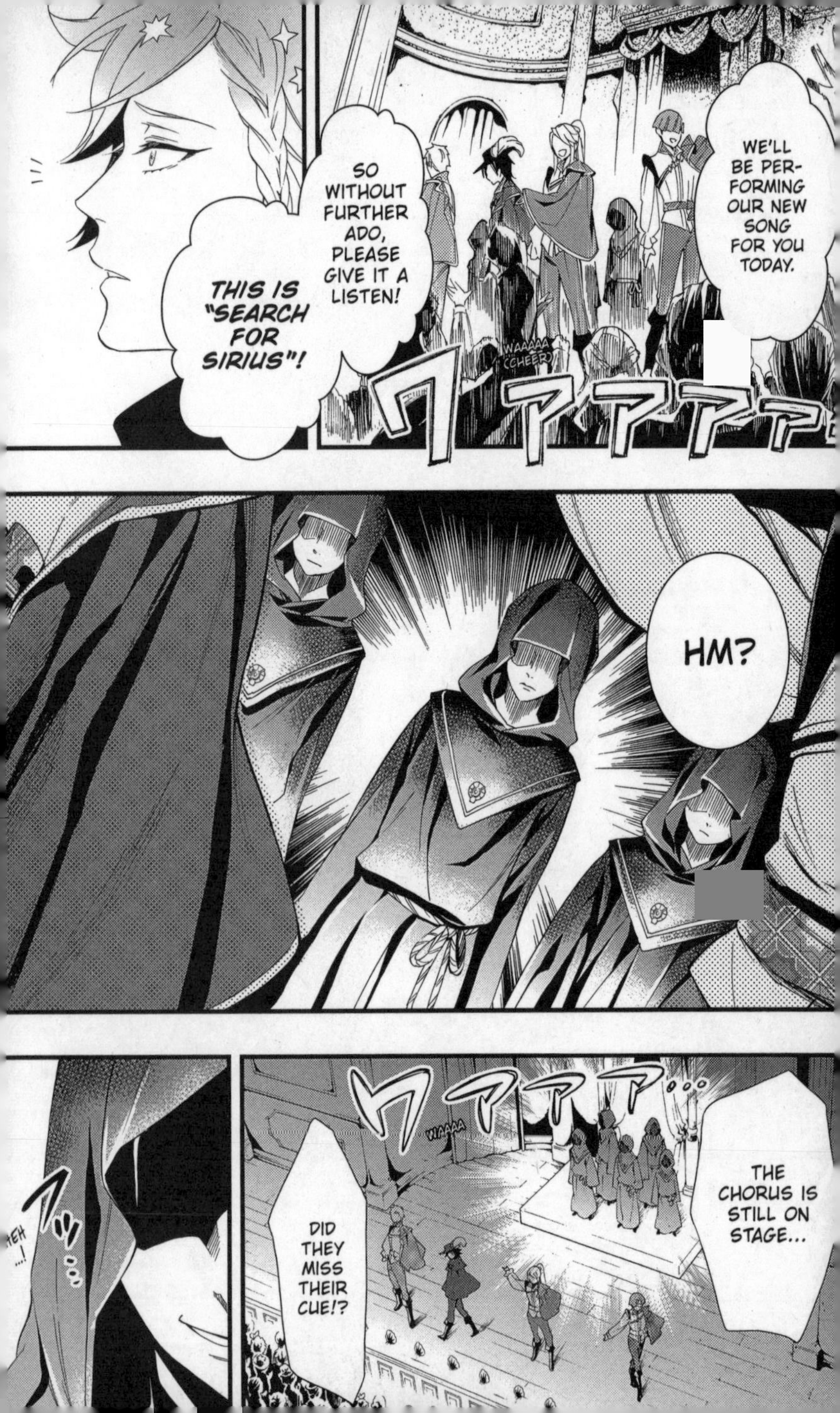
WE'LL BE PERFORMING OUR NEW SONG FOR YOU TODAY.
SO WITHOUT FURTHER ADO, PLEASE GIVE IT A LISTEN!
WAAAAA (CHEER)
ワァァァァ
THIS IS "SEARCH FOR SIRIUS"!
HM?
ワァァァ...
WAAAA
THE CHORUS IS STILL ON STAGE...
DID THEY MISS THEIR CUE!?

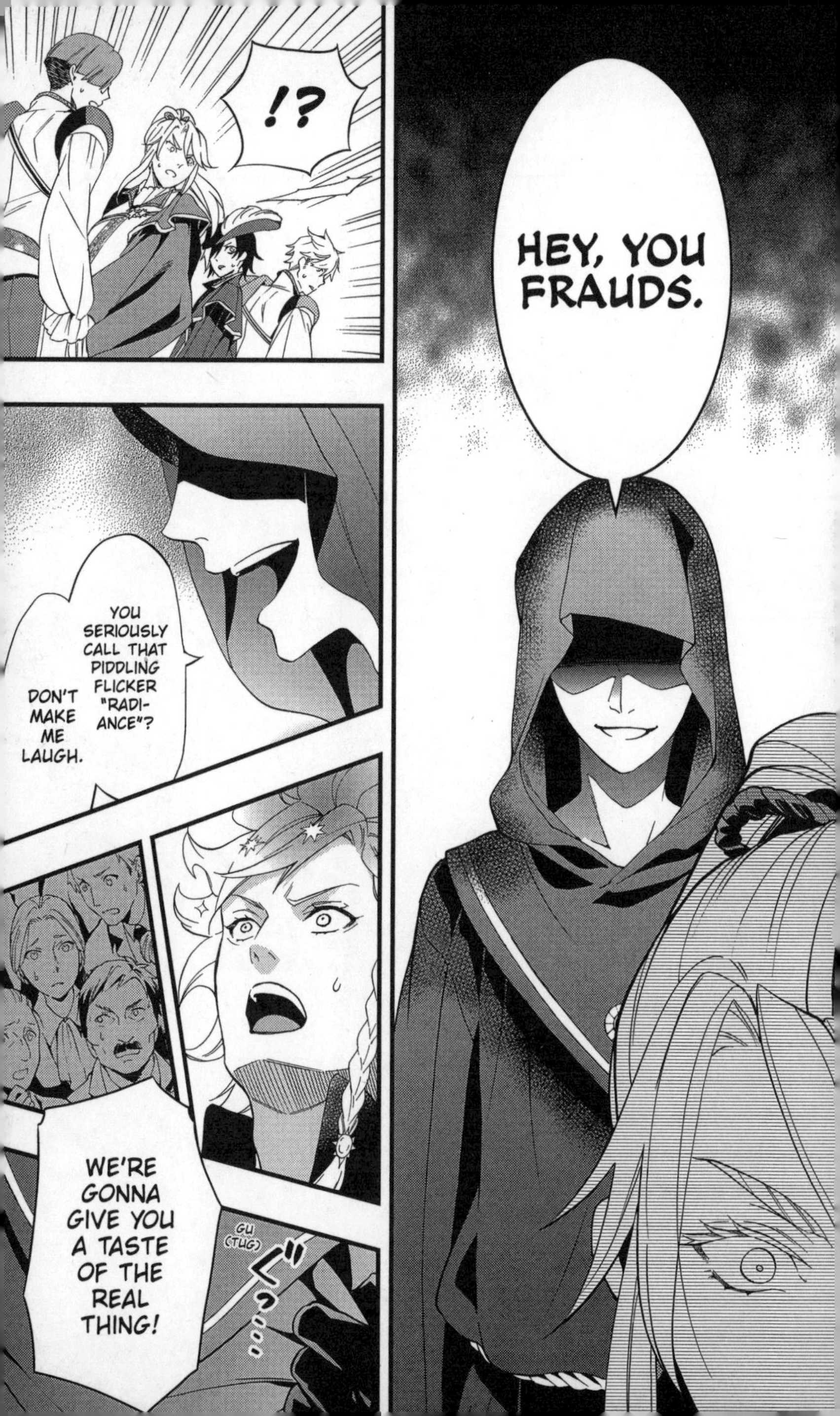
HEY, YOU FRAUDS.
!?
YOU SERIOUSLY CALL THAT PIDDLING FLICKER "RADIANCE"?
DON'T MAKE ME LAUGH.
WE'RE GONNA GIVE YOU A TASTE OF THE REAL THING!
GU (TUG)

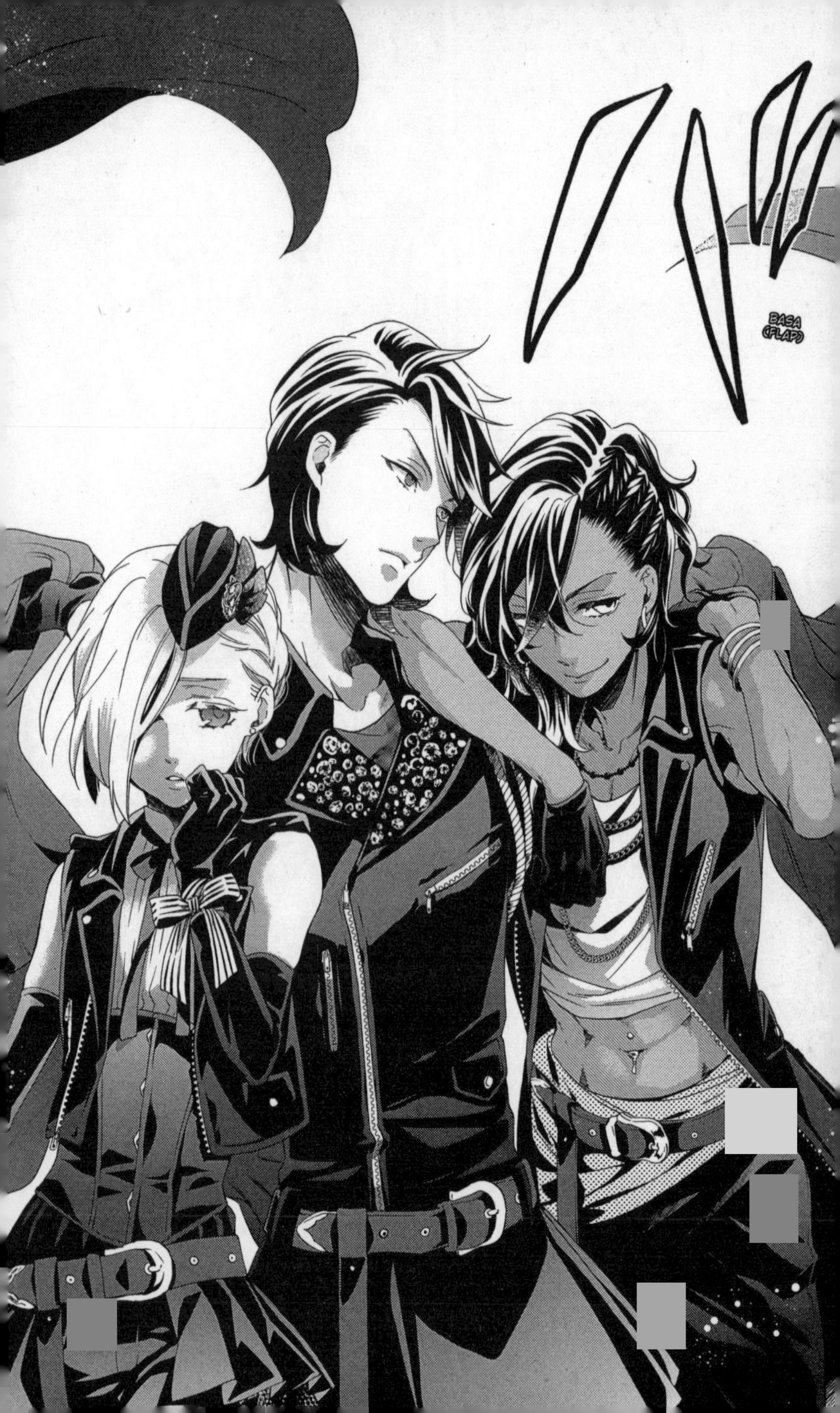
BASA
(FLAP)

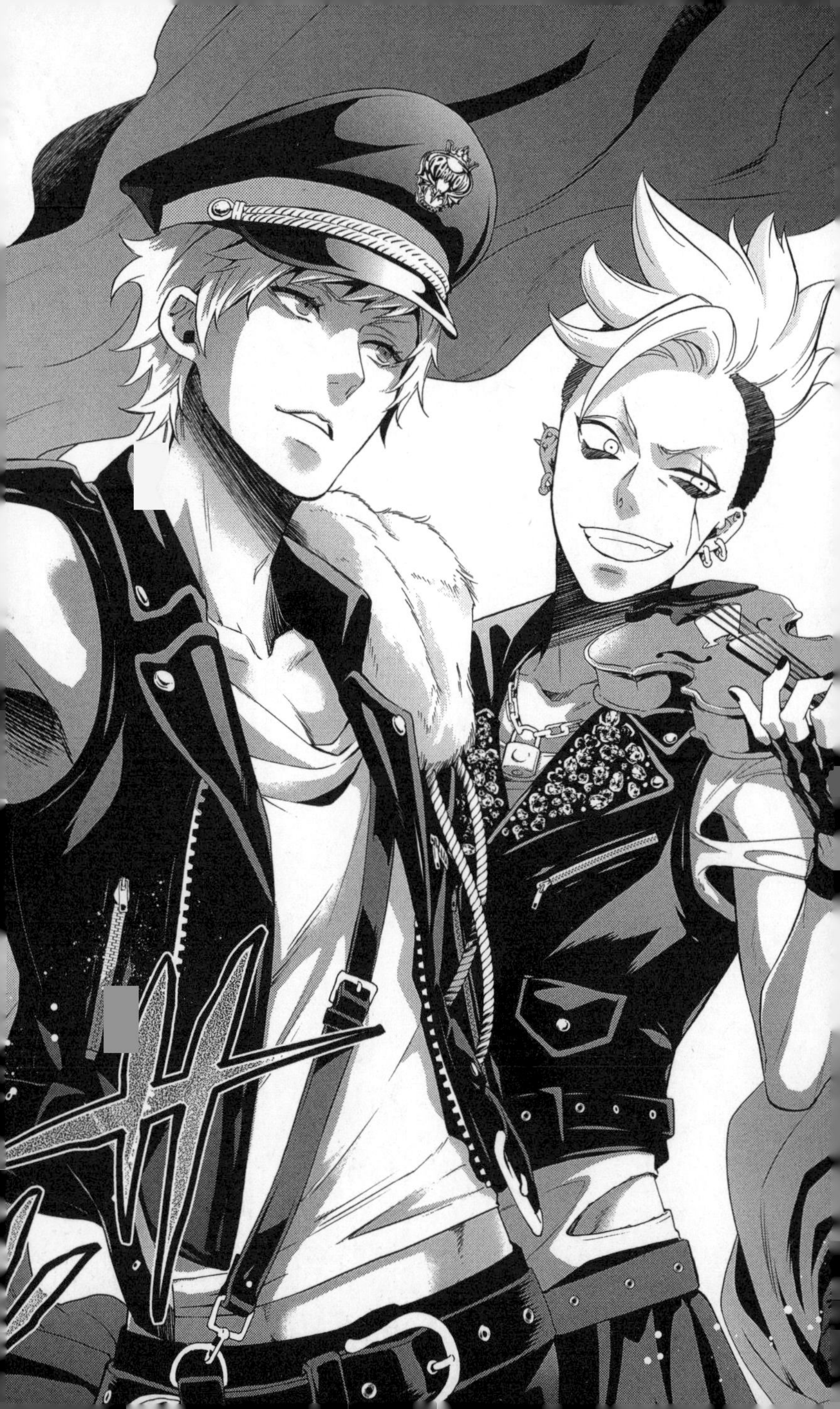

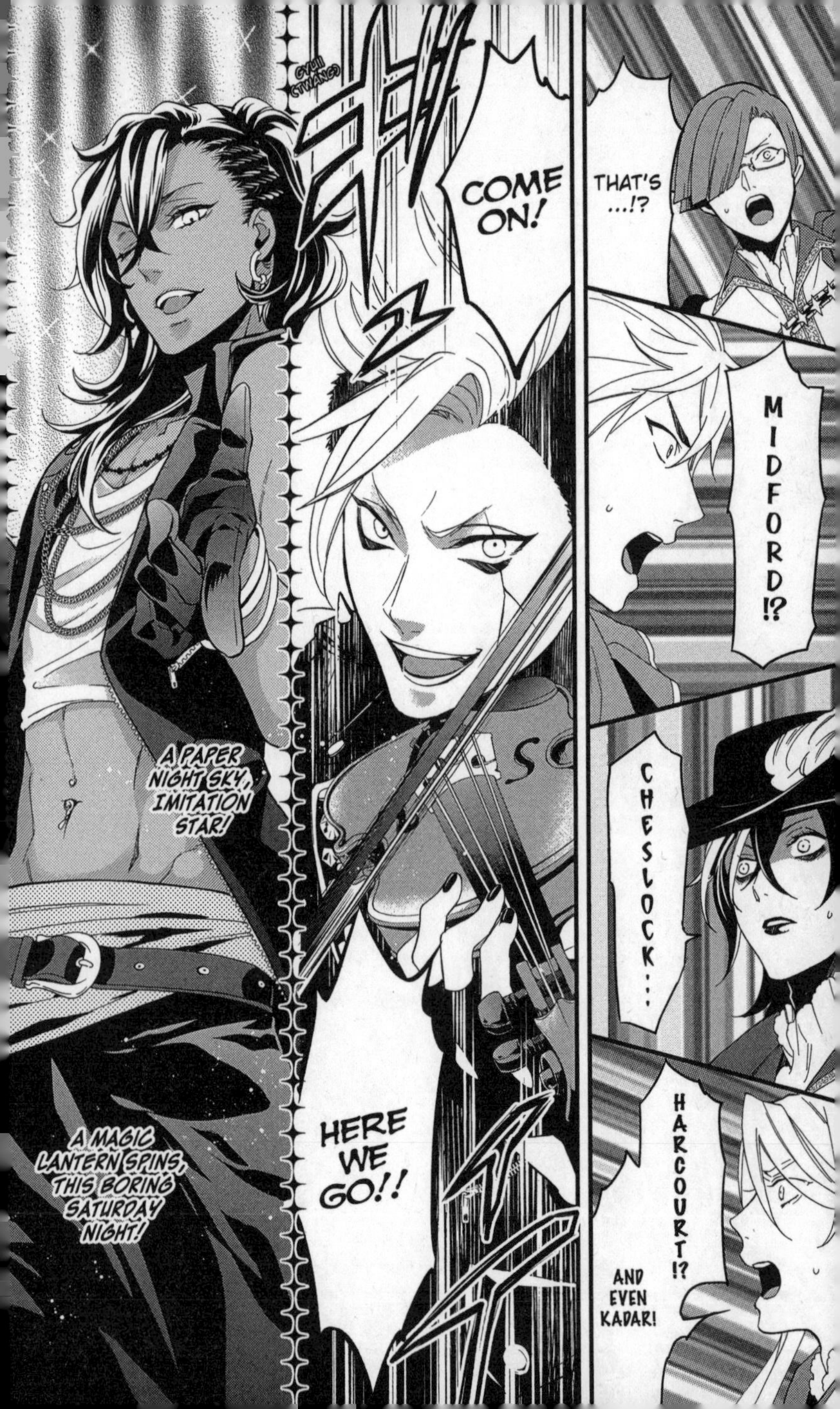
THAT'S ...!?
MIDFORD!?
CHESLOCK...
HARCOURT!?
AND EVEN KADAR!
GYUIII (TWANG)
COME ON!
HERE WE GO!!
A PAPER NIGHT SKY, IMITATION STAR!
A MAGIC LANTERN SPINS, THIS BORING SATURDAY NIGHT!

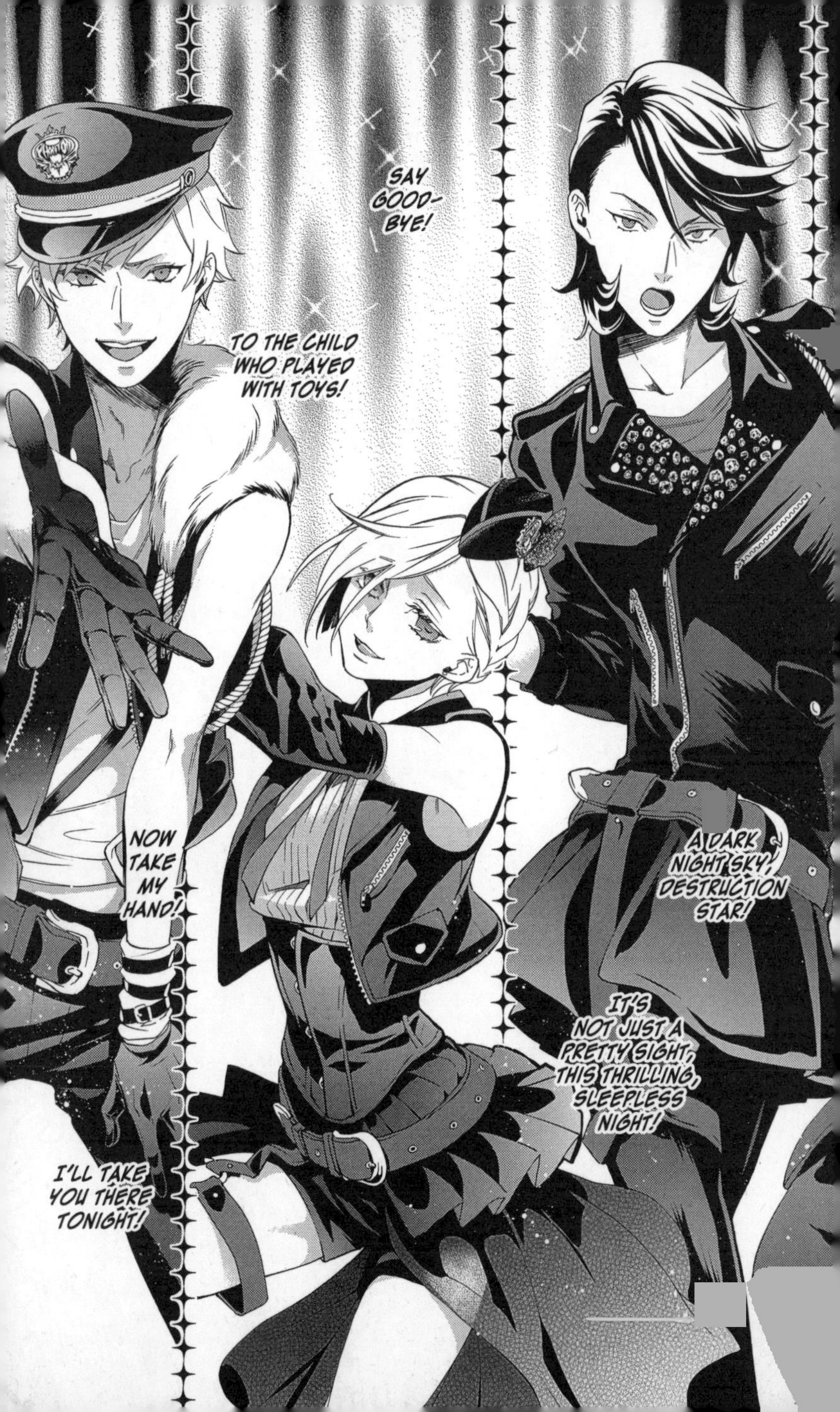
A DARK NIGHT SKY, DESTRUCTION STAR!
IT'S NOT JUST A PRETTY SIGHT, THIS THRILLING, SLEEPLESS NIGHT!
SAY GOOD-BYE!
TO THE CHILD WHO PLAYED WITH TOYS!
NOW TAKE MY HAND!
I'LL TAKE YOU THERE TONIGHT!

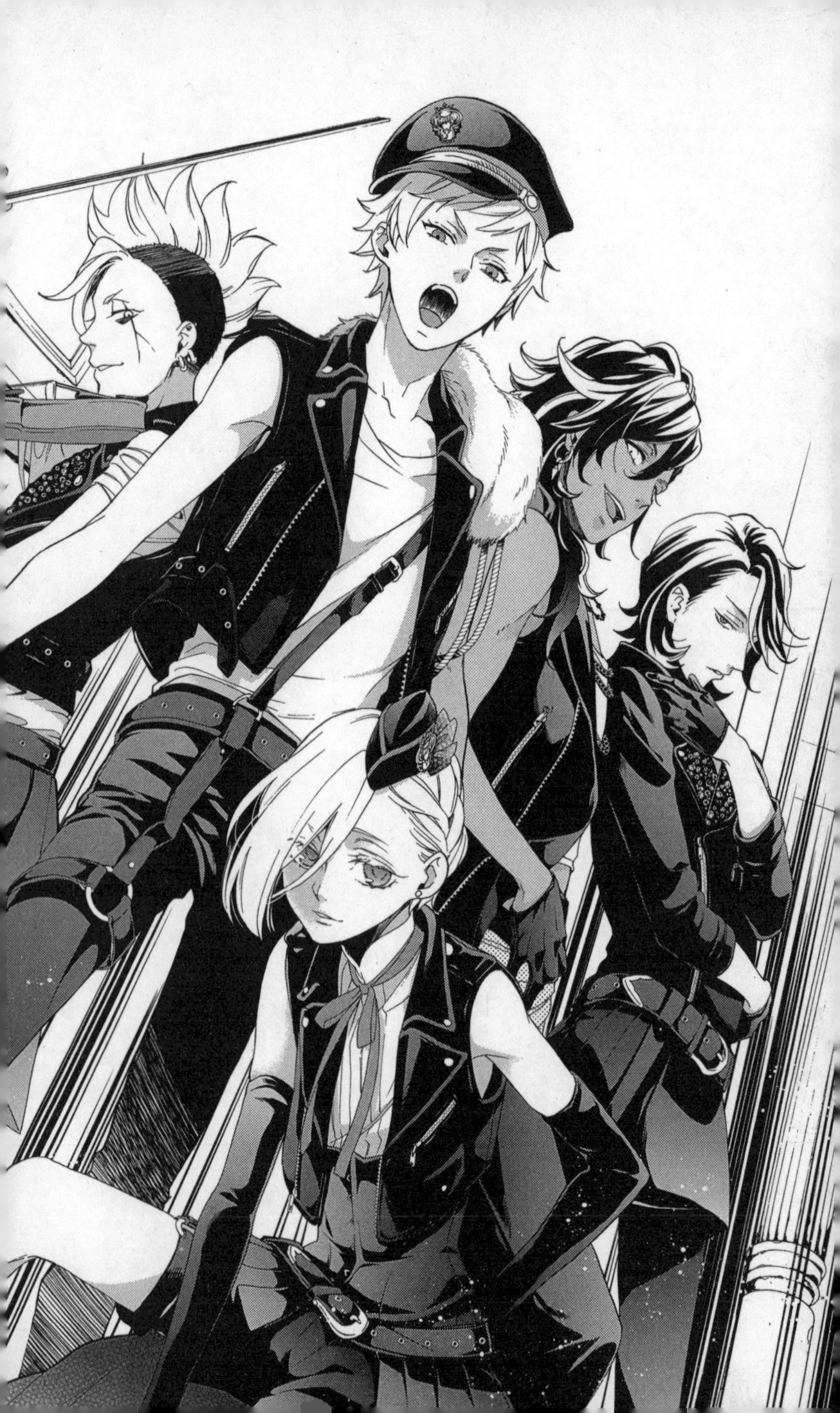

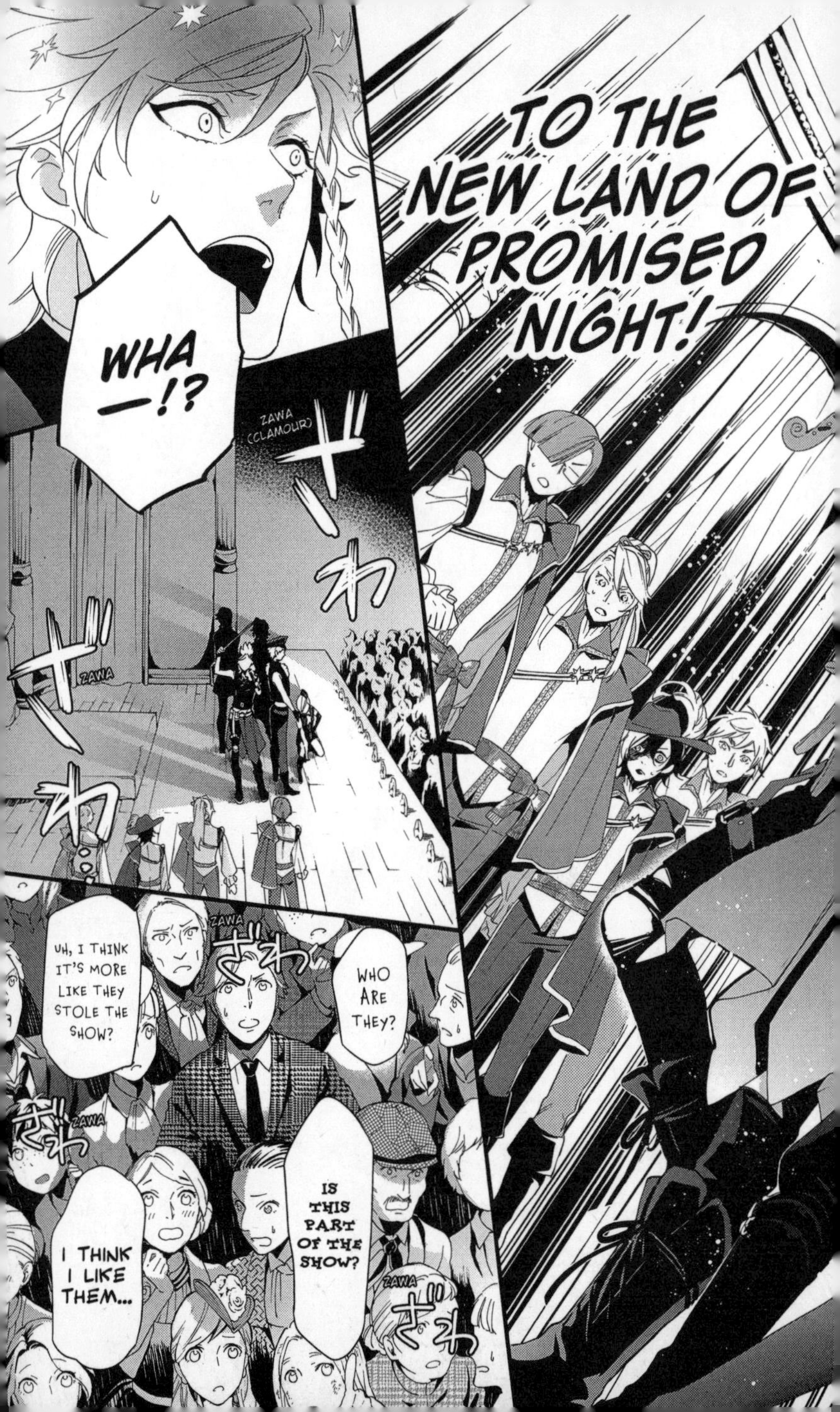
TO THE NEW LAND OF PROMISED NIGHT!
WHA—!?
ZAWA (CLAMOUR)
ZAWA
WHO ARE THEY?
ZAWA
UH, I THINK IT'S MORE LIKE THEY STOLE THE SHOW?
ZAWA
ZAWA
IS THIS PART OF THE SHOW?
I THINK I LIKE THEM...

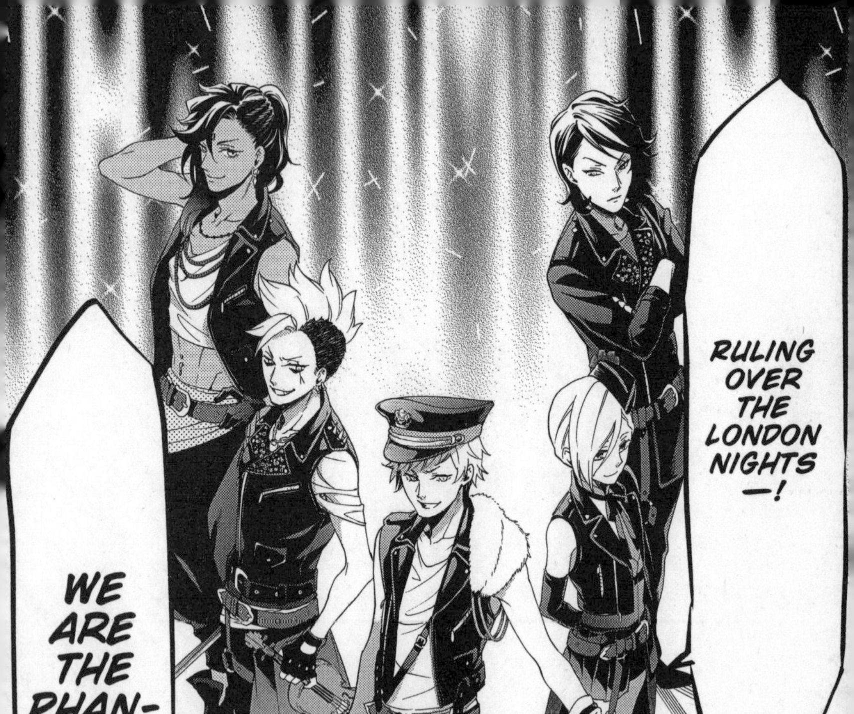
RULING OVER THE LONDON NIGHTS—!
WE ARE THE PHANTOM FIVE!
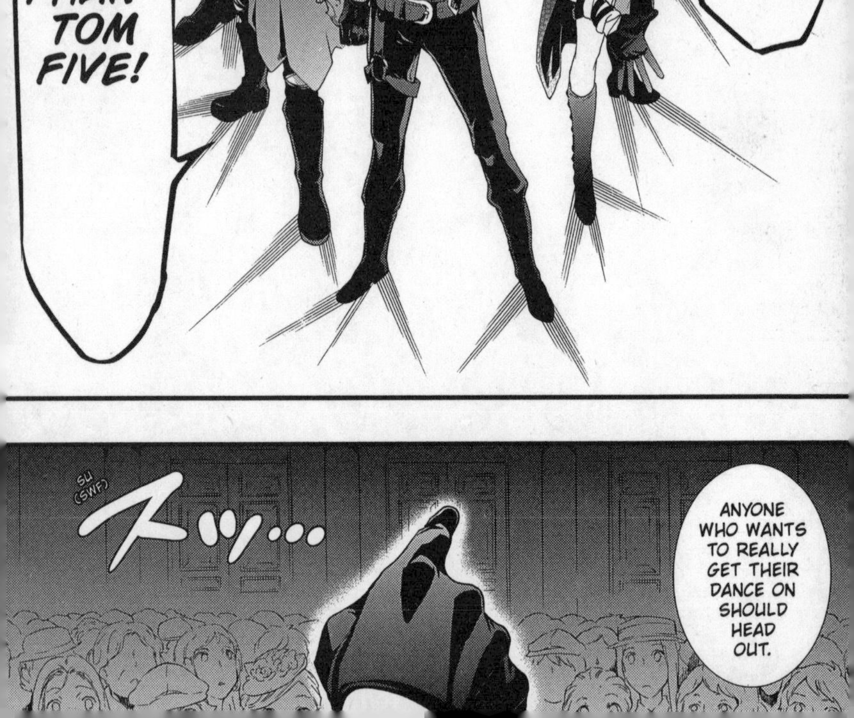
ANYONE WHO WANTS TO REALLY GET THEIR DANCE ON SHOULD HEAD OUT.
SU (SWF)
スッ…

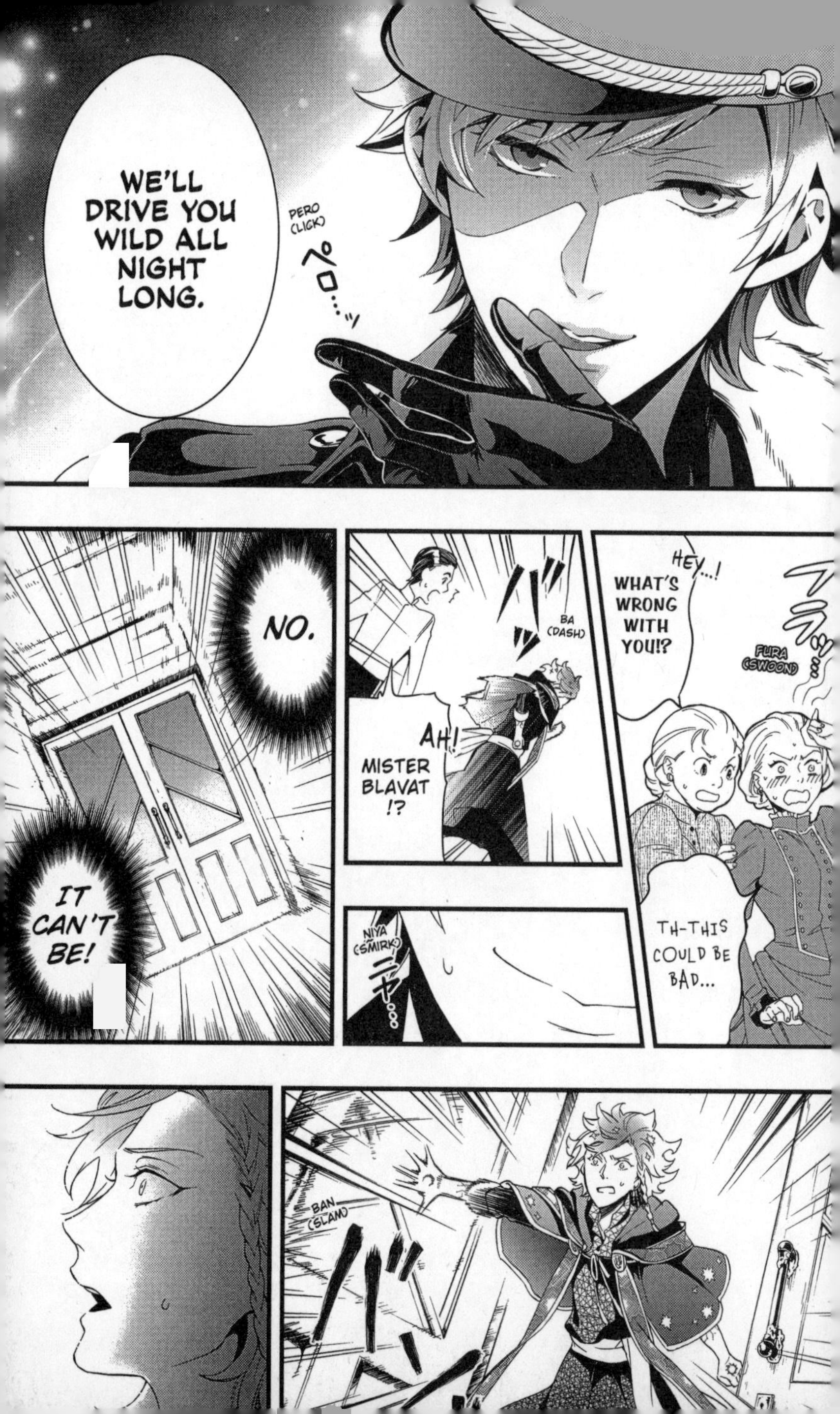

WE'LL DRIVE YOU WILD ALL NIGHT LONG.
PERO (LICK)
ペロ…ッ
HEY...!
WHAT'S WRONG WITH YOU!?
FURA (SWOON)
TH-THIS COULD BE BAD...
BA (DASH)
AH!
MISTER BLAVAT!?
NIYA (SMIRK)
ニヤ…
NO.
IT CAN'T BE!
BAN (SLAM)

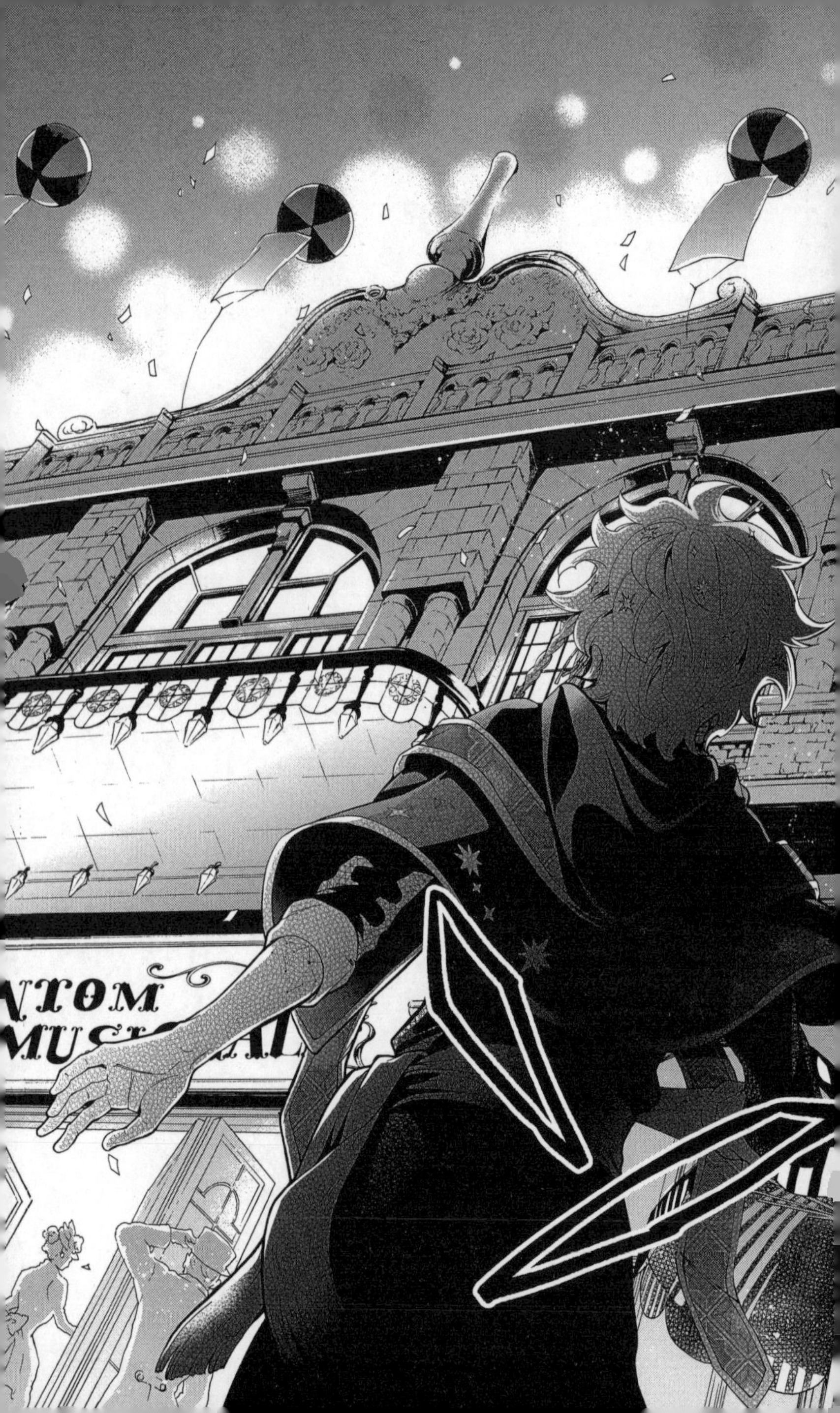

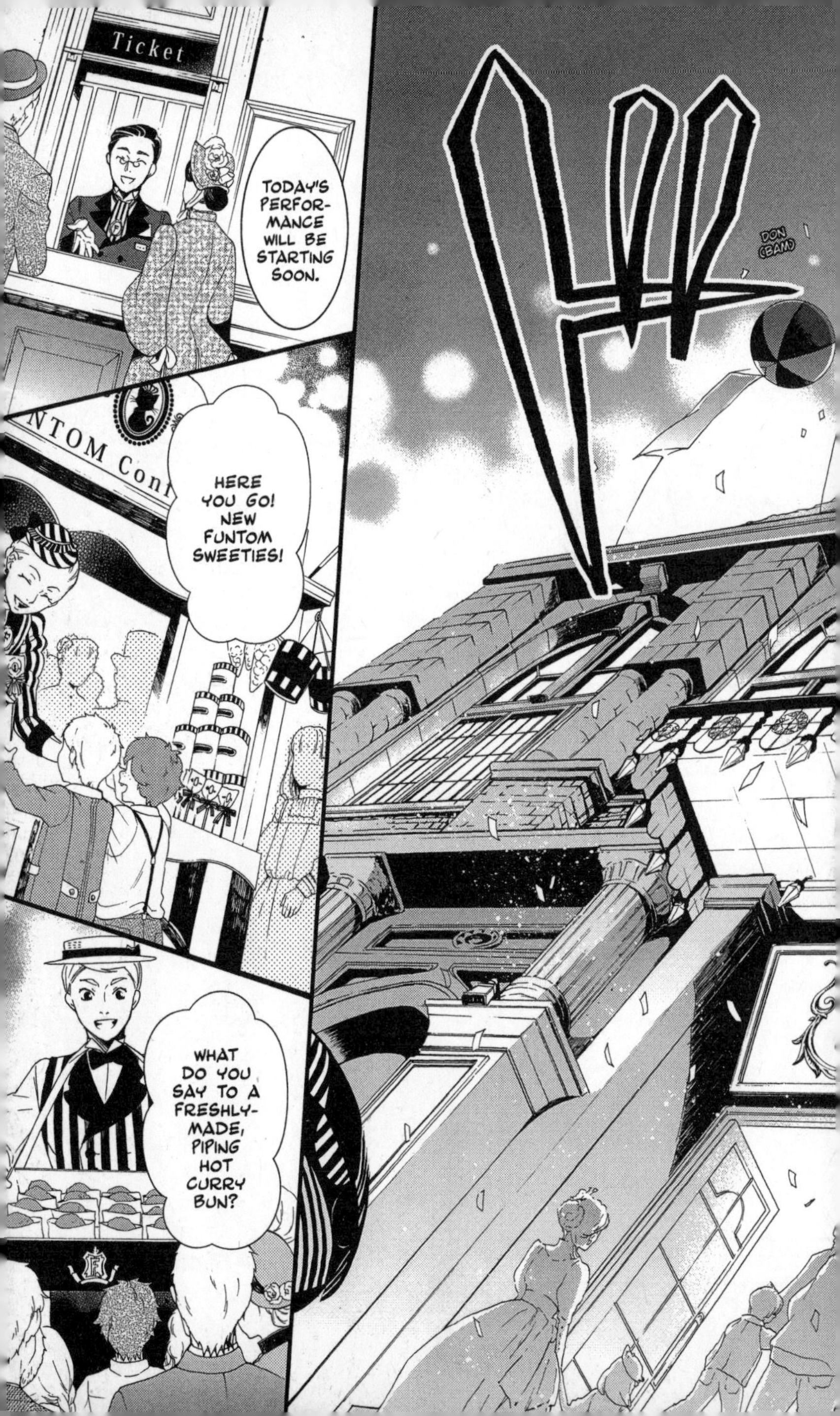
DON (BAM)
Ticket
TODAY'S PERFORMANCE WILL BE STARTING SOON.
NTOM Conf
HERE YOU GO! NEW FUNTOM SWEETIES!
WHAT DO YOU SAY TO A FRESHLY-MADE, PIPING HOT CURRY BUN?

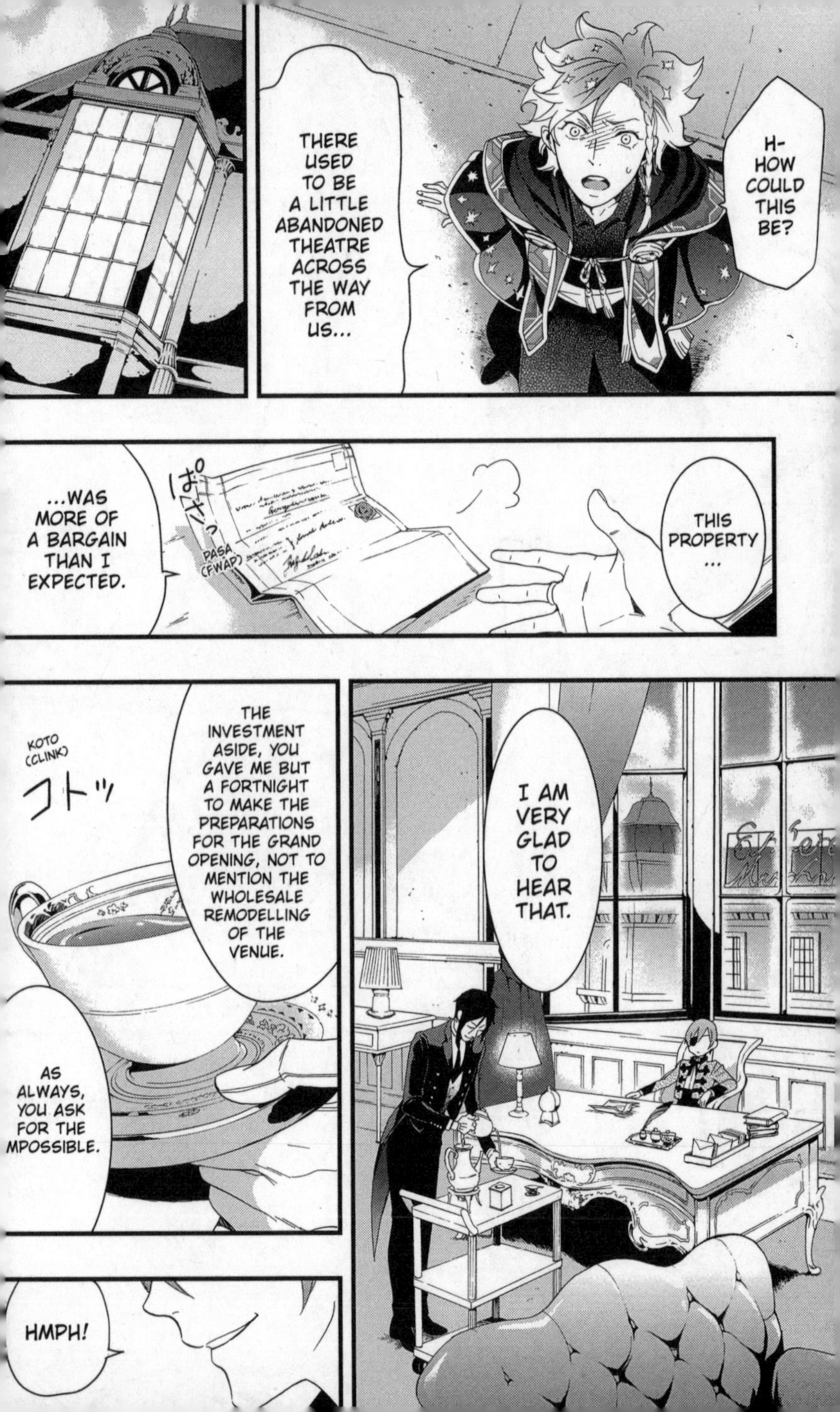
H-HOW COULD THIS BE?
THERE USED TO BE A LITTLE ABANDONED THEATRE ACROSS THE WAY FROM US...
THIS PROPERTY...
ぱさっ
PASA (FWAP)
...WAS MORE OF A BARGAIN THAN I EXPECTED.
I AM VERY GLAD TO HEAR THAT.
THE INVESTMENT ASIDE, YOU GAVE ME BUT A FORTNIGHT TO MAKE THE PREPARATIONS FOR THE GRAND OPENING, NOT TO MENTION THE WHOLESALE REMODELLING OF THE VENUE.
KOTO (CLINK)
コトッ
AS ALWAYS, YOU ASK FOR THE MPOSSIBLE.
HMPH!

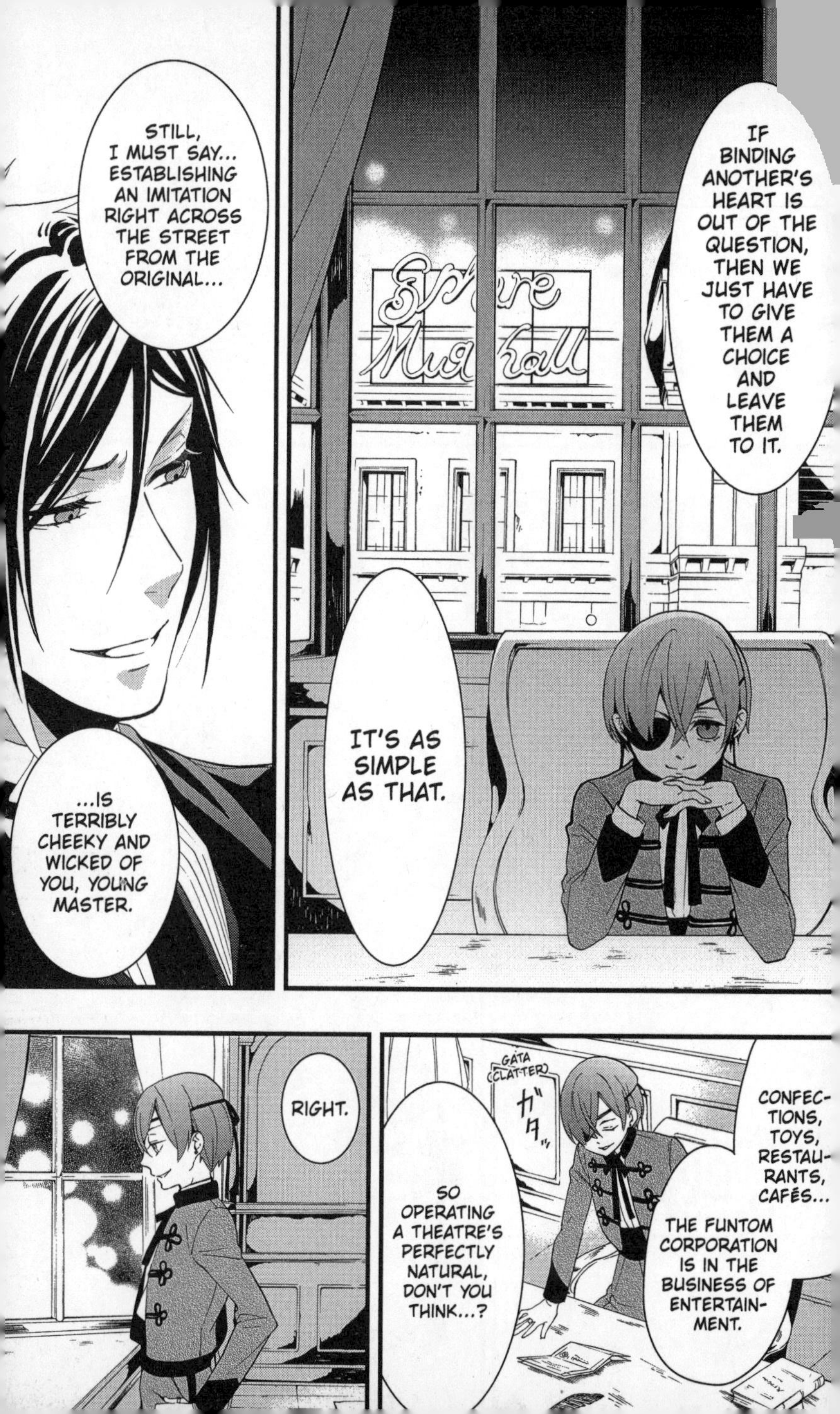
IF BINDING ANOTHER'S HEART IS OUT OF THE QUESTION, THEN WE JUST HAVE TO GIVE THEM A CHOICE AND LEAVE THEM TO IT.
IT'S AS SIMPLE AS THAT.
STILL, I MUST SAY... ESTABLISHING AN IMITATION RIGHT ACROSS THE STREET FROM THE ORIGINAL...
...IS TERRIBLY CHEEKY AND WICKED OF YOU, YOUNG MASTER.
GATA (CLATTER)
ガタッ
CONFEC-TIONS, TOYS, RESTAU-RANTS, CAFÉS...
THE FUNTOM CORPORATION IS IN THE BUSINESS OF ENTERTAIN-MENT.
SO OPERATING A THEATRE'S PERFECTLY NATURAL, DON'T YOU THINK...?
RIGHT.

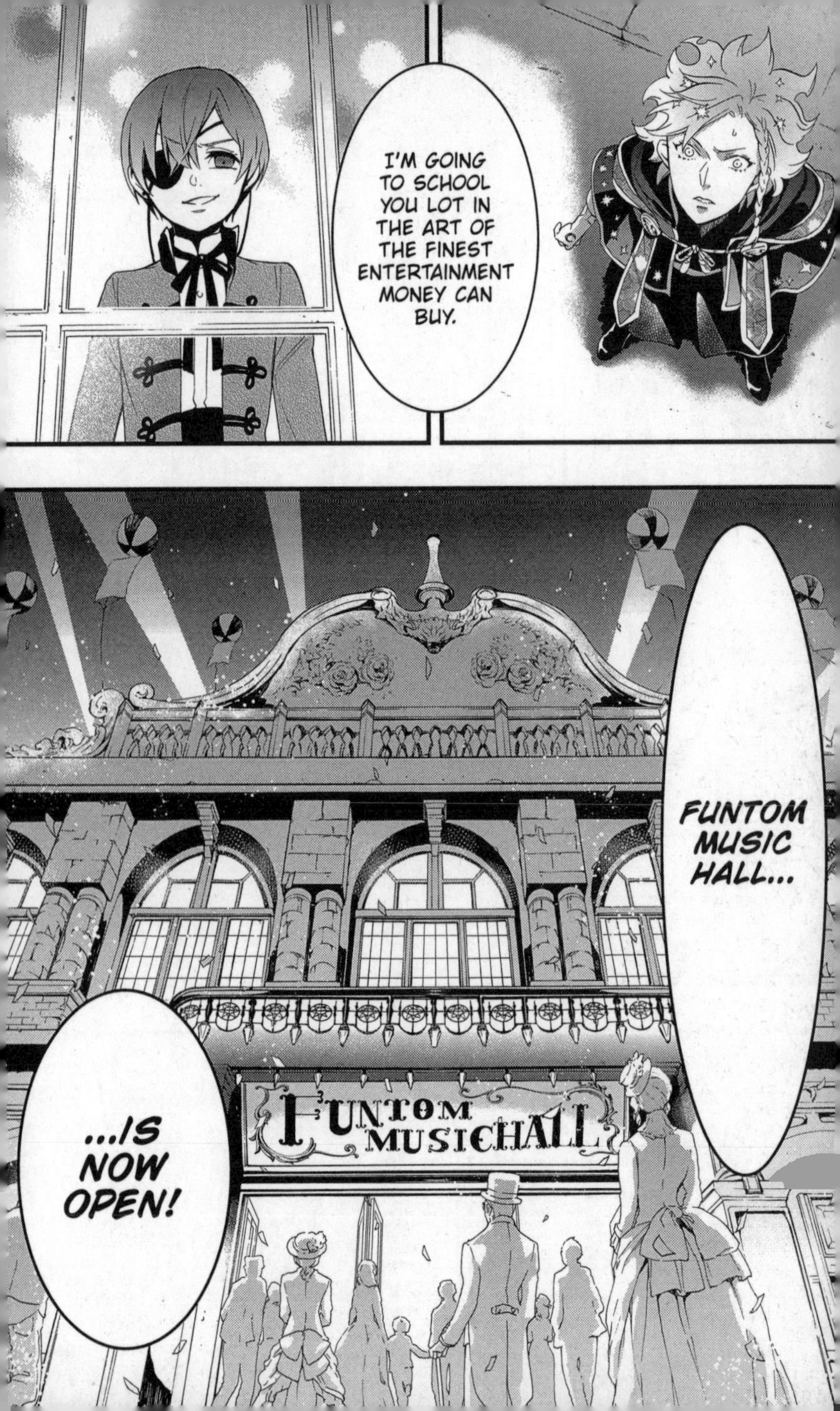
I'M GOING TO SCHOOL YOU LOT IN THE ART OF THE FINEST ENTERTAINMENT MONEY CAN BUY.
FUNTOM MUSIC HALL...
FUNTOM MUSICHALL
...IS NOW OPEN!

Black Butler

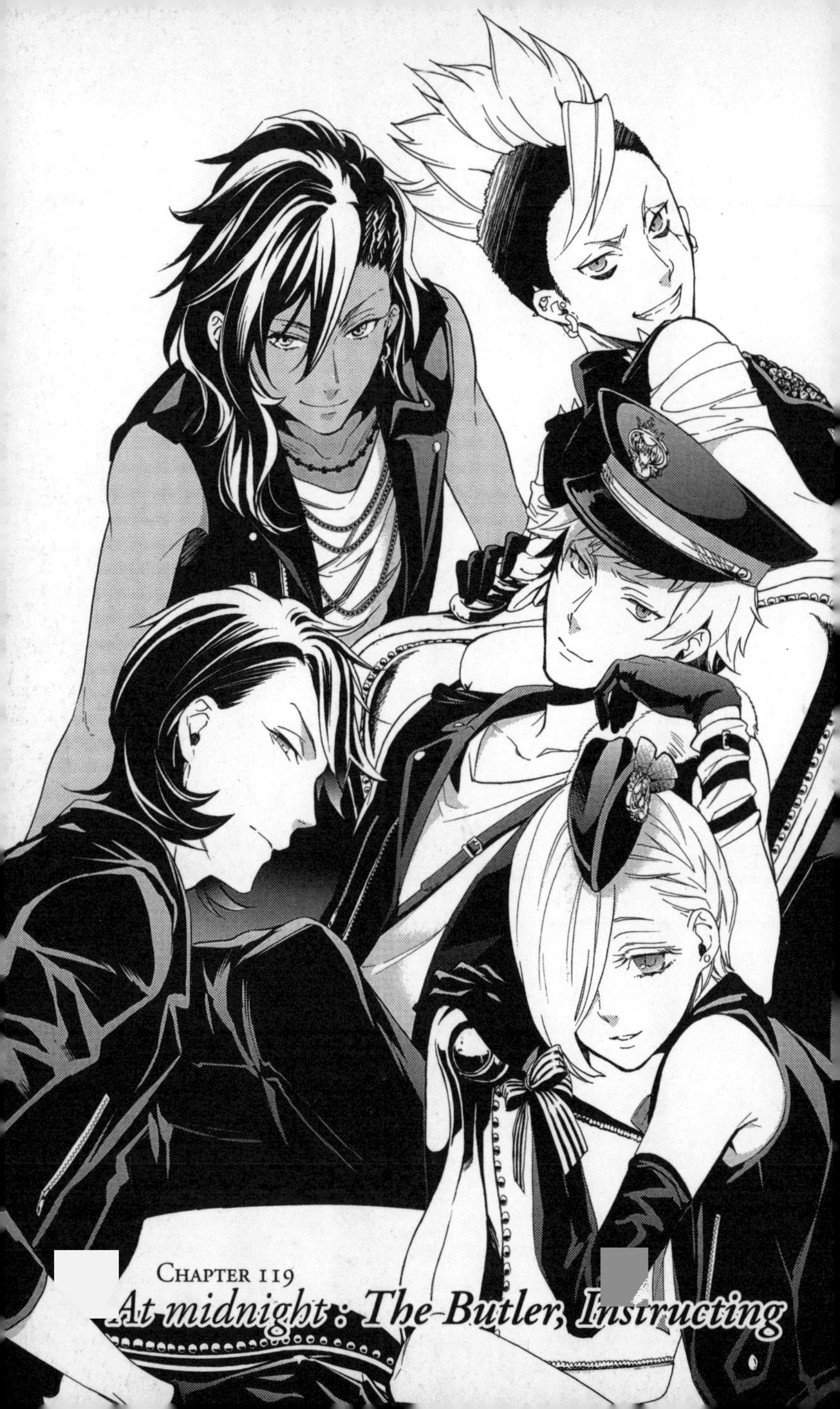

Chapter 119
At midnight : The Butler, Instructing

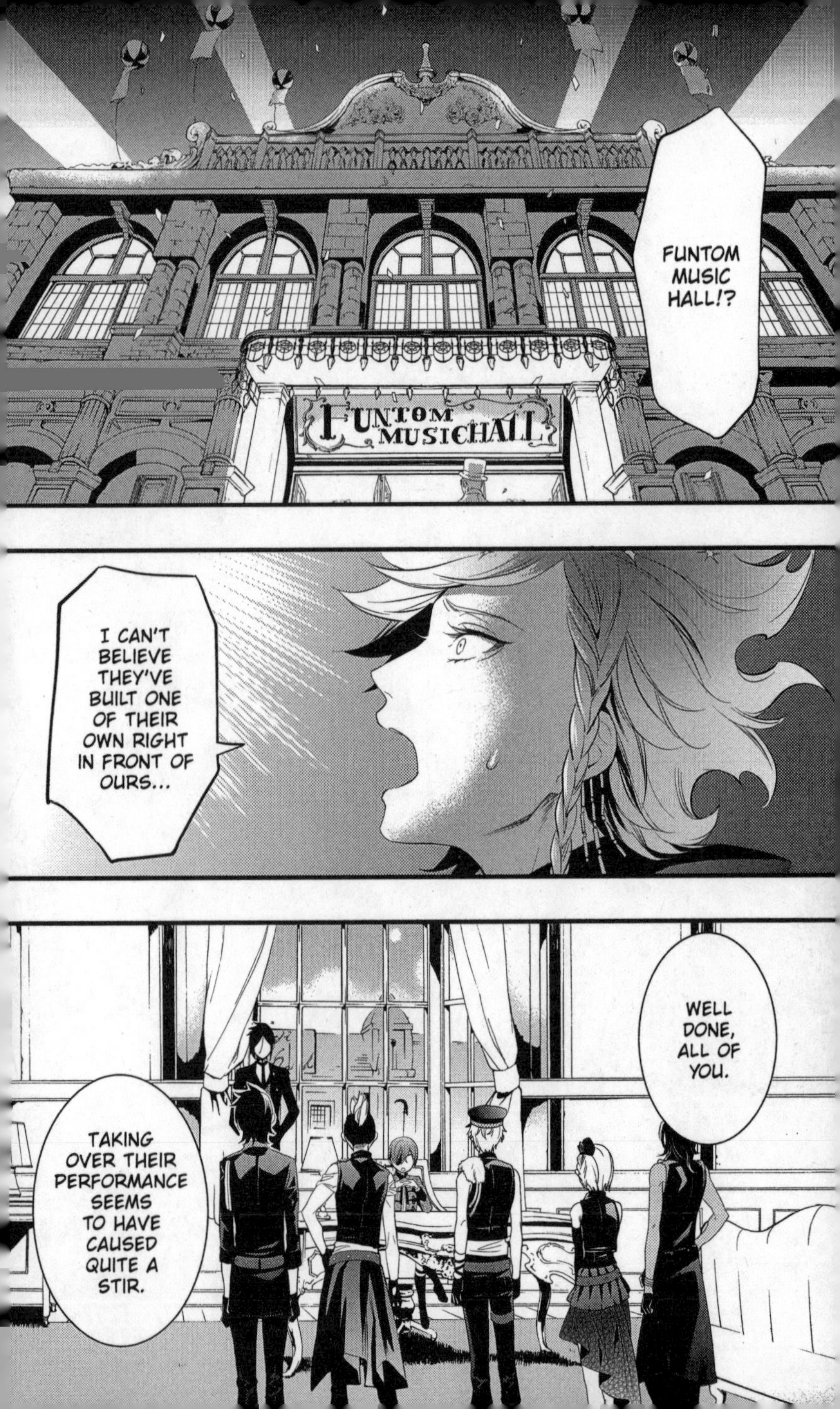
FUNTOM MUSIC HALL
FUNTOM MUSIC HALL!?
I CAN'T BELIEVE THEY'VE BUILT ONE OF THEIR OWN RIGHT IN FRONT OF OURS...
WELL DONE, ALL OF YOU.
TAKING OVER THEIR PERFORMANCE SEEMS TO HAVE CAUSED QUITE A STIR.

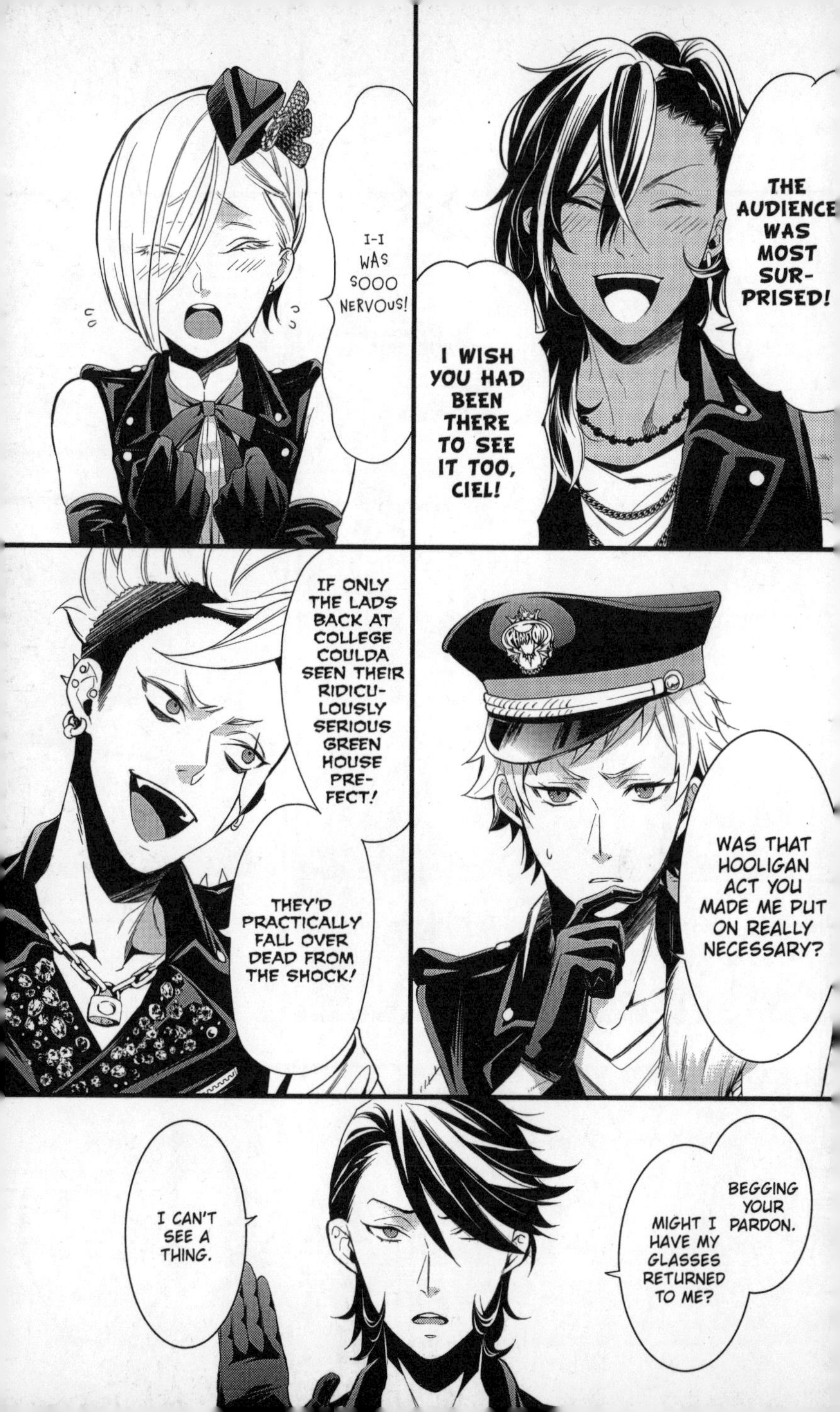
THE AUDIENCE WAS MOST SUR-PRISED!
I WISH YOU HAD BEEN THERE TO SEE IT TOO, CIEL!
I-I WAS SOOO NERVOUS!
WAS THAT HOOLIGAN ACT YOU MADE ME PUT ON REALLY NECESSARY?
IF ONLY THE LADS BACK AT COLLEGE COULDA SEEN THEIR RIDICU-LOUSLY SERIOUS GREEN HOUSE PRE-FECT!
THEY'D PRACTICALLY FALL OVER DEAD FROM THE SHOCK!
BEGGING YOUR PARDON.
MIGHT I HAVE MY GLASSES RETURNED TO ME?
I CAN'T SEE A THING.

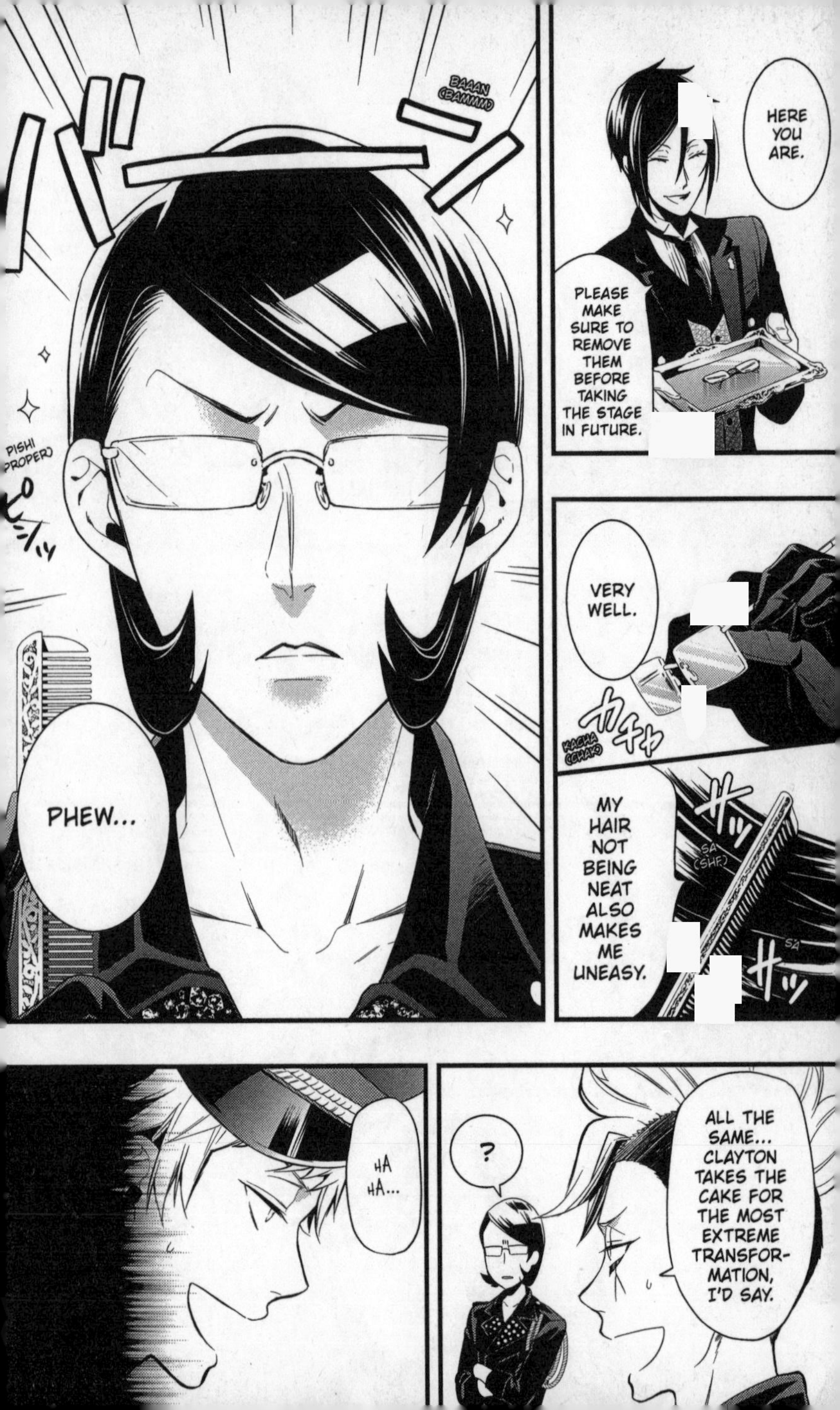
HERE YOU ARE.
PLEASE MAKE SURE TO REMOVE THEM BEFORE TAKING THE STAGE IN FUTURE.
VERY WELL.
KACHA (CHAK)
MY HAIR NOT BEING NEAT ALSO MAKES ME UNEASY.
SA (SHF.)
SA
BAAAN (BAMMM)
PISHI (PROPER)
PHEW...
ALL THE SAME... CLAYTON TAKES THE CAKE FOR THE MOST EXTREME TRANSFOR-MATION, I'D SAY.
?
HA HA...

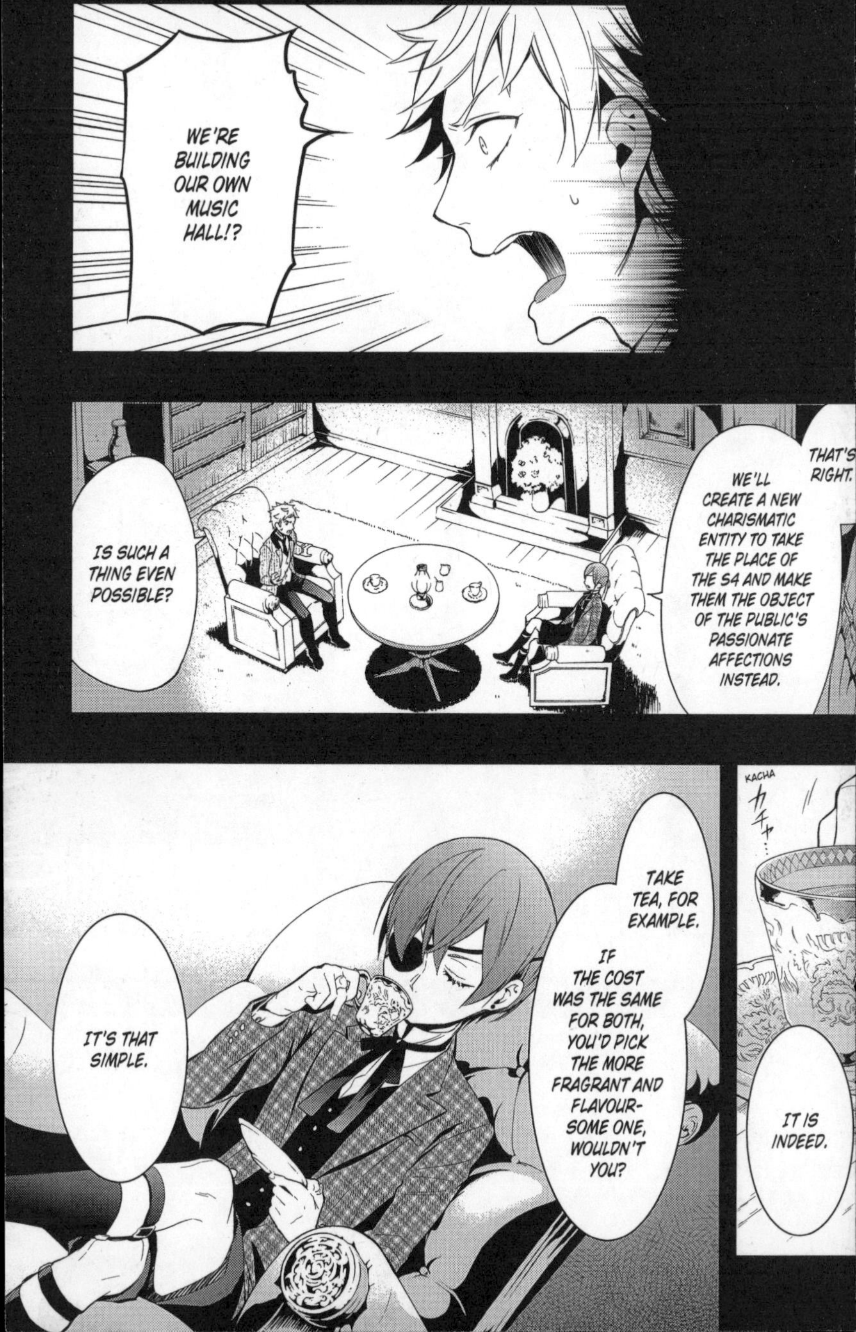
WE'RE BUILDING OUR OWN MUSIC HALL!?
THAT'S RIGHT.
WE'LL CREATE A NEW CHARISMATIC ENTITY TO TAKE THE PLACE OF THE S4 AND MAKE THEM THE OBJECT OF THE PUBLIC'S PASSIONATE AFFECTIONS INSTEAD.
IS SUCH A THING EVEN POSSIBLE?
KACHA
カチャ…
TAKE TEA, FOR EXAMPLE.
IF THE COST WAS THE SAME FOR BOTH, YOU'D PICK THE MORE FRAGRANT AND FLAVOUR-SOME ONE, WOULDN'T YOU?
IT IS INDEED.
IT'S THAT SIMPLE.

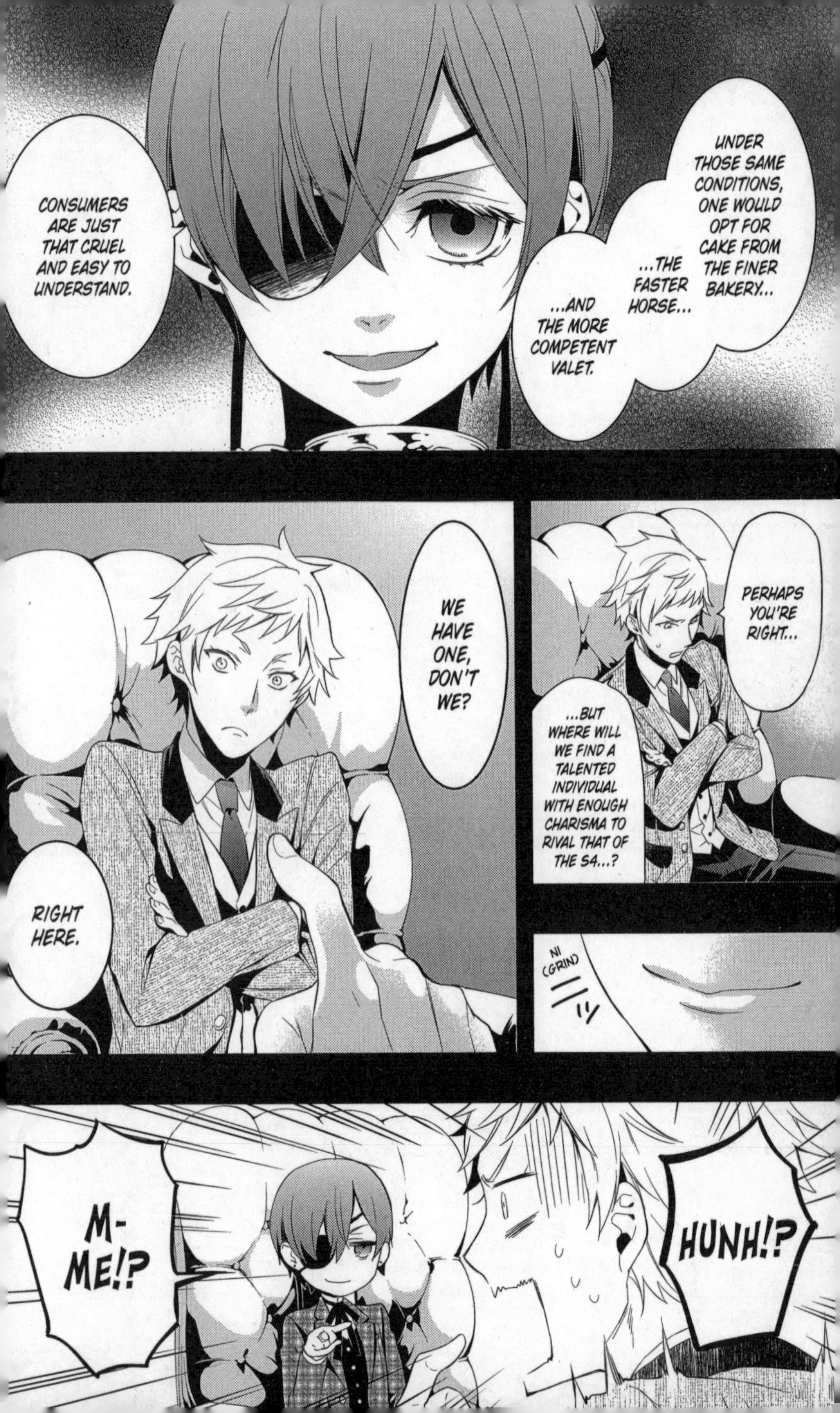
UNDER THOSE SAME CONDITIONS, ONE WOULD OPT FOR CAKE FROM THE FINER BAKERY...
...THE FASTER HORSE...
...AND THE MORE COMPETENT VALET.
CONSUMERS ARE JUST THAT CRUEL AND EASY TO UNDERSTAND.
PERHAPS YOU'RE RIGHT...
...BUT WHERE WILL WE FIND A TALENTED INDIVIDUAL WITH ENOUGH CHARISMA TO RIVAL THAT OF THE S4...?
NI (GRIN)
WE HAVE ONE, DON'T WE?
RIGHT HERE.
HUNH!?
M-ME!?

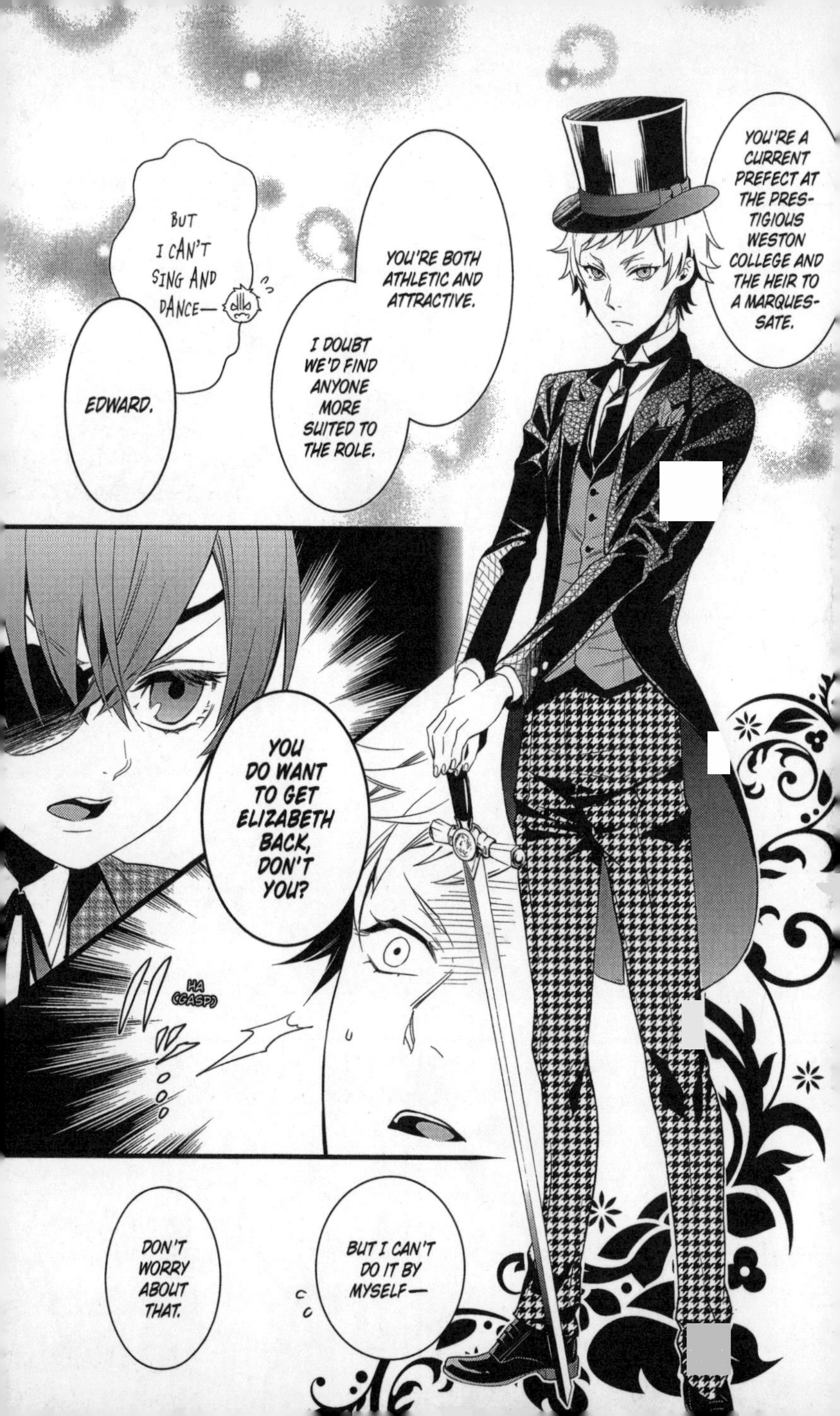
YOU'RE A CURRENT PREFECT AT THE PRES-TIGIOUS WESTON COLLEGE AND THE HEIR TO A MARQUES-SATE.
YOU'RE BOTH ATHLETIC AND ATTRACTIVE.
I DOUBT WE'D FIND ANYONE MORE SUITED TO THE ROLE.
BUT I CAN'T SING AND DANCE—
EDWARD.
YOU DO WANT TO GET ELIZABETH BACK, DON'T YOU?
HA (GASP)
BUT I CAN'T DO IT BY MYSELF—
DON'T WORRY ABOUT THAT.

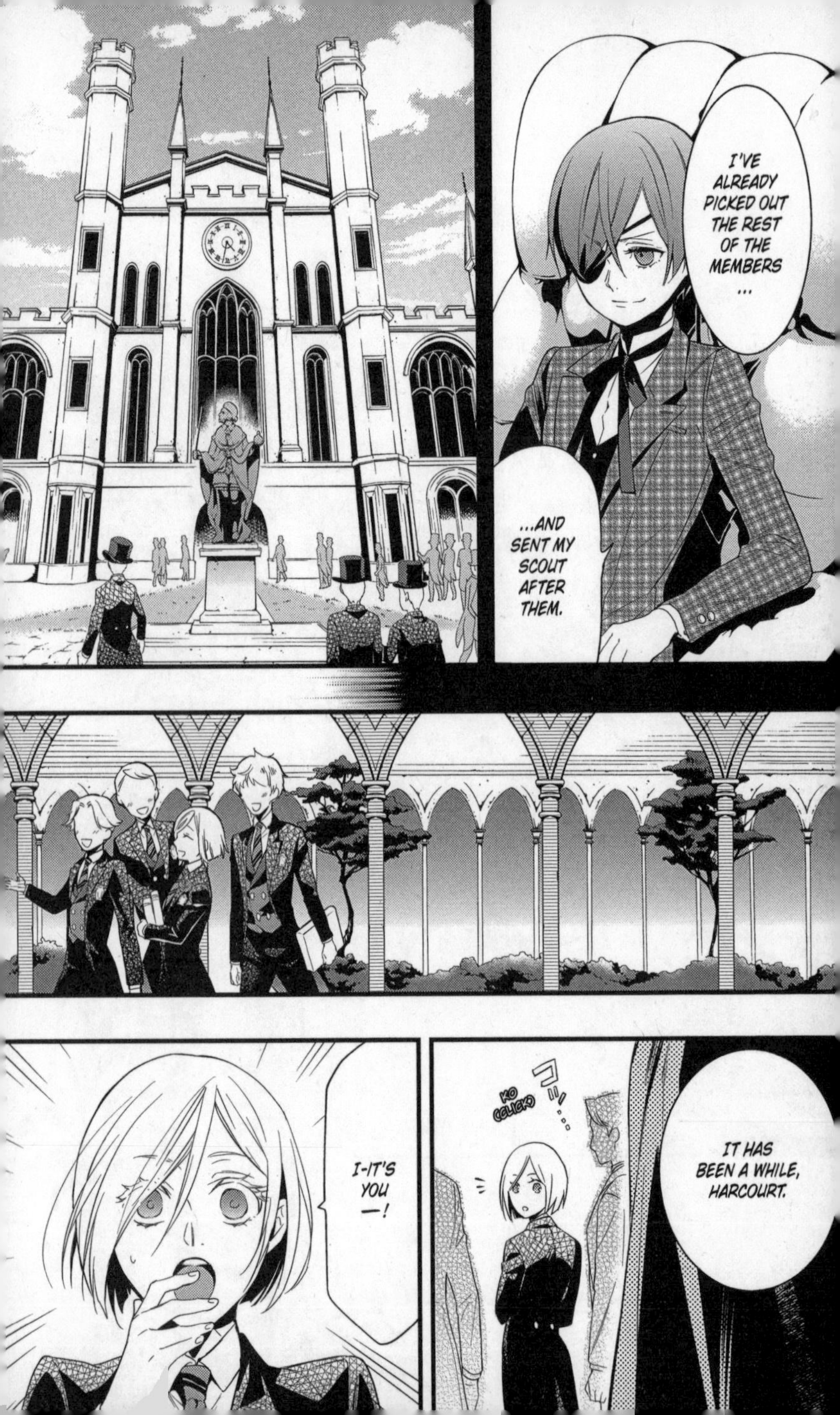
I'VE ALREADY PICKED OUT THE REST OF THE MEMBERS...
...AND SENT MY SCOUT AFTER THEM.
KO (CLICK)
IT HAS BEEN A WHILE, HARCOURT.
I-IT'S YOU—!

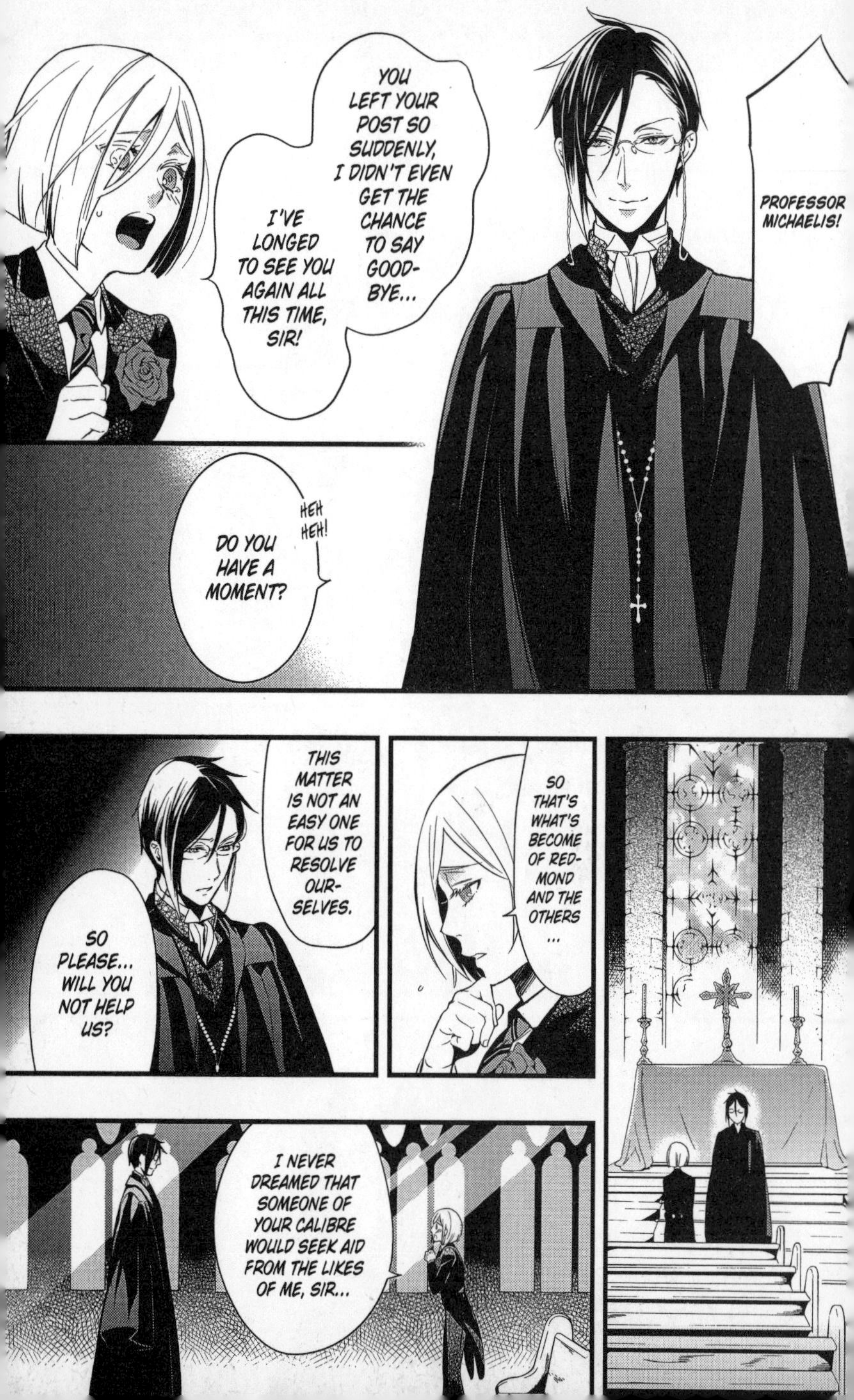
PROFESSOR MICHAELIS!
YOU LEFT YOUR POST SO SUDDENLY, I DIDN'T EVEN GET THE CHANCE TO SAY GOOD-BYE...
I'VE LONGED TO SEE YOU AGAIN ALL THIS TIME, SIR!
HEH HEH!
DO YOU HAVE A MOMENT?
SO THAT'S WHAT'S BECOME OF RED-MOND AND THE OTHERS...
THIS MATTER IS NOT AN EASY ONE FOR US TO RESOLVE OUR-SELVES.
SO PLEASE... WILL YOU NOT HELP US?
I NEVER DREAMED THAT SOMEONE OF YOUR CALIBRE WOULD SEEK AID FROM THE LIKES OF ME, SIR...

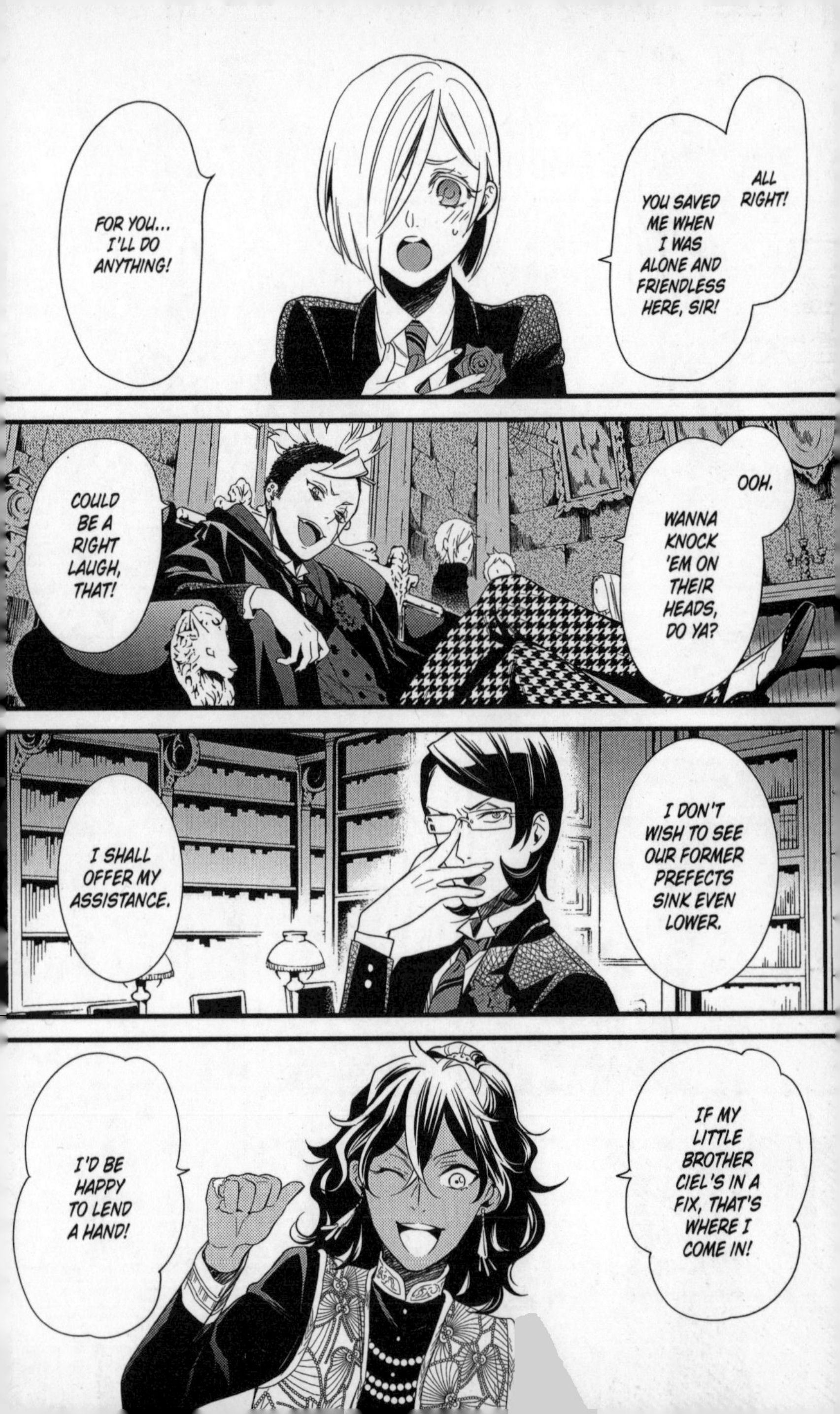
ALL RIGHT!
YOU SAVED ME WHEN I WAS ALONE AND FRIENDLESS HERE, SIR!
FOR YOU... I'LL DO ANYTHING!
OOH.
WANNA KNOCK 'EM ON THEIR HEADS, DO YA?
COULD BE A RIGHT LAUGH, THAT!
I DON'T WISH TO SEE OUR FORMER PREFECTS SINK EVEN LOWER.
I SHALL OFFER MY ASSISTANCE.
IF MY LITTLE BROTHER CIEL'S IN A FIX, THAT'S WHERE I COME IN!
I'D BE HAPPY TO LEND A HAND!

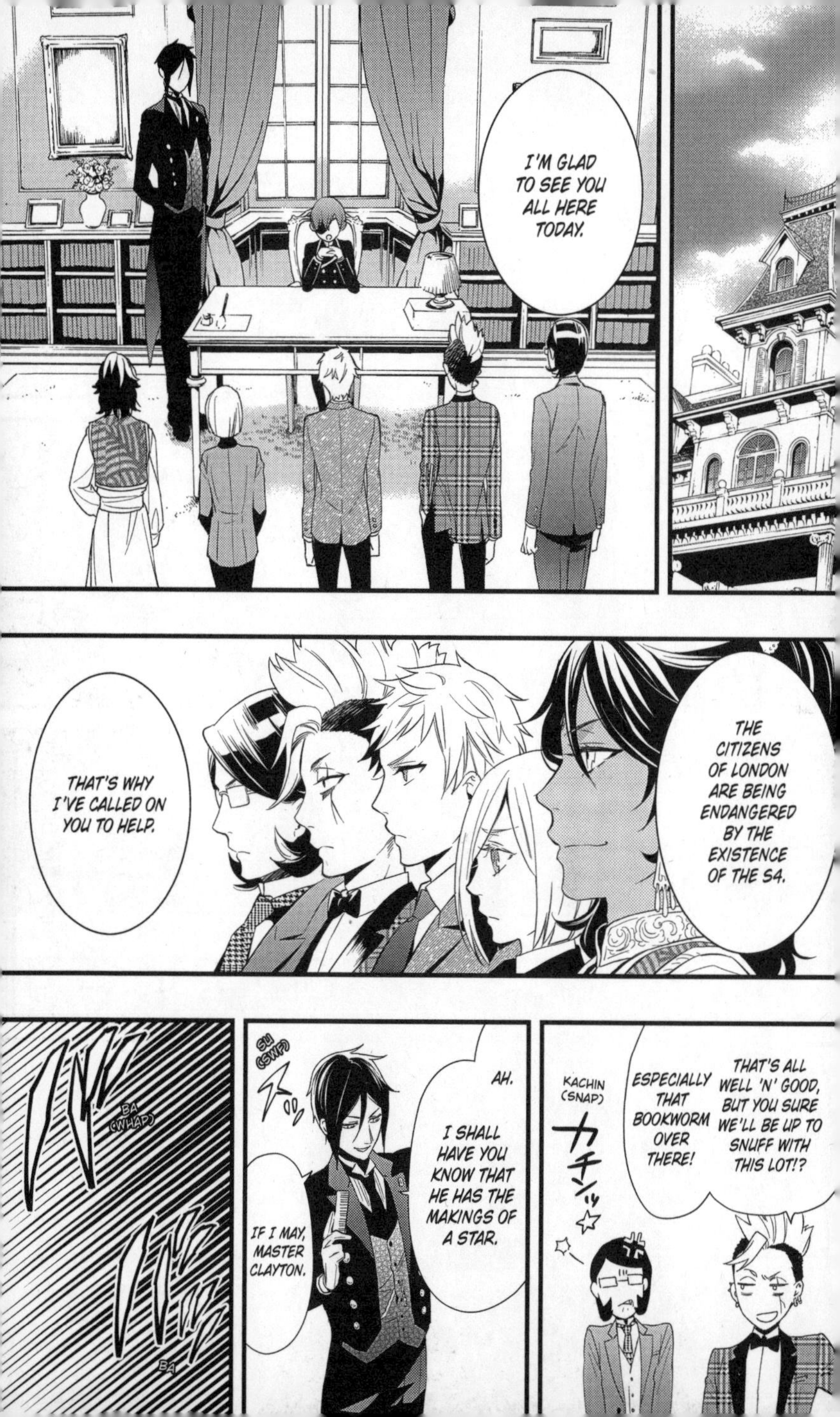
I'M GLAD TO SEE YOU ALL HERE TODAY.
THE CITIZENS OF LONDON ARE BEING ENDANGERED BY THE EXISTENCE OF THE S4.
THAT'S WHY I'VE CALLED ON YOU TO HELP.
THAT'S ALL WELL 'N' GOOD, BUT YOU SURE WE'LL BE UP TO SNUFF WITH THIS LOT!?
ESPECIALLY THAT BOOKWORM OVER THERE!
KACHIN (SNAP)
カチン
AH.
I SHALL HAVE YOU KNOW THAT HE HAS THE MAKINGS OF A STAR.
IF I MAY, MASTER CLAYTON.
SU (SWIP)
BA (WHAP)
BA

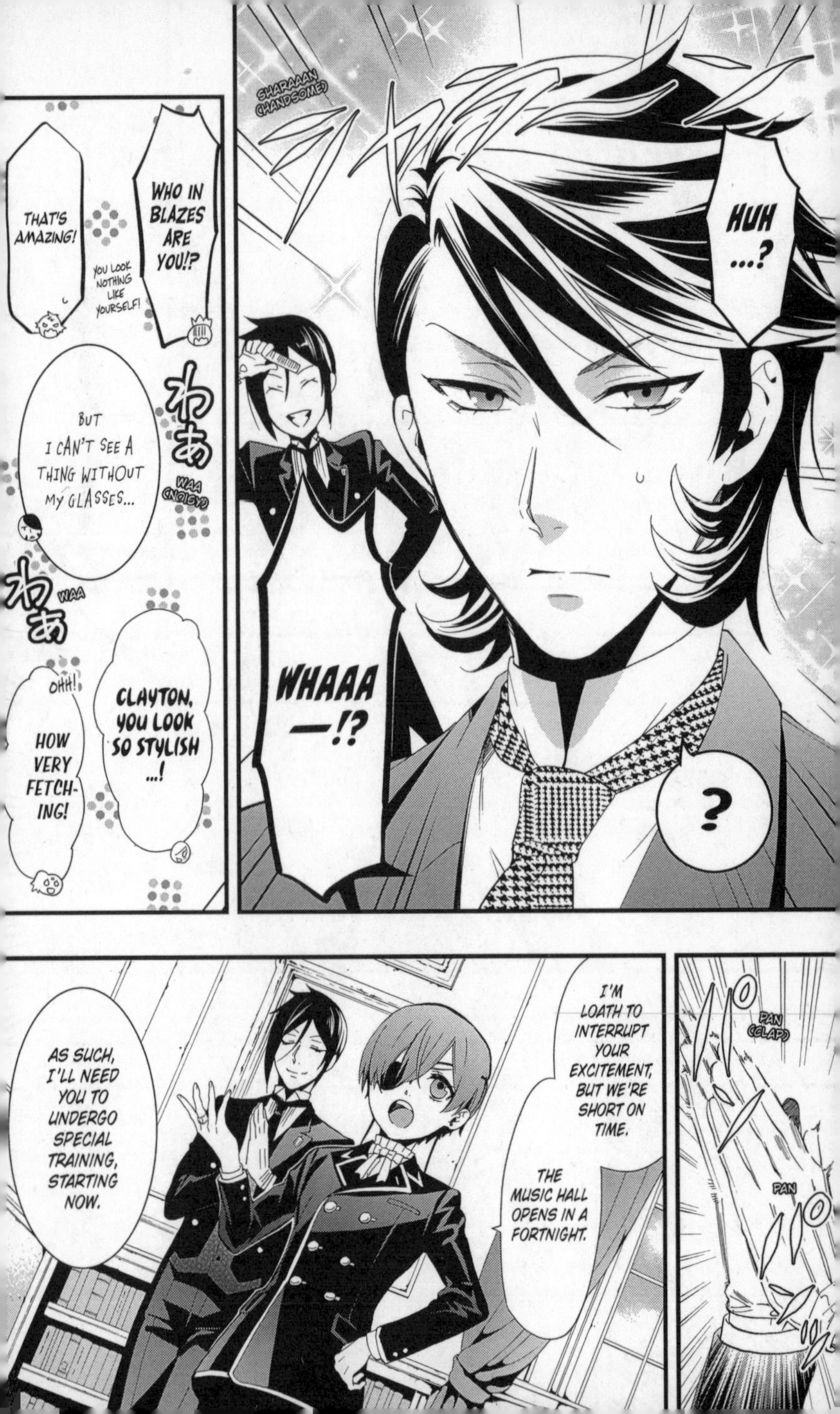
HUH ...?
SHARAAAN (HANDSOME)
?
WHAAA —!?
WHO IN BLAZES ARE YOU!?
THAT'S AMAZING!
YOU LOOK NOTHING LIKE YOURSELF!
わあ
WAA (NOISY)
BUT I CAN'T SEE A THING WITHOUT MY GLASSES...
わあ
WAA
CLAYTON, YOU LOOK SO STYLISH ...!
OHH!
HOW VERY FETCHING!
PAN (CLAP)
PAN
I'M LOATH TO INTERRUPT YOUR EXCITEMENT, BUT WE'RE SHORT ON TIME.
THE MUSIC HALL OPENS IN A FORTNIGHT.
AS SUCH, I'LL NEED YOU TO UNDERGO SPECIAL TRAINING, STARTING NOW.

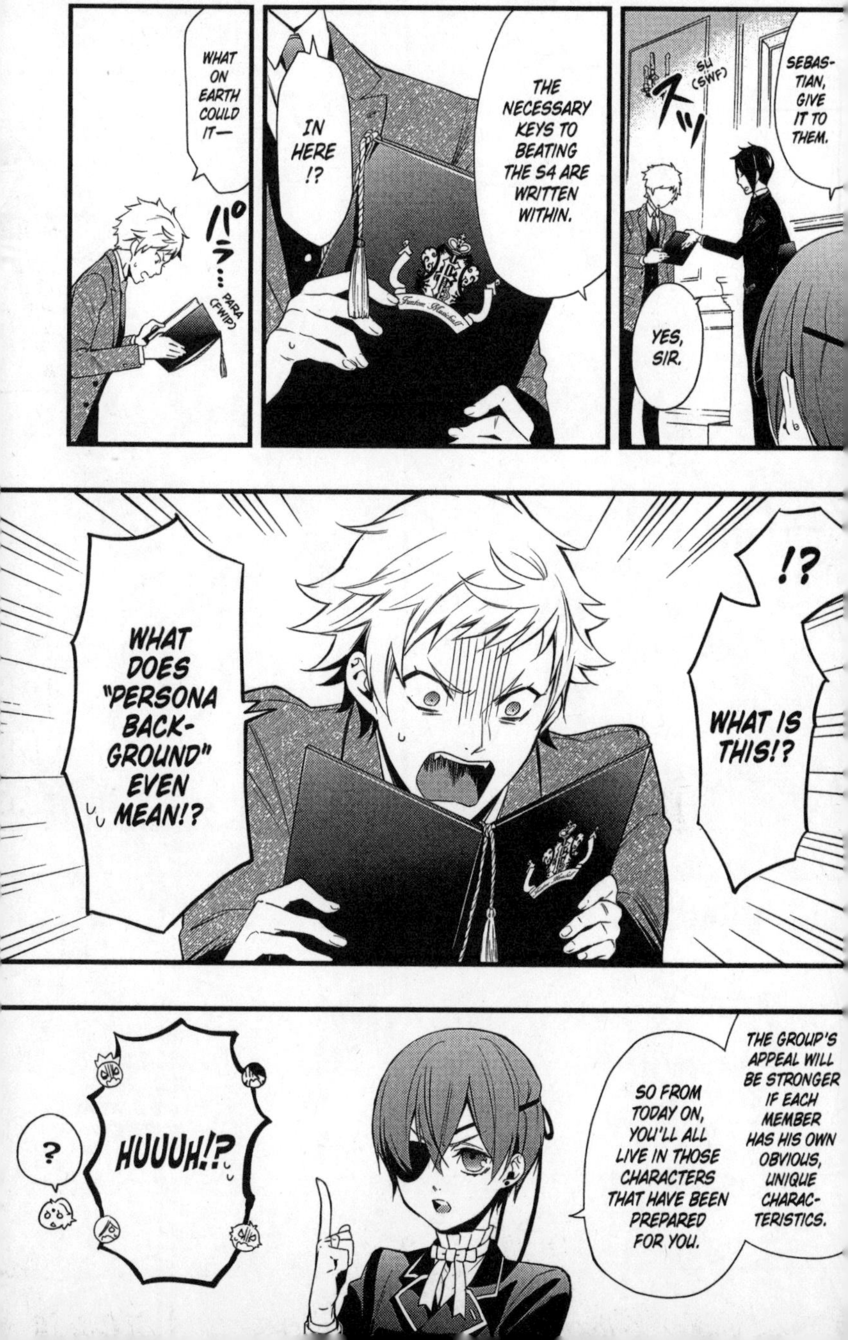
SEBASTIAN, GIVE IT TO THEM.
SU (SWF)
YES, SIR.
THE NECESSARY KEYS TO BEATING THE S4 ARE WRITTEN WITHIN.
IN HERE!?
WHAT ON EARTH COULD IT—
PARA (FWIP)
!?
WHAT IS THIS!?
WHAT DOES "PERSONA BACKGROUND" EVEN MEAN!?
THE GROUP'S APPEAL WILL BE STRONGER IF EACH MEMBER HAS HIS OWN OBVIOUS, UNIQUE CHARACTERISTICS.
SO FROM TODAY ON, YOU'LL ALL LIVE IN THOSE CHARACTERS THAT HAVE BEEN PREPARED FOR YOU.
HUUUH!?
?

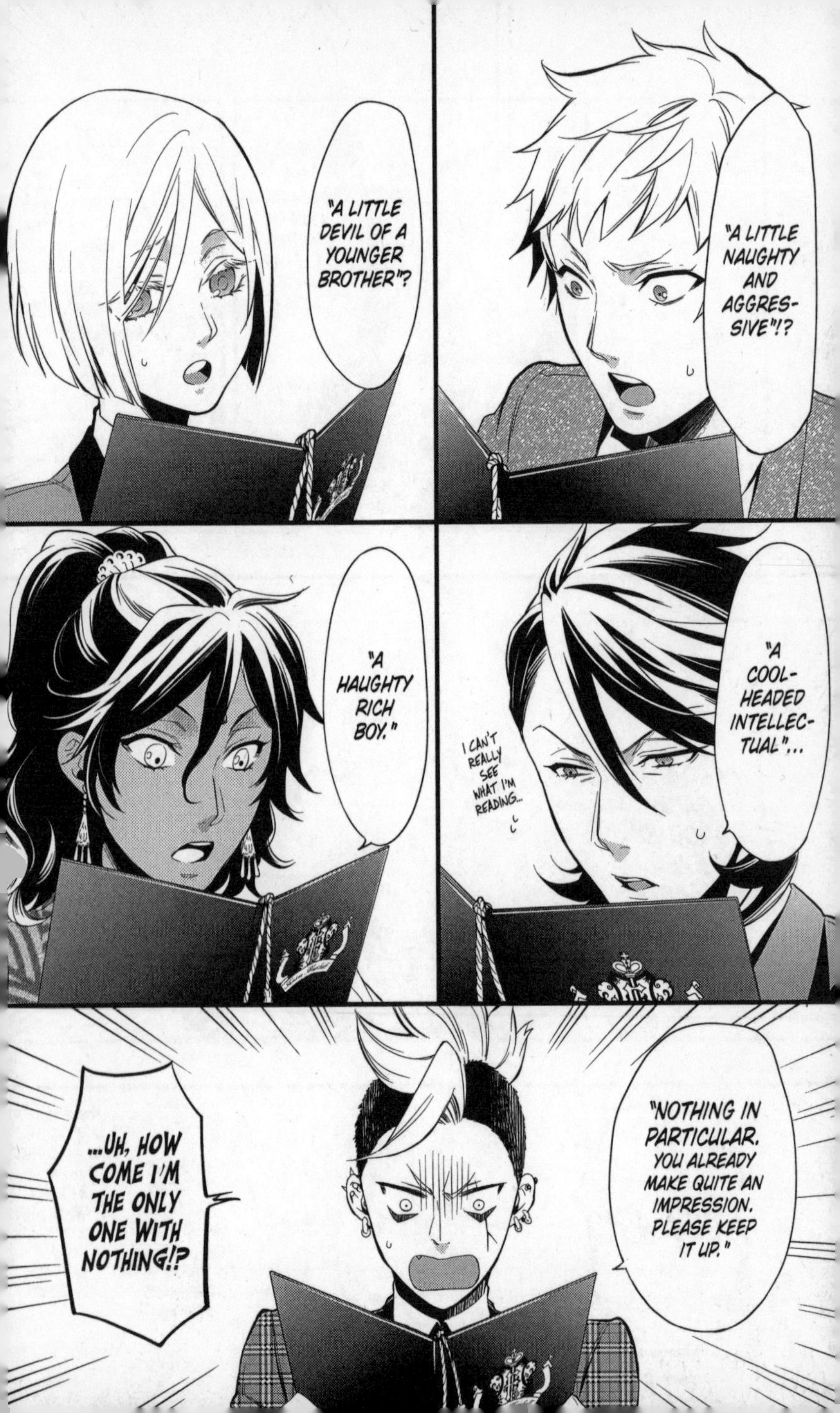
"A LITTLE NAUGHTY AND AGGRES-SIVE"!?
"A LITTLE DEVIL OF A YOUNGER BROTHER"?
"A COOL-HEADED INTELLEC-TUAL"...
I CAN'T REALLY SEE WHAT I'M READING...
"A HAUGHTY RICH BOY."
"NOTHING IN PARTICULAR. YOU ALREADY MAKE QUITE AN IMPRESSION. PLEASE KEEP IT UP."
...UH, HOW COME I'M THE ONLY ONE WITH NOTHING!?

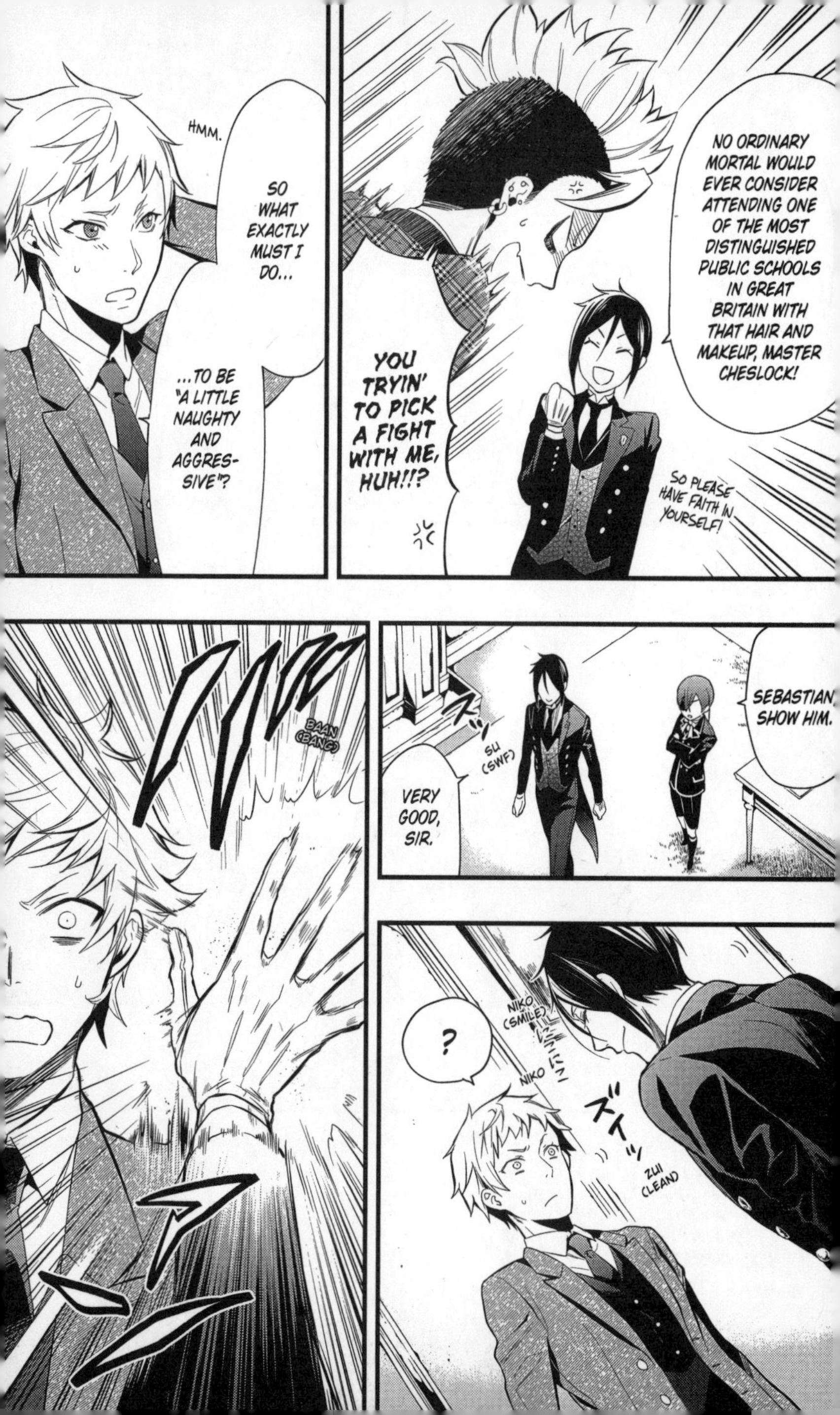
NO ORDINARY MORTAL WOULD EVER CONSIDER ATTENDING ONE OF THE MOST DISTINGUISHED PUBLIC SCHOOLS IN GREAT BRITAIN WITH THAT HAIR AND MAKEUP, MASTER CHESLOCK!
SO PLEASE HAVE FAITH IN YOURSELF!
YOU TRYIN' TO PICK A FIGHT WITH ME, HUH!!?
HMM.
SO WHAT EXACTLY MUST I DO...
...TO BE "A LITTLE NAUGHTY AND AGGRES-SIVE"?
SEBASTIAN, SHOW HIM.
SU (SWF)
VERY GOOD, SIR.
?
NIKO (SMILE)
NIKO
ZUI (LEAN)
BAAN (BANG)

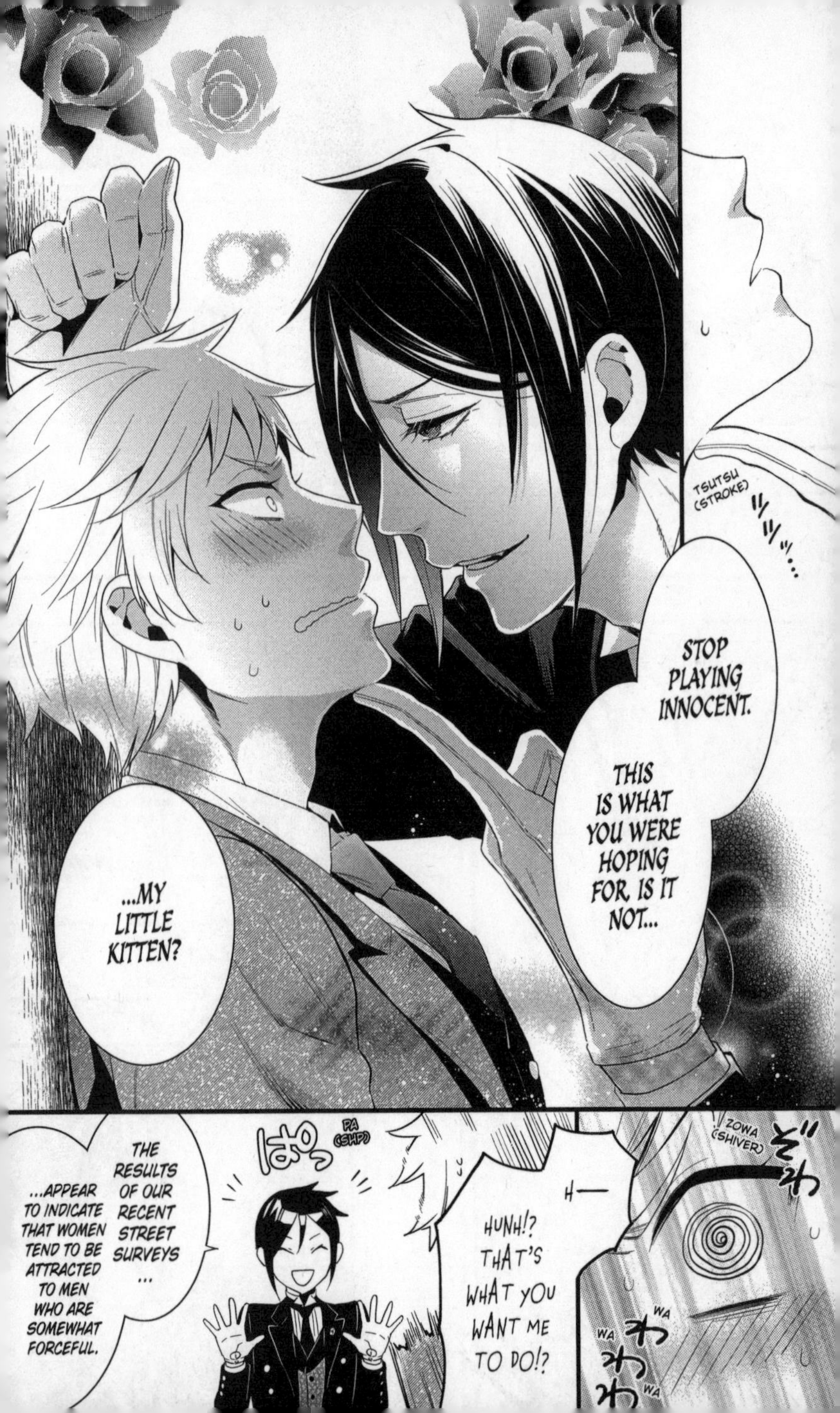

TSUTSU (STROKE)
STOP PLAYING INNOCENT.
THIS IS WHAT YOU WERE HOPING FOR, IS IT NOT...
...MY LITTLE KITTEN?
ZOWA (SHIVER)
WA WA WA
H—
HUNH!? THAT'S WHAT YOU WANT ME TO DO!?
PA (SHP)
THE RESULTS OF OUR RECENT STREET SURVEYS...
...APPEAR TO INDICATE THAT WOMEN TEND TO BE ATTRACTED TO MEN WHO ARE SOMEWHAT FORCEFUL.

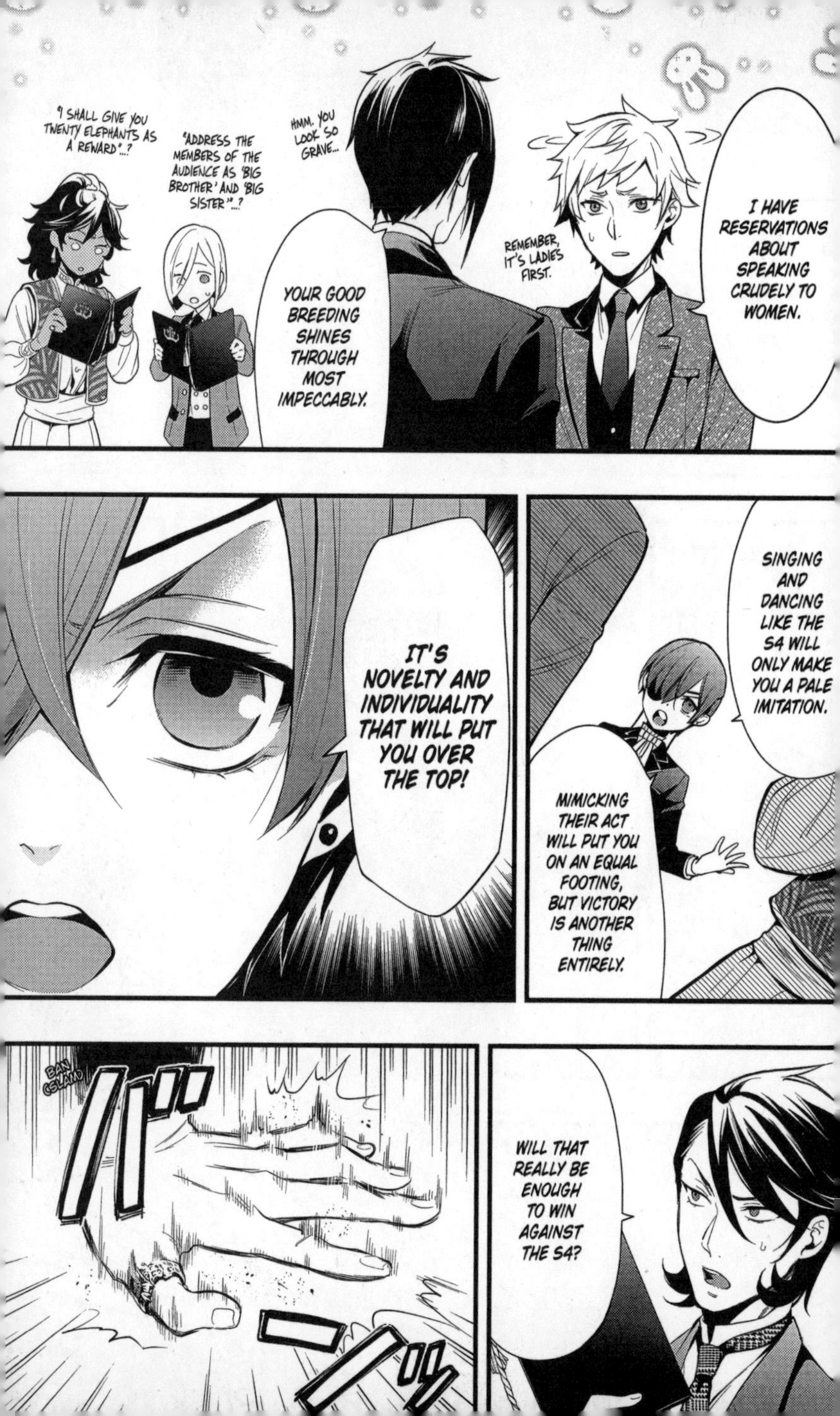
I HAVE RESERVATIONS ABOUT SPEAKING CRUDELY TO WOMEN.
REMEMBER, IT'S LADIES FIRST.
HMM. YOU LOOK SO GRAVE...
YOUR GOOD BREEDING SHINES THROUGH MOST IMPECCABLY.
"ADDRESS THE MEMBERS OF THE AUDIENCE AS 'BIG BROTHER' AND 'BIG SISTER'"...?
"I SHALL GIVE YOU TWENTY ELEPHANTS AS A REWARD"...?
SINGING AND DANCING LIKE THE S4 WILL ONLY MAKE YOU A PALE IMITATION.
MIMICKING THEIR ACT WILL PUT YOU ON AN EQUAL FOOTING, BUT VICTORY IS ANOTHER THING ENTIRELY.
IT'S NOVELTY AND INDIVIDUALITY THAT WILL PUT YOU OVER THE TOP!
WILL THAT REALLY BE ENOUGH TO WIN AGAINST THE S4?
BAN
SLAM

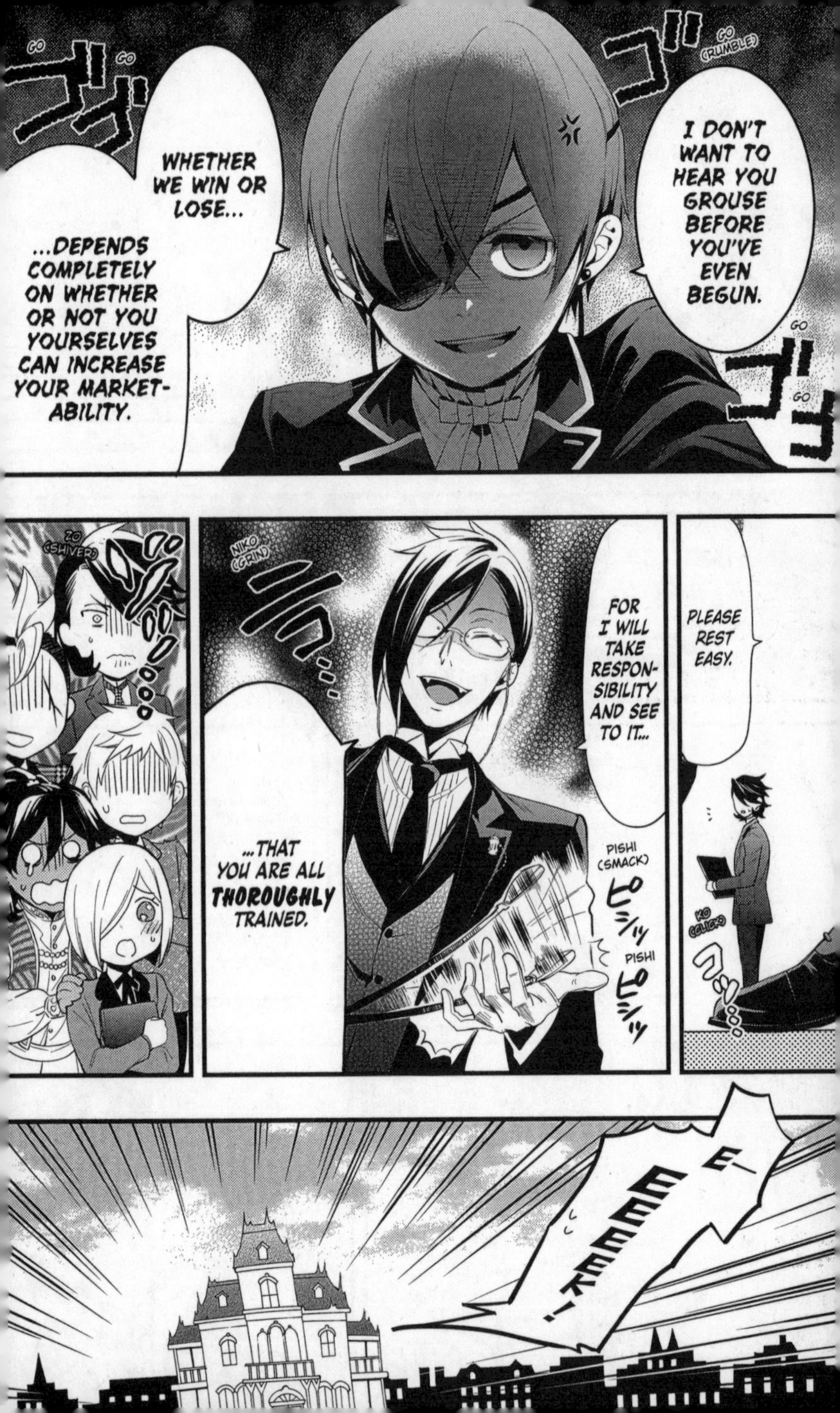
GO (RUMBLE)
I DON'T WANT TO HEAR YOU GROUSE BEFORE YOU'VE EVEN BEGUN.
GO
GO
WHETHER WE WIN OR LOSE...
...DEPENDS COMPLETELY ON WHETHER OR NOT YOU YOURSELVES CAN INCREASE YOUR MARKET-ABILITY.
GO
GO
PLEASE REST EASY.
KO (CLICK)
FOR I WILL TAKE RESPON-SIBILITY AND SEE TO IT...
NIKO (GRIN)
...THAT YOU ARE ALL **THOROUGHLY** TRAINED.
PISHI (SMACK)
PISHI
ZO (SHIVER)
E– EEEEEEK–!

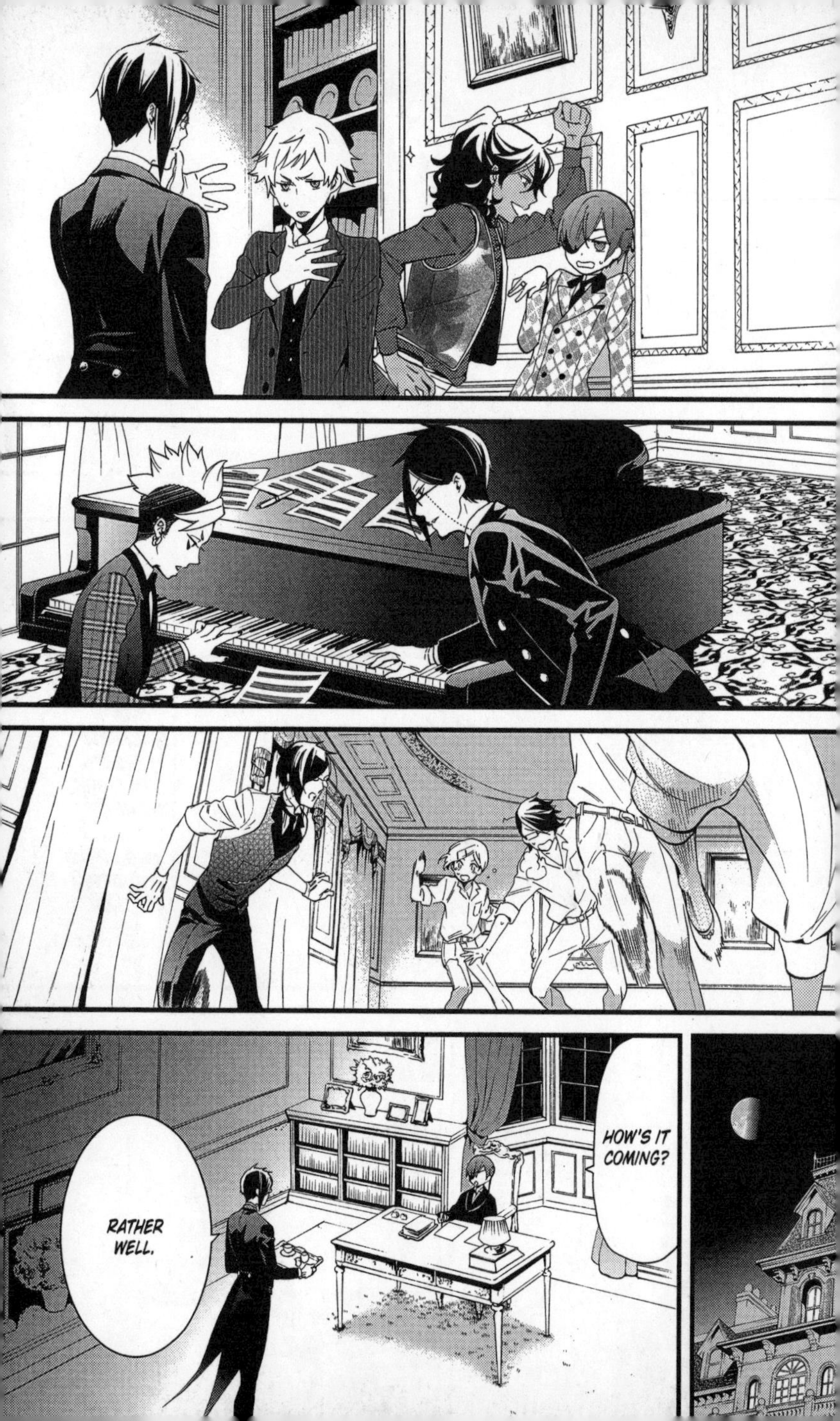
HOW'S IT COMING?
RATHER WELL.

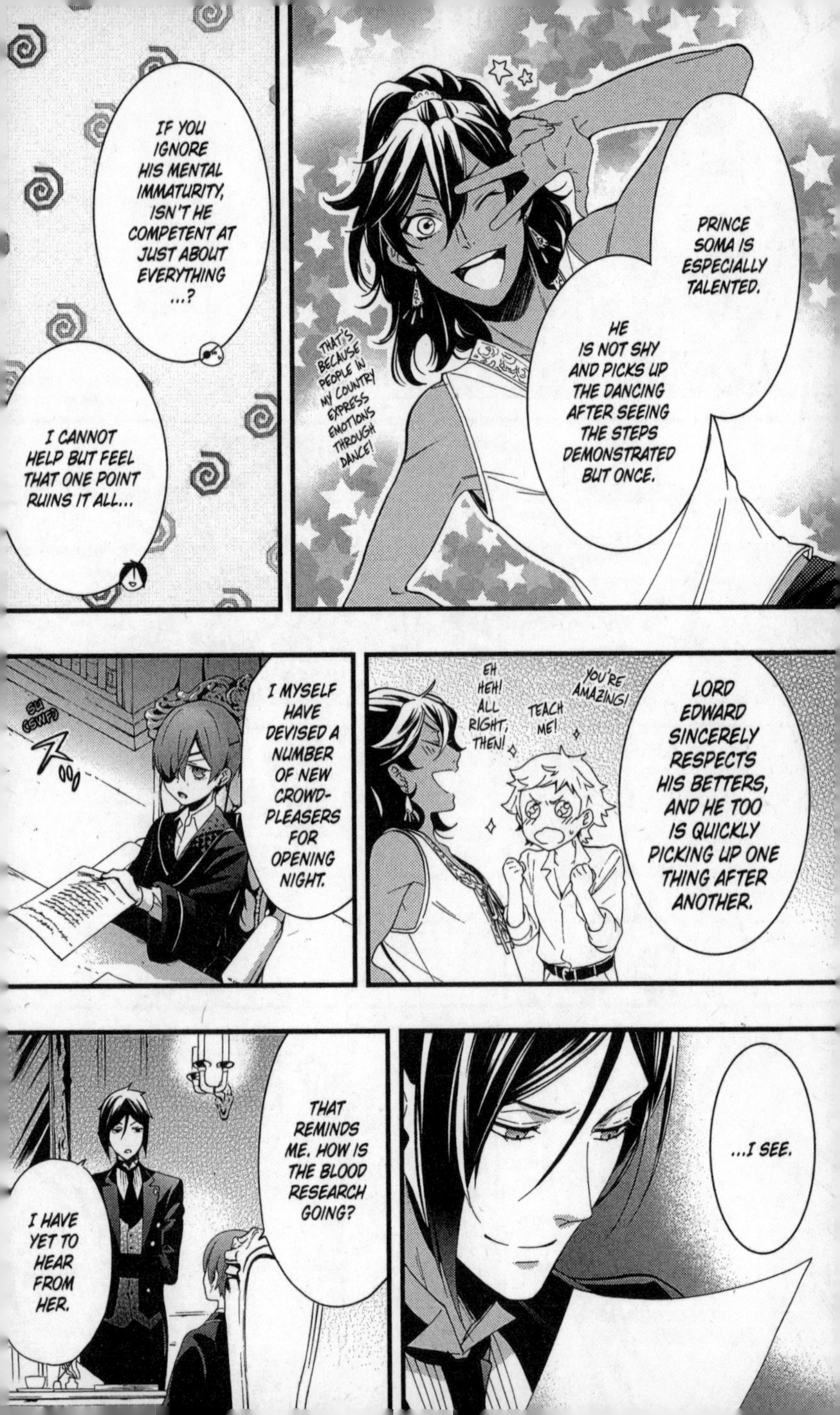
PRINCE SOMA IS ESPECIALLY TALENTED.
HE IS NOT SHY AND PICKS UP THE DANCING AFTER SEEING THE STEPS DEMONSTRATED BUT ONCE.
THAT'S BECAUSE PEOPLE IN MY COUNTRY EXPRESS EMOTIONS THROUGH DANCE!
IF YOU IGNORE HIS MENTAL IMMATURITY, ISN'T HE COMPETENT AT JUST ABOUT EVERYTHING ...?
I CANNOT HELP BUT FEEL THAT ONE POINT RUINS IT ALL...
LORD EDWARD SINCERELY RESPECTS HIS BETTERS, AND HE TOO IS QUICKLY PICKING UP ONE THING AFTER ANOTHER.
YOU'RE AMAZING!
TEACH ME!
EH HEH! ALL RIGHT, THEN!
I MYSELF HAVE DEVISED A NUMBER OF NEW CROWD-PLEASERS FOR OPENING NIGHT.
SU (SWF)
...I SEE.
THAT REMINDS ME. HOW IS THE BLOOD RESEARCH GOING?
I HAVE YET TO HEAR FROM HER.

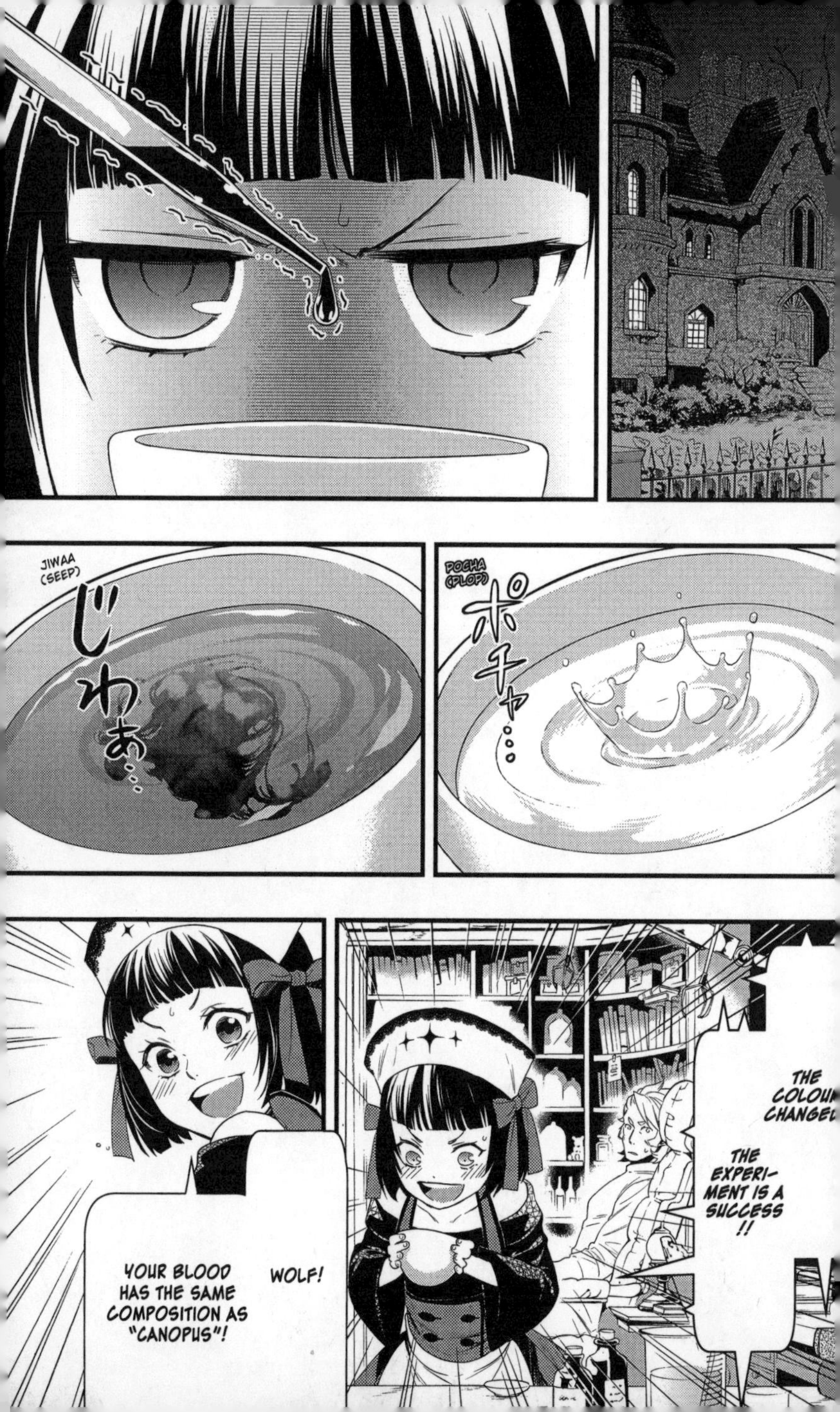

POCHA (PLOP)
ポチャ...
JIWAA (SEEP)
じわぁ...
THE COLOU CHANGE
THE EXPERIMENT IS A SUCCESS!!
WOLF!
YOUR BLOOD HAS THE SAME COMPOSITION AS "CANOPUS"!

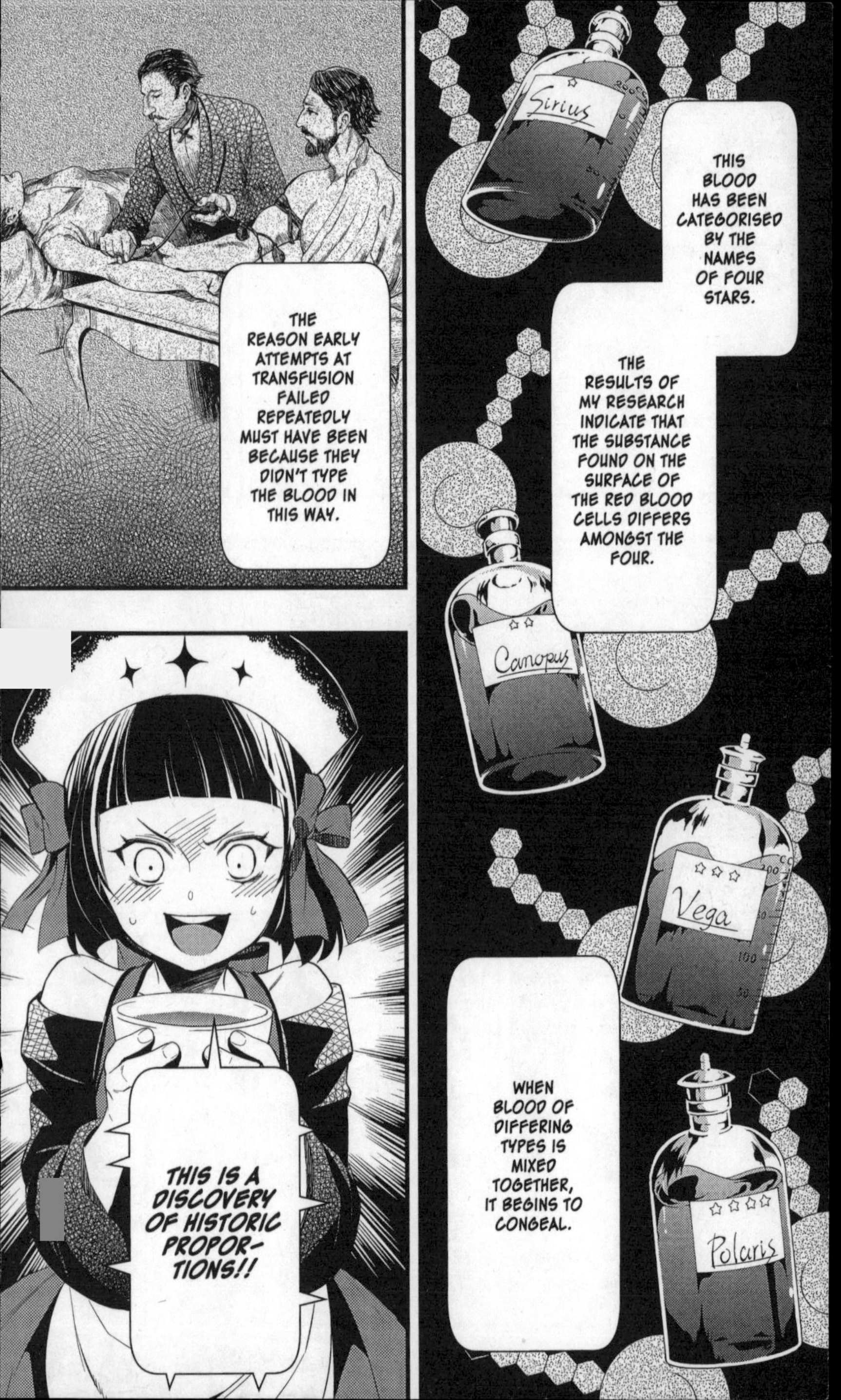
Sirius
THIS BLOOD HAS BEEN CATEGORISED BY THE NAMES OF FOUR STARS.
THE RESULTS OF MY RESEARCH INDICATE THAT THE SUBSTANCE FOUND ON THE SURFACE OF THE RED BLOOD CELLS DIFFERS AMONGST THE FOUR.
Canopus
Vega
WHEN BLOOD OF DIFFERING TYPES IS MIXED TOGETHER, IT BEGINS TO CONGEAL.
Polaris
THE REASON EARLY ATTEMPTS AT TRANSFUSION FAILED REPEATEDLY MUST HAVE BEEN BECAUSE THEY DIDN'T TYPE THE BLOOD IN THIS WAY.
THIS IS A DISCOVERY OF HISTORIC PROPOR-TIONS!!

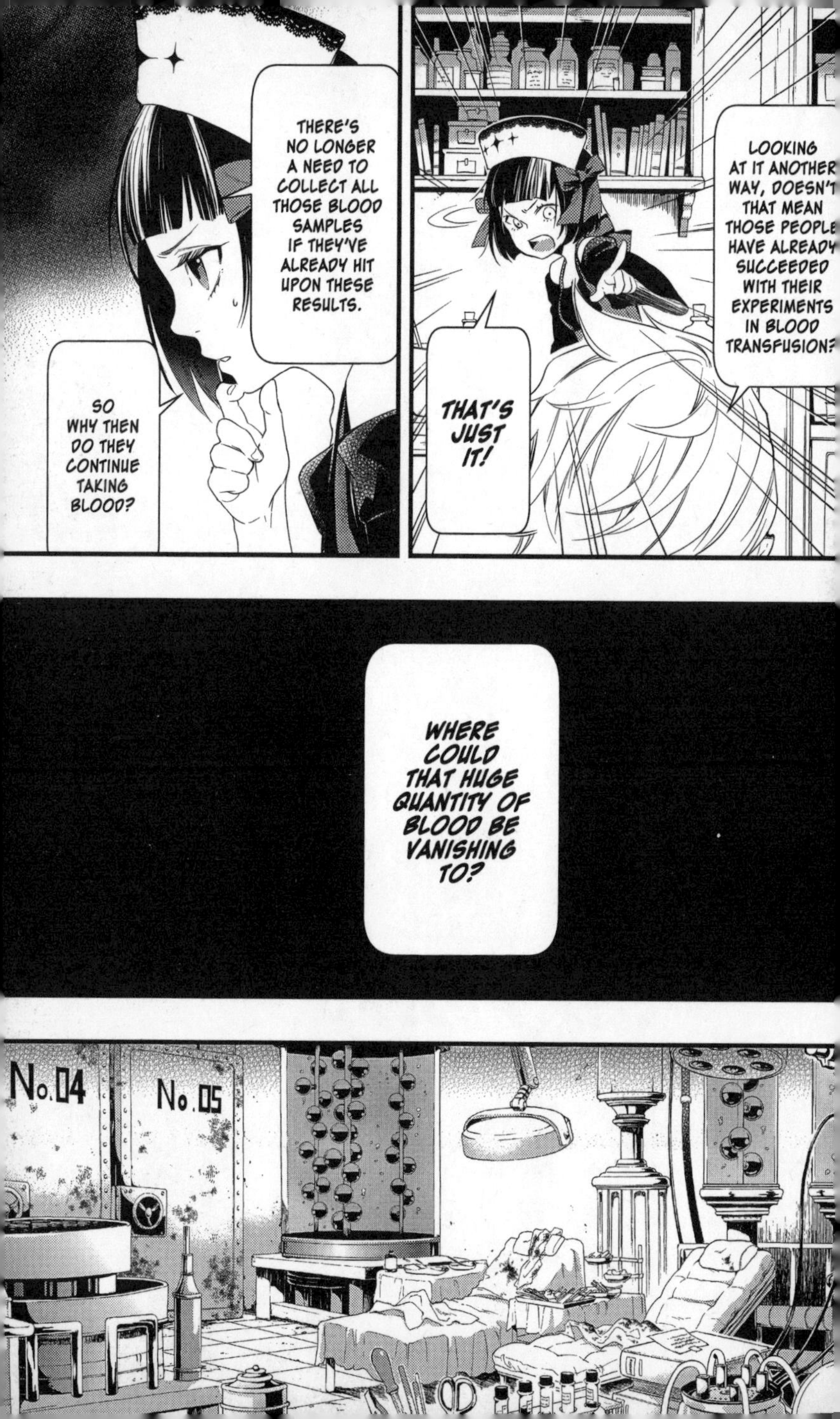
LOOKING AT IT ANOTHER WAY, DOESN'T THAT MEAN THOSE PEOPLE HAVE ALREADY SUCCEEDED WITH THEIR EXPERIMENTS IN BLOOD TRANSFUSION?
THAT'S JUST IT!
THERE'S NO LONGER A NEED TO COLLECT ALL THOSE BLOOD SAMPLES IF THEY'VE ALREADY HIT UPON THESE RESULTS.
SO WHY THEN DO THEY CONTINUE TAKING BLOOD?
WHERE COULD THAT HUGE QUANTITY OF BLOOD BE VANISHING TO?
No.04
No.05

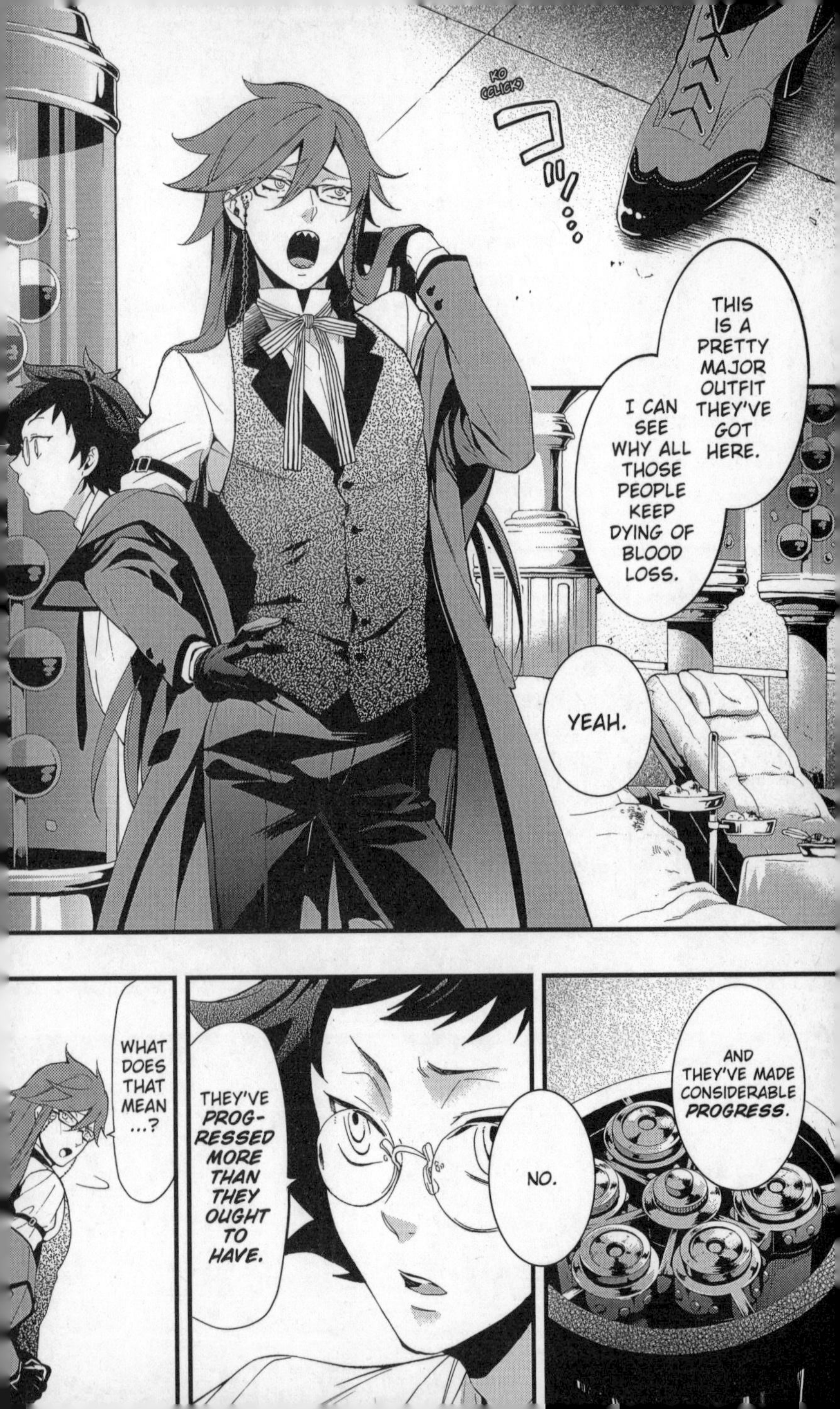
KO (CLICK)
THIS IS A PRETTY MAJOR OUTFIT THEY'VE GOT HERE.
I CAN SEE WHY ALL THOSE PEOPLE KEEP DYING OF BLOOD LOSS.
YEAH.
AND THEY'VE MADE CONSIDERABLE *PROGRESS*.
NO.
THEY'VE *PROGRESSED MORE THAN THEY OUGHT TO HAVE.*
WHAT DOES THAT MEAN ...?

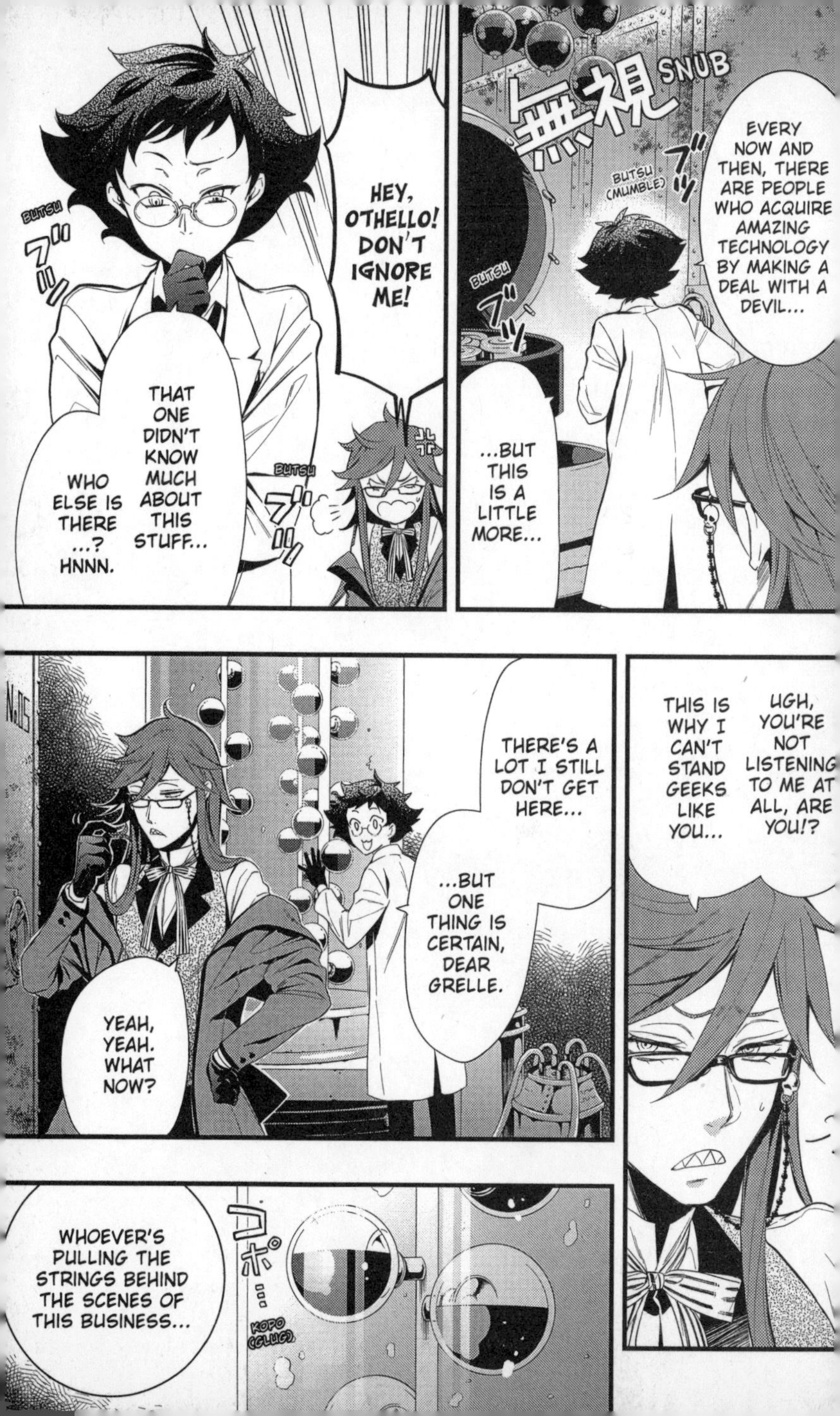
無視
SNUB
EVERY NOW AND THEN, THERE ARE PEOPLE WHO ACQUIRE AMAZING TECHNOLOGY BY MAKING A DEAL WITH A DEVIL...
ブツ
BUTSU (MUMBLE)
ブツ
BUTSU
...BUT THIS IS A LITTLE MORE...
HEY, OTHELLO! DON'T IGNORE ME!
ブツ
BUTSU
THAT ONE DIDN'T KNOW MUCH ABOUT THIS STUFF...
WHO ELSE IS THERE ...? HNNN.
ブツ
BUTSU
UGH, YOU'RE NOT LISTENING TO ME AT ALL, ARE YOU!?
THIS IS WHY I CAN'T STAND GEEKS LIKE YOU...
THERE'S A LOT I STILL DON'T GET HERE...
...BUT ONE THING IS CERTAIN, DEAR GRELLE.
YEAH, YEAH. WHAT NOW?
WHOEVER'S PULLING THE STRINGS BEHIND THE SCENES OF THIS BUSINESS...
コポ...
KOPO (GLUG)

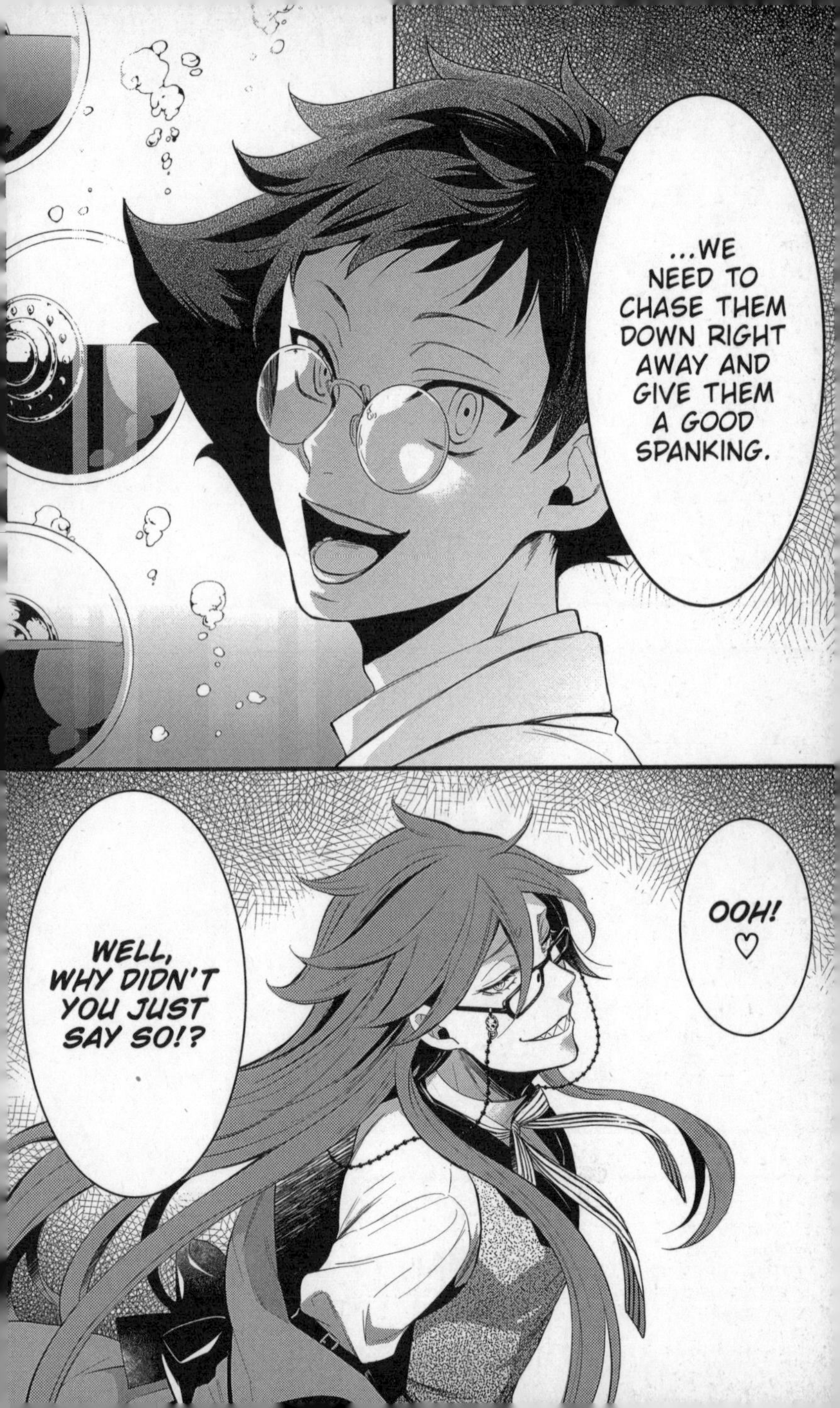
...WE NEED TO CHASE THEM DOWN RIGHT AWAY AND GIVE THEM A GOOD SPANKING.
OOH! ♡
WELL, WHY DIDN'T YOU JUST SAY SO!?

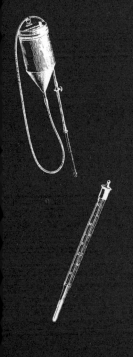

Black Butler

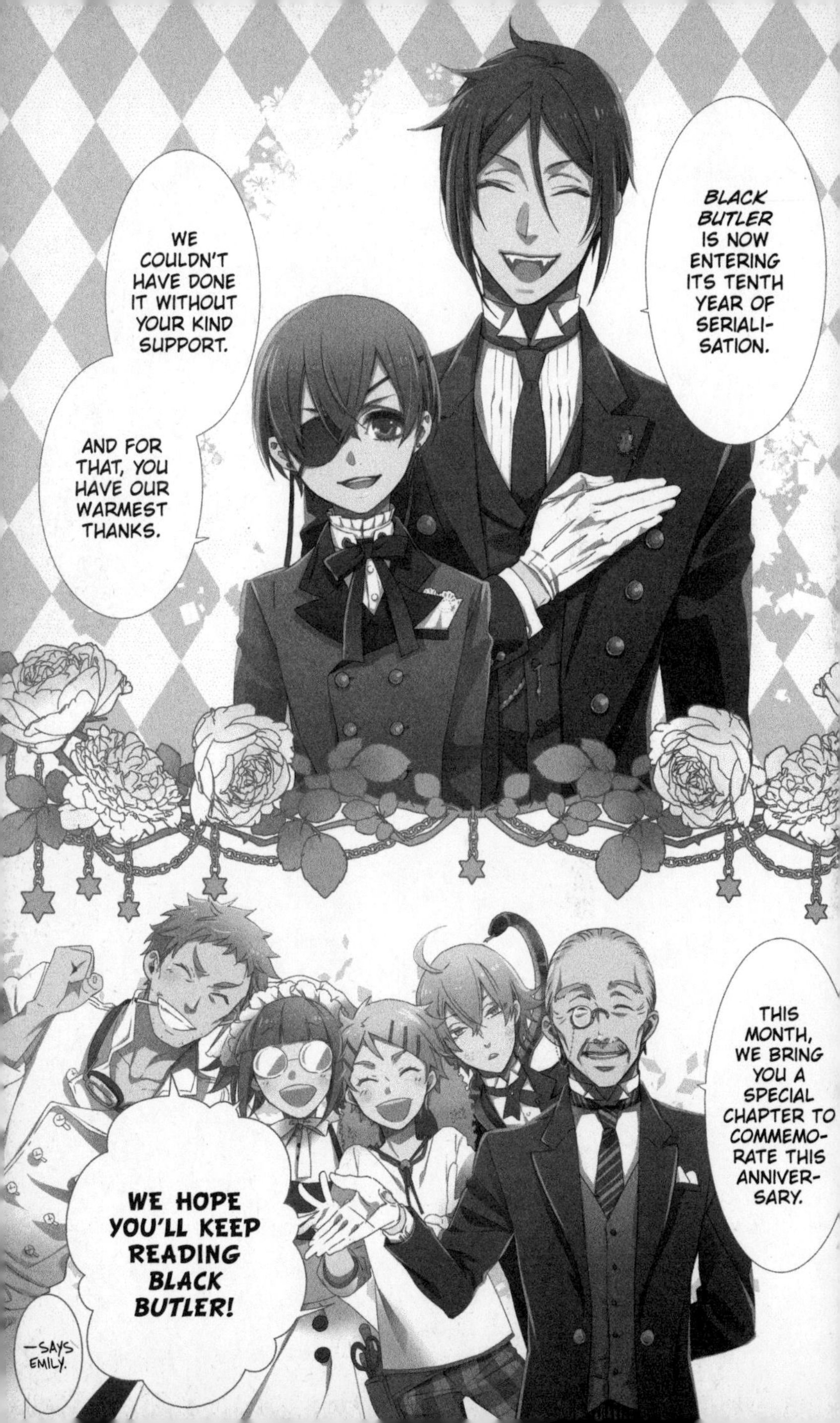
BLACK BUTLER IS NOW ENTERING ITS TENTH YEAR OF SERIALI-SATION.
WE COULDN'T HAVE DONE IT WITHOUT YOUR KIND SUPPORT.
AND FOR THAT, YOU HAVE OUR WARMEST THANKS.
THIS MONTH, WE BRING YOU A SPECIAL CHAPTER TO COMMEMO-RATE THIS ANNIVER-SARY.
WE HOPE YOU'LL KEEP READING *BLACK BUTLER*!
—SAYS EMILY.

Bonus Chapter
On a special day : The Butler, Lyrical

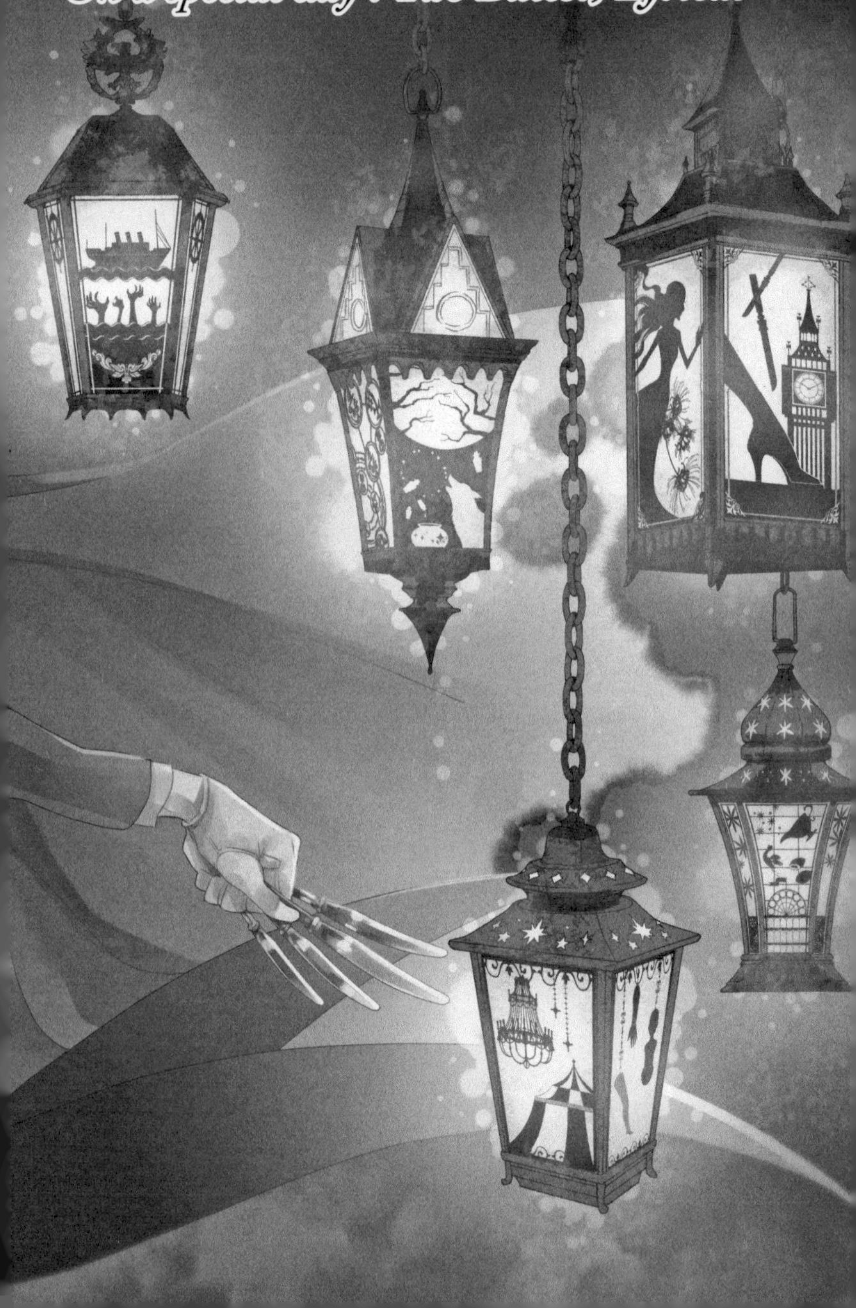

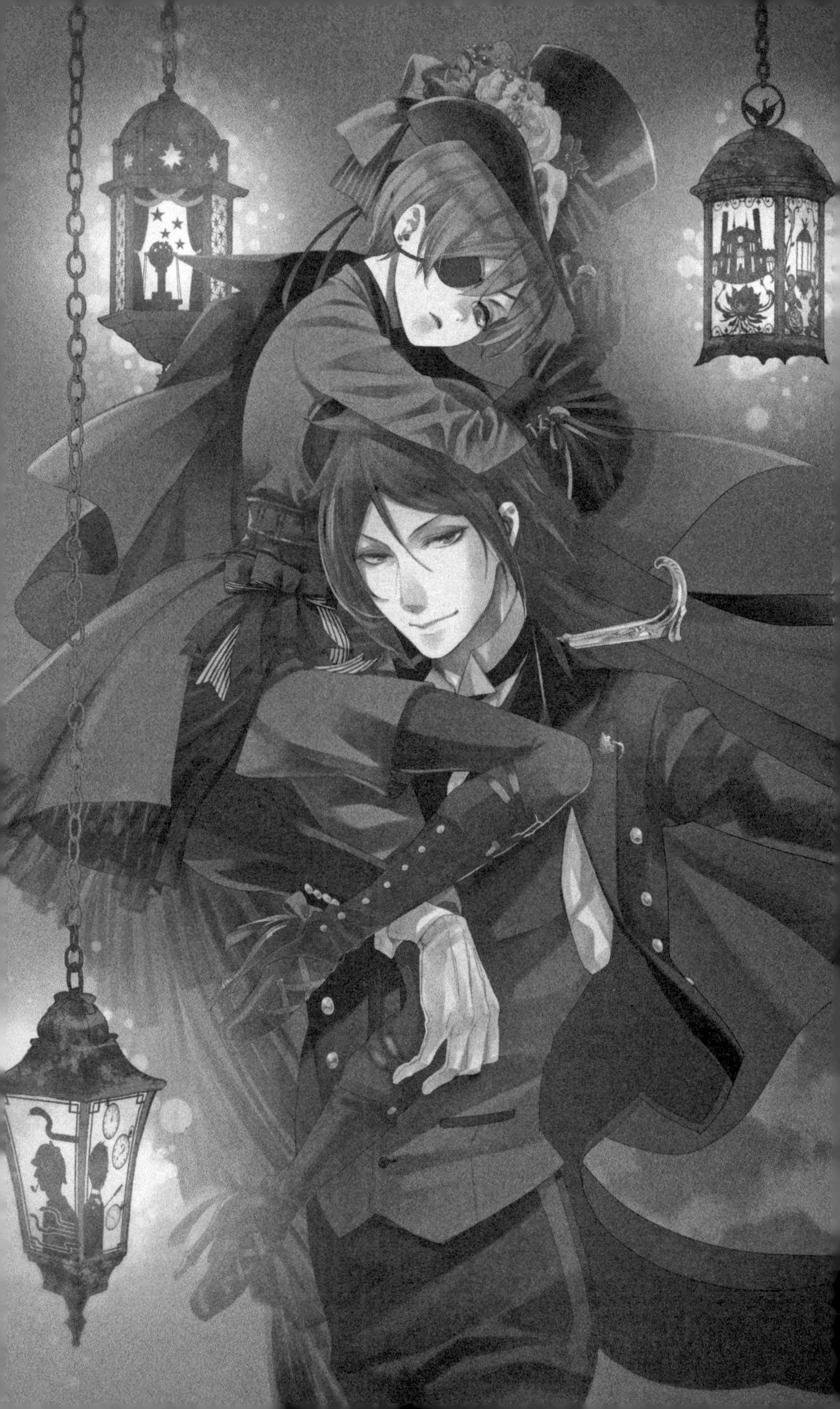

Black Butler

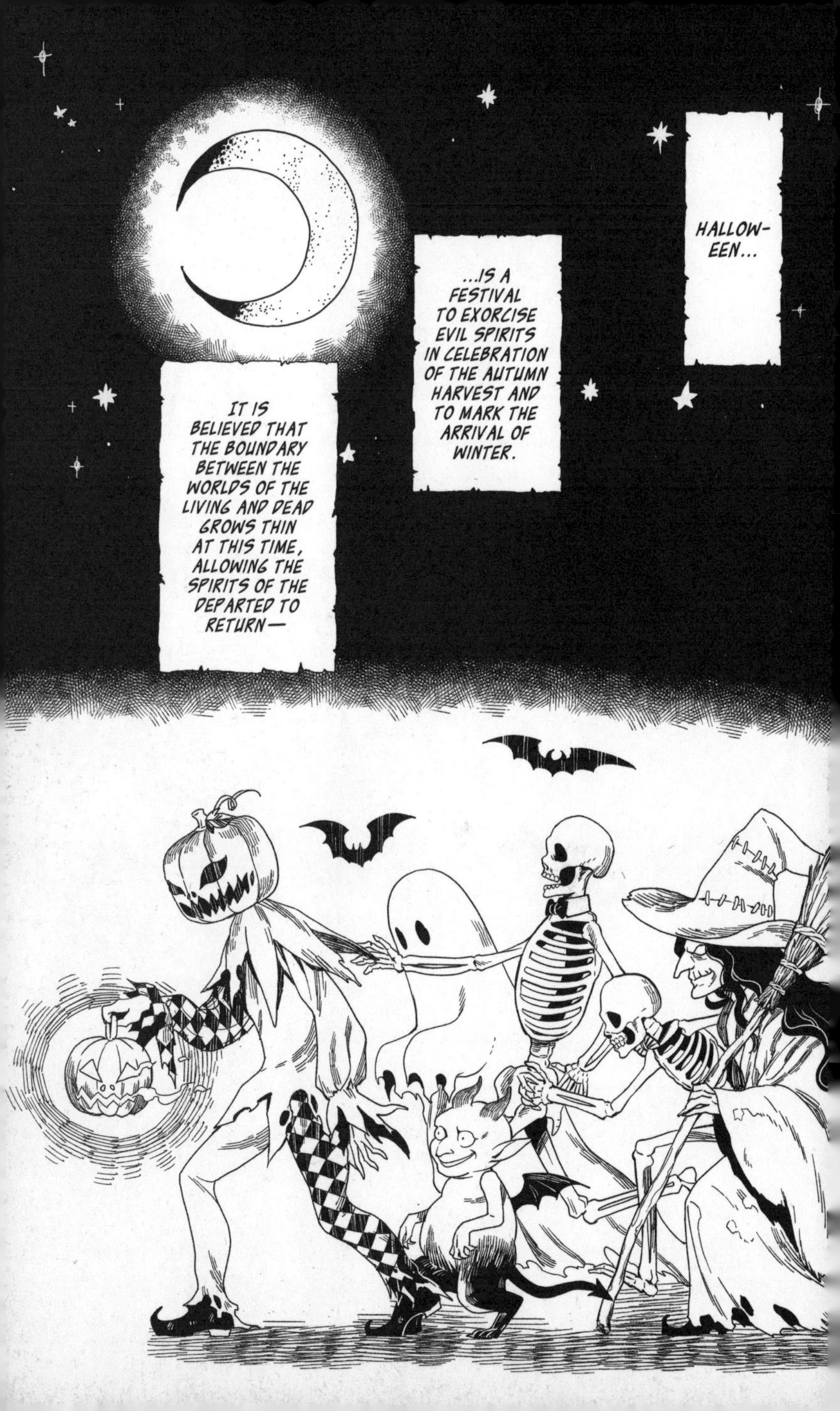
HALLOWEEN...
...IS A FESTIVAL TO EXORCISE EVIL SPIRITS IN CELEBRATION OF THE AUTUMN HARVEST AND TO MARK THE ARRIVAL OF WINTER.
IT IS BELIEVED THAT THE BOUNDARY BETWEEN THE WORLDS OF THE LIVING AND DEAD GROWS THIN AT THIS TIME, ALLOWING THE SPIRITS OF THE DEPARTED TO RETURN—

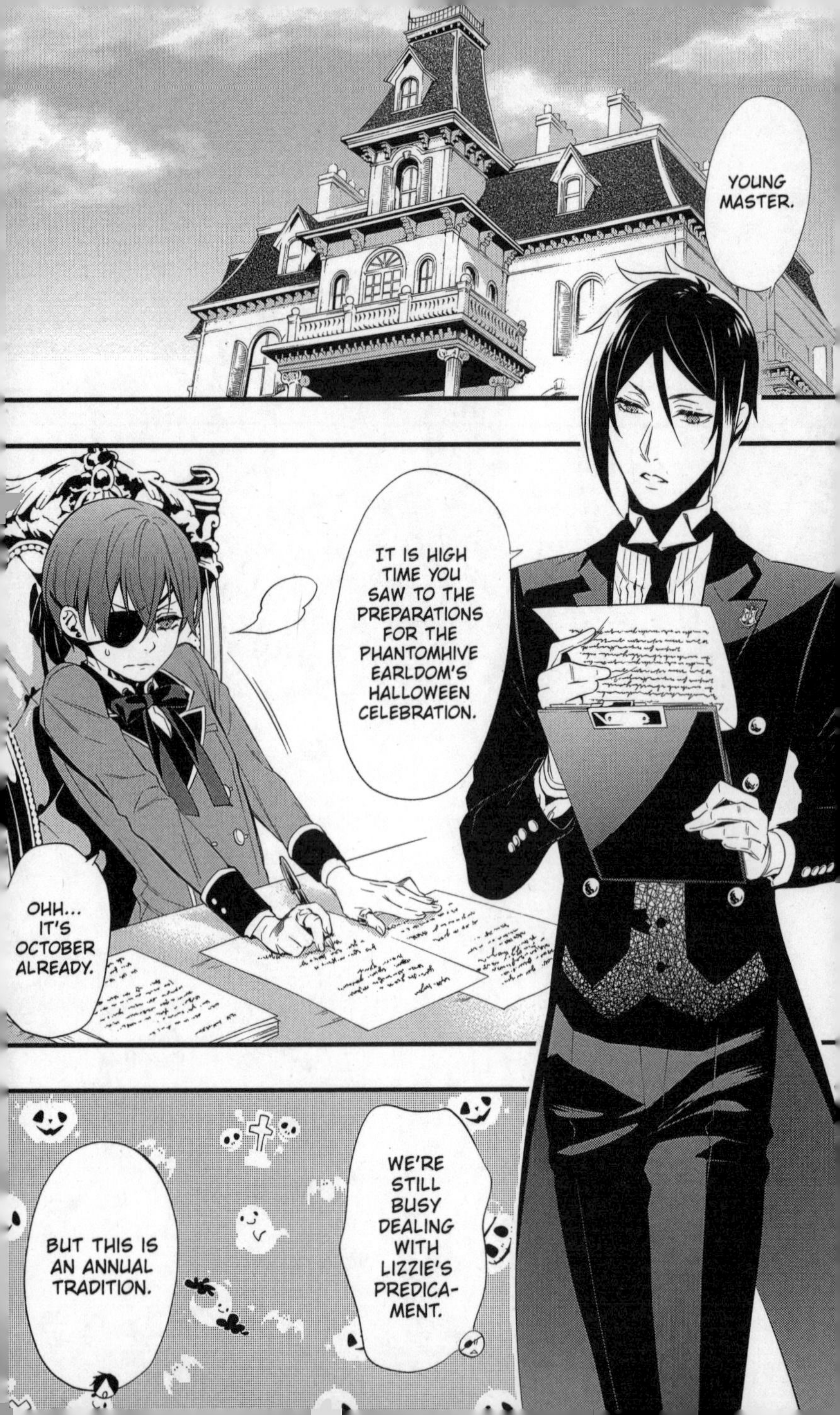
YOUNG MASTER.
IT IS HIGH TIME YOU SAW TO THE PREPARATIONS FOR THE PHANTOMHIVE EARLDOM'S HALLOWEEN CELEBRATION.
OHH... IT'S OCTOBER ALREADY.
WE'RE STILL BUSY DEALING WITH LIZZIE'S PREDICA-MENT.
BUT THIS IS AN ANNUAL TRADITION.

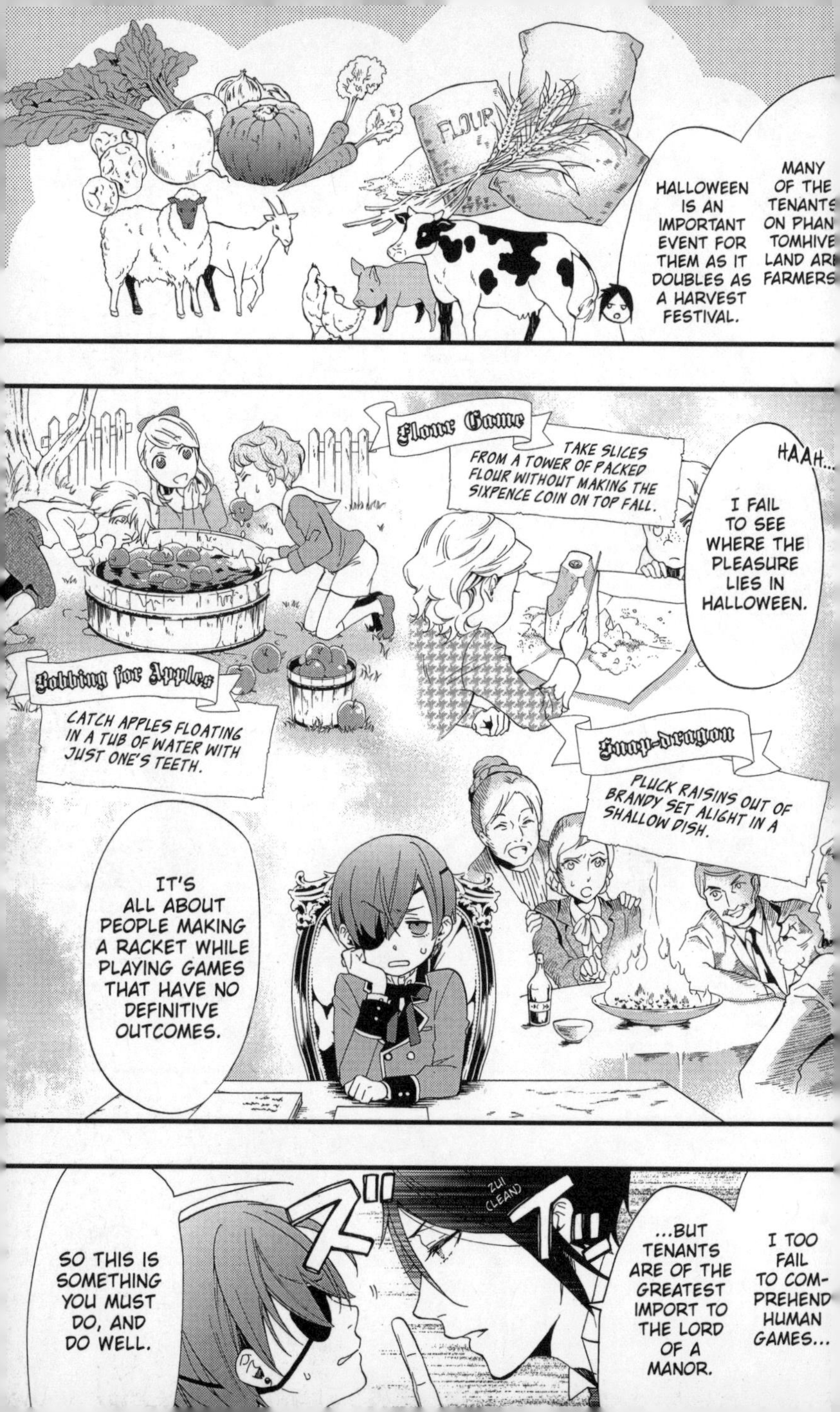

MANY OF THE TENANTS ON PHAN TOMHIVE LAND AR FARMERS
HALLOWEEN IS AN IMPORTANT EVENT FOR THEM AS IT DOUBLES AS A HARVEST FESTIVAL.
FLOUR
HAAH...
I FAIL TO SEE WHERE THE PLEASURE LIES IN HALLOWEEN.
Flour Game
TAKE SLICES FROM A TOWER OF PACKED FLOUR WITHOUT MAKING THE SIXPENCE COIN ON TOP FALL.
Bobbing for Apples
CATCH APPLES FLOATING IN A TUB OF WATER WITH JUST ONE'S TEETH.
Snap-dragon
PLUCK RAISINS OUT OF BRANDY SET ALIGHT IN A SHALLOW DISH.
IT'S ALL ABOUT PEOPLE MAKING A RACKET WHILE PLAYING GAMES THAT HAVE NO DEFINITIVE OUTCOMES.
I TOO FAIL TO COMPREHEND HUMAN GAMES...
...BUT TENANTS ARE OF THE GREATEST IMPORT TO THE LORD OF A MANOR.
ZUI (LEAN)
SO THIS IS SOMETHING YOU MUST DO, AND DO WELL.

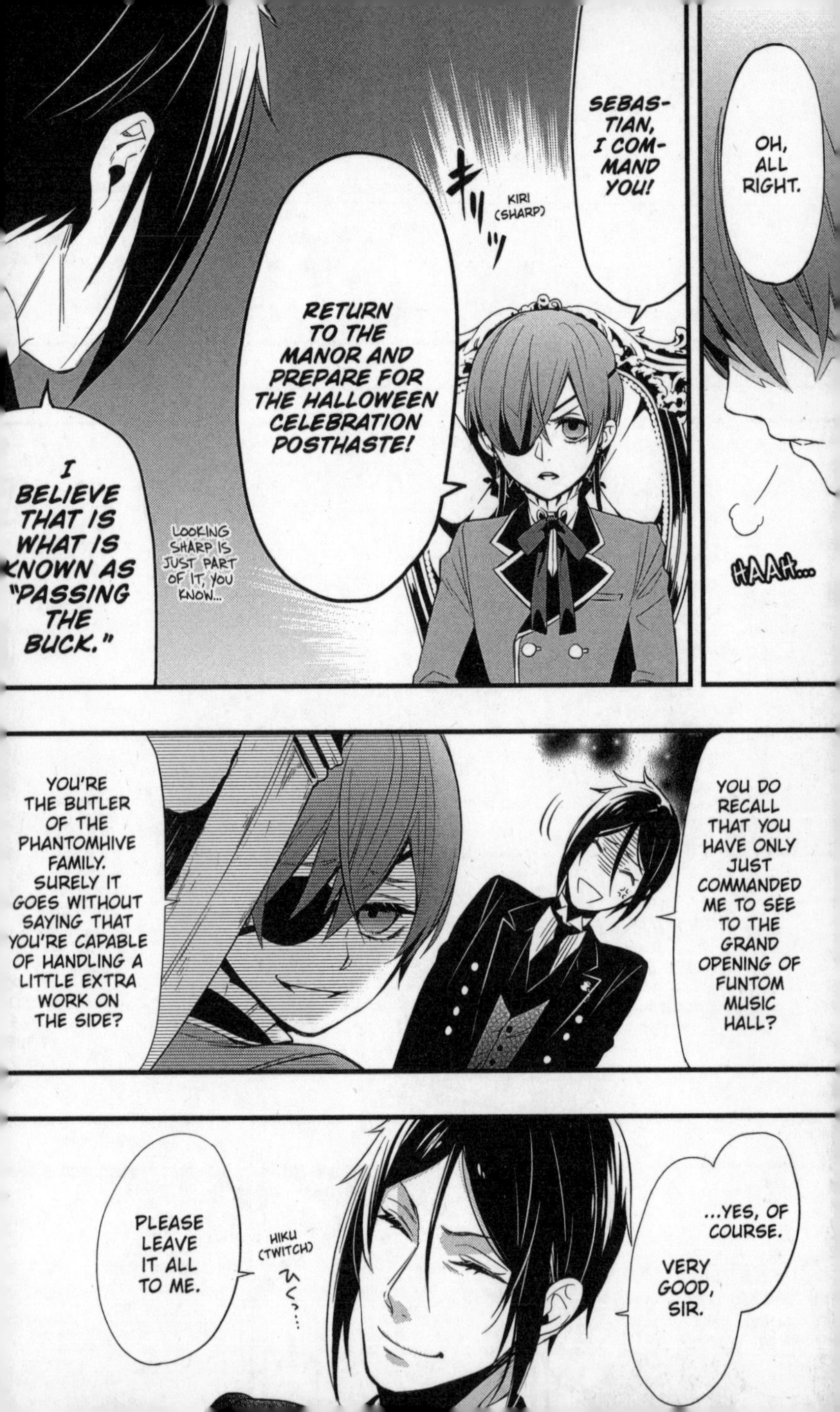

OH, ALL RIGHT.
HAAH...
SEBASTIAN, I COMMAND YOU!
KIRI (SHARP)
RETURN TO THE MANOR AND PREPARE FOR THE HALLOWEEN CELEBRATION POSTHASTE!
I BELIEVE THAT IS WHAT IS KNOWN AS "PASSING THE BUCK."
LOOKING SHARP IS JUST PART OF IT, YOU KNOW...
YOU DO RECALL THAT YOU HAVE ONLY JUST COMMANDED ME TO SEE TO THE GRAND OPENING OF FUNTOM MUSIC HALL?
YOU'RE THE BUTLER OF THE PHANTOMHIVE FAMILY. SURELY IT GOES WITHOUT SAYING THAT YOU'RE CAPABLE OF HANDLING A LITTLE EXTRA WORK ON THE SIDE?
...YES, OF COURSE.
VERY GOOD, SIR.
HIKU (TWITCH)
PLEASE LEAVE IT ALL TO ME.

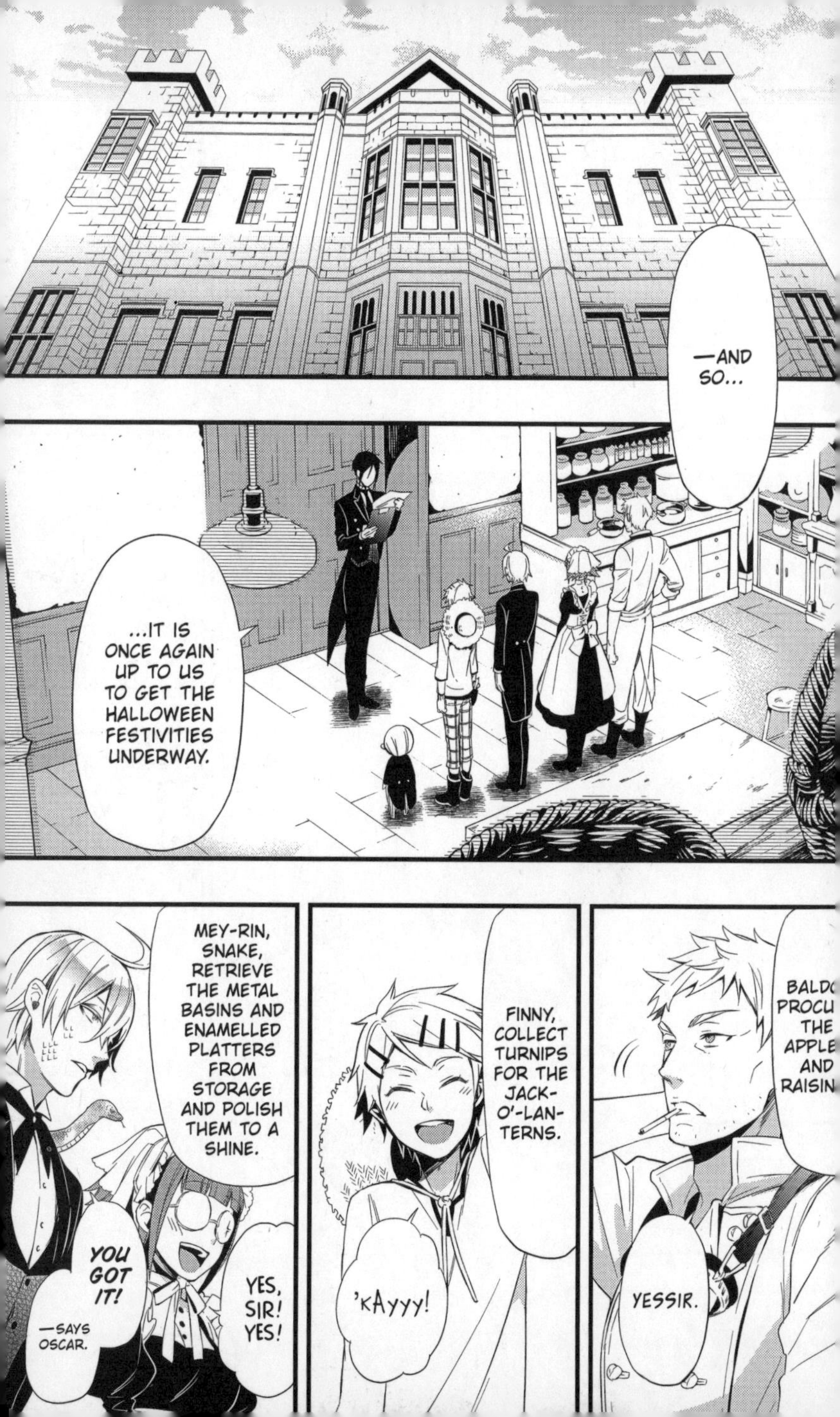
—AND SO...
...IT IS ONCE AGAIN UP TO US TO GET THE HALLOWEEN FESTIVITIES UNDERWAY.
BALDO PROCU THE APPLE AND RAISIN
YESSIR.
FINNY, COLLECT TURNIPS FOR THE JACK-O'-LANTERNS.
'KAYYY!
MEY-RIN, SNAKE, RETRIEVE THE METAL BASINS AND ENAMELLED PLATTERS FROM STORAGE AND POLISH THEM TO A SHINE.
YES, SIR! YES!
YOU GOT IT!
—SAYS OSCAR.

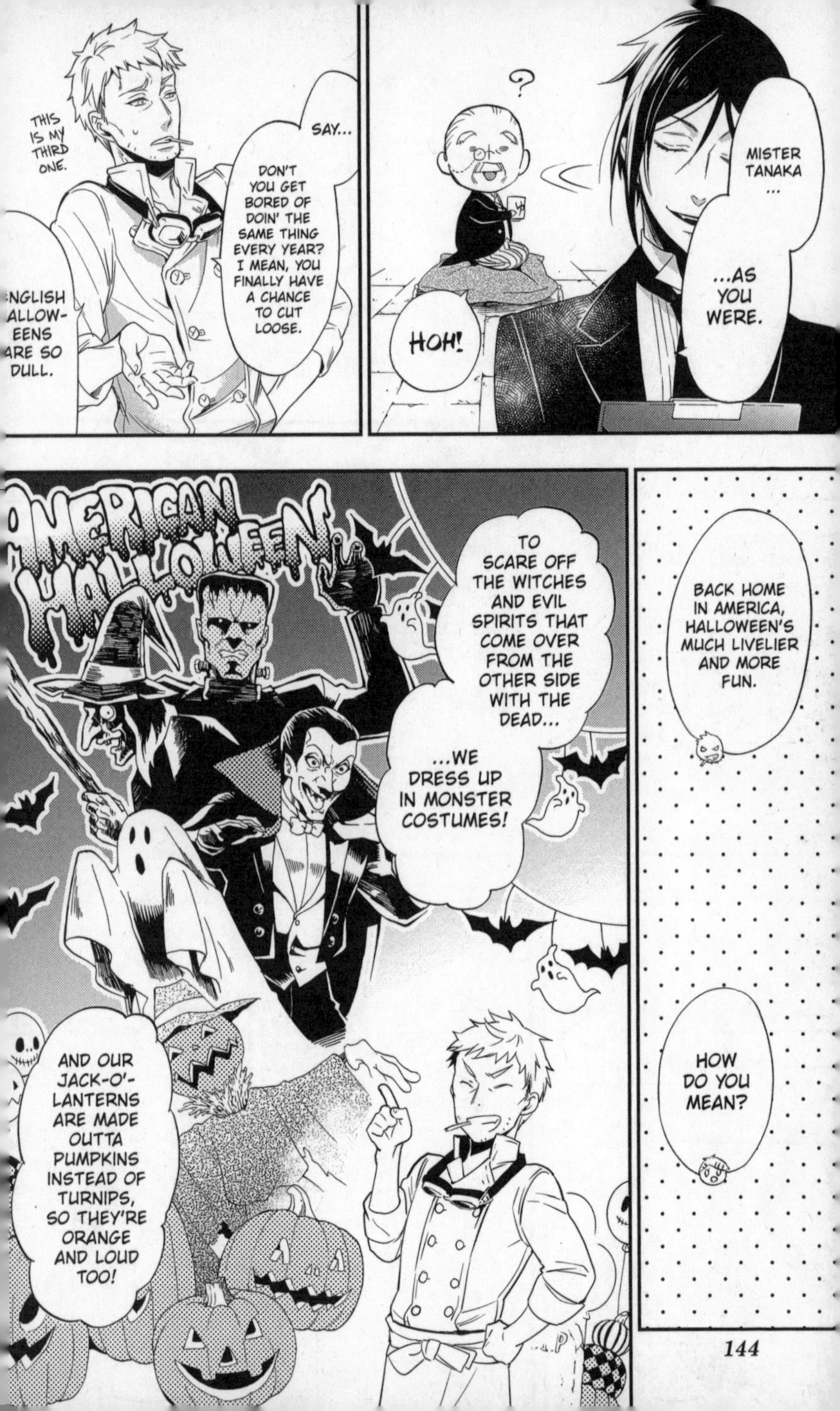
MISTER TANAKA ...
...AS YOU WERE.
?
HOH!
SAY...
DON'T YOU GET BORED OF DOIN' THE SAME THING EVERY YEAR? I MEAN, YOU FINALLY HAVE A CHANCE TO CUT LOOSE.
THIS IS MY THIRD ONE.
NGLISH HALLOWEENS ARE SO DULL.
BACK HOME IN AMERICA, HALLOWEEN'S MUCH LIVELIER AND MORE FUN.
HOW DO YOU MEAN?
MERICAN HALLOWEEN
TO SCARE OFF THE WITCHES AND EVIL SPIRITS THAT COME OVER FROM THE OTHER SIDE WITH THE DEAD...
...WE DRESS UP IN MONSTER COSTUMES!
AND OUR JACK-O'-LANTERNS ARE MADE OUTTA PUMPKINS INSTEAD OF TURNIPS, SO THEY'RE ORANGE AND LOUD TOO!

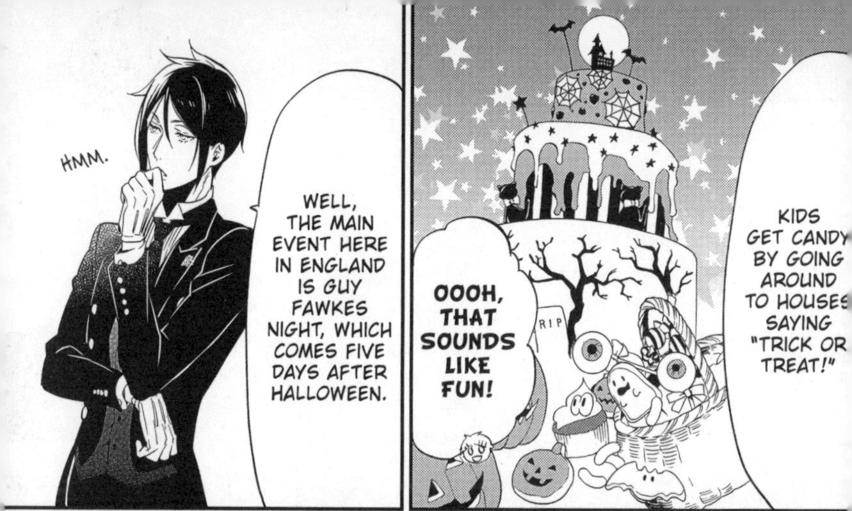
KIDS GET CANDY BY GOING AROUND TO HOUSES SAYING "TRICK OR TREAT!"
OOOH, THAT SOUNDS LIKE FUN!
RIP
WELL, THE MAIN EVENT HERE IN ENGLAND IS GUY FAWKES NIGHT, WHICH COMES FIVE DAYS AFTER HALLOWEEN.
HMM.

※GUY FAWKES NIGHT: THE ANNIVERSARY OF THE ARREST OF GUY FAWKES, A MEMBER OF THE PLOT TO BLOW UP THE HOUSE OF LORDS AND ASSASSINATE KING JAMES I

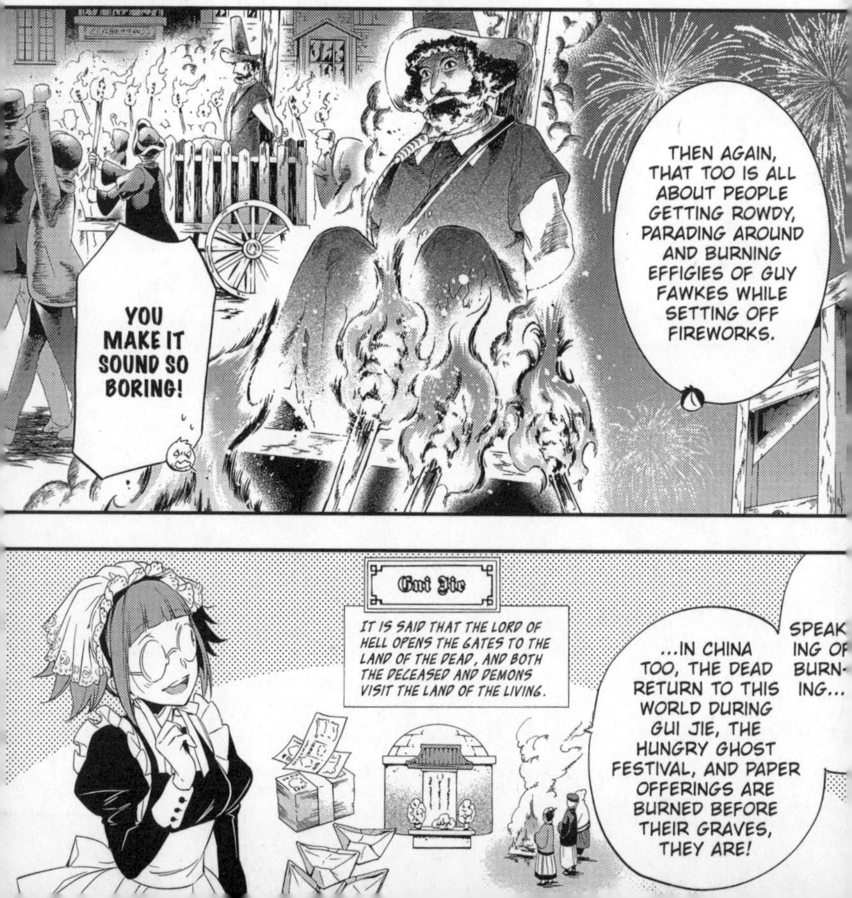
THEN AGAIN, THAT TOO IS ALL ABOUT PEOPLE GETTING ROWDY, PARADING AROUND AND BURNING EFFIGIES OF GUY FAWKES WHILE SETTING OFF FIREWORKS.
YOU MAKE IT SOUND SO BORING!
SPEAKING OF BURNING...
...IN CHINA TOO, THE DEAD RETURN TO THIS WORLD DURING GUI JIE, THE HUNGRY GHOST FESTIVAL, AND PAPER OFFERINGS ARE BURNED BEFORE THEIR GRAVES, THEY ARE!
Gui Jie
IT IS SAID THAT THE LORD OF HELL OPENS THE GATES TO THE LAND OF THE DEAD, AND BOTH THE DECEASED AND DEMONS VISIT THE LAND OF THE LIVING.

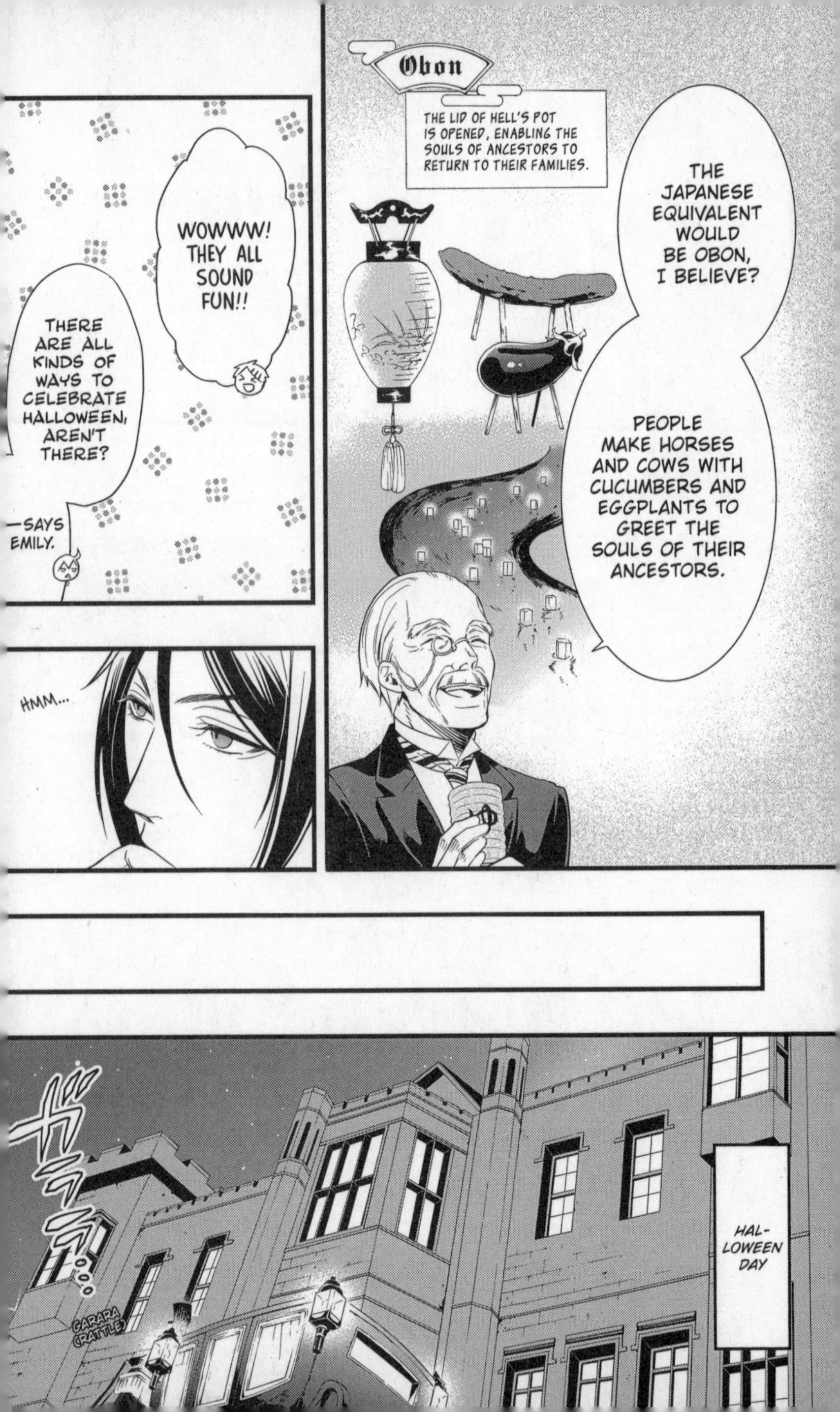
Obon
THE LID OF HELL'S POT IS OPENED, ENABLING THE SOULS OF ANCESTORS TO RETURN TO THEIR FAMILIES.
THE JAPANESE EQUIVALENT WOULD BE OBON, I BELIEVE?
PEOPLE MAKE HORSES AND COWS WITH CUCUMBERS AND EGGPLANTS TO GREET THE SOULS OF THEIR ANCESTORS.
WOWWW! THEY ALL SOUND FUN!!
THERE ARE ALL KINDS OF WAYS TO CELEBRATE HALLOWEEN, AREN'T THERE?
—SAYS EMILY.
HMM...
HAL-LOWEEN DAY
GARARA (RATTLE)

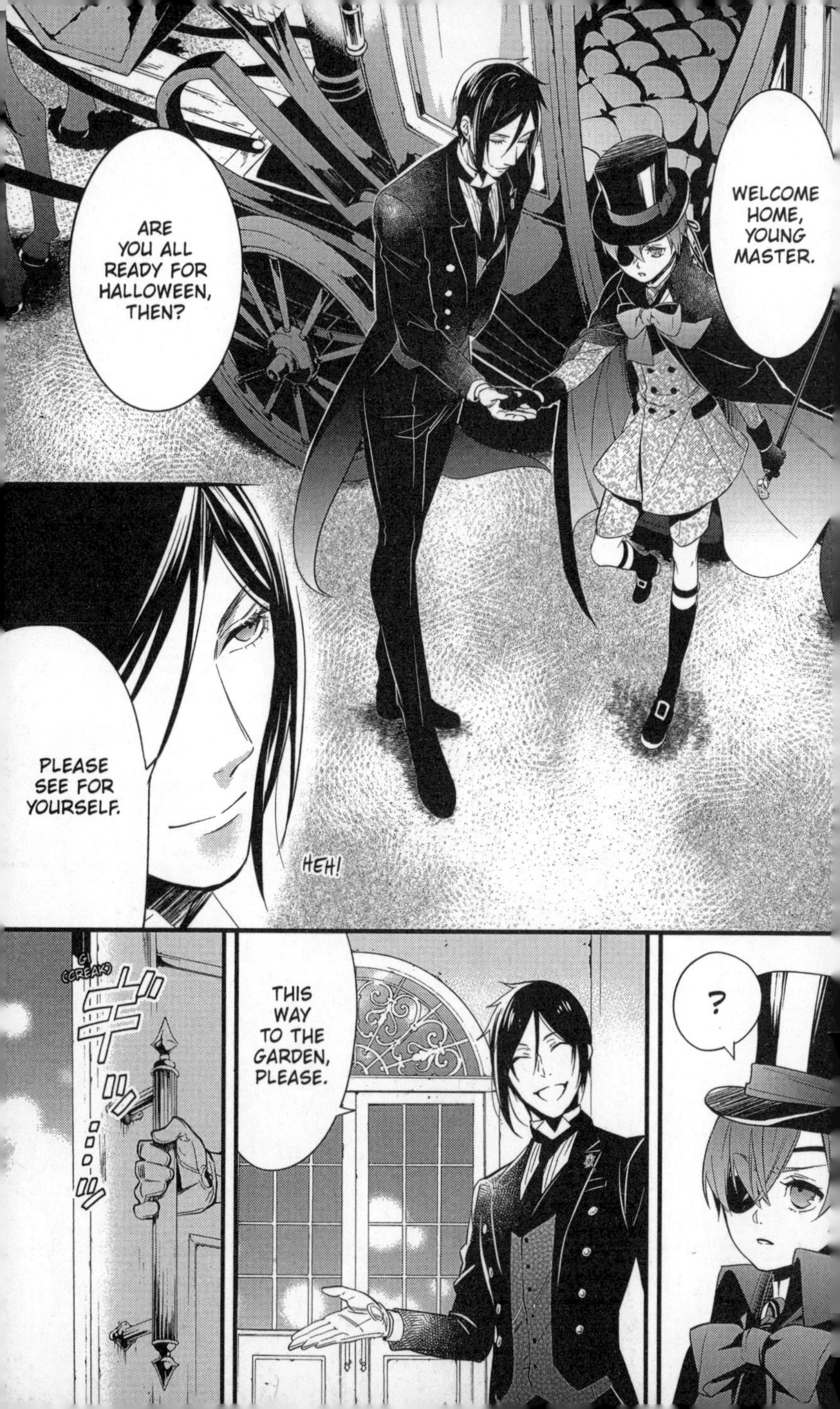
WELCOME HOME, YOUNG MASTER.
ARE YOU ALL READY FOR HALLOWEEN, THEN?
PLEASE SEE FOR YOURSELF.
HEH!
?
THIS WAY TO THE GARDEN, PLEASE.
GI (CREAK)

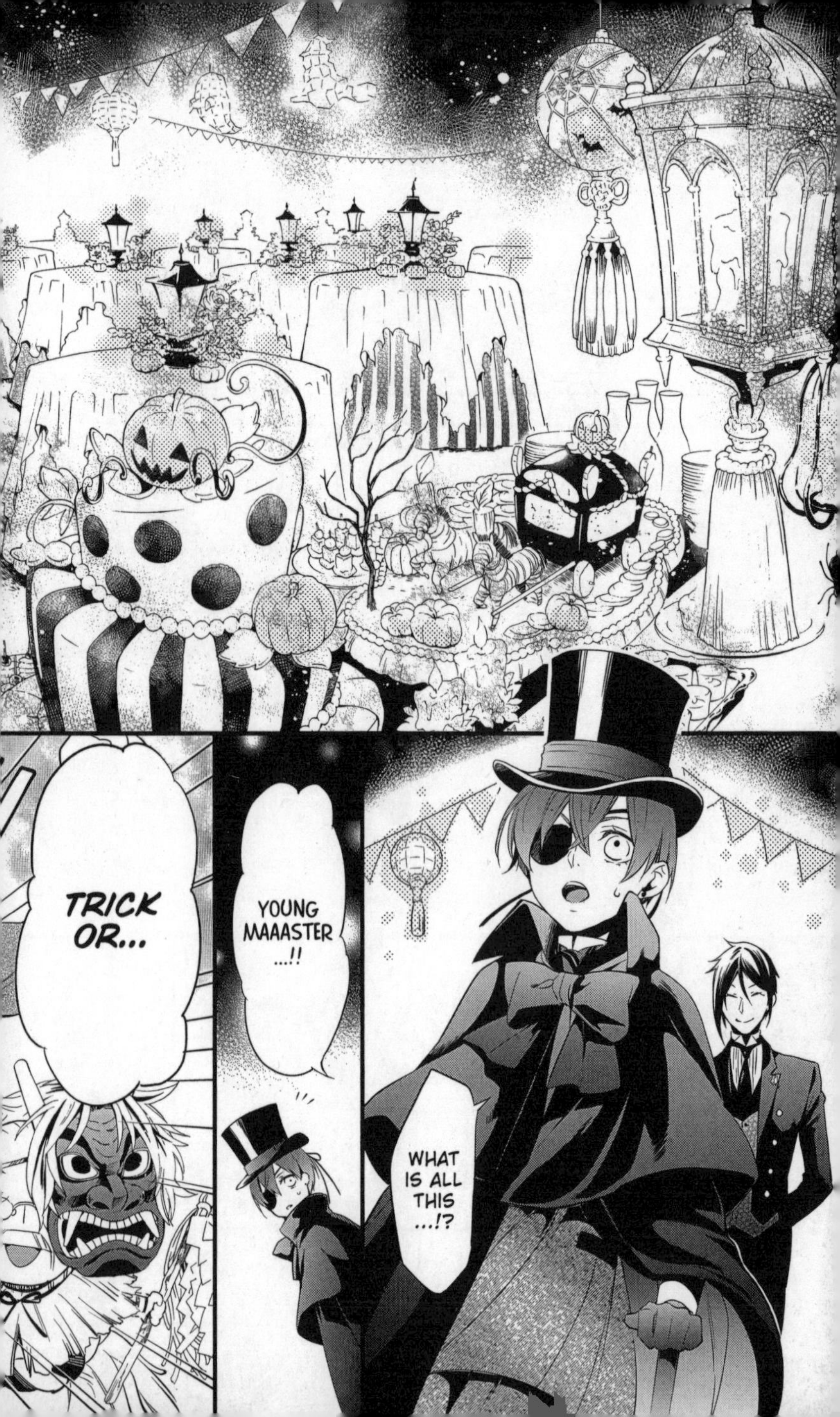
WHAT IS ALL THIS ...!?
YOUNG MAAASTER ...!!
TRICK OR...

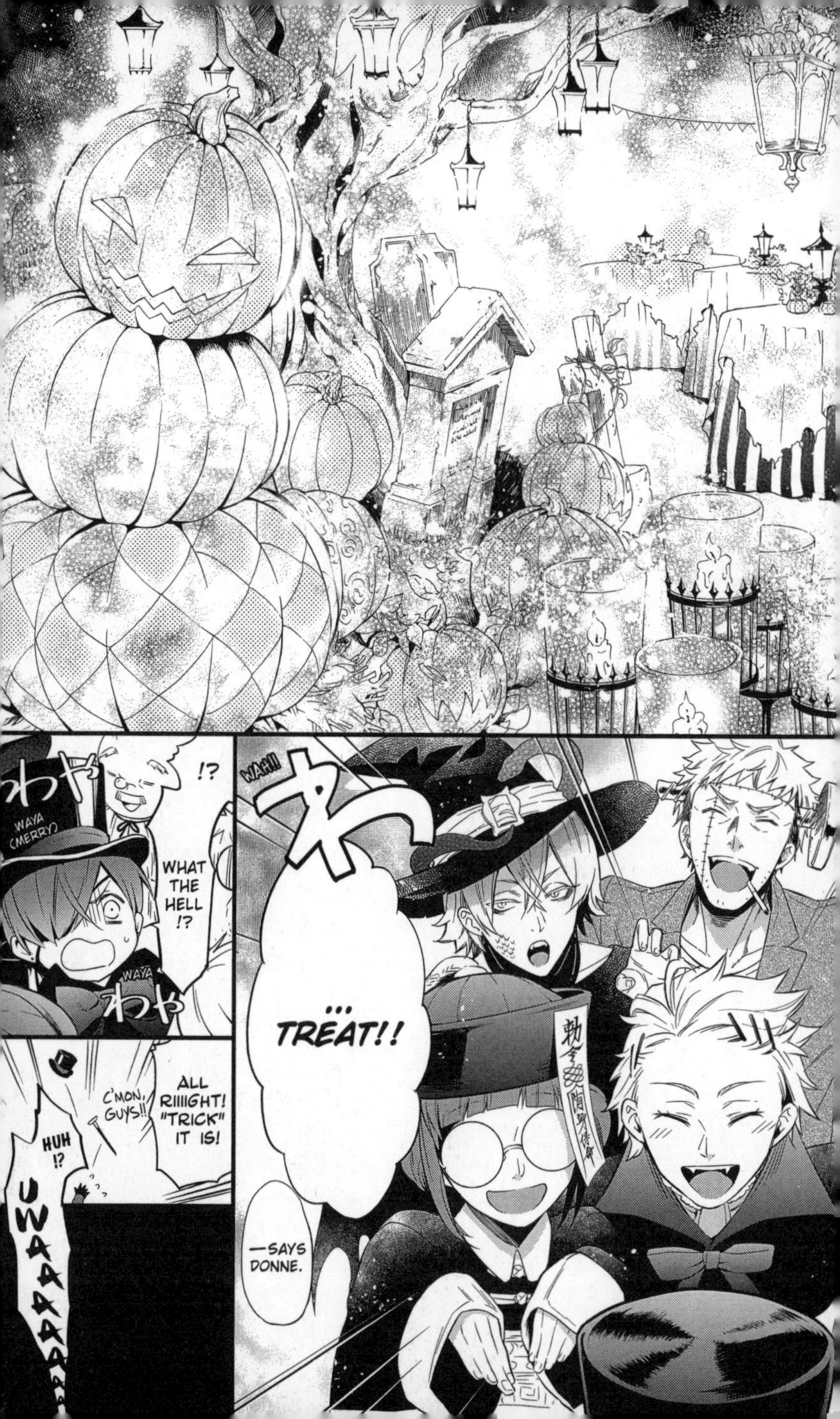
WAH!!
...TREAT!!
—SAYS DONNE.
わや
WAYA (MERRY)
!?
WHAT THE HELL !?
WAYA
わや
ALL RIIIIGHT! "TRICK" IT IS!
C'MON, GUYS!!
HUH !?
UWAAAAAAA

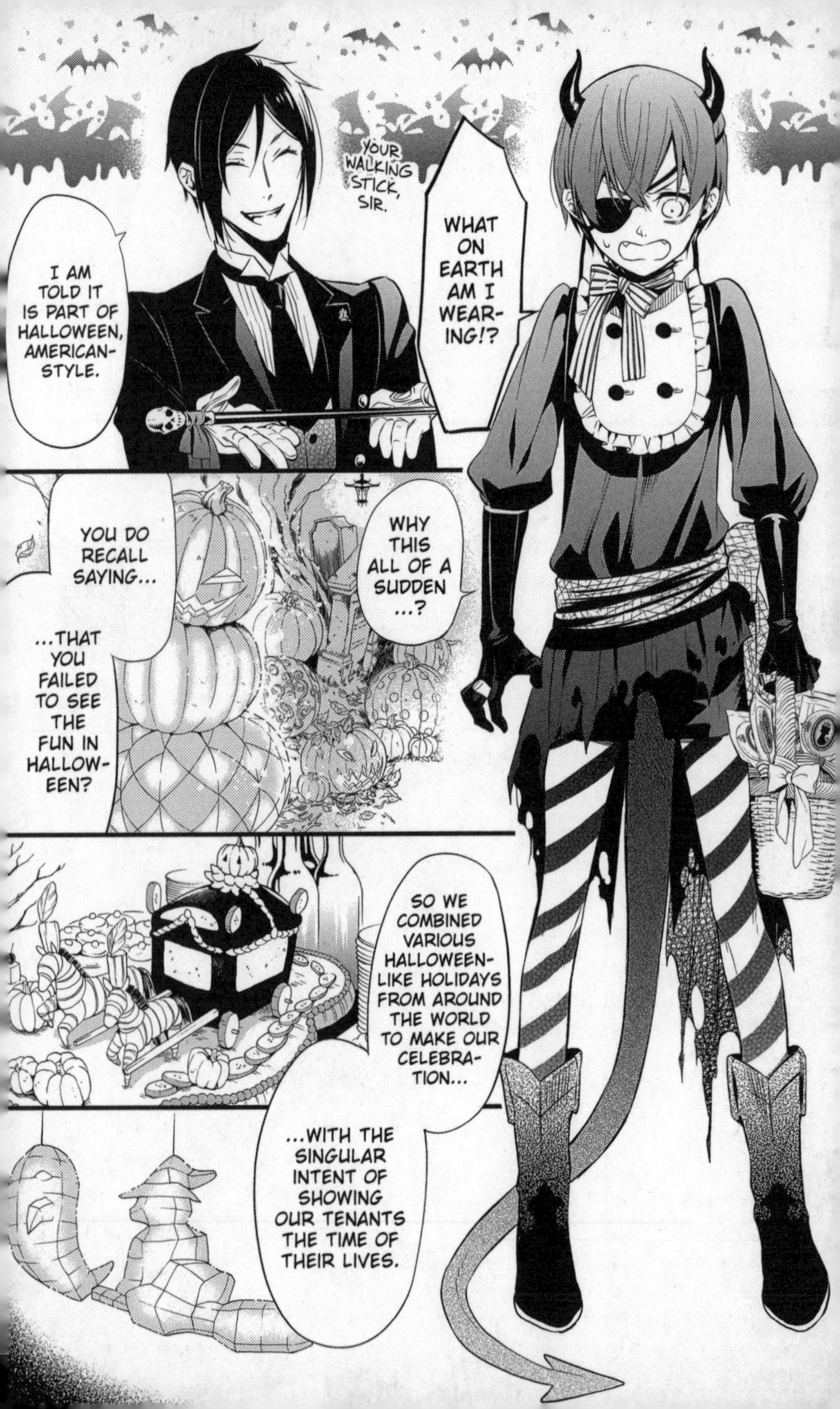
WHAT ON EARTH AM I WEAR-ING!?
YOUR WALKING STICK, SIR.
I AM TOLD IT IS PART OF HALLOWEEN, AMERICAN-STYLE.
WHY THIS ALL OF A SUDDEN ...?
YOU DO RECALL SAYING...
...THAT YOU FAILED TO SEE THE FUN IN HALLOW-EEN?
SO WE COMBINED VARIOUS HALLOWEEN-LIKE HOLIDAYS FROM AROUND THE WORLD TO MAKE OUR CELEBRA-TION...
...WITH THE SINGULAR INTENT OF SHOWING OUR TENANTS THE TIME OF THEIR LIVES.

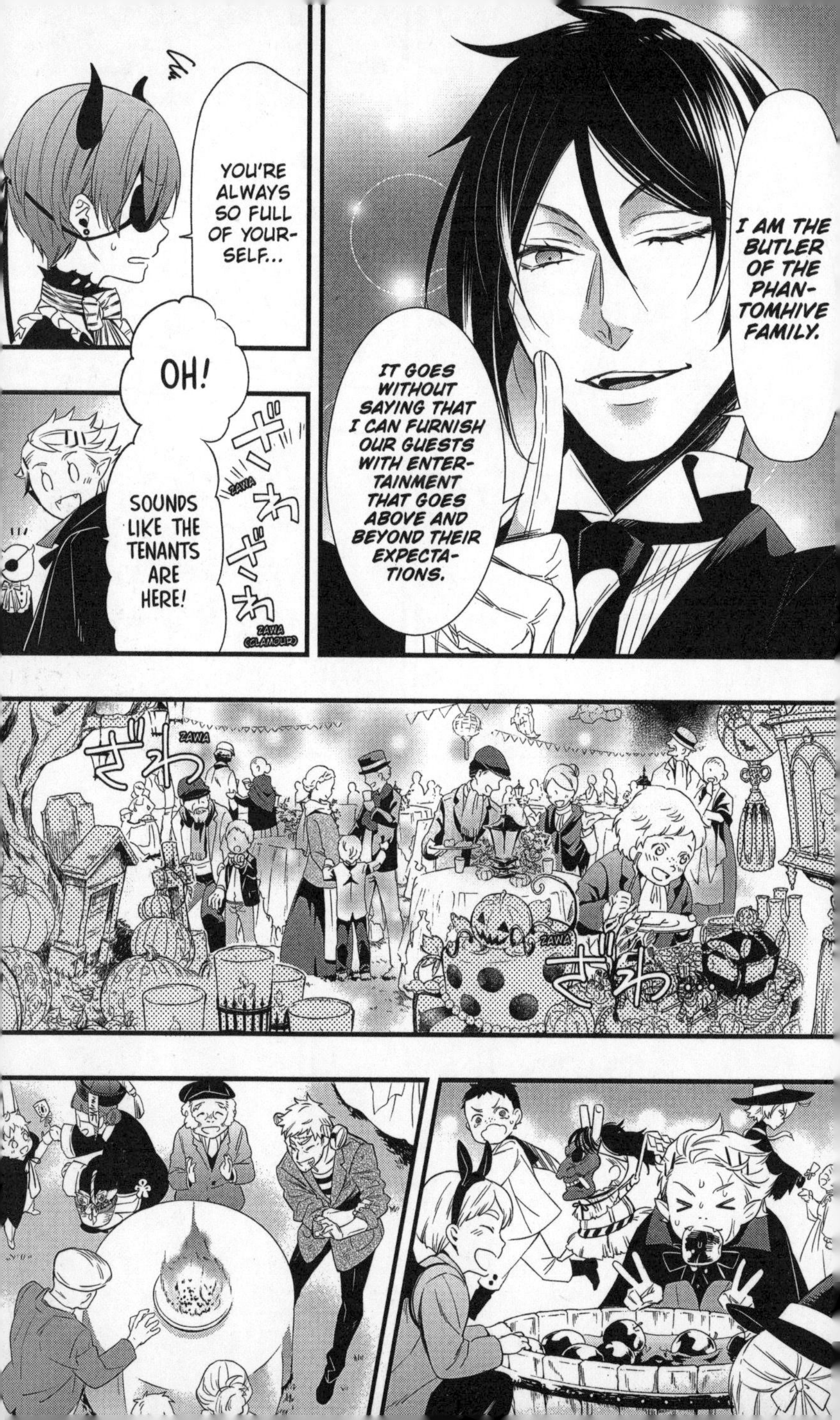
I AM THE BUTLER OF THE PHANTOMHIVE FAMILY.
IT GOES WITHOUT SAYING THAT I CAN FURNISH OUR GUESTS WITH ENTERTAINMENT THAT GOES ABOVE AND BEYOND THEIR EXPECTATIONS.
YOU'RE ALWAYS SO FULL OF YOURSELF...
OH!
SOUNDS LIKE THE TENANTS ARE HERE!
ざわざわ
ZAWA
ZAWA (CLAMOUR)
ざわ
ZAWA
ざわ
ZAWA

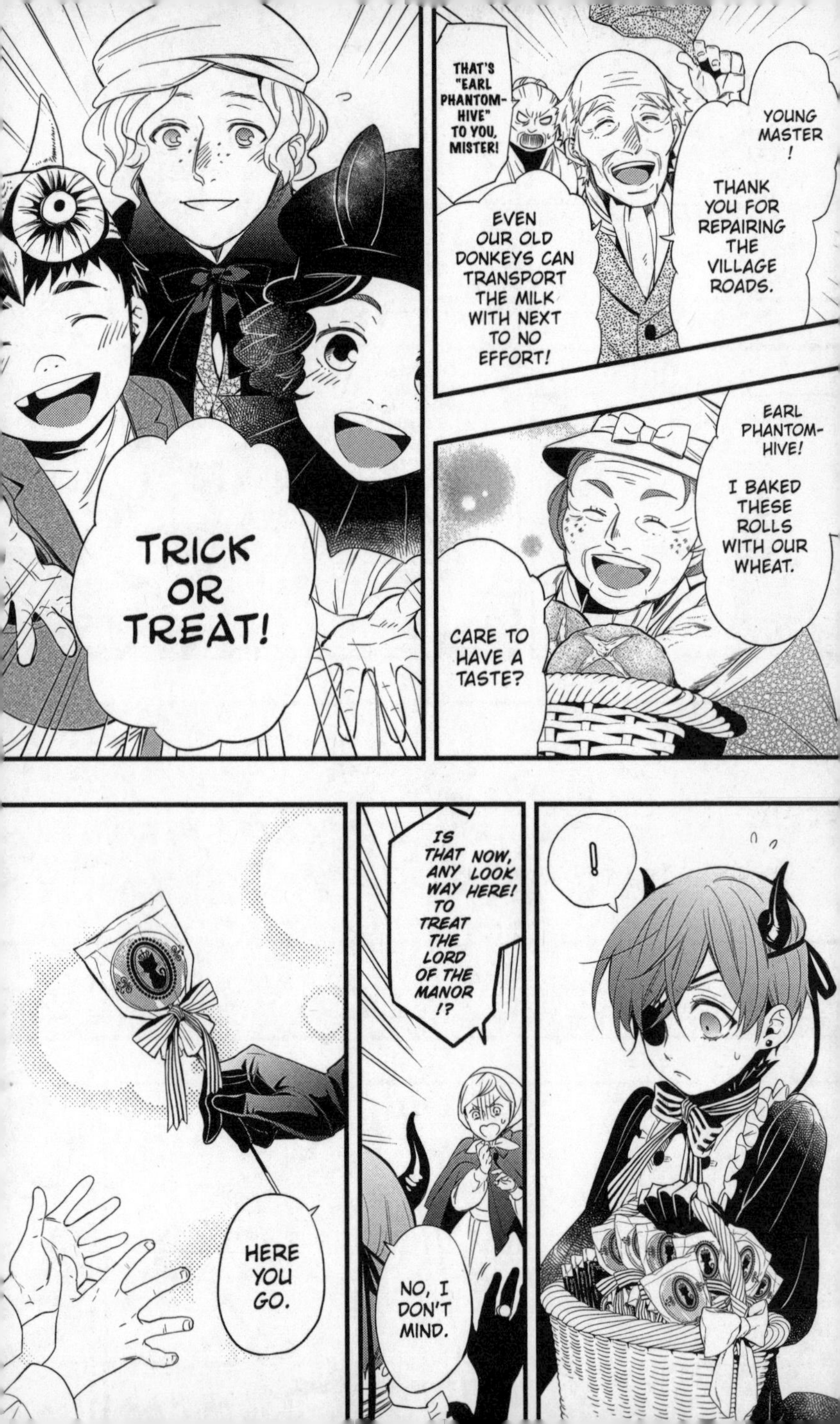
YOUNG MASTER!
THANK YOU FOR REPAIRING THE VILLAGE ROADS.
EVEN OUR OLD DONKEYS CAN TRANSPORT THE MILK WITH NEXT TO NO EFFORT!
THAT'S "EARL PHANTOMHIVE" TO YOU, MISTER!
EARL PHANTOMHIVE!
I BAKED THESE ROLLS WITH OUR WHEAT.
CARE TO HAVE A TASTE?
TRICK OR TREAT!
!
NOW, LOOK HERE!
IS THAT ANY WAY TO TREAT THE LORD OF THE MANOR!?
NO, I DON'T MIND.
HERE YOU GO.

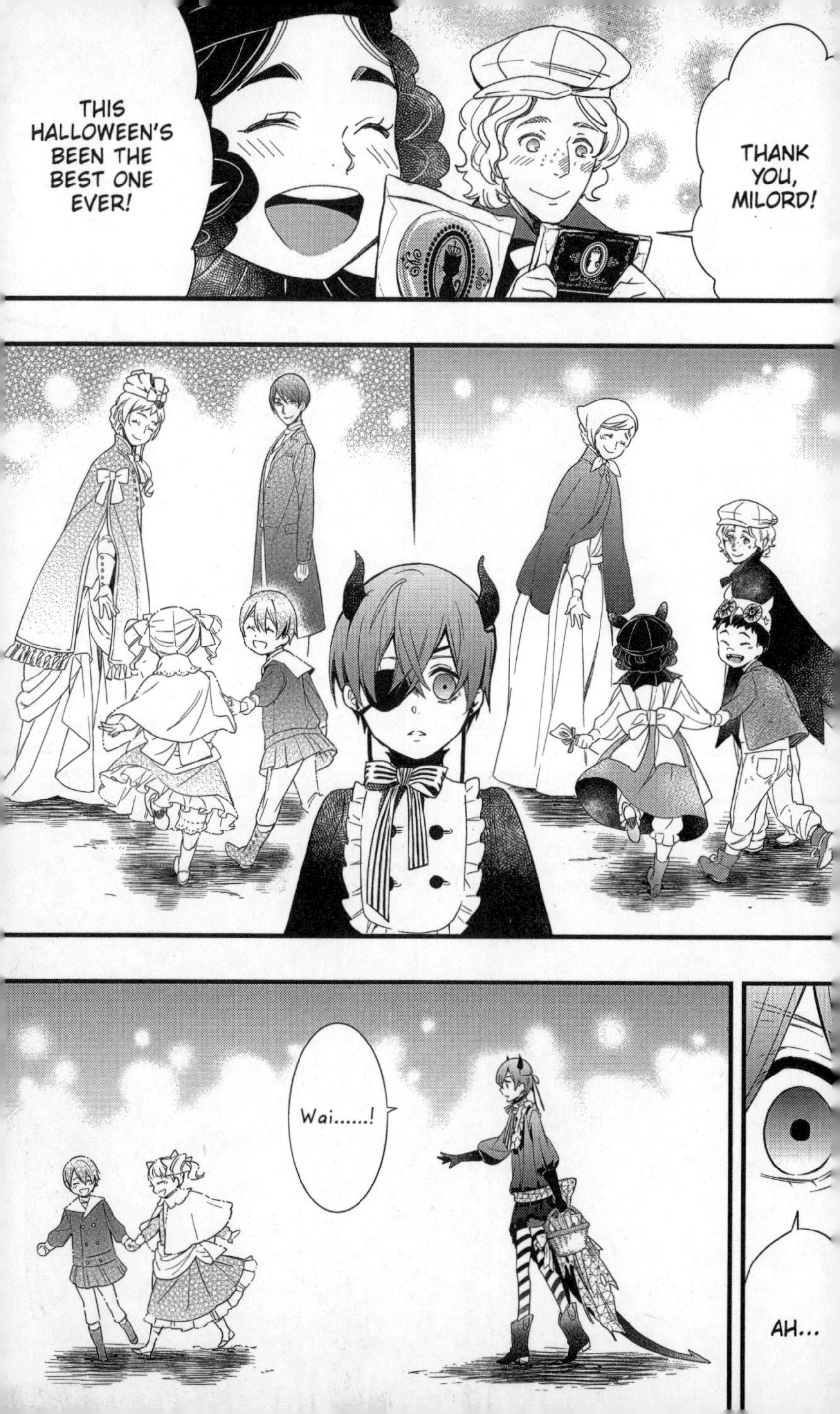
THANK YOU, MILORD!
THIS HALLOWEEN'S BEEN THE BEST ONE EVER!
AH...
Wai......!

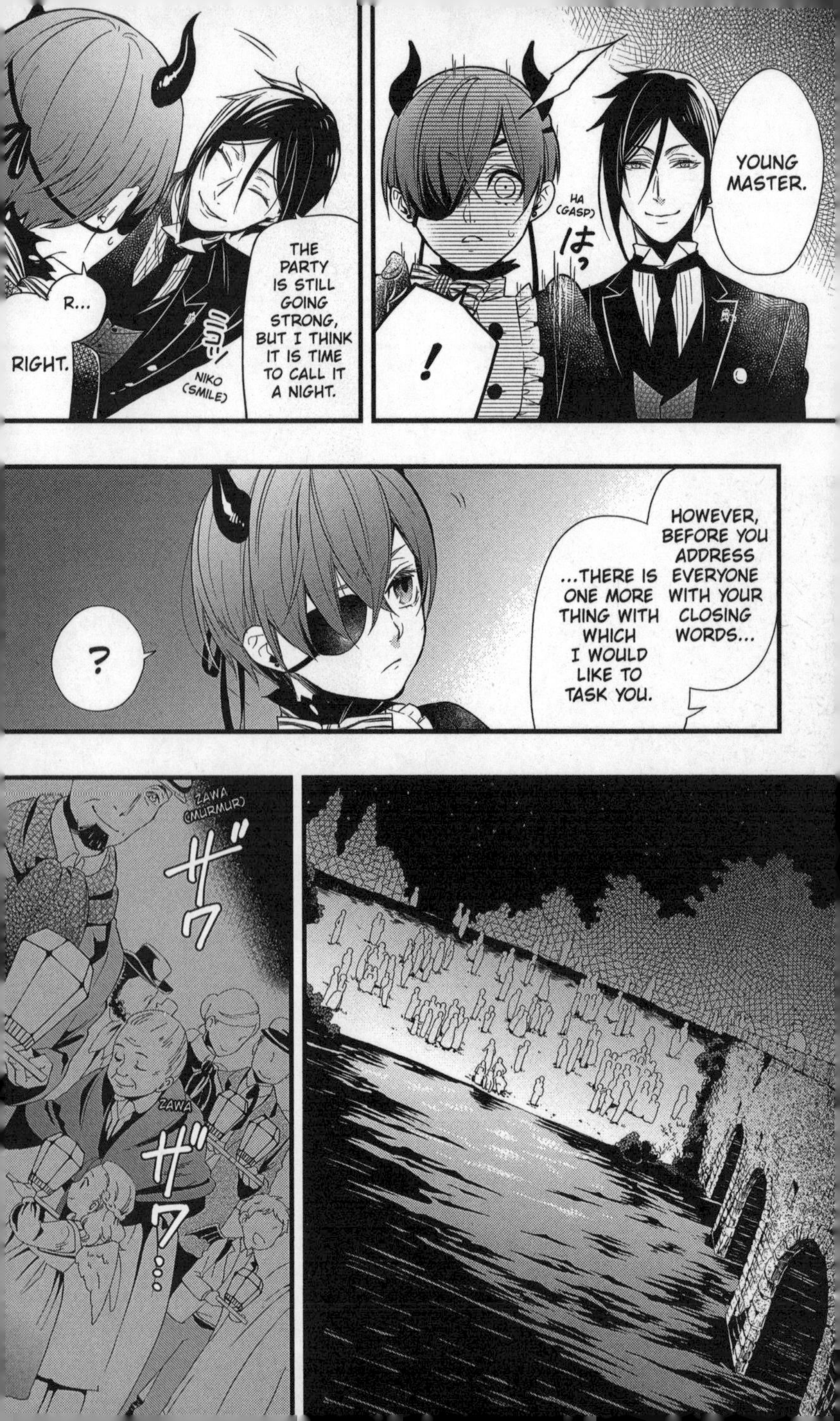
YOUNG MASTER.
HA (GASP)
はっ
!
THE PARTY IS STILL GOING STRONG, BUT I THINK IT IS TIME TO CALL IT A NIGHT.
NIKO (SMILE)
ニコッ
R...
RIGHT.
HOWEVER, BEFORE YOU ADDRESS EVERYONE WITH YOUR CLOSING WORDS...
...THERE IS ONE MORE THING WITH WHICH I WOULD LIKE TO TASK YOU.
?
ZAWA (MURMUR)
ザワ
ZAWA
ザワ...

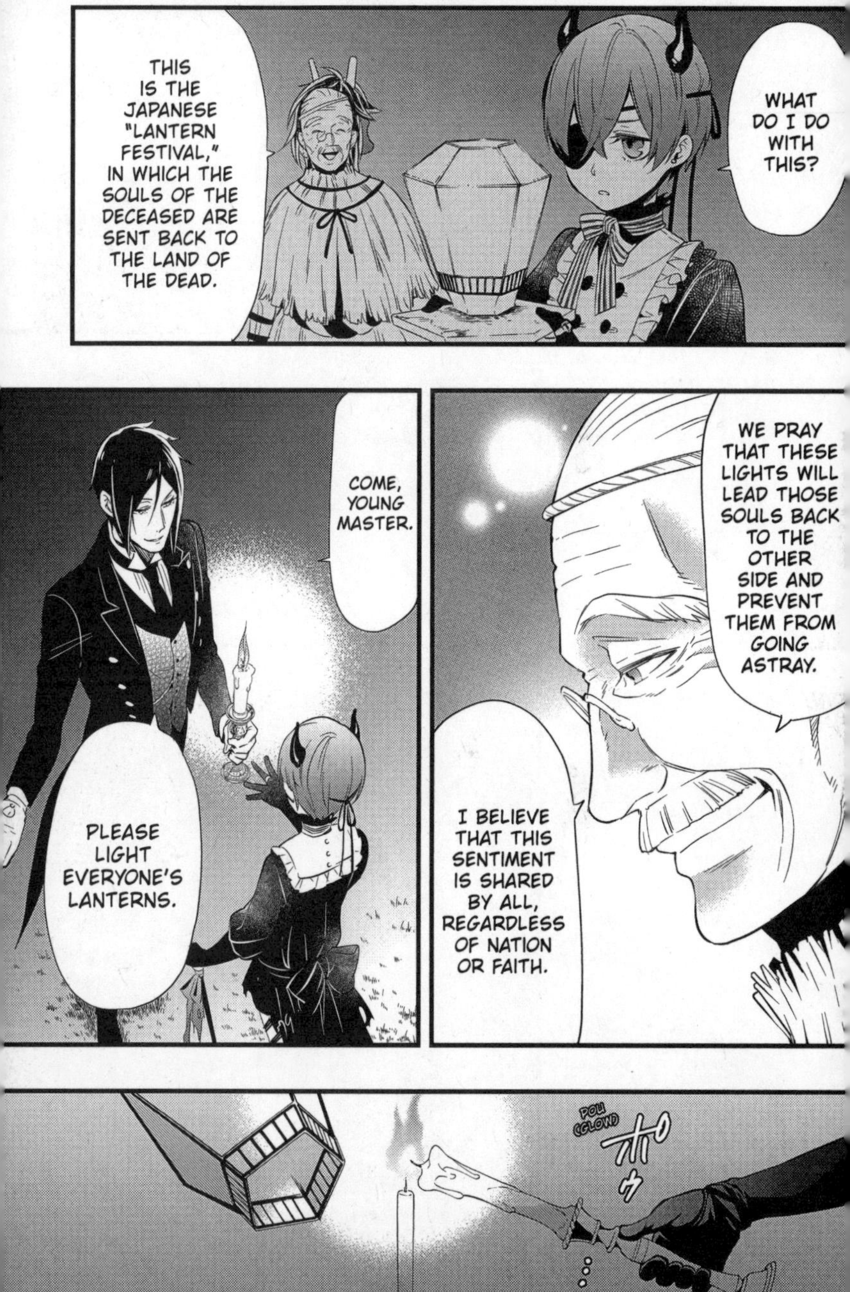
WHAT DO I DO WITH THIS?
THIS IS THE JAPANESE "LANTERN FESTIVAL," IN WHICH THE SOULS OF THE DECEASED ARE SENT BACK TO THE LAND OF THE DEAD.
WE PRAY THAT THESE LIGHTS WILL LEAD THOSE SOULS BACK TO THE OTHER SIDE AND PREVENT THEM FROM GOING ASTRAY.
I BELIEVE THAT THIS SENTIMENT IS SHARED BY ALL, REGARDLESS OF NATION OR FAITH.
COME, YOUNG MASTER.
PLEASE LIGHT EVERYONE'S LANTERNS.
POU (GLOW)

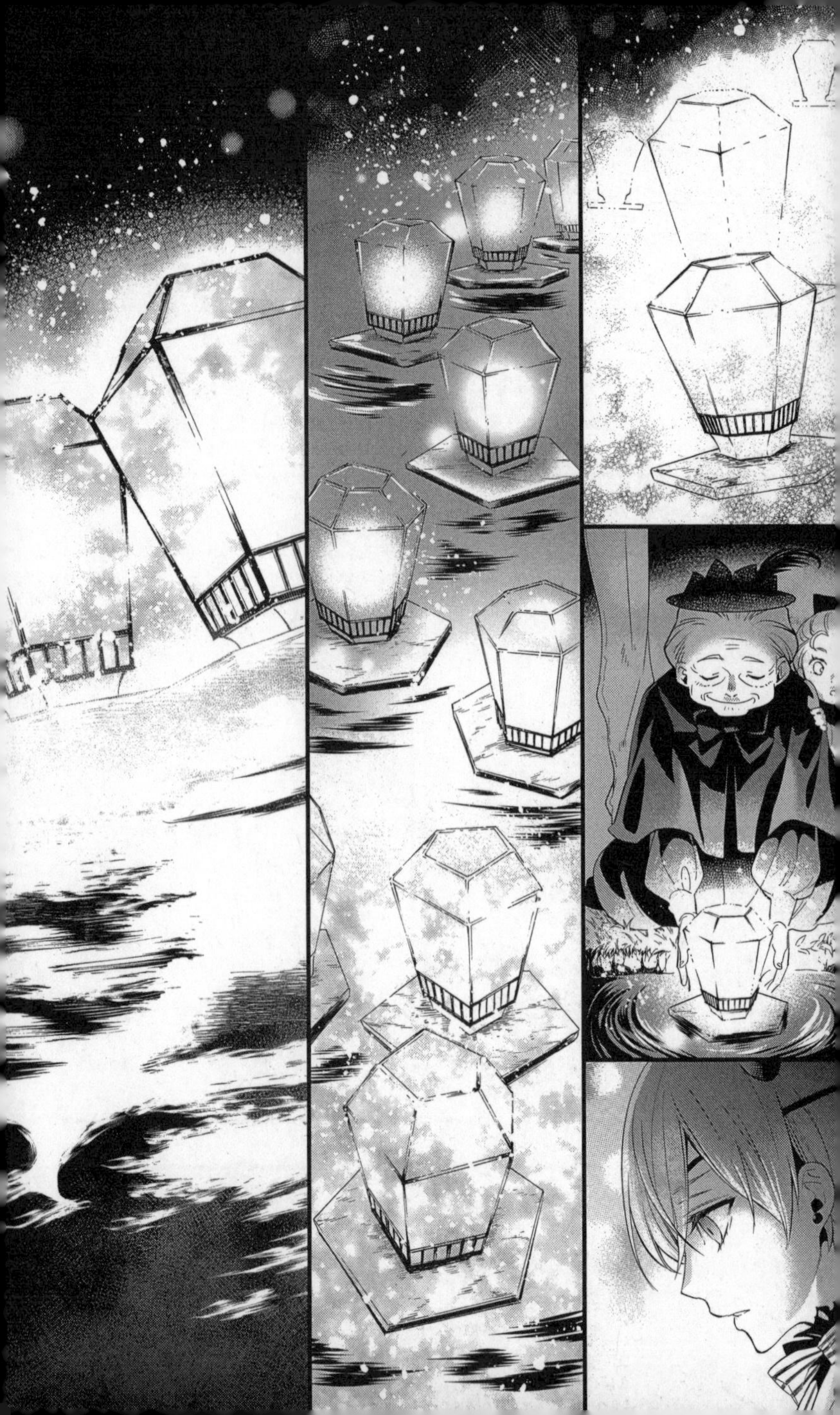

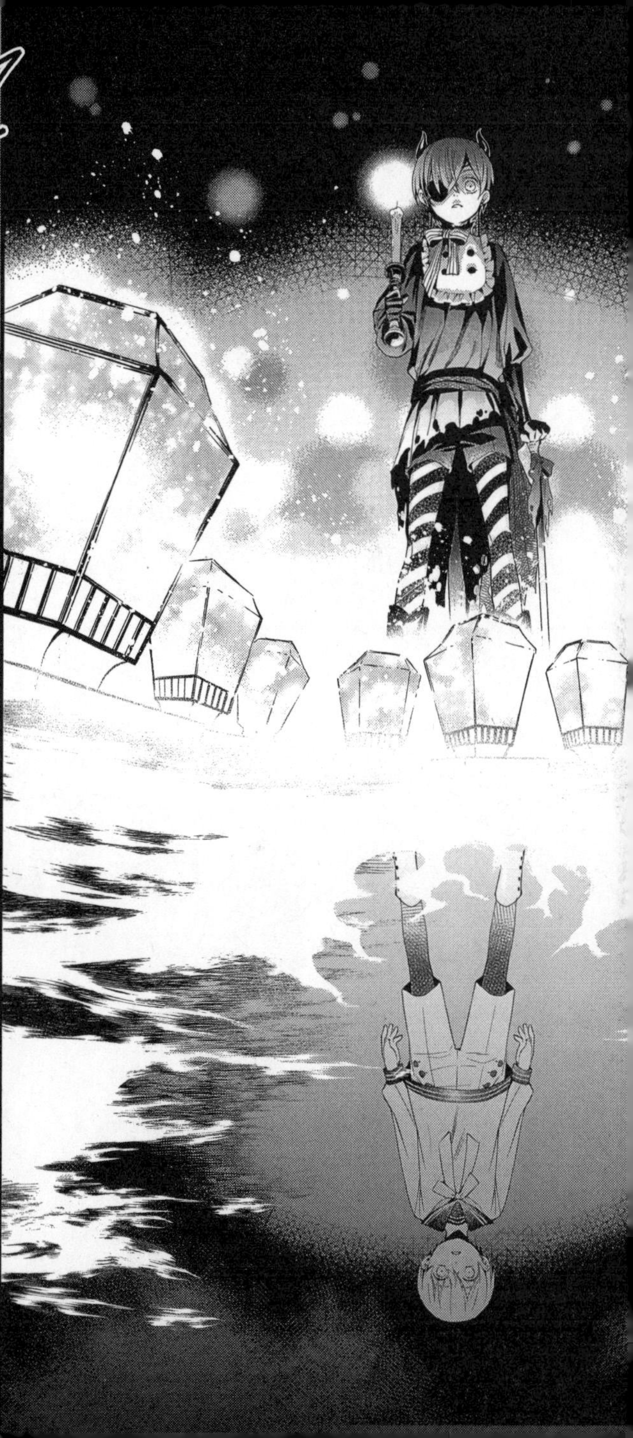

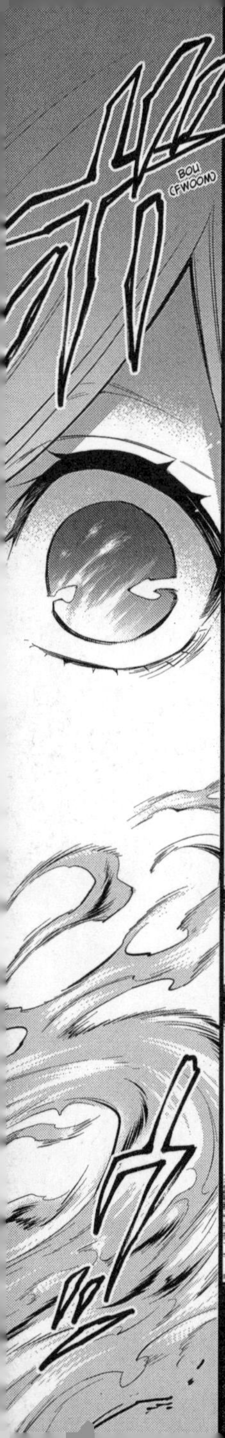
BOU
(FWOOM)

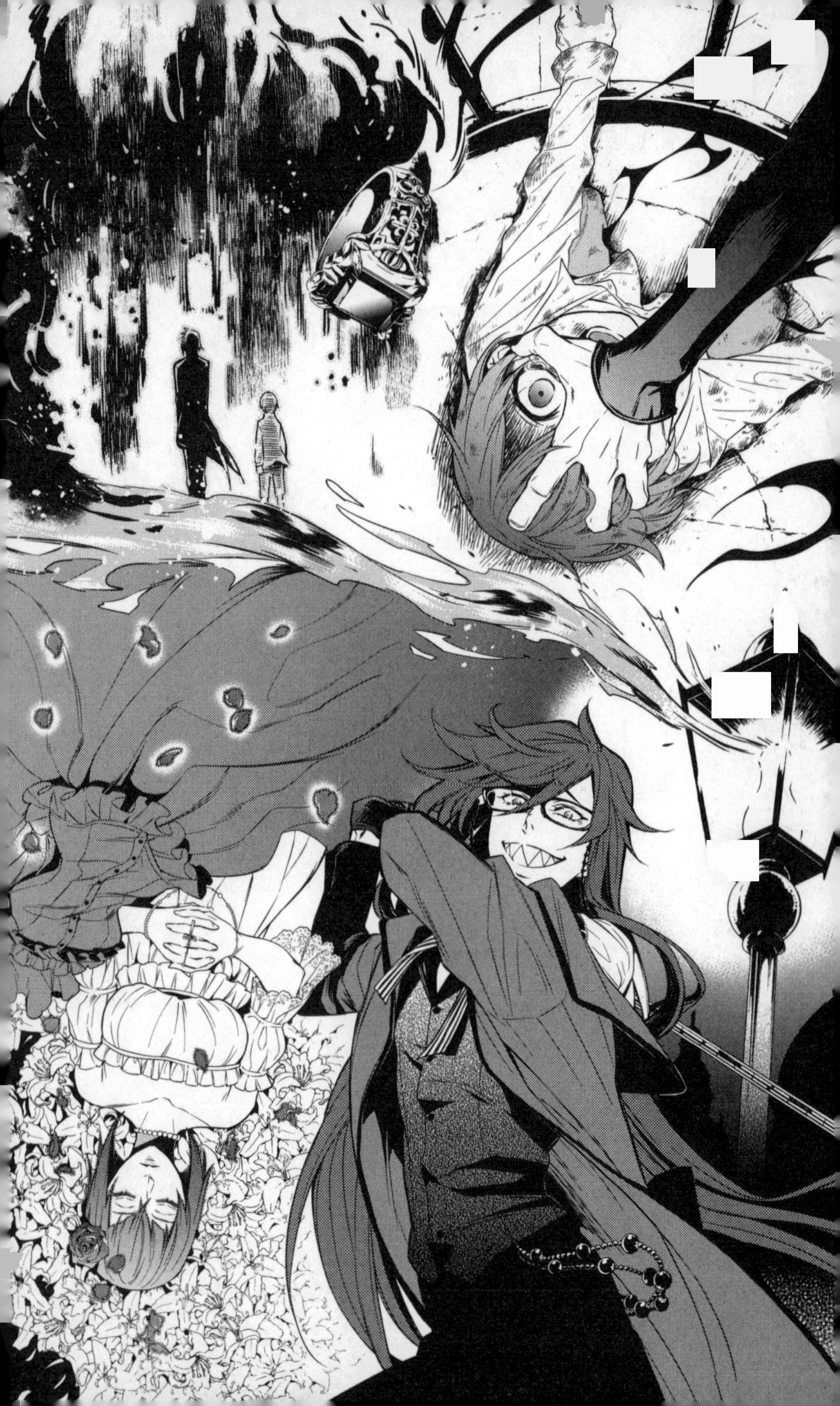

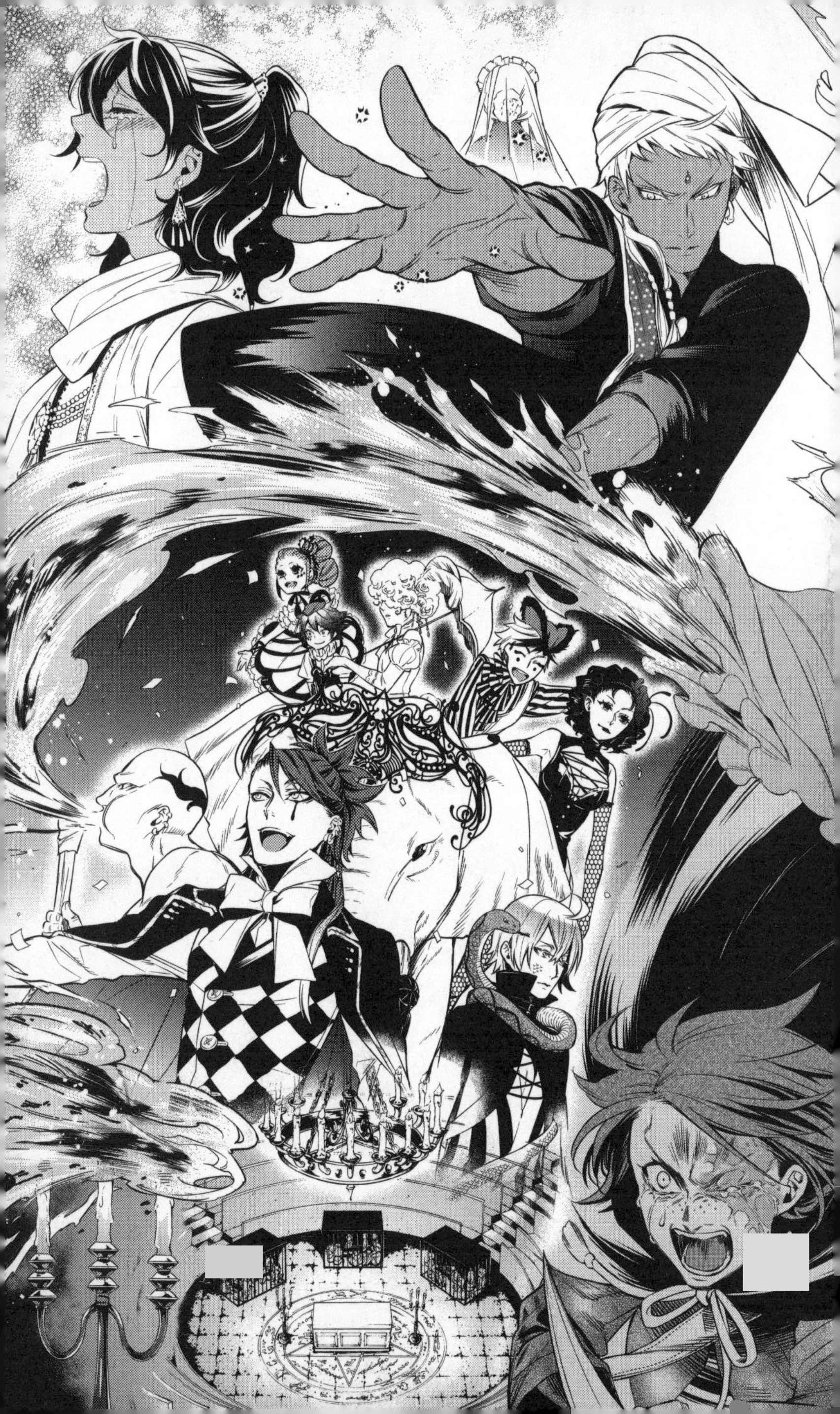

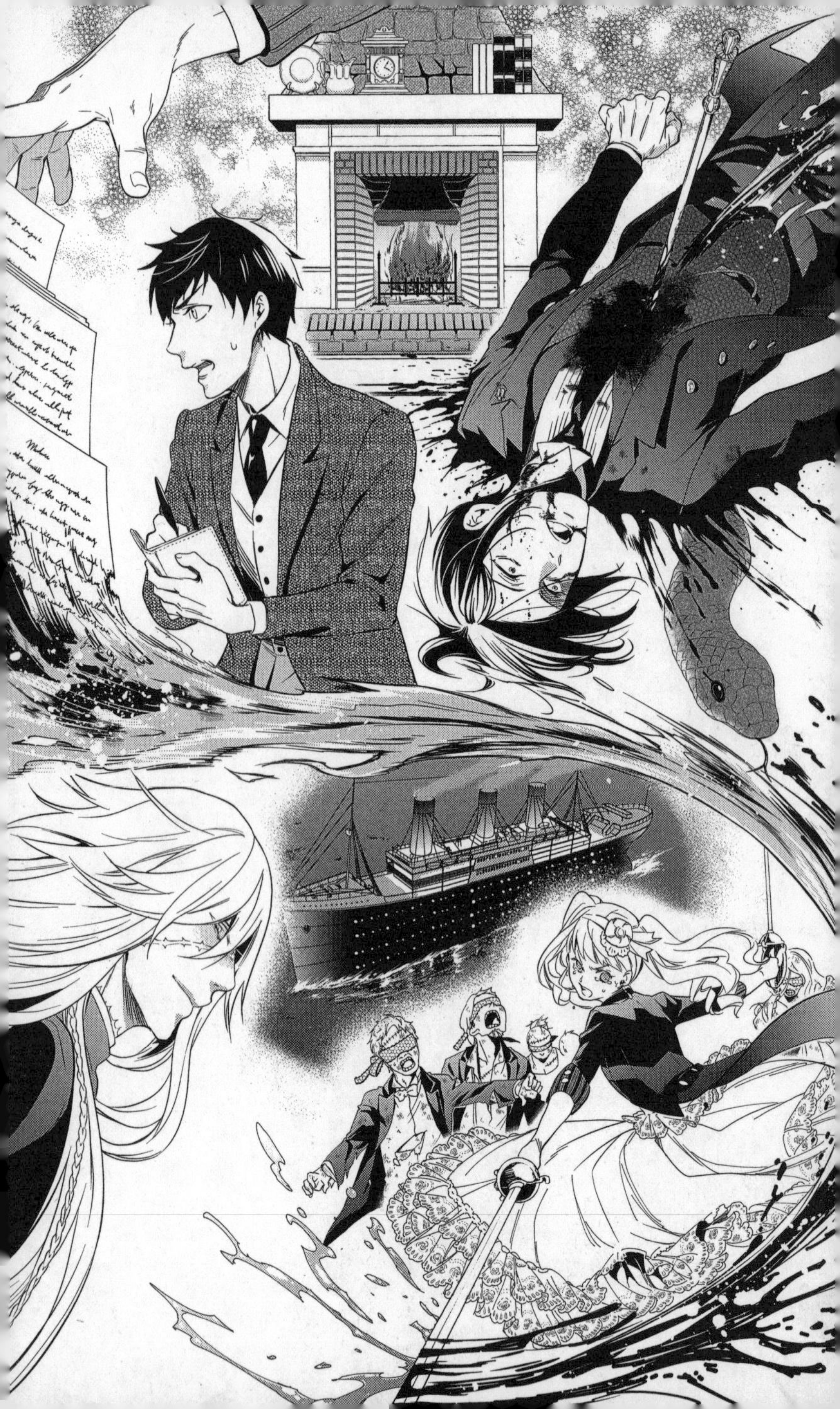

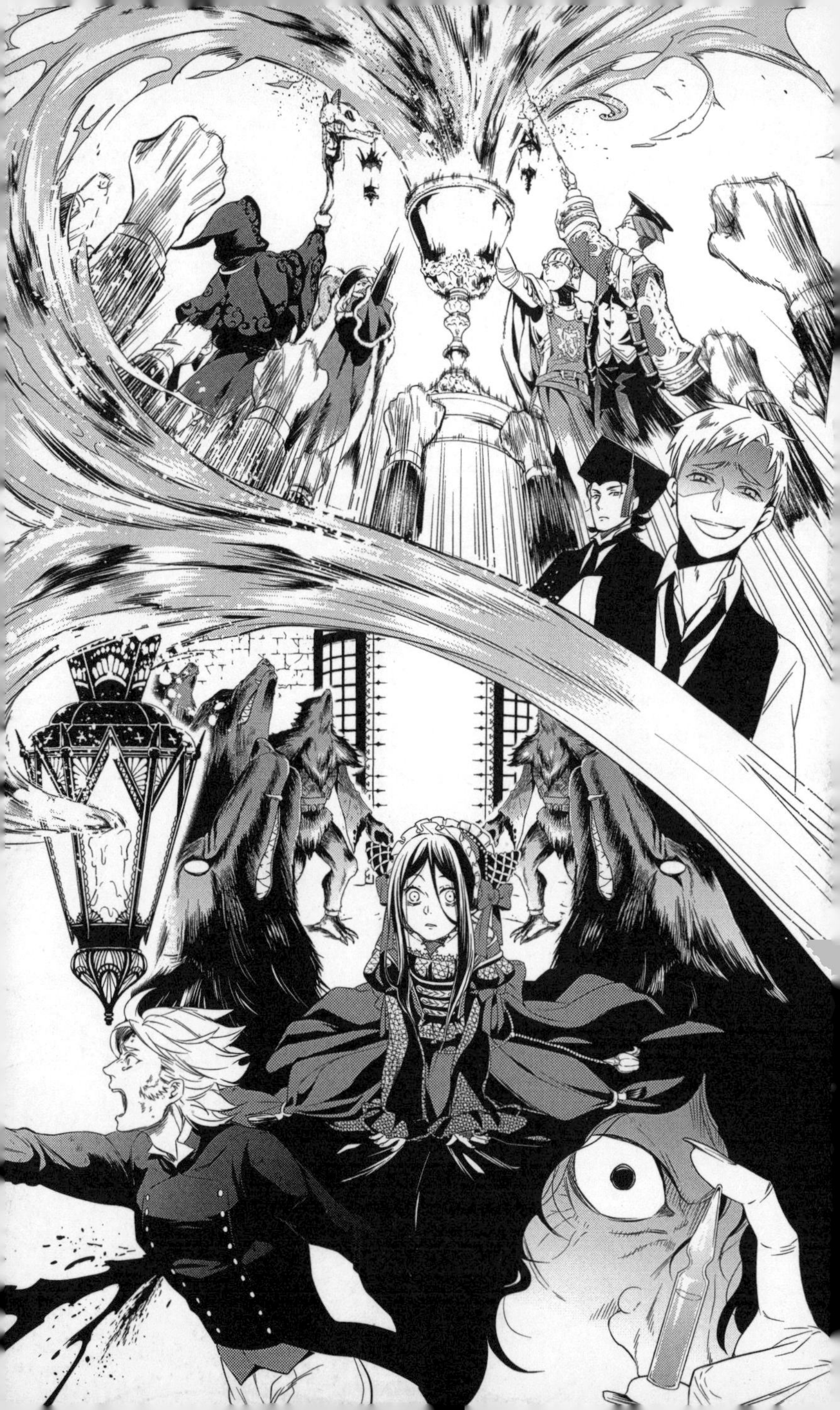

HA
CGASP)

THE
CANDLE
BURNS
AWAY TO
KEEP ITS
FLAME
ALIVE—

NOT
UNLIKE
...

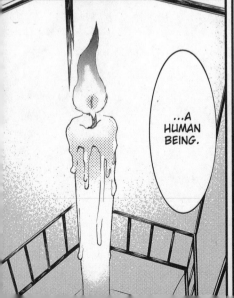

...A
HUMAN
BEING.

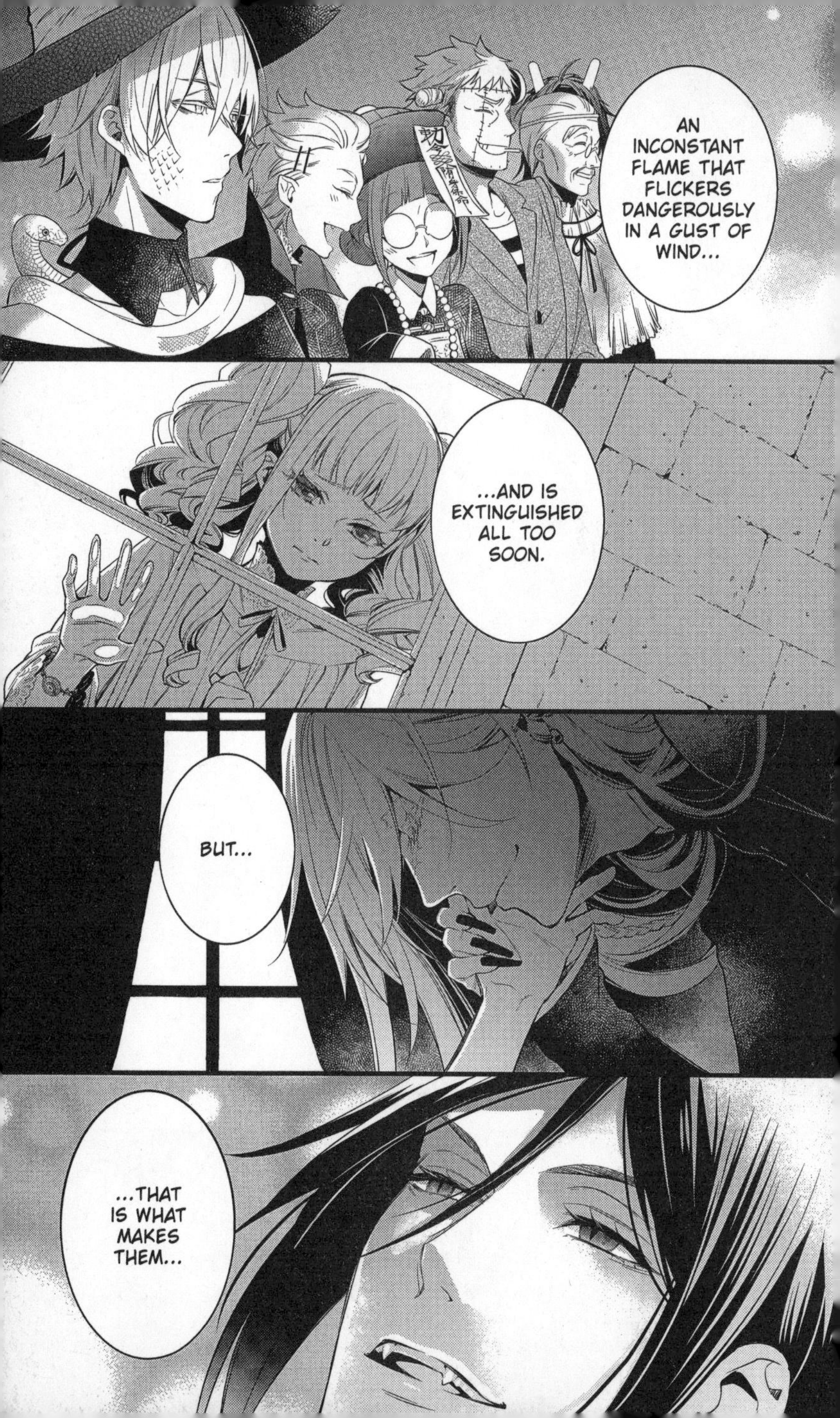
AN INCONSTANT FLAME THAT FLICKERS DANGEROUSLY IN A GUST OF WIND...
...AND IS EXTINGUISHED ALL TOO SOON.
BUT...
...THAT IS WHAT MAKES THEM...

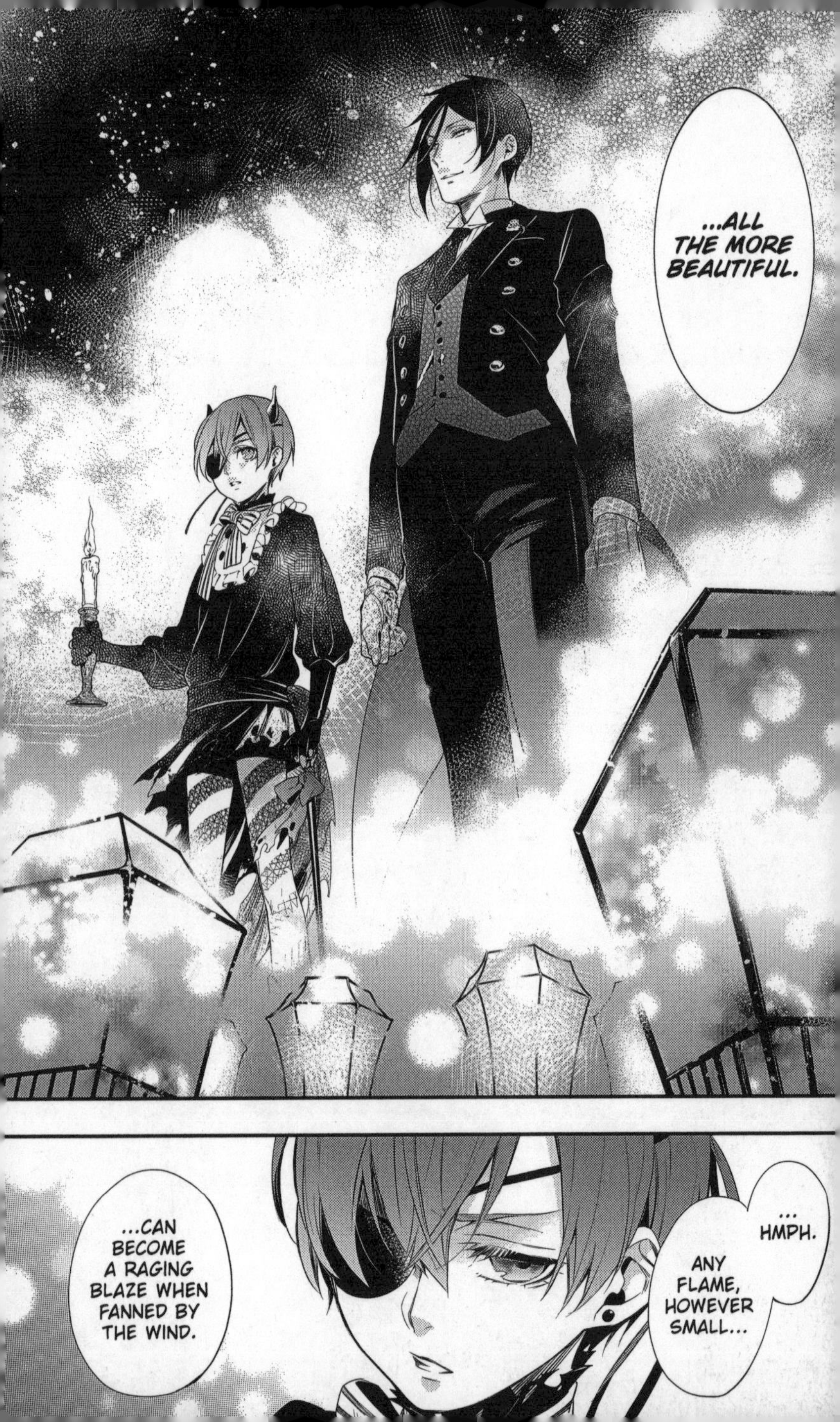
...ALL THE MORE BEAUTIFUL.
... HMPH.
ANY FLAME, HOWEVER SMALL...
...CAN BECOME A RAGING BLAZE WHEN FANNED BY THE WIND.

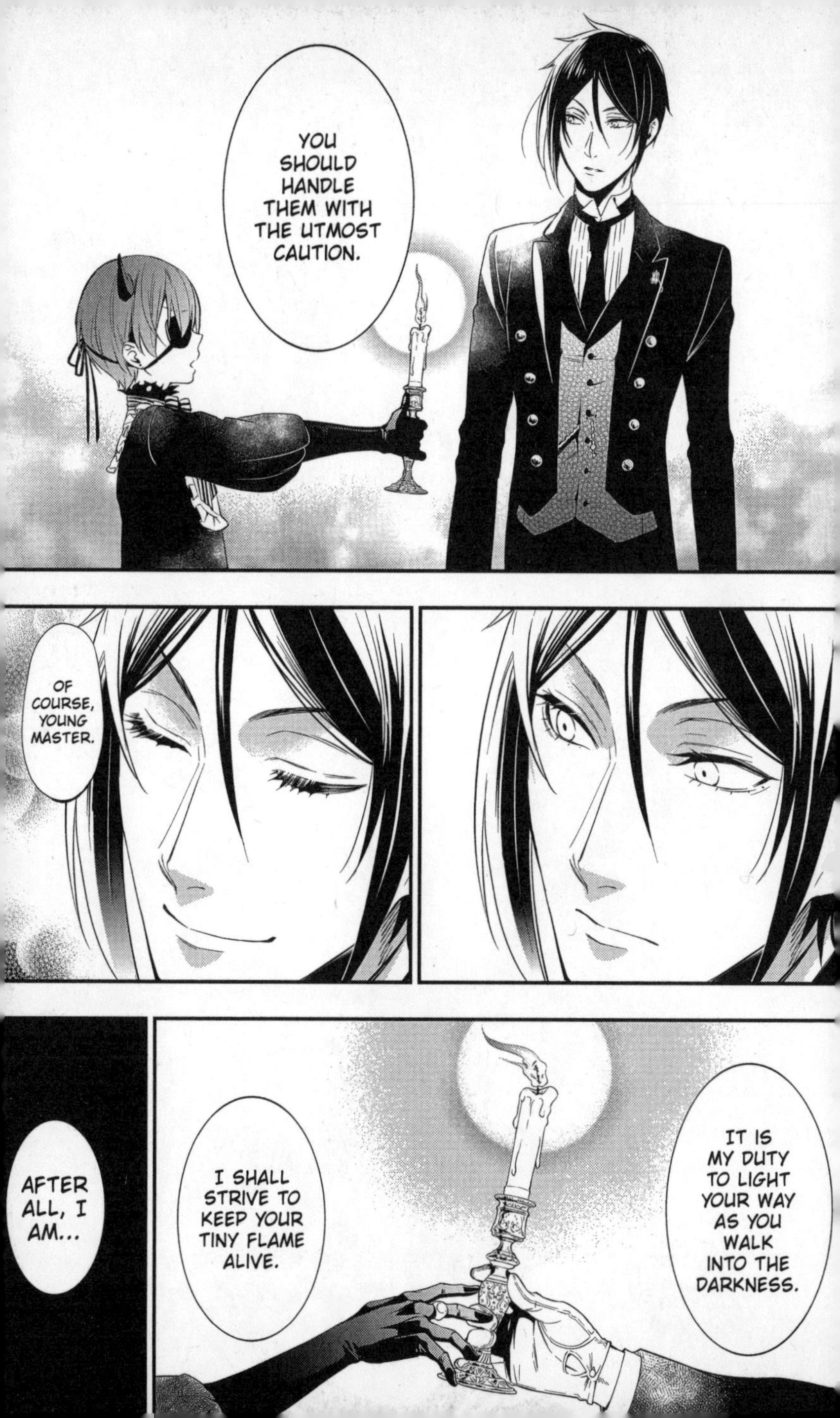
YOU SHOULD HANDLE THEM WITH THE UTMOST CAUTION.
OF COURSE, YOUNG MASTER.
IT IS MY DUTY TO LIGHT YOUR WAY AS YOU WALK INTO THE DARKNESS.
I SHALL STRIVE TO KEEP YOUR TINY FLAME ALIVE.
AFTER ALL, I AM...

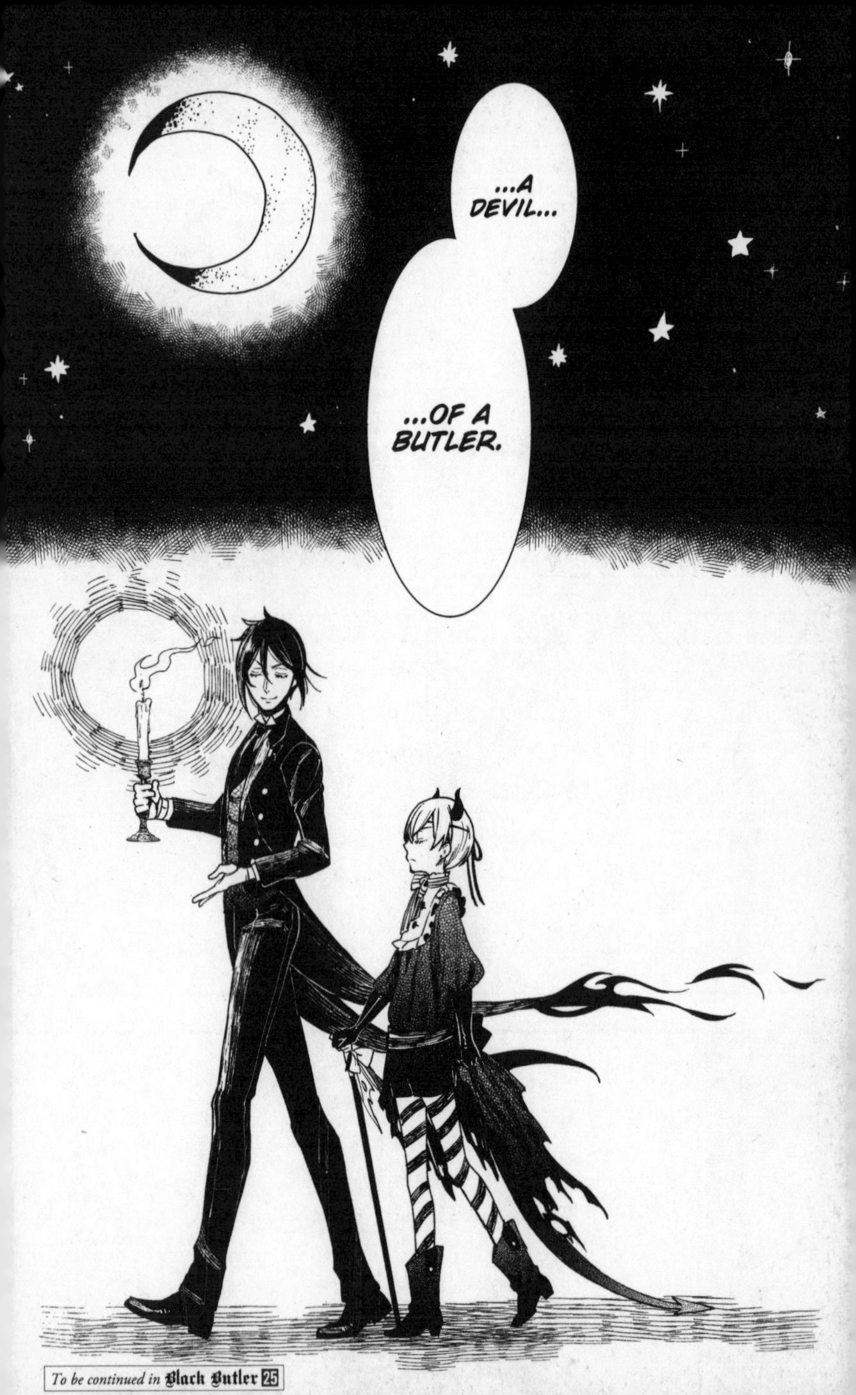
...A DEVIL...
...OF A BUTLER.

To be continued in Black Butler 25

Black Butler

黒執事

Downstairs

Wakana Haduki
7
Tsuki Sorano
Chiaki Nagaoka
Zen
Sanihiko
*
Takeshi Kuma
*
Yana Toboso

Adviser
Rico Murakami

Special thanks to You!

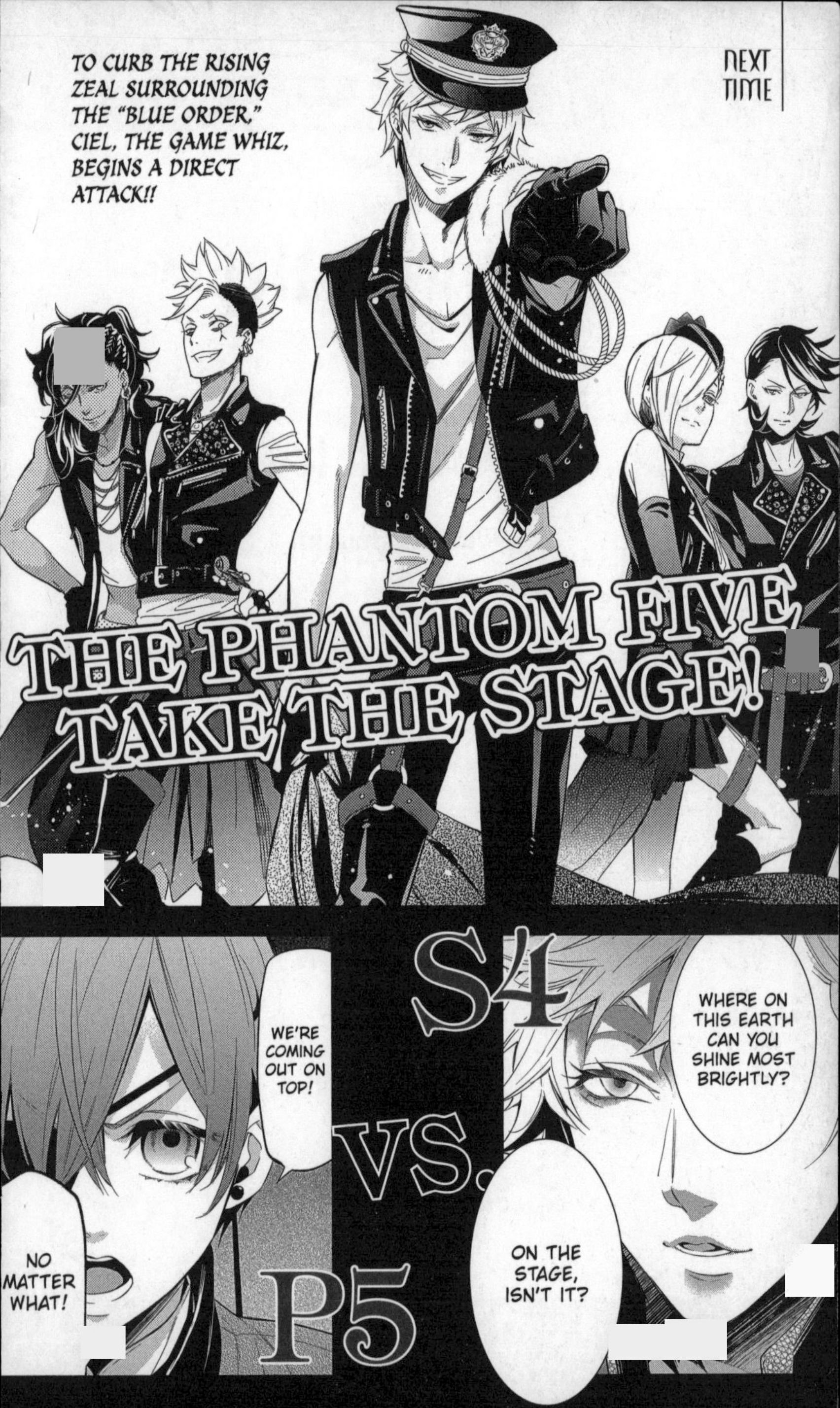
NEXT TIME
TO CURB THE RISING ZEAL SURROUNDING THE "BLUE ORDER," CIEL, THE GAME WHIZ, BEGINS A DIRECT ATTACK!!
THE PHANTOM FIVE TAKE THE STAGE!
WHERE ON THIS EARTH CAN YOU SHINE MOST BRIGHTLY?
ON THE STAGE, ISN'T IT?
S4 VS. P5
WE'RE COMING OUT ON TOP!
NO MATTER WHAT!

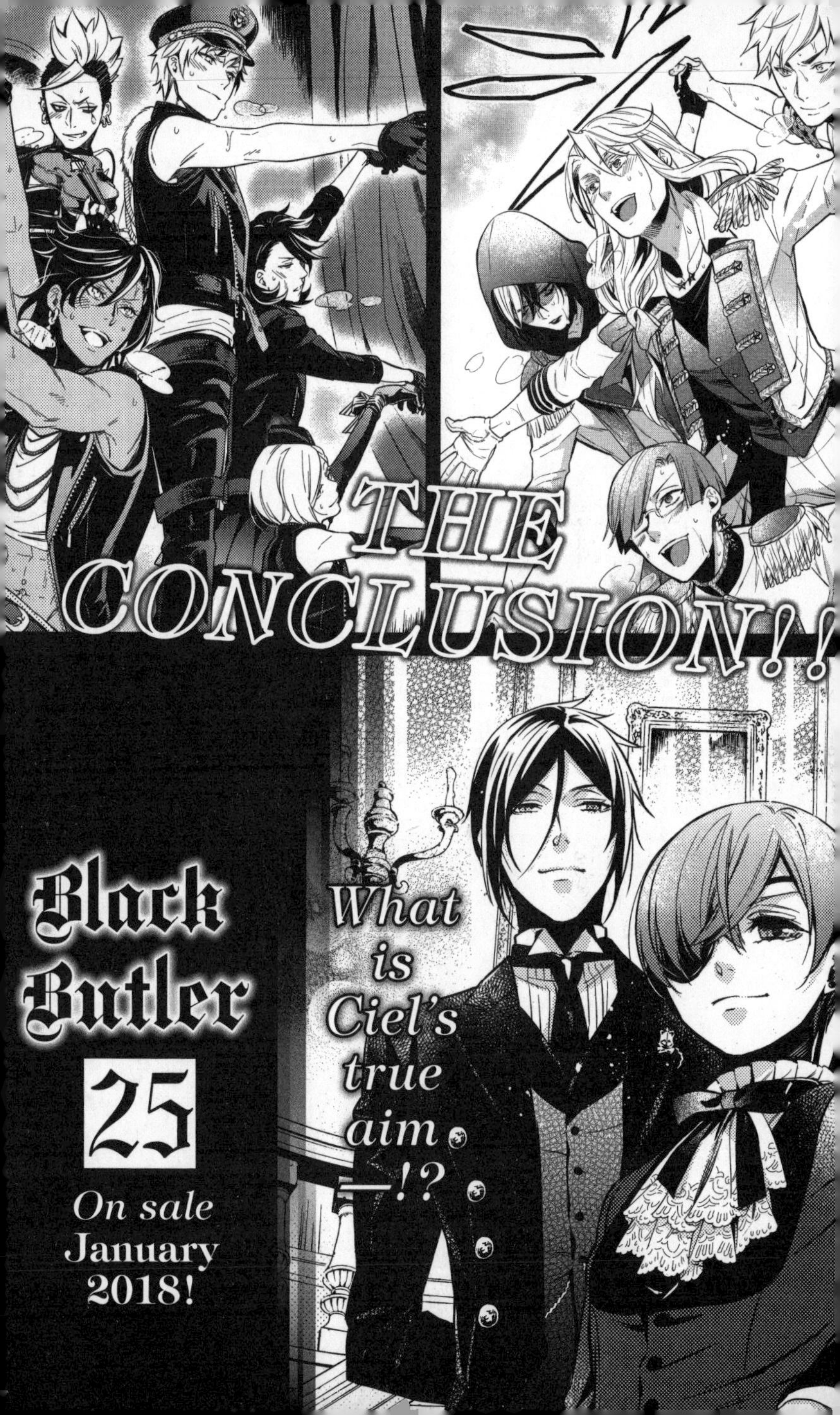
THE CONCLUSION!!
What is Ciel's true aim—!?
Black Butler
25
On sale January 2018!

Black Butler

Yana Toboso

AUTHOR'S NOTE

Serialised Chapter 120 (the last chapter in this volume) marks exactly ten years since I began drawing *Black Butler*. I never imagined I'd be drawing this series for such a long time. I also never imagined I'd still find it difficult drawing Sebastian. But I've grown fond of him over our decade together, so I'd like to grapple with him and his hair's center part for a while longer. And so, here's Volume 24!

The Phantomhive family has a butler who's almost too good to be true... or maybe he's just too good to be human. And now you can find him in two places at once!

Read the latest chapter of

Black Butler

on the same day as Japan!

Available now worldwide at your favourite e-tailer!

THE BEAT OF THE SOUL CONTINUES...

VOL. 1 - 5 AVAILABLE NOW!

Soul Eater Not! ©Atsushi Ohkubo/SQUARE ENIX

BLACK BUTLER ㉔

YANA TOBOSO

Translation: Tomo Kimura
Lettering: Bianca Pistillo

KUROSHITSUJI Vol. 24 © 2016 Yana Toboso / SQUARE ENIX CO., LTD. First published in Japan in 2016 by SQUARE ENIX CO., LTD. English translation rights arranged with SQUARE ENIX CO., LTD. and Yen Press, LLC through Tuttle-Mori Agency, Inc.

English translation © 2017 by SQUARE ENIX CO., LTD.

Yen Press
1290 Avenue of the Americas
New York, NY 10104

Visit us!
† yenpress.com
† facebook.com/yenpress
† twitter.com/yenpress
† yenpress.tumblr.com
† instagram.com/yenpress

First Yen Press Edition: October 2017
The chapters in this volume were originally published as ebooks by Yen Press.

Yen Press is an imprint of Yen Press, LLC.
The Yen Press name and logo are trademarks of Yen Press, LLC.

The publisher is not responsible for websites (or their content) that are not owned by the publisher.

Library of Congress Control Number: 2010525567

ISBNs: 978-0-316-51120-9 (paperback)
       978-0-316-51124-7 (ebook)

10 9 8 7 6 5 4 3 2 1

BVG

Printed in the United States of America